Literature and the Image of Man

Literature and the Image of Man

Communication in Society, Volume 2

LEO LOWENTHAL

Transaction Publishers

New Brunswick (U.S.A.) and London (U.K.)

First paperback printing 2016.
Copyright © 1986 by Transaction Publishers, New Brunswick, New Jersey.

This book is printed on acid-free paper that meets the American National Standard for Permanence of Paper for Printed Library Materials.

Library of Congress Catalog Number: 85-20687
ISBN: 0-88738-057-3 (cloth); 978-1-4128-5700-0 (paper)
eBook: 978-1-4128-2763-8
Printed in the United States of America

Library of Congress Cataloging in Publication Data

Lowenthal, Leo.
  Literature and the image of man.
  (Communication in society / Leo Lowenthal; v. 2)
  Bibliography: p.
  1. Literature and society—Europe. 2. European literature—History and criticism. I. Title. II. Series: Lowenthal, Leo. Communication in society; v. 2.
PN51.L6   1986b   809.03
ISBN 0-88738-057-3   85-20687

Contents

Acknowledgments

Part II of this volume as well as Excursus B in Part I and the last section, "Reception," in chapter 7 were translated from German into English, especially for this volume, by Christine Schoefer, to whom I am profoundly grateful. I also acknowledge with thanks James Porter's English rendition of Helmut Dubiel's "Afterword."

Part I was originally published under the title, *Literature and the Image of Man,* Beacon Press, 1956. Part II appeared in German under the title *Erzählkunst und Gesellschaft,* Luchterland, 1971.

The essays on Ibsen, Strindberg, and Hamsun in Part I had appeared in a German version in the *Zeitschrift für Sozialforschung* in the 1930s.

Preface:
Social Meanings in Literature

Creative literature conveys many levels of meaning, some intended by the author, some quite unintentional. An artist sets out to invent a plot, to describe action, to depict the interrelationships of characters, to emphasize certain values; wittingly or unwittingly, he stamps his work with uniqueness through an imaginative selection of problems and personages. By this very process of selection—an aspect of creativity that is most relevant to the theme of this book—he presents an explicit or implicit picture of man's orientation to his society: privileges and responsibilities of classes; conceptions of work, love, and friendship, of religion, nature, and art. Through an analysis of the works included in this volume, an image may be formed of man's changing relation to himself, to his family, and to his social and natural environment, from the beginning of the seventeenth to the threshold of the twentieth century.

The writer indeed develops believable characters and places them in situations involving interaction with others and with the society in which they live. He must present what he considers to be the essentials of the individual largely through the behavior of particular characters as they face concrete situations. Of course, the historian does not neglect such considerations. But he often depersonalizes the reaction of the individual to other individuals and to society in order to reveal the broader political, economic, and social forces at work. At the other extreme, memoirs, autobiographies, diaries, and letters might be offered as sources of data at least as personal and specific as the contents of imaginative literature. In such personal documents, however, rationalization and, particularly, self-justification often blur or distort the image of social reality. It is the artist who portrays what is more real than reality itself.

One of the concerns which the creative writer shares with the theoretician is to describe and name new experience. The artist's desire to re-create the unique and the important often leads him to explore hitherto nameless anxieties and hopes. He is neither an articulate recording machine nor an inarticulate mystic but a specialized thinker, and it is often only after his creative tasks have been performed that society recognizes its predicaments. The specific treatment which a creative writer gives to nature or to love, to gestures and moods, to gregariousness or solitude, is a primary source for a study of the penetration of the most intimate spheres of personal life by social forces. It is the task of the sociologist of literature to relate the experience of the writer's imaginary characters and situations to the historical climate from which they derive. He has to transform the private equation of themes and stylistic means into social equations.

Certainly, other sources describe the occupations and preoccupations of the bourgeois at the time of Molière; but only Molière reveals what it was like to live this experience. Similarly Goethe depicts the social and occupational problems which faced the sensitive bureaucrat or white-collar worker of his time. But the writer not only reports how the individual reacts to the pressures of society; he also offers a picture of changing views about the comparative importance of psychic and social forces. Corneille, the spokesman for the French absolute monarchy, viewed man as naturally incapable of imposing order on himself and his affairs without the guidance of a powerful state authority. Ibsen, on the other hand, living in the heyday of a competitive society, portrays individuals who are highly competitive in all their affairs, both public and private, and who ascribe their conduct to their innate natures. In fact, most generalized concepts about human nature found in literature prove on close inspection to be related to social and political change.

In the late sixteenth and early seventeenth centuries, the values of the national state and the monarchy were almost universally accepted by authors who saw in them not only a cure for the evils of the remnants of feudalism, but also a delimiting framework for the boundless aspirations characteristic of the time. It was only later that republican ideals appeared in literature, and later still that the elaborate social critique of an Ibsen could make its debut.

Authors may look forward or backward to a different age, but they tend to do so within the confines of an existing or foreseeable reality. Because the writer is not so much concerned with objects, events, or institutions as with attitudes and feelings which his characters have about them, any social or political "bias" he may have is far from the severe handicap that it would appear to be at first sight. Man is born, strives, loves, suffers, and dies in any society, but it is the protrayal of *how* he reacts to these common human experiences that matters, since they almost invariably have a social nexus. Precisely because great literature presents the whole man in depth, the artist tends to justify or defy society rather than to be its passive chronicler.

All literary materials, including those hitherto considered beyond the province of the sociologist, therefore assume social meanings. The idea of "nature," for example, at different moments of history has had these very different connotations: the non-human world to which one goes for relaxation from the human scene; a Utopia which idealizes an extra-historical space as opposed to society in corruption; the sanctuary for those in flight from a frustrating situation. Sometimes the style of the artist provides significant clues, as when Ibsen's people use almost identical terms to describe competition between husband and wife and competition in the professional world. Or again it may be the emotions which assume social relevance. Thus, for example, Cervantes displays a number of sentiments and actions denoting extreme personal insecurity, ranging from worry about professional status to moral and philosophic doubts. Such fears in turn can be related, more or less directly, to the unprecedented social mobility which followed the disintegration of the feudal world, and they indicate how profoundly the individual was affected by this dramatic change.

The literature of any period gives its audience meaningful portraits of human types. The Spaniards to whom Cervantes spoke, the Englishmen who saw Shakespeare's plays, and the French audiences of Corneille, Racine, and Molière had no difficulty in identifying their dramatis personae or in recognizing their nuances. Because of this representational quality, all literature, whether first or second rate, can be subjected to social analysis. But the works of a Cervantes or Ibsen present problems quite different from those of the hack.

The writer achieves greatness because of the depth of his insight into the human condition. The fact that literary genius is rare and its audience small, presents in itself a sociological problem, but this in no way detracts from the writer's role as interpreter. More important is the question of his relation to various population groups, as a participant or observer. For if a group has no opportunity to express its own emotional or intellectual experiences, and is isolated from the literate sector of society, it may lie beyond the artist's range of observation. To the Greek tragedian, for example, the feelings and thoughts of slaves were of little significance. The contemporary American writer, on the other hand, has almost unlimited access to behavior on all social levels, from the industrial tycoon to the migrant farm laborer. The problem here is simply to be as clear as possible about the scope of the author's view. For most of the periods studied, members of the lower classes of the European population rarely appear as fully drawn characters in works of literature. There are exceptions; Cervantes and Shakespeare both went to considerable pains to create individuals from the lower classes, and Cervantes surely had unusual opportunities to observe them closely. But the bulk of the fictional characters considered here are from the middle and higher levels of society.

This analysis of three centuries of European literature begins with the breakdown of feudalism and the rise of absolutist governments, then turns to the growth and consolidation of the middle classes, and ends with the foreshadowings of modern totalitarian orders. As social history, it suggests an arc, curving upward in the first tentative gropings toward modern individualism, rising to a plateau of confidence in the individual, and finally declining at the point where the individual feels threatened by technological and social forces. Each end of the trajectory marks a period of stress.

The breakdown of the feudal order forced man to fall back upon himself; he had to learn how to cope with countless problems and decisions that were once taken care of by worldly and spiritual hierarchies. But together with the anxieties generated by this new autonomy he sensed a great promise, for in the period of the formation of the national state and the development of a mercantile economy his own future seemed to have infinite possibilities. At the end of the curve, in our own century, he begins to feel threatened by the encroachment of powerful social forces emanating not only from his own corner of the earth but from every part of a contracting world.

This curve, as illustrated in the works studied here, also describes the context of the individual's growing awareness of his own history and of the social conditioning of his roles. In Shakespeare's day, men tended to be aware of society mainly through face-to-face encounters with others; human bonds, whether of pity or sympathy, were felt to be freely assumed. From the time of Corneille onward, however, the individual learned to see himself as irrevocably involved in a social order, whether he subjected himself to it or revolted against it in the name of a different order. After Molière, social awareness increased to the point where the problem of adaptation to organized society became a central theme of literature; Goethe and Ibsen were both concerned with the price this adaptation exacted from the individual, and at times each writer went to great pains to reveal the social determinants of private problems. Ibsen's works explicitly portray persons as they experience the all-pervasive force of their society.

For the beginning of the period, Lope de Vega, Cervantes, and Calderon represent Spain; Shakespeare, England; and Corneille, Racine, and Molière, France. Strict chronological sequence has been sacrificed for the sake of preserving national groupings. The Spanish writers are dealt with first, since Spain remained closest to feudalism and did not succeed in developing a viable national state or a successful capitalist economy.

The effect on Spain of its conquests in the New World was dramatic; and the three writers considered display three different ways of facing the social changes brought about by this development. Calderon accepted the *status quo* with a kind of fatalism, while Lope de Vega adopted a more dynamic social orientation in glorifying the benefits of an absolute monarchy; Cervantes rejected it.

The Spain of Cervantes' novels is a highly mobile and competitive society. Man has become the measure of a world which is losing its theological determinants; he can now judge what he sees in strictly human rather than theological terms. He rejects much of his society, particularly those deformations of character that are the result of competition and insecurity, but he does so in the name of a manmade ideal. Despite the obvious fact that Don Quixote is presented as a feudal knight, the ideals and observations of Cervantes are too modern, too secular, and too close to the Renaissance concept of the individual for us to call him a sentimentalist. Unlike Cervantes, Lope de Vega is very much the successful and active man of his times, and very much at home in his world. He is intoxicated, in a sense, by the splendor of Spanish power at its peak. But by the middle of the seventeenth century only the deluded could maintain a glorious image of the declining empire: Calderon no less than Lope endorses monarchism; his allegiance, however, is colored by nostalgia for medieval values, caused perhaps by his awareness of diminishing Spanish strength.

Shakespeare in *The Tempest* presents a paradigm of the condition of man at the beginning of the modern era. Shakespeare's age was still characterized by the spirit of an adventurous, mercantile economy which preceded the consolidation of the middle class. He provides the most complete picture of the Renaissance individual who interprets the world almost exclusively in the light of his own needs and to whom outward events appear as tests of an inward adequacy and dynamism.

While Shakespeare advocated the importance of competent rulers, he simultaneously perceived their subjects enmeshed in a new pattern of social mobility which could push the individual downward as well as up.

The French writers, too, reacted to the radical social changes of their times. Their viewpoints, however, are focused on a progressive state where the monarchy is firmly established and the middle classes have begun to flourish. Corneille's individual stands in need of a powerful state authority for guiding his acts—a dependency on outside authorities that would have been alien to Shakespeare. Racine rebels against all authority in favor of the individual, whom he sees as frustrated by submission to the powers that be. Molière sees man feeling his way through the new order to individual autonomy. The French dramatists thus represent three stages in the middle of the development of increasing social control: the bourgeois ethos is more apparent in Racine than in Corneille, and in Molière it is virtually all-pervasive.

Sociologically, Goethe is Molière's direct successor. His work is a progression from the revolt of the Storm and Stress period to his acceptance of middle-class responsibility in *Wilhelm Meister's Travels.* His final view is that the individual is worthy of the name only if he performs a useful social task. Goethe knew the price of adaptation, however, and in his old age became particularly concerned with the growing problem of the alienation of the artist from society at large.

The curve ends with Ibsen and Hamsun. Ibsen was an incisive critic of middle-class society, and the main question he posed was whether society has lived up to the claims of its apologists. His answer was almost invariably negative. In every sphere of life he found the results of competition and specialization to be pernicious. In all of their personal and social encounters, his characters emerge as losers. The institutions and façades of public life become incompatible with individual needs, and man is torn by this conflict. Ibsen explores the classical image of the autonomous individual found in Shakespeare and Cervantes, only to see him break apart under the impact of the very forces that were supposed to help him to realize his potentialities.

If Ibsen presents the dilemma of liberalism, Knut Hamsun implies its authoritarian resolution. There is, in all his novels, an anticipation of the Nazi ideology. He rejects modern, urban, industrial society with its frustrations and responsibilities. His solution is a flight to nature in the form of submission to forces beyond human control, with which he combines admiration of "blood, race, and soil." Such values led him finally into the Nazi movement.

It is striking that in the works of all these periods—underneath the fashions of classicism and romanticism, of rationalism and empiricism in taste and thought—there is a certain continuity in the changing relationships of the individual to his society. Studied separately, the works of each writer yield impressive insights into seemingly timeless universals. Considered together, they testify that man, as he has grappled with the ever-changing problems of his adaptation to society, has become increasingly preoccupied with his own integrity and increasingly aware of the forces which threaten it. The Western ideal of freedom that emerged in the late Renaissance was at first thought to be boundless. That this ideal was found to be subject to the manifold limitations of economic laws, social pressures, and the vagaries of political history may in part account for the fact that pain and anxiety are predominant themes of creative literature. The question the artist asks of mankind is whether pain and anxiety are necessary elements of human destiny, or whether they are mainly a consequence of social conditions.

Part I

Studies on the European
Drama and Novel
from the Renaissance to the
Threshold of Modernity

1

The Spanish Dramatists

Paradoxically, the nation that more than any other inaugurated the modern age did not long enjoy the fruits of this era but fell rapidly into economic and political decline. Spain is closely linked to the discovery of North and Central America, to the ensuing importation of colonial products, and, above all, to the increase of precious metal in Europe. But Spain's brief period of unprecedented expansion was badly mismanaged; neither the court nor the nobility recognized that only the creation of strong national industries and a firmly centralized government could guarantee her continuance as a major world power. The ruling strata had developed a type of economic parasitism which found ample nourishment in the wealth of the old and new worlds. But with the devaluation of precious metals, what had for a brief period been a comfortable over-abundance for parasites now became a ruinous overabundance of parasites.

Although Spain played an ever more negligible role in the new order, the three most eminent Spanish writers of the sixteenth and seventeenth centuries represent the three social points of view prevailing in the Europe of that time. The chronology of their appearance is, however, the reverse of what one would expect. The oldest, Cervantes, is the most critical and the most forward looking of the three while the youngest, Calderon, looks to a society that has already been superseded, Lope de Vega, as spokesman for the absolute monarchy, looks neither backward nor forward but tries to adjust to the prevailing conditions. Of the three, Cervantes is the most rewarding for the purpose of our analysis, namely, to trace the social origins of individual expectations and anxieties.

Lope de Vega, 1562–1635

Background

Lope's life might be described as that of an intellectual entrepreneur. He was born into a family of the metropolitan aristocracy, with excellent

3

connections at court. Educated by the Jesuits, he enjoyed the special tutelage of an uncle who, as Inquisitor, belonged to the upper bureaucracy of the Church of Spain. Then, in quick succession, Lope became active as a soldier, bishop's page, and secretary to the Duke of Alba, a most influential political figure of his time. In early middle age he suffered the sole setback of his career when scandals about his love affairs resulted in a few years' exile from the capital. This trouble, however, seems to have cast no shadow on Lope's future; he returned to Madrid neither sadder, wiser nor more chaste, and there he comfortably spent the last forty years of his life still pursuing his erotic activities. After two marriages, terminated by the death of both wives, Lope was ordained a priest and assigned to one of the fashionable metropolitan churches. His deviations from the moral code did not prevent his earning many honors; he enjoyed the favor of the current power cliques, and the Pope bestowed upon him an honorary doctorate for having extolled Mary Queen of Scots as a Catholic martyr in one of his innumerable plays.

Lope participated in the proceedings of the Inquisition, and was able to reconcile his religious activities with the colorful private life to which seven illegitimate children bore witness. His literary production, too, was nearly inexhaustible. More than two thousand plays came from his pen, of which a third have been preserved. Cervantes (whom Lope snubbed all his life, only to eulogize him fourteen years after his death) with some justice called him "a monster of nature." Lope died in 1635, in his seventy-third year. His funeral was as spectacular as his life had been; the obsequies lasted nine days, with three bishops in attendance.

Lope's work portrayed the ambiguities in the social position of the Spanish ruling groups in his time. The Spanish monarchy and the worldly and ecclesiastical aristocracy bound up with it were able to maintain their luxuries for a while on the proceeds of the great Spanish explorations, especially on the proceeds of colonial wealth and the booty acquired in victorious campaigns. This prosperity was bound to be frustrated sooner or later, if only because the mode of production which was beginning to replace feudalism demanded not luxury but industriousness—that is, industry in both senses of the word. The internal inconsistency between the medieval and the modern ways of social life which characterized the Spanish aristocracy—its attempt to subordinate essentially capitalistic types of production and consumption to an antiquated feudal system—furnishes Lope with his underlying theme.

The Maintenance of Order: Authority

For an understanding of this inner contradiction as it manifests itself in Lope and in the group of which he was a part, the reader might refer to almost any one of the dramas. Consider, for example, *The Duke of Viseo*. The play begins with the triumphant return of a general of the army from his successful African campaign. He is welcomed by the king in a manner somewhat less than friendly, however, for he and his brothers have been accused by the favorite courtier of high treason. The courtier plans to marry a lady attached to the court, who makes the mistake of asking the general's advice on the desirability of the match. The courtier's grandmother having been discovered to be a Moor, the general thinks the marriage ill-advised, and swears the lady to secrecy in the matter of the African grandmother. Of course, the lady talks; the court circles teem with gossip and internecine quarrels break out. In these intrigues, the Duke of Viseo, brother-in-law to the king and the epitome of loyalty to his in-laws, becomes unhappily involved. The outcome for the duke is death; the king has him destroyed, along with the general who began it all, as well as the general's brothers. A young lady, in love with the duke, dies of sorrow at his bier. The denouement, however, is the king's acknowledgment of the duke's innocence; to mend matters as best he can, he confers the honors due to the unjustly condemned duke upon the duke's brother and, in fact, pronounces him heir-apparent to the throne. It is taken for granted that the king has behaved with propriety and justice and, in his eleventh-hour restitutions, has shown an ample degree of forbearance and good sportsmanship.

The play is typical of Lope, its authoritarian structure reconciling social values of the medieval type with the emerging values of monarchical absolutism. At no point is there doubt that Lope sides with the principle of absolute authority. The matter could not be pinpointed more specifically than it is in a conversation between the duke and one of his peers, a member of the duke's camarilla, both of whom are eventually put to death by the king whose praises are being sung:

> *Guimarans*:   Viseo,
> Such honorable thought in you's the issue
> That we and you in war and peace were both
> Restrained by law, and by the law impell'd
> To hold in high esteem our king, for that
> He stands for God in our country. As for ourselves,
> We princes are on earth what in the heavens above
> The Angels are unto God's countenance.
> Therefore we owe him all obedience
> And thanks for aught he does.[1]

And the duke takes it up from there:

> *Viseo:*   It is a lofty and a noble thought
> That you observe in our earthly hierarchy
> An image of the heavenly.[2]

Sublime or banal, the observation is commonplace enough to the Renaissance with its highly schematic system of analogues. But what is of interest is that this respect for the traditional order, for authoritarian force, is an absolute for Lope; the king is respected even when he is transparently in the wrong. Once he has his grandees murdered, he need only appoint the murdered man's brother to be his successor to set everything straight again. Similarly, in another of Lope's dramas, the well-known *Jewess of Toledo,*[3] a Spanish king falls in love with a beautiful young Jewish girl; the innocent heroine is put to death and, although the king causes her downfall, the murder is justified because it recalls the king to his duties as ruler and father.

One need only compare, for instance, Viseo's ethos with Don Quixote's to recognize the degree of Lope's conformism. Don Quixote symbolizes a conflict in which the individual is finally shattered by the authority of social facts. This conflict is to become a pervasive motif in literature throughout the ensuing modern era. But Lope's theme is one which plays on the potential compatibility of the individual's private and public life; in case of doubt, however, it is society that has the final say. When the Jewess is put to death, the state benefits by her removal; and what is the death of one Jewess, no matter how innocent, when measured against the welfare of the state?

In Lope's glorification of the absolute monarchy we do not find any longer the moralistic compulsion of the Middle Ages, nor do we, on the other hand, find the artist a spokesman for individual freedom. Like Corneille in France, Lope is a poet of the new nationalism. The medieval sense of inner duty is replaced by an attitude of dependence on a secular power from without. In another of Lope's plays, *The Sheep Well,* the king is shown as coming to the aid of the people against the depredations of a feudal lord. Here, as elsewhere in the plays, we get a picture of a society in which almost anything can happen, and it is the will of the king that imposes a pattern on events, insures order and, occasionally, promotes justice. It has been thought by some that Lope was indirectly giving lectures to kings on justice and on reparations for injustice. However that may be, it is just as certain that he was equally concerned with absolute allegiance to the monarch.

But while Lope raises the issue of conformism, he at the same time obscures the conflict between individual wishes and the claims of the state. He persistently portrays victory as on the side of the ruler in the struggle between good and evil, right and wrong, honor and caprice, virtue and vice. With the dice thus loaded, we can do no more than infer the price of conformity to his protagonists; Lope is too rigid a monarchist to display it at any length.

The Threat to Order: Passion

The concern of Lope's protagonists is to placate the powers-that-be in order to stave off complete destruction. The realities of the social world, however, tend constantly to be veiled by metaphysics. The essential characteristics of the modern era—industriousness, professional concerns, the conflict between rich and poor, the importance of private property and competition in trade and industry—all are absent, or appear only incidentally, in his work. All those aspects of social observation which in Cervantes' novels are so rich are either left out of account or made part of an inscrutable human destiny. Accidents of every description, even miracles and magic tricks, recur repeatedly.

Lope's fatalism was a response to the mobility of seventeenth-century society, with its chance meetings and its possibilities for accidents, including sudden downward movements on the social ladder; it is a fatalism that has more in common with Calvin's doctrine of predestination than with medieval Catholic dogma. Yet Lope's fatalism proves remarkably inconsistent. At times, tragic human events are viewed as the unforeseeable results of destiny but, on other occasions, they are viewed as springing from human passions. At one point we get the lines:

> Even if fate's intent could be discovered
> Its reach no human being could escape.
> So soon as man has found his enemy in fate
> Not even the firmest will can then withstand it.[4]

But in the same play we read this interchange:

King:	Elvira then is dead?
Don Luis:	Aye, cold, my lord.
	There's not a breath upon her to be felt.
King:	Why, has she killed herself?
Don Leonardo:	My lord,
	She did not.
King:	What then, was the cause?
Leonardo:	Immeasurable love.[5]

Lope portrays love as a force that cannot be brought into harmony with the existing social order—a motif which, as we shall see, will frequently form the point of departure for an implied social critique, e.g., in Racine and in the Goethe of *Werther.* In Lope's plays the idea of absolute monarchy, the principle of the existing order, always wins out; nevertheless such an expedient resolution, as, for instance, in *The Jewess of Toledo,* must have been pale in comparison with the dramatic effect of the passion with which the king loves first his wife and later the Jewess. This passion engulfs him to such a degree that he is ready to discard all obligations. Once the Jewess has been brought to him he renounces all thought of a campaign against the Moors. In the conflict between his duty as a commander and his desires as a lover, the lover—until duty conquers all—is victorious. An unbridgeable gulf opens between social order and the individual.

Pessimism

Thus for Lope, society is formalized into a value in itself, against which passion is viewed as a fateful, if not fatal, accident. Cervantes, on the other hand, makes a clear distinction between a bad society and one which is beneficial to human beings. The world which mocks Don Quixote is in many respects a useful world; only insofar as it stunts human morality does it deserve to be rejected by Cervantes and the Knight alike. But behind the hilarity of the Knight's adventures, Cervantes has managed to express the hope that there may some day emerge a society in which people will no longer laugh at Don Quixotes, and in which individual freedom and the collective good may be maintained side by side. In this sense, *Don Quixote* is not only a non-conformist but also an optimistic document, the more optimistic in that it provides a framework within which right action and wrong action are clearly distinguishable from each other.

Far otherwise with Lope. Bascially he distrusts the individual's capacity for self-discipline and right social action, and he implies the need for a rigidly binding relationship between governor and governed. What he demands is ready submission to the will of the ruler who, once having been designated to keep peace in the social body, must be inviolable. Since man is incapable of self-government, the only reasonable solution is for him to abdicate the task to the state. Lope, like Hobbes and Machiavelli, begins with an assumption of innate disorder in human nature.

However sympathetic he is to the *status quo,* Lope nevertheless registers the bewilderment of the man of his century in a way that is more bleakly sad than that of either Cervantes, with his bagful of Utopian possibilities, or Calderon, with his strong religious ties and his (even if deceptively) firm medieval moorings. And at times a genuinely desperate note can be caught in Lope; it is heard quite distinctly in such lines as the following, from the monologue of a young gardener (Belardo) in *The Jewess of Toledo:*

> How foolish is the world, and how ridiculous
> Are the illusions to which it surrenders.
> All is delusion and hypocrisy,
> Stupidity or else presumptuousness.
> God in His Heaven is addressed as "thou,"
> Base man is titulate' "Your Highness,"
> A wife sans shame and honor's now a courtesan;
> Depravity may pass for youthful folly,
> Thieving's misnamed dexterity; poverty, dishonor,
> Honorable he alone who's rich and fortunate.
> Foolhardiness assumes the name of bravery,
> And vulgar cunning's likened to discretion.
> Madness and avarice take on ambition's name . . .
> Thus have all designations been confounded,
> But death alone cannot be altered by this world,
> For he alone does level all whom he encounters.[6]

The feeling of futility in Lope's distress is sharpened if we contrast the lines with another work of the same period: Lope's theme is sufficiently similar to that of Shakespeare's Sixty-sixth Sonnet to justify their analysis side by side:

> Tir'd with all these, for restful death I cry
> As to behold desert a beggar born,
> And needy nothing trimm'd in jollity,
> And purest faith unhappily forsworn,
> And gilded honour shamefully misplac'd,
> And maiden virtue rudely strumpeted,
> And right perfection wrongfully disgraced,
> And strength by limping sway disabled,
> And art made tongue-tied by authority,
> And folly—doctor-like—controlling skill,
> And simple truth miscall'd simplicity,
> And captive good attending captain ill:
> Tir'd with all these, from these would I be gone,
> Save that, to die, I leave my love alone.[7]

It will be noticed that in Belardo's monologue the world's madness is characterized by a confusion and corruption of terminology. The uses of language have been perverted and defiled; distinctions have broken down; coherence is gone; anything can be made to equal anything else; meanings can be reversed at will; language has become an instrument of deception, hypocrisy, falsification, disguise. Death alone can neither be changed as a reality, nor can it be falsified by language. It remains the sole safeguard and certainty to which man has access in a world gone mad. It has literally "gone" mad; for there is a certain dynamic quality in Belardo's words which allude to a time when the world was neither absurd nor insane, and the suggestion, though undeveloped, is very strong that things have not always been this way.

While Belardo's words bear a highly generalized impress, in Shakespeare's sonnet the entire atmosphere is to a very marked degree personalized. Shakespeare's "I" is in the foreground of the recital continuously. Moreover, the defects which the sonnet stigmatizes are not corruptions of language but corruptions of institutions, attitudes, actions. In other words, Shakespeare deals with a more or less specific historical development into which the individual is thrown and in which something happens to him. It is not, as in the case of Lope, a phenomenon of general misorientation which is being indicted, a case of linguistic aberration, the perversion of speech as the genuine tool of truth, but rather the corruption of a way of life. Insofar as the abuse of language is at all criticized in Shakespeare's verse, the criticism really sidesteps language in order to get at something else: the wicked reality. Lope's words betray a certain desperate explosiveness; they might almost be interpreted as the outburst of a man at his wit's end. Shakespeare's words—raising the truisms of contemporary tavern philosophers to artistic consciousness—sound a very articulate protest indeed against conditions that have overwhelmed the individual; they are capable, however, of being changed—they are historical phenomena, societal facts and tendencies that contain their own possibilities for change.

The two excerpts reveal the difference not only between two poetic temperaments but between two social situations as well. Lope de Vega typifies a transitional period. His philosophy still shows the influence of the medieval brand of realism, according to which the essence of reality consists in universal concepts which are, as creations of God, fixed and static; the world does not change.

Shakespeare, on the other hand, stands in the more advanced position of the nominalist. For him such names as honor, virtue, fame—although they may temporarily have no phenomena to which they can be related—denote human attributes which can again become part of reality. One might say that for Shakespeare man's measure—the very definition of man—lies in his ability to change. And change is brought about by the force of love. Lope's ultimate lines aver only the invincibility of death; Shakespeare's project the individual toward life. To the man of the Renaissance the concept of love bears distinctly revolutionary aspects. It indicates uniqueness, specificity, particularity; it can neither be inherited nor transmitted. It is no more grounded in tradition than it can be taught for future use: in short, it is the very essence of individuality.

Calderon, 1600–1681

Background

Calderon's life spans the final stages of Spain's decline as a world power, her loss of supremacy to France and England and the economic decay that followed the first phases of colonization. Calderon neither gave his endorsement to this state of affairs, nor, since he was a loyal servant of the Crown, did he attack it. Of the three possible positions—to sympathize with the existing order, to criticize it, or to withdraw from it—Calderon's was the latter, an escape into the past; to all intents, his is the viewpoint of medieval man.

Like Lope, Calderon was educated by the Jesuits. His family enjoyed intimate connections at court, his father having served as under-secretary in two successive reigns. After his military service, Calderon became poet laureate to the court and like the glamorous Lope, who befriended him, was knighted in due time, became a priest, and spent the last years of his life in increasingly eminent positions assigned to him by the Crown. Unlike Lope, however, he seems to have led a personally honorable life and to have confined himself to the pattern of the well-behaved courtier.

The idea of monarchy which Calderon exalted had little in common with the modern power-state as Lope conceived it. What Calderon portrays is, in substance, the feudal state, now prolonged in the Inquisition, in league with the Church. The concept of honor that lies at the center of his reaction has an artificial character: it means not merit but a prestige like that of the Spanish Empire itself, backward looking and without intrinsic strength. There are two classes: the feudal lords, and the rest who are their subordinates. Only among the former do we find pure passion, excellence of conduct, bravery, and virtue. In the lower strata nearly everybody is vulgar, cowardly, and dissolute. Nothing could more pointedly mark the contrast between Calderon and Cervantes: Cervantes at times places his final truths in the mouths of gypsies and robbers; Calderon would shrug off these dregs of humanity as unworthy candidates for prestige and honor.

The Concept of Honor

Calderon has occasionally been described as an author who glorified emerging middle-class values, and his play, *The Mayor of Zalamea*, has been cited in support of this interpretation. A close examination of the drama will not, however, bear out this view. The play portrays the infatuation of a captain, who is a member of the gentility, for the daughter of the mayor of Zalamea, a wealthy farmer in whose house the captain is billeted. When the affair comes to light, the father insists that the captain restore his daughter's violated honor by marrying her—an unusual request because of the social distance between the gentry and a peasant, however wealthy and respected he may be in his community. Since the captain rejects this request the peasant has him murdered and petitions the king to sanction this avengement of his daughter.

A superficial analysis of the play might suggest that Calderon's intention was to take the part of the mayor and his class against the gentry. If nothing else the mayor's request to the king to approve his drastic action rules out this view. It also becomes increasingly clear that the model of "honor" in this case is not middle-class virtue, but a concept that originates in and chiefly refers to the highest feudal circles, from which the subsidiary orders derive their raisons d'être. In a conversation between the mayor and the captain's commanding officer, the peasant raises the point of honor three times in quick succession in an atmosphere heavy with tension; he has made up his mind not to stop short of the most drastic measures if his demands are ignored:

Crespo:	And I tell you, whoever points his little finger at my honour, I'll cut him down before hanging.
Lope:	Know you not, you are bound by your allegiance to submit?
Crespo:	To all costs of property, yes; but of honour, no, no, no! My goods and chattels, aye, and my life—are the king's; But my honour is my own soul's.[8]

What enables these two people, miles apart socially, to communicate with each other is the commonly understood reference to a traditional hierarchy of values that is impervious to any practical exigencies. They both know what "honor" entails, and this keeps the conversation going. At the same time—though so faintly as to be just audible—a new concept of man is caught in the peasant's remonstrances: his readiness to relate honor to his private individuality, to his "soul." But it would be too far-fetched to interpret this passing allusion as the same attitude as that which found expression in the paeans to the individual and his soul, and which was developed in the philosophies of Cervantes and Shakespeare. The most Calderon is saying is that honor belongs to any one, given the sanction of higher authority. He is not having the peasant formulate a new insight, as Cervantes might have done. The peasant is, on the contrary, merely repeating lessons about honor he has learned and that have been passed down to him from on high.

Calderon and Lope

In Calderon's play, the peasant's son, conversant with the devices for attaining upward mobility in the decaying years of the bankrupt and money-hungry Spanish monarchy, suggests to his father that he might easily avoid the discomforts of having his house used for billeting army personnel by simply buying a title of nobility. But the father says:

> A patent of gentility; upon thy life now dost think there's a soul who doesn't know that I'm no gentleman at all, but just a plain farmer? I should only prove I was worth so many thousand royals, not that I had gentle blood of my veins, which can't be bought at any price. . . . If a fellow's been bald ever so long, and buys him a fine wig, and claps it on, will his neighbors think it his own hair a bit more? . . . They know his bald pate is safe under it all the while. That's all he gets by it.

Still the son objects:

> Nay, sir, he gets to look younger and handsomer, and keeps off sun and cold.

Whereupon the father says:

> I'll have none of your wig honour at any price. My grandfather was a farmer, so was my father, so is yours, and so shall you be after him.[9]

Quite obviously, the father's argument is extra-rational and depends solely for its persuasiveness on identification with the concepts of those who have the highest prestige.

Literary historians have suggested that the peasant's speech may have been inspired by the following passage in one of Lope's plays:

> He that was born to live in humble state
> Makes but an awkward knight, do what you will.
> My father means to die as he has liv'd
> The same plain collier that he always was;
> And I too must an honest ploughman die.
> 'Tis but a single step or up or down;
> For men there must be that will plough or dig,
> And when the vase has once been fill'd, be sure
> 'Twill always savour of what first it held.[10]

Although it is obvious that Lope and Calderon are likeminded in their benevolent view toward the *status quo,* as opposed to Cervantes who of the three stands alone as its critic, nevertheless between the former two we find significantly different motivations. Lope's argument for things as they are is based on considerations of utility: "for men there must be that will plough or dig." He is not unaware of the factor of upward (or, for that matter, downward) mobility, but in justifying the division of labor in his own society he sidesteps the issue by pointing to the quite honorable, concrete social tasks of the peasant. For Calderon, however, social mobility is something beyond the pale; a man's station and role in life is transcendentally determined: "gentle blood . . . can't be bought at any price." The different reasons for supporting the social order may perhaps be explained by the contrast between a social climate of confidence in the future of the *status quo,* as Lope had known it in earlier years, and that of a power system in rapid decline, which was the heritage of Calderon.

The difference between the two writers emerges most clearly when we consider the over-all qualities of their works. Lope wrote count-less plays with a contemporary setting (though his social observations were far less rich and realistic than those of Cervantes). Calderon, on the other hand, was attracted by feudal settings. When he does deal with a contemporary theme, the language seems stilted and codified.

In *The Great World Theater* (*El Gran Teatro del Mundo*), Calderon shows God assigning people their professional status before placing them on earth. Quite naturally, only the king is satisfied with the role given him; all the others strongly object. Their objections are pointless because the will of God cannot be contradicted. The beggar, in particular, finds it hard to accept his status, but he is assured that it is not the role itself that matters but how well it is played. In the end, the conclusion is that life on earth will, in any case, be brief and will be followed by an eternity in heaven for those who play their parts well. The drama makes quite apparent that no one can change his role without incurring divine wrath; the beggar can only hope to be a good beggar, the king a good king. The rewards, if there are any, spring from acceptance. The play exemplifies the formalism, rigidity and, at the same time, the dreamlike quality of the decaying Spanish empire.

Artificial Traditionalism

In *The Physician of His Honour* Calderon has an impetuous prince lose his dagger in the bedroom of a noble lady. The prince is being impetuous to no great purpose; the woman retains her innocence. But the dagger having been discovered, the intrigue must be resolved and honor restored. The transparent fact that no honor has been lost to begin with is quite beside the point; the rite must go on. The husband is denied the possibility of a duel with the prince, for it is not within the rules of the game for a grandee to take bodily revenge on a son of the royal house. Instead, the husband restores his honor by opening the veins of his sleeping wife; and he does so with the complete approval of the king, whose son has thus in effect murdered the one innocent party in the cabal.

The play reads like an indictment; the very absurdity of the murder speaks of the meaninglessness of the traditional code. But the over-all character of Calderon's works testifies to the fact that no irony is intended (although the phantastic element in his plays suggests that he himself may have been, at some level, aware of the hollowness of the social system he was glorifying). One's role may be absurd; nevertheless the advice is to accept it and to play it well. The situation reminds one of Lessing's *Emilia Galotti*, written roughly a hundred years later. In the German writer's drama, a patrician kills his own daughter rather than allow the tyrant of a petty Italian state to dishonor her. But Lessing's temperament was critical and his message revolutionary. In his drama the rising middle class indicts the arbitrariness of absolute monarchy; there could not have been any doubt in the minds of the audience that the dagger which struck Emilia should have been aimed at the prince. Calderon's play, on the other hand, inadvertently depicts the decay of a once respectable value system that is degenerating to the status of a private ritual. To paraphrase a well-known *mot:* in Lessing's world the situation is serious but not hopeless; in Calderon's it is hopeless but not serious.

The social position of Calderon may perhaps be illuminated by a comparison of the moral values expressed in *The Mayor of Zalamea* with those which prevail in a story by Cervantes, wherein a rich peasant boy dishonors a young girl and refuses to marry her. In the former, as we remember, the stubborn Crespo has the captain executed because the captain, equally stubborn, refuses to marry the peasant's daughter. In *Don Quixote*, however, the claims of restitution of honor as a traditional moral value lose out to the prerogatives inherent in the possession of private property: the lord of the region is unable to force the rich peasant's son to marry the girl—because the lord is the peasant's debtor. Calderon's peasant, on the other hand, where honor is involved, imitates to an almost grotesque degree the professed ideologies of medieval chivalry in words like these:

> You shall forthwith take all my substance, without reserve of a single farthing for myself or my son, only what you choose to allow us; you shall even brand us on back or forehead, and sell us like slaves or mules by way of adding to the fortune I offer you—all this, and what you will beside, if only you will with it take my daughter to wife, and restore the honour you have robbed. . . . And what is my demand? But that you should restore what you have robbed: so fatal for us to lose, so easy for you to restore.[11]

The reactionary character of the speaker is further underscored by the way in which he refers to the new social order, the rule of law, the protection of certain rights enforced by sane and solid magistrates. He will not violate the traditional hierarchy by taking recourse to orderly procedures of law, so as to have redress

> which I could myself now wrest from you by the hand of the law but which I rather implore of you as a mercy on my knees![12]

The unbending rigidity with which a privileged group tries to cling to antiquated concepts may be noted again in the captain's evasive and impertinent reaction to the old peasant's plea:

> As to the wrong you talk of, if you would avenge it by force, I have little to fear. As to your magistrate's stick there, it doesn't reach my profession at all.[13]

The final sanction of the mayor's act of retribution is unequivocal. The king himself forgives the peasant, because he has, "if unusually, not unjustly," acted in the spirit of the Spanish monarchy. As a parting symbol of a mentality which abhors nothing more than change, the king appoints Crespo "perpetual Mayor of Zalamea. And so fare well."[14]

Calderon's greatness as a literary artist is not, of course, under question here. But it may be interesting to note in this context that Goethe, who had the highest respect for Calderon's art, in the end repudiated him. According to Goethe, the audience was forced into an attitude of total passiveness, obliged to accept the contents, spirit, characters, and morals of Calderon, as if they were ingredients of so much spoon-fed medicine.[15] Goethe speaks here for the progressive middle-class critic, who rejects not only the reactionary authoritarian values of Calderon but also, in the last analysis, the rigidity of the art forms through which they are manifest.

In some of Calderon's plays, ironically enough, there is a quixotic element of doubt about reality, and wherever we encounter it even the courtly pomp with which in his own life he was surrounded seems to take on a dream-like quality. But such ambiguity with regard to reality is far removed in its social meaning from the phantasy of Cervantes, whose idealism does not prevent him from acutely observing the world around him.

Notes

1. Lope de Vega, *El Duque de Viseo,* Act II.
2. Ibid.
3. Spanish title: *Las Paces de los Reyes y Yudia de Toledo.*
4. *El Duque de Viseo,* Act I.
5. Ibid., Act III.
6. Lope, *Las Paces de los Reyes,* Act II (translation by Edgar Rosenberg).
7. Shakespeare, *The One Hundred Fifty-Four Sonnets* (New York: Crowell, 1944), p. 65.
8. Calderon, *The Mayor of Zalamea,* Act I, Scene 3. From *Rubaiyat of Omar Khayyam and Six Plays of Calderon,* translated by Edward Fitzgerald (London: Everyman's Library, 1928, p. 260). All quotations from this book are reprinted by permission of E. P. Dutton & Co., Inc.
9. Ibid., Act I, Scene 2, p. 254.
10. Lope de Vega, *Wise Man at Home,* quoted in Calderon's *Plays,* p. 284.
11. Calderon, *Plays,* Act III, Scene 3, p. 277.
12. Ibid.
13. Ibid.
14. Ibid., Act IV, Scene 5, p. 283.
15. See, Goethe, "Calderon's 'Daughter of the Air'" (1822) in *Goethe's Literary Essays,* ed. J. E. Spingarn (New York, 1921), pp. 208–11.

2

Cervantes, 1547–1616

Don Quixote is read today primarily as a collection of humorous adventures. Its author nevertheless experienced the bitter uncertainty of the small man in post-medieval society. Cervantes attempted perpetually, and in vain, to shake off the conditions of poverty into which he was born. His father, coming from the lowest ranks of gentility, was a man of somewhat obscure professional qualifications, part lawyer, part physician; he was both deaf and destitute. Cervantes wavered for a time between attempts to make a career in the papal bureaucracy of Rome and efforts to hew out a place for himself in the military by enlisting in the Spanish Navy, which just then was readying to engage the Turkish fleet at Lepanto. During this battle the poet all but lost his life.

After a partial recovery, Cervantes again joined the fleet, only to be captured by Algerian pirates; the next twelve years he spent in captivity. His various attempts to escape brought him near to hanging, burning, and impaling. When finally his widowed mother scraped together the needed ransom, Cervantes returned to his homeland and found a modest position as collector of taxes and procurer of military provisions. At this time he married, and it seems that for the next few years he was able to support his growing family (though barely) by various additional jobs, some of them literary. The last twenty years of his life were spent trying to survive on the meager proceeds from his writing and from occasional government posts, none of which he was able to hold for any length of time. This was his routine, interrupted periodically by imprisonment for debt, for unsubstantiated charges of civil disorder or embezzlement. On one of these occaions (he was then under suspicion of murder) he had to take his entire family to jail with him. He died in a state of utter destitution the same year Shakespeare died—tradition has it that they died the same day.

Cervantes' life, in a way, symbolizes the plight of the non-aristocratic individual in a society that is no longer bound by the fixed relationships of the medieval worldly and ecclesiastical hierarchy, but has become impersonal and abstract. Fundamentally the themes of his novel are those of an old way of life being replaced by a new order. Cervantes stresses the resulting conflicts in two ways: through the struggles of the Knight, and through the contrast between him and Sancho Panza. Don Quixote lives in a phantasy world of the vanishing feudal hierarchy; the people with whom he deals, however, are merchants, minor functionaries in the government, unimportant intellectuals—in short, they are, like Sancho, people who want to get ahead in the world and, therefore, direct their energies to the things which will being them profit.

But common sense, this altogether correct answer to the challenge of organized society, tends to obscure a quality which Don Quixote possesses in ample degree—humaneness, which always protests injustice. It is from Don Quixote's humaneness that certain tendencies, antiauthoritarian and, for his time revolutionary, derive. The protest takes the form of an ironical twist: Don Quixote is always wrong, the others always right. A shaving bowl is not really a helmet, nor is a windmill a dragon. The wineskins are no more giants than the innkeeper is a knight. It is absurd to want to free the galley slaves, because they will only commit more crimes and finally take their liberty out on their liberator. The people are "right" in protecting their belongings against the onslaughts of a Don Quixote and in guarding against his interference in their private affairs. Common sense has a higher authority than his absurd pretensions.

This is not to say that Don Quixote is not a hero, any more than it is to say that Cervantes is nostalgically oriented toward the past. If we examine the novel closely, we see that Cervantes' concept of man is in every way contrary to the medieval concept. True, Don Quixote does pay lip service to obsolete structures—the hierarchy of the Church and the feudal social system, together with the conceptions of virtue and chivalry associated with them. But he does not accept them in their old meanings; he recasts them to suit his own purpose. One might say that Don Quixote is the first figure in Renaissance literature who seeks by action to bring the world into harmony with his own plans and ideals. Cervantes' irony lies in the fact that while overtly his hero battles against the new (the early manifestations of middle-class life) in the name of the old (the feudal system), actually he attempts to sanction a new principle. This principle consists, basically, in the autonomy of individual thinking and feeling. The dynamics of society have come to demand a continuous and active transformation of reality; the world must be perpetually constructed anew. Don Quixote recreates his world even though he does so in a phantastic and solipsistic fashion. The honor for which he enters the lists is the product of his thinking, not of socially established and accepted values. He defends those whom he considers worthy of his protection and assails those he believes to be wicked. In this sense he is a rationalist as well as an idealist.

Despite his feudal accouterments the Knight shares another attribute with the new post-medieval character—solitude. His opponents, too, are isolated, but for a quite different reason: their atomization is a consequence of the fact that each is pursuing his own selfish motives. Don Quixote is isolated because what he wants to accomplish is impossible: he wants to suppress those who are evil, to do away with force, to free men, to realize his feeling of devotion for humankind in his love for Dulcinea. He runs head-on into conflict with all authority as soon as he begins to put such good intentions into effect.

His idealism has two sides, metaphysical and moral. The world as he sees it, he sees on the basis of his own ideas, and his ideas reside simply, sometimes simple-mindedly, in his impressions. The world, as he reconstructs it, is in truth his private property. The peasant is not a peasant but an Arab; the windmill and the wine-skins are dragons and giants; the innkeeper is a lord of the castle; the peasant girl a noble lady. This world, which he has created, he then evaluates by his own moral ideals. The outcome for him personally can only be failure, since his adversary is no less than the expedient relativism of the common-sense world.

But while *Don Quixote* ends on a note of sad resignation, this solution seems not to have reflected the author's convictions. Cervantes had in fact a practical, first-hand knowledge of the forces of hunger, of money, of private property. In some instances he raised quite specific demands for reform; in this he may have been stimulated by manifestoes on natural rights to be found in Catholic literature, which not only traced the authority of the king to that of the people but enunciated more or less outspoken demands for radical economic change. (For example, statements may be found in these broadsides which appear to call for cooperative farms.) Whether Cervantes was directly familiar with the writings of Mariana and Suarez, we have no way of ascertaining; but we do know that he envisioned a Utopia roughly along the lines indicated by these writers. As already noted, his critique of the *status quo* was essentially cloaked in images of artistic irony. Thus, he stressed in many variations the society of the poor as the only place where genuine human feelings still exist, because there people remain uncorrupted by interests in worldly goods. In the "exemplary" tale of *Rinconete and Cortadillo,* he even allowed himself the extended jest of picturing a society of robbers and thieves as exemplars of true human solidarity.

Mobility: Sancho Panza

The New World Picture

Midway through *Don Quixote,* the noble Knight takes it into his head to reward Sancho Panza, the peasant servant whom his errant mind has transformed into a medieval squire, by conferring upon him the governorship of an island. The island is, of course, imaginary. For some time Don Quixote and Sancho have gone their separate ways, but the expectation of the good fortune of the governorship brings the servant back to his master. He tells his wife that he has been offered the job of running an entire island by himself and that, although the job entails his separation from his family, it would be criminal to turn it down on that account. It is quite "necessary" that he take the job, he says,

> And then, too, I like to think that I may be able to come upon another hundred crowns to take the place of those we've spent, although, naturally, it makes me sad to have to leave you and the young ones. . . . I can tell you one thing, wife, said Sancho, that if I did not expect to see myself the governor of an island before long. I would die right here and now.[1]

By implication, Sancho is raising an issue that will later become a fundamental one in middle-class society, the issue of social mobility. Granted that the peasant's phantasies about the extent of his mobility are extreme—the possibilities open to a peasant at the turn of the sixteenth century certainly did not range from utter destitution to high political positions—they nonetheless serve to reveal areas of feelings and perceptions which are real enough despite the rather absurd event that occasions them.

It is difficult for us today to imagine and to reconstruct the uncertainties to which Western man was exposed during the century-long revolution which marked the transition to middle-class life. The feudal society of the late Middle Ages had brought its own vicissitudes; but uncertainty had not been notably one of them. The peasant, for better or worse, was no more than a subunit of the feudal pyramid—born into it and replaced in it by his offspring. His position was both specifically defined and predictable. But with the waning of the closed system of an agricultural society people found themselves increasingly freed from the securities as well as the bondages that inhere in an unchangeable social location.

By the turn of the sixteenth century most of the former touch-stones—social, cultural, religious, and economic—had become questionable or entirely useless. Man had to begin, again, from scratch: he had to learn to orient himself to a situation in which he was increasingly thrown back upon his own resources. He found himself between two worlds, "one dead, the other powerless to be born." John Donne was to formulate this sense of frustration in a famous passage from his *Anatomie of the World*:

> And new Philosophy calls all in doubt,
> The Element of fire is quite put out;
> The Sun is lost, and th'earth, and no man's wit
> Can well direct him where to look for it.
> And freely men confess that this world's spent,
> When in the Planets and the Firmament
> They seek so many new; they see that this
> Is crumbled out again to his Atomies.
> 'Tis all in pieces, all coherence gone;
> All just supply, and all Relation:
> Prince, Subject, Father, Son, are things forgot,
> For every man alone thinkes he hath got
> To be a Phoenix, and that then can be
> None of that kind, of which he is, but he.
> This is the world's condition now.[2]

Everything seemed, in Cervantes' day, to be possible at every moment; catastrophe impended, but so did success. The notion that "*tout est dangereux ici-bas*" had all the force of an ever-present, acutely-felt state of mind although the other half of Voltaire's observation, "*et tout est nécessaire*," had not yet been added. And it is precisely this inner reflection of mobility which Sancho Panza's words convey: failure or glory, far beyond the normal expectation of a peasant's career, both seem accessible, perhaps equally accessible to him.

Now this upward or downward mobility (for which the phantasy knows no limit) has certain decisive consequences for human relationships. Consider first the peasant's attitude toward his employer, the Knight. Sancho's words betray the fact that he can no longer quite clearly separate motives of personal loyalty from motives of self-interest. Even while he stammers a trifle defensively about some felt "necessity," his acquisitive mind is drawn toward the possibility of a monetary windfall. This is no longer the feudal peasant who unquestioningly surrenders his life to the tasks and purposes of the person one step above in the hierarchy; he is instead a being who must rely on an entirely new set of motivations. It is, suddenly, the motivation of modern man, in whom self-interest and friendly feeling are often closely allied. The relationships among individuals are now determined by uncertainties and ambiguities, and private decisions must be based on a relativist concept of social reality.

Mobility penetrates even the intimate sphere of family relations. In the peasant's ruminations the drive for sucess and the concern for wife and children are at once separate and complementary forces. While Sancho, in his chatter about having to leave Teresa and the little ones, pays lip service to family responsibilities, this emotional drive is quite clearly subordinated to the drive for acquisition and success, the means for obtaining luxury as well as security for the family unit. The lines between the egoism of the thriving middle-class individual and the altruism of the family man have become blurred in Sancho's declaration—but in case of doubt he will defend the governorship against the claims of his wife.

Secularization of Family and State

Turn now to the wife's answer to Sancho's argument:

> No, not that, my husband, Teresa protested. Let the hen live even though she may have the pip, and in the same way you should go on living and to the devil with all the governorships in the world. Without a governorship you came out of your mother's belly, without a governorship you've lived up to now, and without a governorship you will go, or they will carry you, to your grave when God so wills. There are plenty of folk in this world who manage to get along without being governors . . . but [they] are still numbered among the living. The best sauce in the world is hunger, and since this is something they never lack, the poor always have an appetite.[3]

The passage reveals a number of added features characteristic of post-medieval society; we may confine ourselves briefly to three.

First, the secularization of feelings. There is no pious traditionalism in Teresa's reply, which is directed toward individual needs and pragmatic ways to gratify them. The casual reference to the Deity is hardly more than a stock response; but while the identification of man and animal is not uncommon in medieval literature, Teresa's opening sentence inaugurates a new theme: she avails herself of a private metaphor which is all the more convincing for being part and parcel of her whole outlook. The goal of life is survival, not transcendental salvation. What matters are the hens, not God. Teresa's points of orientation are not the great powerful institutions of society, or religious convictions, but rather are to be found in concrete and cogent life situations which must be maintained and possibly bettered, if the improvement can be brought about on a realistic, sensible level.

Second, the passage tells us something about woman's role in the society of Cervantes' day. Teresa's reaction is conservative; social mobility frightens her. She foreshadows the dual role of the wife in the middle-class family: exclusion from social processes outside the family while remaining a touchstone for the husband's ability to assert himself in his role of breadwinner. When Sancho works up the anticipation of grandiose personal success, the woman acts as the representative of common sense, which seems to be required for the survival of the family unit. Even as she considers the unlikely event that her husband should realize his dreams, her attitude remains one of down-to-earth reasonableness:

> But look, Sancho, if by any chance you do fall in with a governorship, don't forget me and your children. Remember that little Sancho is already turned fifteen, and it is only right that he should go to school. . . . Remember, too, that your daughter, Mari-Sancha, would not drop dead if we married her off.[4]

Sancho immediately toys with the idea of marrying the children into high society, but the wife, true to form, advises him to stick to his own station: "You bring home the money, Sancho, and leave the marrying of her to me." The wife acts throughout as manager of the family, which in turn functions as the only stabilizing element in the turmoil social mobility has created among the Panzas. The family is conceived of as having its own norms, in line with the mores and conventions of the social group for which the husband qualifies; for the wife the bonds of the family guarantee stability and serve as a counterforce to the dangers inherent in both upward and downward mobility. Teresa warns Sancho that their daughter might make blunders in marrying

> some great count or high and mighty gentleman who every time he happened to feel like it would call her an upstart . . . she will be a stranger to others and to herself.[5]

25

The third issue raised by Teresa's reply to Sancho is a suspect view of government. Her remark takes place in the context of the social condition in which the national state has replaced the feudal order. It was largely tradition that had bound the individual to the feudal hierarchy, but the new national state must enforce its claims to power. Not since the time of the late Roman Emperors had Europe experienced to such a degree the force and strength of the state apparatus—its magistracy, its military, its police—in a series of harsh and demanding laws that regulated work and possession. This new political milieu was experienced simply as harshness and toil by the broadest stratum of the population, who were almost always its victims and seldom its beneficiaries. We need only consider how, even in a lenient democracy, the attitude of the ordinary citizen toward the state is compounded of a certain ambivalence in order to infer that the first centuries of modern history must have been a time of extreme uneasiness and aversion toward a rigid monarchy.

Sancho's attitude toward the organs of government is identical with his attitude toward society as a whole. He wants to get on; he wants to be part and parcel of the small group of masters. By masters he more or less unconsciously means people who have a lot of money, and he is inclined to identify a high office of government with money. Teresa's attitude, on the contrary, reflects a wife's skepticism of these risky schemes and stratagems, and an acute anxiety lest the head of the family drift away from home and lose himself in dubious adventures. Cervantes merely hints at these tensions, as he merely hints at all social topics, but they are present in his work in germinal form.

Creativity: Dulcinea

Illusion or Reality?

An intriguing scene occurs in the thirty-second chapter of the second part of *Don Quixote*. Here we are introduced to a social rank far above that of Sancho Panza and his wife as the Knight argues politely with his hosts, the Duke and Duchess. When the conversation turns to Don Quixote's relationship to his beloved, the Lady Dulcinea del Toboso, the Duchess observes:

> if we are to believe the tale about Senor Don Quixote that was recently published in these parts and that won the praise of all—we are to gather from this tale, if I remember rightly, that your Grace has

never seen the lady Dulcinea, that there is, in fact, no such lady in existence, or, rather, that she is a purely fanciful one, created in your Grace's own mind, whom you have endowed with all the charms and perfections that you chose to give her.[6]

The Duchess thus ceases to talk as a fictitious character may be expected to, within the story; instead, she talks about the story (by virtue of which she exists at all) and discusses *Don Quixote* with Don Quixote. Today, we are not so startled as Cervantes' contemporaries must have been by the device; it is a kind of irony that has been used often since, although his must certainly be a very early example.[7] In any case, enough of the mood of ambiguity survives to give us a sudden feeling of uncertainty. For a moment, we no longer know whether we are inside the novel or out of it, and the demarcation between existence and phantasy becomes problematic, as indeed it is in the Knight's world. The question: does Dulcinea exist? points to the heart of Cervantes' ambiguous philosophical position, a position that betrays the fundamental uncertainty of his time.

In the Middle Ages, the world and everything in it had been viewed as created and guaranteed by God. The hierarchy of society, perceptions of the "real" and even the imagination of man, all had their fixed places in this ordering. The figure of Don Quixote arises in a world that has lost this theological compass, a world in which man must create his own ordered meanings so that he can locate himself, others, and the external world. Don Quixote does this by embracing two seemingly irreconcilable philosophies—those of sensualistic empiricism and rational idealism—but the two complement each other as orientation courses in the new order. To Don Quixote, Dulcinea exists. She represents the Knight's perception as well as her own (after all, she is his creation), and the Knight's and her own rational and moral criteria. Don Quixote is man placed at the center of things after the fall of the feudal hierarchy. To him, only that exists which man creates, perceives, imagines, or anticipates.

The evaluation Cervantes makes of Don Quixote (and of himself) is also one he applies to others, in a moral sense: man is the offspring of his own works. The Knight, in a conversation with a peasant boy at a strategic point early in the novel, asserts "the fact that every man is the son of his works."[8] The same words are used by the Knight's servant when, much later in the story, Sancho Panza reminds himself that "each one is the son of his own works, and being a man I may become to be pope, not to speak of being governor of an island; for my master may win so many that there will not be people enough to give them to."[9] Similarly, all the love of a Don Quixote would not be enough to create the shining image of Dulcinea if she did not herself act out the infinite potentialities of her inner being, if she were not "the daughter of her works."[10] There is hardly a concept more generic to the modern style of life in the Western world than this which burdens the individual with the responsibility for his own life and for the life of man.

The ideal of man as the center of his acts brings us close to modern concepts of democracy. The social world comes into being by virtue of the individual's creative acts; and it is in this recognition, morally, that the foundation of human equality resides. Man, any man, contains a creative potential, although his condition, his social role, may not allow him to realize it.

Two basic concepts of human nature run through modern moral beliefs. The one, represented by Machiavelli, Luther, and Hobbes, endows the human being with innate qualities of evil—or, at least, brutishness—and prescribes rigid coercive measures. The other, whose chief spokesmen are artists, endows man with the primary quality of innocence. Of course, the Christian dogma of Original Sin was taken seriously by artists of the Renaissance and it was often a potent factor in their lives; indeed, if there is one commonplace of which the schoolboy in Cervantes' or Shakespeare's time was daily reminded, it was:

> In Adam's fall
> we sinnèd all.

But it may be laid down that for Cervantes and such artists as Shakespeare, Racine, Schiller, and Ibsen, the original kindness and benevolence of man shines through all his manifestations—his acts as well as his attributes. Cervantes, nevertheless, while he believes human beings are by nature good, admits that they often are not. The original kindness is constantly jeopardized.

The Jeopardy

It is society at large that confronts the idealism of the creative individual with the reality of competitiveness. In place of the egoism of the creative artist, or of a Don Quixote, it imposes the egotism of private gain. It is no mere coincidence that Cervantes, the highly fanciful literary artist, was also an excellent reporter of the social realities of the Renaissance. If he was interested in the individual who was the "son of his own works," he was also an observer of the conditions that threatened him. In *The Man of Glass,* a crazy young student expatiates at length on the professions, specifically on laborers, lawyers, and physicians. Repeatedly he emphasizes instances of human coldness and competitiveness that result in spiritually and materially damaging others.

In speaking of "lads with mules for hire," for example, the student says:

> All you lads have in you something of the pimp, something of the thief, and something of the mountebank. If your masters (for such is the name you give to those you carry upon your mules) chance to be simpletons, you play more tricks on them than this city has known for many years past; if they are foreigners, you rob them; if they are students, you curse them; if they are religious, you blaspheme against them; and if they are soldiers, you tremble from fear.[11]

The carter comes off no better:

> Half the time he is singing and the other half he is cursing or yelling "Get behind there!" when someone tries to pass him. And if by any chance he has to stop to get one of his wheels out of a rut, two good round oaths are of more use to him than three mules.[12]

The sailors

> are a fine lot, though unversed in city ways, and they know no other language than that which is used aboard ship. In fair weather they are diligent, but they are lazy in a storm. In a tempest they give many orders and obey few. Their god is their seaman's chest and their grub, and they find amusement in watching the seasick passengers.[13]

And the carriers, finally, are indicted in language scarcely less restrained:

> They have been divorced from sheets and have married packsaddles. They are so industrious and have such an eye for business that they would lose their souls rather than a day's haul. Their music is that of hoofs, their sauce is hunger, their matins consist in speaking their mind, and they go to mass by hearing none.[14]

All of these Theophrastian characters are drawn from the growing class of transport workers who had arisen with the revival of European trade and were now in evidence on a vast scale as the economy of Europe expanded. All show traits of rudeness and indifference to fellow men. Anxious to counter the exploitations to which they are subjected, these people respond by exploiting others in turn—in ways that are petty and limited, certainly, for that is all their depressed station in society allows. Moreover, they share another dehumanizing trait: a shrunken capacity for speech. The mule drivers "blaspheme"; the carters are "cursing or yelling"; the sailors speak only in the crude language "which is used aboard ship"; the carriers substitute "speaking their mind" for prayers. Language, the principal tool of human communication, is being used only to convey aggression and hostility. These socially useful working men have reduced language to a point where they, as social men, are silent.

No less interesting are the student's remarks about a second vocational group peculiar to the new society: the free professions—the physicians and lawyers, both of whom are inseparable from the basic features of the emerging social picture. The physicians come to the fore as practitioners of the natural sciences, the lawyers as the executors and administrators of the law with jurisdiction over substantial areas of land—counties, states, even international areas—a jurisdiction that makes possible and facilitates the mechanics of a commercial economy. The Man of Glass ironically acknowledges their respectability, at the same time indicting them for concealing ignorance and self-interest behind the masks of expert knowledge.

> The judge may pervert or delay justice; the man of law may in his own interest plead an unjust cause; the merchant may drain off our property—in short, all those with whom we must necessarily deal may do us some wrong, but there is none of them other than the doctor who is in a position to deprive us of life itself, without punishment. Physicians may and do kill without fear or running away and without unsheathing any other sword than that of a prescription; for there is no means of discovering their crimes, since they at once bury them underground.[15]

It should be noted that the Man of Glass speaks in one and the same sentence of "the merchant" and the learned professions. What they have in common is the self-seeking monetary drive:

> He charged lawyers and solicitors with being negligent and ignorant, comparing them to doctors who, whether or not the patient recovers, collect their fee; these gentlemen of the legal profession did the same regardless of whether they won or lost their case.[16]

But there is one group of professions of which the Man of Glass has only good things to say—authors and actors. In the course of the story, someone remarks that "there are many actors who are well-born and sons of somebody"; to this, the Man of Class replies with his customary lucidity:

> That is true enough, but what the stage stands least in need of is individuals of gentle birth. Leading men, yes, who are well mannered and know how to talk, that is another matter. For it might be said of actors that they earn their bread by the sweat of their brows, with an unbearable amount of labor, having constantly to memorize long passages, and having to wander from town to town and from one inn to another like gypsies, losing sleep in order to amuse others, since their own well-being lies in pleasing their public. Moreover, in their business, they deceive no one, inasmuch as their merchandise is displayed in the public square, where all may see and judge of it.[17]

And as for authors, they

> too, have an incredible amount of work to perform and a heavy burden of care; they have to earn much in order that by the end of the year they may not be so far in debt that they will have to go into bankruptcy; yet for all of that, they are as necessary to the state as are shady groves, public walks, and parks, and other things that provide decent recreation.[18]

Cervantes, if anyone, knew the artist's calculated risks, the constant threats of economic disaster; but that is by the way. What is very much to the point is the defensiveness, even the defiance, of Cervantes' attitude. From the very beginning of the new era the artist finds himself socially and economically—and thus psychologically—in a position of jeopardy, which forces him to articulate and to press his claim, not merely for toleration but for recognition of his unique role. The nature of the argument is transparent; art is as important to the maintenance of the social equilibrium as are all other public institutions and activities. Above and beyond that, the artist has something to bring to society which neither the tradesman nor the professional brings. His task is to serve men by giving them pleasure; thus his function is not one of exploiting his fellows but, on the contrary, of socializing them. And he is continuously creative. Wherever he goes—if he is an actor—or whatever he achieves—if he is a writer—he helps men to maintain their identity and integrity in this strange new world.

And yet, at the same time, no other professions had to fight so persistent a battle for respectability and recognition as did the actor and the freelance literary artist.

Who is Dulcinea?

With this background in mind, we can appreciate the serious side of the otherwise comic conversation between the Knight and his hosts, the Duke and Duchess. According to Don Quixote, something has happened to Dulcinea; some baffling and awful metamorphosis has taken place in her:

> I found her under a magic spell, converted from a princess into a peasant girl, from a beautiful creature into an ugly one, from an angel into a devil, from a fragrant-scented being into a foul-smelling wench, from a fine-garbed, dignified lady into a rustic clown, leaping in the air—in short, from Dulcinea del Toboso into a Sayago country woman.[19]

He goes on to say that certain terrifying influences that can be neither accurately named nor controlled are the cause of this kind of sudden downward fate of a human being. But, unlike the explanations provided in the old fairy tales, such causes as the Knight assigns can scarcely be interpreted as supernatural in origin; if anything, they are social. "Who is it," asks the Duke, "could have done such a wrong to the world?"

> Who? Don Quixote repeated. Who could it have been except some malign enchanter of the many envious ones who persecute me? That cursed race of beings was born into the world to darken it, to frustrate the achievements of the virtuous and exalt those of the wicked.[20]

Thus enter the anonymous forces of reality, thinly veiled in poetic symbols. These are the threat to human creativity, these as yet indefinable and hence all the more troubling agents—"some malign enchanters." Sancho can dream of upward mobility, but he can all too easily fail disastrously—and so can the Knight. The world teems with unknown enemies, with accidents and unaccountable misfortunes, with human injustice, expediency, and greed.

On the other side of the ledger is the infinite power of creativity. A human being develops his own fulfillment out of his own activity. Who is Dulcinea? She is never completely real since there are always possibilities which must remain latent: neither is she completely unreal since some possibilities have been realized. As Don Quixote puts the matter:

> God knows whether or not there is a Dulcinea in this world or if she is a fanciful creation. This is not one of those cases where you can prove a thing conclusively. I have not begotten or given birth to my lady,

although I contemplate her as she needs must be, seeing that she is a damsel who possesses all those qualities that may render her famous in all parts of the world, such as: a flawless beauty; dignity without haughtiness; a tenderness that is never immodest; a graciousness due to courtesy and a courtesy that comes from good breeding; and, finally, a highborn lineage, for beauty is more resplendent and more nearly perfect in those of lofty extraction than in creatures of a humbler origin.[21]

The last lines in this passage might sound like a refutation of democratic philosophy, since the Knight takes recourse to such issues as "highborn lineage" and "lofty extraction." He introduces them, however, merely to disparage them in what follows. Part of Cervantes' genius is that he invites the reader's participation in the creative process: Don Quixote, seeming suddenly to realize that he has allowed himself to relapse into the prejudices of an obsolete social order, stops and catches up with himself by observing:

I can say only that Dulcinea is the daughter of her works, that virtues shed luster upon the bloodstream, and that a person of low degree who is possessed of them is more to be esteemed than the vicious one who has risen to high station. Moreover, Dulcinea has qualities that well may bring her to a crown and scepter; for a woman who is at once beautiful and virtuous may by her merits come to work miracles, and has locked within her, potentially if not actually, a higher fortune than the one she knows.[22]

The argument is now restated: a person of low degree deserves high praise if he develops his capacities; "high station" in itself is not a mark of virtue.[23] The figure of Dulcinea as she finally emerges symbolizes the new concept of man: the question of Dulcinea as real "in this world" or as "a fanciful creation" is resolved when the Knight describes her as "the daughter of her works," thus tipping the scale in favor of man's fulfilling his meaning by activity. Man becomes the creator of his world rather than a mere creature in it. This is true of Don Quixote and his Dulcinea, as well as of Cervantes himself, who has entered the scene by way of the Duchess' remarks and who is the creator of them both. But the reliability of one's own constructs is precarious, and so is the moral desire to recreate the world in a genuine human image. Hence, the philosophical ambiguity that arises at the beginning of the modern erea. The artist as the prototype of the idealist takes this risk of ambiguity.

By the time of the Renaissance the world has come to be viewed as an immense *tabula rasa.* It has no prior and accepted guarantes.

Intellectuals, philosophers, bellelettrists, as well as geographers and explorers, all tried to begin *ex nihilo* and to discover the very nature of the universe, both inside and outside the human realm. When Pascal enunciated his famous confession of terror, *"les silences éternels de ces espaces infinis m'effraient,"* he may have been thinking along cosmological lines, but he also gave utterance to the fears of the late Renaissance individual. The infinite spaces needed replenishing. The historical absurdity in which Don Quixote engages and revels replaces all factual concreteness with a world made new by him.

Cervantes, in sum, is in all his works on the road to the discovery of human nature. The process is critical and non-conformist, realistic in method and idealistic in intention. This journey toward the discovery of the individual takes place in two stages: the first seeks to observe reality; the second defines the ideal. The concluding sections of this chapter will deal with these two stages respectively.

Property: The Gypsies

Beset by economic uncertainties, haunted by accident and misfortune, Cervantes speaks for the little man of his time when he says in one of his prefaces to *Don Quixote:* "I will have profit, for without it fame is not worth a farthing." Repeatedly he describes private property and particularly money as the new regulators of social relationships which had once been determined by feudal fealty. In the second part of *Don Quixote,* he tells the story of "a most dignified duenna" who has fallen on hard times and whose daughter has been disgraced. Here is a story that must have happened many times over:

> The son of a very rich farmer, in a village not far from here that belongs to my lord the duke, fell in love with her. How it happened I do not know, but they came together and, under promise of marrying her, he made a fool of my daughter and now is unwilling to keep his word.[24]

Formally, the feudal order shows itself in such passages as this. Ostensibly, the farmer owes loyalty to the lord of the region, but, in reality, the impoverishment of the landed aristocracy has destroyed the validity of an artificially maintained social system. The duenna, steeped in the tradition of mutual responsibility, has pleaded her cause with the lord, but in vain:

> My lord the duke is aware of this, for I have complained to him not one but many times, imploring him to order that farmer's son to marry her, but he turns a deaf ear and scarcely listens to me. The reason is

that the young deceiver's father is so rich; he lends the duke money and goes security for his debts from time to time, and so my lord does not wish to offend him or give him trouble of any sort.[25]

What hitherto had been a binding personal relationship has become a cold, anonymous, impersonal dealing, rooted in monetary property. The reiteration of the theme in Cervantes shows the impact of the rapid social change on the ways people looked at the world.

Marginal Man

Cervantes' view of property relations reminds one of the apothecary's speech in Shakespeare's *Romeo and Juliet* and the experiences of Timon and Lear. In the works of both these artists the nature of man comes to the fore when the protagonists are placed in situations of material scarcity; this is true not only of Don Quixote but of a number of lesser figures in the *Novellas,* just as it is true of Timon and Lear in the solitude of nature, and of Prospero, Ferdinand and Miranda on their remote island in *The Tempest.* It is an element of the quasi-Utopian idyl of *As You Like It* that the society which surrounds the exiled duke should be free from the cares and conspiracies attending the larger context of propertied society from which he has been banished.

These incidents of material deprivation point to the function of such marginal situations. A number of writers have, like Cervantes, introduced marginal figures as true representatives of human concerns and as standards for understanding (and criticizing) the central features of their society. One might almost say that the prevailing philosophy of human nature since the Renaissance has been based on the conception of each individual as a "deviant case" whose existence consists very largely in his efforts to assert his personality against the restrictive and leveling claims of society.

Very quickly after the downfall of feudalism, the literary artist developed a liking for figures who look at society not from the viewpoint of a participant but from the vantage point of an outsider. The further these figures are removed from the affairs of society, the greater is likely to be their social failure (which is almost, but not quite, a tautology); they are also more prone, as a result, to display unspoiled, uninhibited, and highly individual characteristics. The conditions—whatever they may be—that remove them from the affairs of society are viewed as the conditions that bring them closer to their inner natures. The more primitive and "natural" the setting into which they are cast, the better are they able to develop and maintain their humaneness.

Cervantes presents an array of such marginal figures and situations. There are, first, the mad people—Don Quixote and the Man of Glass—who though still operating in the social world are in continuous conflict with it by word and deed. Then in *Rinconete and Cortadillo,* we meet petty crooks and beggars who live parasitically off the social world. One step farther from the center we find the gypsies presented in *The Little Gypsy* (*La Gitana*); they are completely outside the main stream of affairs. Finally, we have the situation wherein Don Quixote, the marginal Knight, speaks to the simple goatherds about the Golden Age in which the unity of man and nature reaches its fulfillment.

To this catalog of marginal types and situations, we add the figure of woman, who almost throughout the entire course of modern literature from Cervantes to Ibsen has been treated as an individual closer to her own nature and truth than are men, since man is indissolubly bound up with the competitive processes of work, in contrast to the enforced removal of woman from professional activities. Not accidentally does Cervantes use Dulcinea as a symbol of human creativity.

The Morality of the Marginal Man

There are two, not mutually exclusive, ways of looking at the marginal figures of Cervantes; they are the refuse of a society that has cast them aside, and they are, in their own right, moralists.

In a world in which man is taught common sense and skills leading to wealth and position, those devoid of property or common sense have no place; they are actually or potentially outside the social limits. They might just as well not exist. But since, manifestly, they do exist (though somewhat *in absentia),* society protects itself against them by an elaborate system of controlling devices, above all by punishing those who do not respect property and isolating those who do not respect common sense. The latter provide the basis for a large range of comedy (as we shall find in our analysis of Molièrere).

All these marginal creatures, the beggars, the crooks, the gypsies, the insane, constitute "overheads" of society, to which they are either unwilling to belong or from which they are forcibly cast out. But while they are accused, indicted, and confined, they themselves in turn are accusers. Their very existence denounces a world they never made and which wants no part of them. The artist, in giving these people a voice, may seek to inspire uneasiness on the part of those who have profited by the prevailing order. The artist's voice, in sum, is most often not the voice of the victors who arrogate their spoils. His is the voice of the losers.

The other aspect in which the marginal figures may be viewed leads us back to the concept of idealism. The marginal figures not only serve the negative function of indicting the social order; they also positively demonstrate the idea of man. They all serve to show the possibilities of Utopia, where everyone has the freedom to be his own deviant case—with the result that the very phenomenon of deviation disappears. The outcast society of robbers and thieves who are plying their trade on the fringes of Sevilla, and the society of gypsies encamped on the outskirts of Madrid, are grotesque Utopian prototypes: everybody works according to his talents, and everything is shared by everybody. Paradoxically enough, the robber, whom we would expect to place a high valuation on possession, displays only indifference to worldly goods. Money as such has no meaning for him; the principles which govern his life are honor among thieves and responsibility to his fellows. The highest moral law he recognizes is that of solidarity. The society of the robbers calls itself a "brother-hood"; the society of the gypsies obeys the "law of friendship." The acting chief of the "brotherhood" describes two older members of the club as if he were recommending them for membership to some respectable alumni group: "very truthful and upright individuals, God fearing and conscientious; they led model lives and enjoyed a good reputation."[26] Add the quality of "leadership," and you have all the customary prerequisites.

The meaning of Cervantes' critical idealism is even clearer in *The Little Gypsy.* During a performance in Madrid, a young man with an unimpeachable social background falls in love with a gypsy girl. He follows the tribe to its camp outside the city. Like Shaw's young ideal-ist in *Major Barbara,* he plans to join the gypsies in order to be united with his beloved. The tribal chief teaches the young aspirant the code by which the group lives.

> We observe inviolably the law of friendship; no one solicits the object of another man's affection; we live free from the bitter curse of jealousy. [27]

By implication, human traits are conceived of as unchangeable: if man is left to himself, the *lumen naturale* is bound to shine forth, and its rays are as self-evident as all other natural phenomena. Friendship derives from human nature itself. Jealousy is a symptom of property coveted; it may operate in the "normal" world where private property rules, but it should have no place in human relationships. Implied is the view that each person possesses his own inviolable individuality; he makes choices freely—in this case, of the other sex. (We shall see presently how Cervantes provides a corrective for masculine superiority, the remaining defect in an otherwise egalitarian society.)

Later the gypsy chief describes to the young man the means of livelihood available. They fall roughly into two categories, spoils gained from nature, and those acquired from the civilized world. As for the natural spoils:

> We are lords of the plains, of the crops, of the woods, of the forests, of the wells, and of the streams. The forests supply us wood free of cost, the trees fruit, the vine grapes, the gardens vegetables, the fountains water, the streams fish, and the preserves game, the rocks shade, the hills fresh air, and the caves houses. For us the inclemencies of the weather are breezes, the snow a refreshment, the rain baths, the thunder music, and the lightning torches. For us the hard clods of earth are feather beds.[28]

The means for satisfying human needs are detailed here in a spirit completely removed from the anxious concern for survival and self-assertion which is everywhere evident in the conversation of Sancho Panza and his wife. The gypsies experience their intercourse with nature as pleasures, "breezes," "refreshment," "music." In contrast, all the paraphernalia of civilization, whether they be respectable values like honor or mere devices of conspicuous living, appear as so many infringements on the freedom of man:

> We are not harassed by the fear of losing honour, nor are we kept awake by the desire to increase it, nor do we keep up parties, nor do we rise before daybreak to present memorials, or accompany grandees or solicit favours. We esteem these shanties and movable encampments more than gilded ceilings and sumptuous palaces.[29]

As for the livelihood acquired from the "inside society" of the civilized world, it is gained by illegal means. But again, the very way in which their thievery is described mocks the concept of private property which they neither practice nor respect.

> For us the beasts of burthen are reared in the fields; and pockets are cut in cities. There is no eagle or other bird of prey which swoops down more speedily on the victim that it spies than we on the opportunities that hold out to us any prospect of gain. And in conclusion we have many talents that promise us a fortunate end. In prison we confess, and in the pillory we are silent; by day we work, and by night we steal, or, to express it better, we warn everyone not to be careless in seeing where he places his property.[30]

The old man sums up the state of affairs in the private Utopia of the gypsies: "We have what we want since we content ourselves with what we have."[31]

Cervantes' marginal figures have in common integrity and responsibility in their human relationships and the serenity and self-reliance with which they cling to their convictions. Don Quixote does what he believes to be right; the Man of Glass speaks out what he believes to be true; the city thieves will not betray each other, and the gypsies are fully at peace with their lot. None of them adjust themselves to social expediency; their very existence is a protest against a mode of life in which the peasant runs after riches, the peasant's wife after desirable mates for the children, the rich farmer after greater riches and yet more desirable mates, and the lord of the mansion after expedient measures by which to satisfy his creditors. Thus at the threshold of the new society Cervantes describes the laws by which it operates and confronts it with its professed measure: the autonomous and morally responsible individual. And behold, this responsible and independent man is to be found only on the margin of society, which at once produces and expels him.

The Soul as Private Property

We might by this time reasonably assume that the highest degree of freedom has been announced with the happy society of the gypsies. But Cervantes has a still more compelling voice at his command. The woman who does not accept so much as the bare minimum of legal authority, who rejects the conventions and conformities even of this quasi-liberated world, is yet more emphatic than the manifesto of the chief. The last word remains the gypsy girl's. The chief of the tribe having set down his principles, the young inamorato declares his intention of permanently attaching himself to the tribe and marrying the girl. The male council has given consent; but now the girl has her say:

> Although these legislators have found by their laws that I am thine, and have handed me over to thee as thine, I have found by the law of my will, which is the strongest of all, that I do not choose to be so, except it is on those conditions that, before thou camest hither, were concerted between us two. Two years hast thou to live in our company before thou enjoyest mine, in order that thou mayest not lightly repent, nor I from haste be deceived. Conditions over-ride laws: those that I have made with thee, thou knowest. If thou dost care to observe them, it may be that I shall be thine, and thou mine.... These gentry can quite well hand over my body to thee, but not my soul, which is free and was born free, and has to be free as long as I wish.[32]

What here comes to the fore is a Renaissance concept which the literary artist will keep alive until the era of Romanticism and well into it; an individual is to be defined by his possession of himself. The soul, ironically, is used here as a quasi-legal term for this inviolable and inalienable property right. The possessor can divest himself of this innermost property-title only at the price of losing his identity. Such a concept of the soul is not formal, but substantial; it has content, and the content is love. And love, in turn, must not be misconstrued to mean some irrational, accidental and therefore ephemeral quality (as we encountered it in Lope's concept of passion); it is indeed the very essence of freedom. The lover makes his decision; the decision once made, its consequences are no longer accidental or irrational.

In a way, the gypsy girl, for all her verbal lucidity, is quite mad. She has no say in the male world, she is young and powerless. The group to which she claims membership has stipulated her course of action; still she says "No." "No, the law of my will is the strongest of all; my soul is free." This attitude is the attitude displayed by Don Quixote. His craziness has its very wellspring in his persistent independence: he will not be bribed by expedient measures; he will not be diverted from realizing his innermost convictions and ideals.

Justice: Don Quixote

Next Year in Utopia

It is not only fitting that Don Quixote should be the one to tell the story of the Golden Age, it is equally appropriate that his audience should be composed of a group of goatherds very much akin to the Utopian gypsies—an audience fit in no ordinary degree for anticipating "the happy age and happy centuries to which the ancients gave the name of golden . . . because those who lived in that time did not know the meaning of the words 'thine' and 'mine'":

> All then was peace, all was concord and friendship; the crooked plow-share had not as yet grievously laid open and pried into the merciful bowels of our first mother, who without any forcing on man's part yielded her spacious fertile bosom on every hand for the satisfaction, sustenance, and delight of her first son.[33]

This is a description of Utopia, certainly, and Don Quixote exalts it as the yardstick for human life which, bafflingly and inexplicably, "as time went on and depravity increased," brought about the exploitation of nature by man, of man by man, of female by male. Don Quixote regards himself as the guardian of this dream—realized once long ago, and to be realized again long hence; it will be up to him to right whatever wrongs time and depravity have wrought; and so,

> It was for the safety of such as these, as time went on and depravity increased, that the order of knights-errant was instituted, for the protection of damsels, the aid of widows and orphans, and the succoring of the needy. It is to this order that I belong, my brothers, and I thank you for the welcome and the kindly treatment that you have accorded to me and my squire. By natural law, all living men are obliged to show favor to knights-errant, yet without being aware of this you have received and entertained me; and so it is with all possible good will that I acknowledge your own good will to me.[34]

One might regard these words as a mere plot paraphrase of the novel or merely as self-summary: to be sure, the Knight is engaged in the deeds he describes. But placed in the context of the episode—the depiction of the Golden Age for the benefit of the goatherds—the Knight's words may be interpreted as a succinct symbol of his age. The psychological and economic uncertainties which in Cervantes' day afflicted the European nations are well known: the sharp upward turn in competitive struggle for primacy in the professions, the trades, the political administrations, the ordinary labor market; the intellectual, moral, and emotional anxieties of the average person in an era of bloody encounters between loyalist states and rebellious states, of struggles between the Mother Church and her dissident offspring, and struggles among the offspring themselves.

At the same time, the ideals of Don Quixote contain germinally the elements of which the new concept of man is to be constituted. They illustrate first of all that triumphant concept of the Renaissance to which Alexander Pope gave the name "the great chain of being": the notion of the universal escalator on which each individual occupies a definite place, the whole continuously engaged in the process of ascension toward the *summum bonum.* To be sure, Don Quixote strikes some important variations of the concept; what he describes is not a continuously upward line but a process that extends from a golden past to a golden future over a deep abyss of depravity. But the golden age is no less a reality for all that, and it guides Don Quixote's every action: at any given moment in the time continuum the golden life is as possible as a continued life of injustice. Moreover, the inner nature of man is so universal and so constant that a leader such as the Knight may speak to the lowliest of his fellow creatures with complete assurance of being understood by them; and he can refer to generations in the dimmest past with the certainty that their behavior and ideas will be comprehended by his contemporaries. Finally, the ideal of the Golden Age is not to be passed off as nostalgic self-indulgence; the universals in man are viable in every individual, and are fulfilled in Don Quixote himself. In his parting words, in which he pledges himself to the cause of justice among men, he takes on a specific responsibility. And there is no principle involved which would prevent any one of these goatherds from becoming a Don Quixote.

The Conditions of Justice

We may call this twofold responsibility of the individual for his own self and for the world the *credo* of the democratic idea. Don Quixote's memorable speech instructing Sancho in the basic rules of government on the eve of the peasant's taking over the long-coveted governorship of the island spells it out clearly:

> Remember, Sancho, that if you employ virtue as your means and pride yourself on virtuous deeds, you will have no cause to envy the means possessed by princes and noble lords; for blood is inherited but virtue is acquired, and virtue by itself alone has a worth that blood does not have.[35]

In other words, men are basically equal; Sancho has hardly more education than have the goatherds, the gypsies, the pastoral citizens of the Golden Age. Whatever Don Quixote can do, Sancho can do as well. To govern does not mean to dominate but to apply insight. The term virtue is decisive in this context. Machiavelli, the archproponent of the pessimistic concept of human nature, had used it merely to indicate rational efficiency and skillful application of the rules by which the majority of men are to be manipulated, domesticated and forced to submit. Cervantes takes virtue far more literally; to him it denotes the human and the manly, and becomes the expression of the inseparability of insight and action.

The very touchstone by which to test the concept of equality among men is to be found in the administration of justice, for the very essence of justice lies in the distribution of power among the parties involved. The legislator, the statesman, and the judge are, as decision-makers, endowed with symbolic and factual power: they occupy a position which by its very function is *de facto* superior to the positions of those to whom their jurisdiction extends. The relationship is here necessarily one between supplicant and grantor; and it is therefore crucial to Don Quixote that Sancho Panza should refrain from abusing the powers which he is about to confer upon him.

We have already seen that Cervantes' critical idealism tends always to be of a very realistic sort; and while it becomes most dear in its intentions whenever it alights on marginal and quasi-Utopian situations, it asserts itself quite as forcibly when dealing with issues central to society, such as property relations and administrative superstructures. The island for which Sancho Panza is about to embark is part and parcel of the contemporary Spanish society which Cervantes describes, and which the Knight wants to bring back to the fold of the human ideal. Don Quixote's parting instructions illuminate the process of reasoning by which a nonconformist intellectual at the threshold of our era undertakes to improve the reality of a middle-class society by an ideal conception of man. We have already considered the Knight's preamble; the rest of the speech follows:

> Never be guided by arbitrary law, which finds favor only with the ignorant who plume themselves on their cleverness. Let the tears of the poor find more compassion in you, but not more justice, than the testimony of the rich. Seek to uncover the truth amid the promises and gifts of the man of wealth as amid the sobs and pleadings of the poverty-stricken. When it is a question of equity, do not bring all the rigor of the law to bear upon the delinquent, for the fame of the sten judge is no greater than that of the merciful one. If the rod of justice is to be bent, let it not be by the weight of a gift but by that of mercy. When you come to judge the case of someone who is your enemy, put aside all thought of the wrong he has done you and

think only of the truth. Let not passion blind you where another's rights are concerned, for the mistakes you make will be irremediable, or only to be remedied at the expense of your good name and fortune.

If some beautiful woman come to you seeking justice, take your eyes from her tears, listen not to her moans, but consider slowly and deliberately the substance of her petition, unless you would have your reason drowned in her weeping and your integrity swept away by her sighs. Abuse not by words the one upon whom punishment must be inflicted; for the pain of the punishment itself is enough without the addition of insults. When a guilty man comes under your jurisdiction, remember that he is but a wretched creature, subject to the inclinations of our depraved human nature, and insofar as you may be able to do so without wrong to the other side, show yourself clement and merciful; for while the attributes of God are all equal, that of mercy shines brighter in our eyes than does that of justice.

If you observe these rules and precepts, Sancho, your days will be long, your fame will be eternal, rewards will be heaped upon you, indescribable happiness shall be yours, you will be able to marry off your children as you like, your children and your grandchildren will have titles to their names, you will live in peace with all men, and in your last days death will come to you amid a ripe and tranquil old age, and the gentle, loving hands of your great-grandchildren will tenderly close your eyes.[36]

In the passage cited, we find three recurring areas of concern. These may be classified—without any particular regard for the logic of parallelism—as *truth, mercy* and *emotionality*. To begin with the last-named class: no less than six times within the relatively brief context of the passage do we encounter the mention of tears or emotional correlates— "tears of the poor," "sobs of the poverty-stricken," "tears of a beautiful woman." "her moans," "her weeping," "her sighs." The category of truth finds expression in the following five variations: "uncover the truth," "think only of the truth," "your reason," "substance of a petition," "human nature." The category of mercy, finally, occurs six times: "compassion in you," "merciful judge," "the weight of mercy." "show yourself clement," "show yourself merciful," "the attribute of mercy."

The configuration of these categories constitutes in almost complete form the philosophy of modern idealism—morally as well as epistemologically. The world in which Sancho has to act is perceived as consisting of people who are rich and poor, beautiful and ugly, tearful and stubborn, ignorant and clever; but all these social and psychological specificities are the mere trimmings of human nature of whose virtue, as well as verity, the judge must be constantly aware. This holds true, for example, with respect to the display of emotions, genuine or simulated, by which the supplicant might turn disadvantage into advantage. Human communication depends upon language which is oriented toward commonly shared experience and insight; tears would substitute accidental, transient, unreflective, and quasi-biological responses for the exercise of reason, and Sancho will do well to make the necessary reduction.

The Knight is the Chief Justice who passes on to Sancho the responsibilities of the legal office. The ultimate function of this office lies in the inseparably related tasks of finding out the truth and following up the new insight by suitable action. Perhaps above all the rule of law, with its underlying egalitarian concept, asserts itself as the most important single manifestation of the secularized order—even of greater weight than the Baconian concept of science. According to the scientific mode, theory and knowledge are potentially the instruments of power, but the theories and experimental findings of the natural scientist merely admit the possibility of practical application. Usefulness is by no means a necessary component of science itself; the scientist may satisfy himself by mere contemplation. But the rule of law is the measure of man's capacity for rational behavior both in theory and in practice. The guarantee for the presence and the perpetuity of the rational mode in human relations resides in legal institutions, and any change in their substance or form presupposes findings on a higher plane of rationality than those which are presently available. The Knight's instructions emphasize this aspect of modern rationality; he wants to safeguard the realm of reason against any form of irrational intrusion, whether it be the arbitrary laws of tyrants and ignoramuses or the emotional outbursts of lovely women. Thus the recurrent appeals to reason are calculated to reinforce the very foundations on which human life is built. The exaltation of the judge's office testifies to the confidence in man's rationality, a faculty which enables him to discover truth unaided by those higher powers that have lately departed.

Needless to say, Cervantes has his hero describe an experiment in government which is a good deal closer to the enlightened monarchies of the eighteenth century than anything before or after. It remains uncertain how the laws, which the governor is supposed to apply in his dual function of administrator and judge, actually come about. What is certain and important is the recognition that the evident and necessary differences in political status within such a body politic in no way detract from the essential equality among all members of the commonwealth.

The Appeal to Mercy

While the confident search for applicable truth shows the optimistic integration of man's thinking and feeling into the strange new world that he is about to recreate, the burdensome aspects of secularized existence also get their due in the Knight's Magna Charta of justice. True, man is endowed with reason; but he is also endowed with morality. In deference to this, Cervantes, like Shakespeare, exalts the unrestrained quality of mercy that former centuries had experienced only as a promise of life after death. Now it gains the features of a solace, not in the hereafter, but in the here-and-now. Man is alone, and as an autonomous, rational individual must assume responsibility for his own moral fate and for the welfare of others. To overcome the feelings of aloneness, one need only become aware of his identification with all mankind in the commonly shared experience of aloneness. The exhortation to mercy as the highest of human attributes may be looked upon, in a way, as the initial phase of the existentialist view: there is positively nothing beyond the human realm; reason can never be absolute and can at best serve as an ever-threatened, precarious weather vane.

The recognition that the other person stands as much in need of certainty as one's self and the acknowledgment that certainty is ultimately impossible lead to another aspect of democratic beliefs. Although it is true that every individual is endowed with reason, by which he is enabled to survive, he is also endowed—and equally endowed—with the ever-present possibility of social or biological catastrophe, with the impending loss of fortune or health. The quality of mercy thus enters as a constituent element of man's rationality; it is in no way opposed to reason but complements its potential power by the acknowledgment of weakness, for this acknowledgment, in turn, strengthens the cohesiveness of man. Recognizing themselves to be both rational and mortal, men must discover in themselves that moral or emotional agency which prevents reason from becoming a new tyrannical force; and in the last analysis they make common cause by confessing to themselves and to each other a condition of need to which the confession itself brings its own gratification. The voluntary tempering of rational prerogatives out of respect for one's own frailty, and out of humility in the face of it, transforms acts and protestations of mercy from a symptom of human weakness into a symbol of man's greatest strength.

Cervantes' conception of mercy as complementary to reason is paralleled in Shakespeare. The rule of law as the manifestation of reason may be circumvented if the circumvention is closer to virtue than is compliance, however "rational" in appearance. In *The Tempest,* Miranda, the most obedient as well as the most dedicated of daughters, tries to induce Ferdinand to disobey her father's orders out of pity for her lover; similarly the Knight does not discourage the tempering of justice with mercy.

Consider the very architecture of the Knight's speech. It begins with the principles by which justice is to be applied; it introduces a number of relevant social and psychological factors; it then balances the merits of truth and mercy; and culminates in a reference to the soul. The speech reduces human relations to their core: the social world is concretely described; the rule of law is justified by the essential equality of all human beings; and the soul is exalted as the central and archetypical concept of man.

The Knight's speech is very much a document of the Renaissance intellectual. The whole orientation is so exclusively toward life in this world, so entirely concerned with filling every moment of life with meaning, that it would be unthinkable on the basis of it to distinguish between pleasure and morality. The dichotomy between moralism and hedonism, which will become one of the most contested issues in the history of middle-class ideologies, has no validity for Cervantes. If Sancho Panza observes the precepts of reason and mercy—the rule of virtue—he will reap the harvest of "indescribable happiness."

Notes

1. Cervantes, *Don Quixote,* 2 vol. (New York: Viking, 1949), vol. 2, pp. 538–39. All quotations from this edition are reprinted by permission of the Viking Press, Inc.
2. John Donne, *"The First Anniversary,"* II.205–18, in: *The Poems of John Donne,* ed. Herbert J. Grierson, 2 vols. (Oxford, 1912), vol. 2, pp. 23–38.
3. *Op. cit.,* Vol. 2, p. 539.
4. *Loc. Cit.*
5. Ibid., vol. 2, p. 540.
6. Ibid., vol. 2, p. 722.
7. The reader may recognize the technique in *Tristram Shandy,* a seminal example for English literature. The German romantic playwrights, notably Tieck, allow their characters similar licenses; most recently the late novels of Mann rely for much of their irony on premising a narrator, who is constantly weaving in and out of his own narrative, upon which he comments; Joseph

and his brothers make it a point to remind each other that they are "in a story," and so forth. Again, the technique of suspending the conventional boundaries functions in a good deal of the post-World War I expressionistic drama, both in Europe and America, in the work of Pirandello, O'Neill, and Wilder; and the very device of allowing characters to trespass the physical confines of their dramatic sphere is now something of a commonplace in stage production.

8. Ibid., vol. 1, p. 43.
9. Ibid., vol. 1, pp. 424–25.
10. Ibid., vol. 2, p. 723.
11. "The Man of Glass," in Cervantes, *Three Exemplary Novels* (New York: Putnam, 1950), p. 103. All quotations from this book are reprinted by permission of the Viking Press, Inc.
12. Ibid.
13. Ibid.
14. Ibid., p. 104.
15. Ibid., pp. 104–5. To be sure, the learned professions were satirized occasionally in medieval literature, but it is in Cervantes that they are subjected for the first time to social criticism.
16. Ibid., p. 112.
17. Ibid., p. 109.
18. Ibid.
19. Ibid., vol. 2, p. 722.
20. Ibid.
21. Ibid., vol. 2, p. 723.
22. Ibid.
23. This concept is pervasive throughout the works of Shakespeare. See especially, *All's Well that Ends Well,* Act II. Scene 3:

> If she be
> All that is virtuous, save what thou dislikest,
> A poor physician's daughter, thou dislikest
> Of virtue for the name: but do not so:
> From lowest place when virtuous things proceed,
> The place is dignified by the doer's deed:
> Where great additions swell's, and virtue none,
> It is a dropsied honor. Good alone
> Is good without a name. Vileness is so:
> The property by what it is should go,
> Not by the title.

24. Ibid., vol. 2, p. 821. See our comparison of this episode with Calderon's treatment of a similar theme.
25. Ibid.
26. "Rinconete and Cortadillo," in Cervantes, *Three Exemplary Novels*, p. 52.
27. "The Little Gypsy," in *The Complete Works of Miguel de Cervantes in Twelve Volumes,* ed. by James Fitzmaurice-Kelly, Glasgow, 1902, vol. 7, p. 38.
28. Ibid.

29. Ibid., pp. 38–39.
30. Ibid., p. 38.
31. Loc. cit.
32. Ibid., pp. 39–40.
33. *Don Quixote,* vol. 1, pp. 81–82.
34. Ibid., p. 82.
35. Ibid., vol. 2, p. 781.
36. Ibid., pp. 781–782.

3

Shakespeare's *The Tempest*

The process of secularization in the Renaissance has intimate connections not only with an emerging individualism but with the problem of authority. This problem is, in turn, closely identified with a typical Renaissance concept of history—an interpretation of events in terms of the passions, drives and inner conflicts of leading historical figures: we can understand Roman history if we know what kind of man Coriolanus, or Caesar, or Anthony was, and we can understand English history by studying the characters of the English kings. This psychologizing was a natural response to secularization; in a sense, no other kind of interpretation was possible, since "society" had not yet come to be viewed as a body of changing institutions. The problem, therefore, was to legitimize secular authority by finding moral guarantees for those who exercise it.

In *The Tempest*, irrational and rational authority are pitted against each other: the one is authority based on social position, property and power; the other is authority that is exercised and submitted to on the basis of mutually recognized attributes and responsibilities, which embody the qualities of virtue and reason. These types of authority are represented most clearly in the figures of the two brothers, Antonio, the scheming and dissolute usurper, and the wise and virtuous Prospero, rightful Duke of Milan. The moral guarantees for those who exercise authority are explicitly stated: learning and power are to be combined in the Baconian sense and are to be applied to the affairs of men rather than to the search for God's will.

The Concept of Human Nature

With the wavering of theological certainties during the Renaissance, the prevailing doctrines of human nature became subject to considerable doubt. The concomitant decline of the hierarchized society of the Middle Ages and the advent of a society with a high degree of social mobility made the question of the essential qualities of human nature truly crucial. The evidence to be found in everyday life was conflicting and untrustworthy. Men did not consciously look to organized society for their norms; the explicit appeal to custom and common sense that later developed with the solidification of middle-class control had little drawing power for the adventurous individualists of Elizabethan England.

The urge to seek out the basic elements of human nature led primarily in two directions: to the study of exemplary situations of the past, particularly as recorded by Plutarch, and the observation of contemporary individuals in marginal situations which would free them from the demands of conformity and ordinary practicality. As we have seen, Cervantes found revelations of human nature among gypsies, robbers, and other outcast groups. *The Tempest* constitutes a marginal phenomenon of an extreme kind, since in it men are removed from a socially predetermined environment and are cast back upon themselves and the elements.

Because of its island setting, reflecting the Elizabethan enthusiasm for the distant corners of an expanding world, *The Tempest* presents what we may look upon as an experimental situation. By its remoteness from organized society human nature is reduced to essentials—allowing Shakespeare's characters to display their deepest and most intimate reactions. Paradoxically, it is their removal from society that makes their behavior an ideal source for sociological interpretation.

The Tempest then is a play of man alone, or rather of man confronted by nature, without the help or interference of social institutions. Its miniature company lives outside history, responding only to the exterior challenges of nature and the interior attributes of man himself. These two sets of influences are symbolized in the stage settings: the first scene shows men facing a storm at sea; the remainder of the play takes place on a small island unaffected by historical and social exigencies of a milieu.

The play is not, however, a vision of an Utopia, as the setting might suggest. It is more on the order of a "laboratory" experiment, demonstrating the true nature of man as Shakespeare had conceived it. The few people on the island live outside the protection of institutions, law or power—whether feudal or monarchical. In many respects. *The Tempest* reminds us of the Robinson Crusoe story. Prospero's island is as isolated as Crusoe's, and both situations pose the problem of man's survival apart from normal life conditions. Shakespeare's and Defoe's heroes both are thrown back to primitive natural conditions (although, due to Prospero's magic, in radically different ways) and everything has to be created anew. In both instances man, against his own volition, has to contend with nature in a raw state.

Ever since the Renaissance, modern man has perpetuated the idea that he carries an infinity of possibilities within himself; their realization is always within reach, at least in his phantasies and dreams. His potentialities are such that, if need be, he could live apart from the rest of society; he could return to nature. Moreover, once Western man gave up the idea that his true life began only with death, once his nervous system no longer was inscribed with hope for eternal life or fear of eternal condemnation, his expectations came to be centered on the natural and the human. Nature supplants God, in a sense, but, unlike God, its ways have not been defined with certainty and finality; once the experiments of *The Tempest* and *Robinson Crusoe* are concluded, the people can return to society with the new knowledge they have gained.

Both stories are dramas of individualism, but with this decisive difference: Shakespeare's play does not deal with the *homo economicus* but with the *homo moralis.* Inherent in the struggles of Robinson Crusoe is the earnest conviction that man's true goal lies in the social, economic, and political institutions of an individualistic and competitive society. Inherent in the moral stubborness of Prospero is the eschatological dream that man can, by continuous introspection, by listening to his soul, achieve harmony for himself and others. When the tempestuous seas have washed away the jetsam of history and society, the people on the island can remake a world from their own essential humanity.

Thus, while *Robinson Crusoe* is oriented to social themes, *The Tempest* is concerned with the nature of man. Although Crusoe is alone, except for Friday, he still remains an eighteenth-century man who is imbued with the desirability of a freely competitive society. The specifically economic focus of the story is the product of a mind that thinks in social terms, the issue is *laissez faire* versus state interference in economic activities. *The Tempest,* on the contrary, is the product of a mind that locates the drama of human existence within the soul of individual man; it is the innermost victory or defeat that determines the success or failure, triumph or tragedy, of man's life. Prospero learns how to reform himself, and it is only by reforming himself that he will make a better duke.

The Tempest presents a wide range of attitudes of Renaissance man. If we keep in mind the given historical setting of the play, it supplies abundant examples of individuals reacting to their environment in the transitional period between feudalism and middle-class society. Indeed, the abundance is such that one is tempted to interpret the play word by word. But since there is no space here for such an enterprise, and since an appendix[1] contains an interpretation of a single scene—the incident of the shipwreck that opens the play—the following analysis is limited to a number of motifs that run throughout the entire play.

We have suggested that *The Tempest* may be looked upon as a "laboratory" experiment to which the characters of the play are exposed. It opens aboard a ship that represents, both literally and symbolically, the last ties to organized society for the group that is destined for the island.

The storm takes place while the established chains of command are still firmly retained. The mariners go about the business of meeting the challenge of the storm in an orderly manner. The captain details his strategy to the boatswain, who then passes on orders to the crew, in an entirely friendly, workmanlike fashion. The noble lords, who are their passengers, are meanwhile anything but calm. They curse out the crew, falsely accuse the boatswain of drunkenness and generally act out of fear and impatience.

For the time being, it is sufficient to note here that the boatswain by his good sense and his workmanlike command of the situation emerges as the hero of the scene. Gonzalo, the counsellor of Alonso, King of Naples, is shown as a man of calm understanding. Although at first sight he does not appear to be much more than a noble who shows conventional loyalty, he is a professional civil servant; he is thus distinguished from the lords, who are merely persons of high status, neither acknowledging any responsibility to, nor having any function in, society. In the behavior of these aristocratic passengers, we find totally lacking the industriousness, humanity, or knowledge that became the progressive values of the Renaissance individual in Shakespeare's day. We see them rather as reminders of the old order, just as Gonzalo and the boatswain personify the new.

Five Themes on the Island

After the shipwreck, we are introduced to the island where Prospero—who has magic powers at his disposal—is telling his daughter Miranda that many years ago he had lost his dukedom to an usurper, how after his exile he had found refuge on the island, and how he now had caused the shipwreck that would put his enemies into his hands. Presently other voices emerge from behind these two: the deformed and treacherous Caliban and the ethereally beautiful Ariel respectively trudge and fly about. We learn that the ship's survivors have now reached the island, and that most of them are in a state of despondency; Alonso's son Ferdinand wanders alone in a state of complete despair until he meets Prospero and Miranda. Here, then is a handful of people living on what is to all intents and purposes a naked planet. But extreme as the situation may be, their biological, psychological, and social needs continue to exist and must be satisfied; they, therefore, must become increasingly socialized. Soon an embryonic society is apparent.

Five aspects of this emerging society on the island are of interest to us here: work, learning, language, sleep, and sex. In the process of examining how the individuals who make up this small society deal with these five human concerns, we shall discover the degree of their success or failure in living up to the image of man which was being developed in Renaissance socicty.

Work

There is no doubt concerning Prospero's role on the island nor of his ability to rule it and assign tasks to its members. He is a wise man, completely at peace with himself and fully aware of the ways of his fellow men after years of introspection into his own nature. By following only his own inner voice he has attained an authority similar to that of the master of the ship in the course of his professional career. Although Prospero no longer has the external trappings of his former power, he emerges as a real "duke," in the literal sense of "leader." Without question he is entitled to be the initial organizer and supervisor of the people on the island.

The person who has reached the highest degree of rationality becomes by this very achievement the maker of decisions. No one but Prospero makes decisions. That they turn out to be the "right" decisions is further evidence of his qualifications. Prospero's mistakes lie in the past; like Lear at the end of the second act, he is now throwing off his self-destructive indifference to the world. His mission is to work out his own salvation, and instead of taking revenge on his enemies, to provide for their safe survival as well as for the welfare of all others for whom he takes responsibility.

Caliban and Ariel: Torpor and Frivolity. As the gods do in Homer, the extra-human creatures in Shakespeare's works—such as the ghosts of Banquo, Caesar, and Hamlet's father—function as visible manifestations of psychic processes. Like Prospero's magic power, Caliban and Ariel are not essential to the plot in *The Tempest;* they are in fact entirely supererogatory. Although such extra-human types may generally symptomize a tedious conscience, in sociological terms they help to round out the image of man by demonstrating outwardly and visibly his interior conflicts and phantasies.

The relationship of Prospero to his helpers may be illuminated by the psychoanalytic schema of the personality. Caliban represents untamed, uncivilized urges and desires. He is the id, as expressed in a number of ways: (1) his primary concern with nourishment—see, for example, his irrelevant introjection of the topic of food into a conversation with Prospero (Act I, Scene 2); (2) his continual resistance to the performance of useful work; (3) his propensity for sexual promiscuity and rape as demonstrated, for example, by his offer to deliver Miranda to the bed of the scoundrel Stephano (III,2); (4) his irrational conduct in general—for example, his drunken stupor once Stephano has given him a bottle, or his serving notice on the values and mores associated with his master (II,2); (5) his view of biological pleasure as an expression of freedom, and his tendency to equate the two. The word freedom is one he loudly parades when all inhibitions are gone (II,2):

Freedom, highday! highday, freedom! highday, freedom!

Ariel is his direct counterpart. His realm is the superego phantasy. In contrast to Caliban, he is continually engaged in considerate acts: he puts the tired seamen to sleep (I,2); he intercedes with his master in behalf of Prospero's enemies, who have now been sufficiently punished, professing that these would be his own actions "were I human" (V,I). Whereas Caliban is all brute instinct, Ariel connotes the moral and esthetic aspirations that are potential in every human being.

Finally, Prospero himself may be viewed as assuming the role of the ego, perpetually engaged in striving to reconcile the two basic psychic forces for the purpose of mastering reality on all levels.

Seen from this viewpoint. Caliban and Ariel help us to visualize the deeper level of that secularized, human-centered new world, the Empire of Man which is in the process of replacing the City of God. At the same time, however, they are individualities in their own right, and it is from this point of view that we look at them now, particularly in regard to their attitude toward work.

Caliban, sometimes called by Prospero a "slave," has not achieved the transition from mere biological sensationism to the sphere of sensibility specific to man. He represents the animal in man that must be tamed, and forced by threats of punishment (I,2):

> If thou neglect'st or dost unwillingly
> What I command, I'll rack thee with old cramps,
> Fill all thy bones with aches; make thee roar,
> That beasts shall tremble at thy din.

Caliban exemplifies the condition from which man must be freed if he is to find salvation (for even a Caliban can be ennobled). The new, secular salvation comes from man's rising to a reflective rationality, by which he recreates the natural world about him and, in the process, discovers his own nature. Caliban's notion of "useful" work is the most perverted imaginable: to kill Prospero and act the part of procurer to Stephano, the drunken butler.

Ariel symbolizes a more affirmative and agreeable aspect of natural man. Playful, imaginative relaxation is to him a well-earned reward for "worthy service," honestly performed; he has "made no mistakings, served without or grudge or grumblings" (I,2). Still it is clear that Ariel's service, though lovable, is performed with a minimum of personal exertion; he wants to enjoy without paying for enjoyment by toil. He would as soon not "work" at all, though he is glad to put the sailors to sleep or move Prospero to pity, and to render whatever service can be rendered easily and enjoyably. With him, too, Prospero must resort to threats (I,2):

> If thou more murmur'st, I will rend an oak,
> And peg thee in his knotty entrails till
> Thou hast howl'd away twelve winters.

Thus, Ariel and Caliban symbolize two disparate pitfalls of the new autonomy of the individual: escape into the lethargy and apathy of unproductive behavior, or escape into the illusion of complete independence without responsibility or exertion. Both Ariel and Caliban would perish without a Prospero.

Ferdinand and Miranda: The Volunteers. As part of his experiment, Prospero has kept Ferdinand in bondage and has imposed on him, as on everybody else, burdensome tasks. In the beginning of the third act we find Ferdinand hard at work with heavy logs (III,1):

> There be some sports are painful, and their labour
> Delight in them sets off; some kinds of baseness
> Are nobly undergone and most poor matters

Point to rich ends. This my mean task
Would be as heavy to me as odious, but
The mistress which I serve quickens what's dead
And makes my labours pleasures.

Ferdinand's response to the test to which Prospero has subjected him (in order to discover the degree of his devotion to Miranda) is a telling example of one who finds within his own soul the meaning of life. Discovering the key to his individuality in his love for Miranda, Ferdinand sees the whole world in terms of this love; the chains of slavery melt away under the sun of a human relationship which transforms labor into "pleasures." Once work is accepted as not merely a means to one's own survival but as a service to those one loves, it becomes a value in its own right, part and parcel of the individual's integrity.

Miranda epitomizes this idea. Untrained for manual labor, a demure young girl, brought up with care and delicacy by a wise father, she nonetheless identifies with Ferdinand to such a degree that she wishes not only to share his harsh task but to take it from him (III,1):

If you'll sit down,
I'll bear your logs the while. Pray, give me that:
I'll carry it to the pile.

Neither tempted by the escapism of Caliban and Ariel, nor forced into a working situation as Ferdinand is, Miranda formulates the virtues of work as a voluntary and free expression of herself and her love (III,I):

It would become me
As well as it does you: and I should do it
With much more ease; for my good will is to it,
And yours it is against.

She does not mean that Ferndinand is unwilling to work, but that he is performing forced labor and is thereby prevented from exercising free choice. She alone is in a position to "volunteer," unhampered by her father's beneficcnt strictures.

The Noble and the Vulgar Drones. It is noteworthy that Alonso the King of Naples, Sebastian his brother, and Antonio the usurper of the throne of Milan, are as idle socially as they are contemptible morally.

This is equally true, despite their menial stations, of Trinculo the jester and Stephano the butler. Ariel says to the first three (III,3):

> You are three men of sin, whom Destiny . . .
> Hath caused to belch up you; and on this island,
> Where man doth not inhabit; you 'mongst men
> Being most unfit to live.

All five are ghosts of the past, parasites from the upper and lower rungs of the feudal ladder. They are unrelated to the productive affairs of men; the nobles do not know how to administer or supervise such affairs, and the two underlings do not know how to execute them. On the possibility of their doing any work themselves, they are all conspicuously silent. On the possibility of utilizing the labors of others for their own ends, they are a bit more articulate. When Stephano first encounters Caliban in the wilderness of the island, he thinks at once of a way to improve his station in life by exploiting Caliban once he is safely back in Milan (II,2):

> I will give him some relief, if it be but for that: if I can recover him and keep him tame and get to Naples with him, he's a present for any emperor that ever trod on neat's-leather.

Learning

The Renaissance concept of work as it appears in seventeenth-century literature is far removed from the theoretical concept of good works performed in the service of God; work becomes the very act of creation, and without it there would be no human world but only Caliban's atavistic chaos. The meaning of learning has gone through a corresponding transformation. In *The Tempest*, certainly, schooling is no longer conceived as a step toward the experience of the infinite wisdom of a heavenly power, but as a prerequisite for the transformation of the world by productive labor. The post-medieval era does away, at a very early stage, with the traditional exaltation of *vita contemplativa* at the expense of *vita activa*.

The Tempest bears witness to this view that man's life centers around productive labor with learning an essential correlate: labor and learning together make possible the discovery of one's own productive potentialities (one's nature), and are basic to the transformation of natural phenomena into a man-controlled and man-centered world.[2]

Learning and Power. In the first scene of *The Tempest,* the skilled manual experts as well as Gonzalo, a skilled intellectual, go about their business on the basis of acquired knowledge. To these men, the application of learning to the task of resisting the forces of nature brings about a state of equanimity—one is almost tempted to say happiness. Performing their duties by the precept of rational decision, they live in harmony with themselves and with their fellow men.

In the experimental context of the island, Prospero may be said to rediscover and reconstruct out of his own reasoning the essentials of the educational process. His first words in the play, in the opening lines of I,2, are words of instruction to Miranda whom he is at pains to inform further on the responsibilities of adulthood:

> I have done nothing but in care of there,—
> Of thee, my dear one! Thee, my daughter!—who
> Art ignorant of what thou art, nought knowing
> Of whence I am; nor that I am more better
> Than Prospero, master of a full poor cell,
> And thy no greater father.

It is noteworthy that nowhere else does Prospero show such signs of pride; only when telling his daughter that he is living up to the task of passing on knowledge to the next generation does he boast:

> and here
> Have I, thy schoolmaster, made thee more profit
> Than other princes can, that have more time
> For vainer hours and tutors not so careful.

For Prospero, the gentleman scholar, the search for truth is not a leisurely pastime but the most serious business of his life. Prior to his exile, however, he had been unable to relate theory and practice, unable to apply his learning to the conduct of the affairs of state. When he describes to his daughter the injury inflicted on him by his brother Antonio, whom he had deputized to "manage the state," he admits that he had prized his "library" above his "dukedom" and that he was "reputed"

> In dignity, and for the liberal arts,
> Without a parallel.

But by living as a secularized monk, lost in books, abandoned to the *vita contemplativa,* he had actually invited his brother's outrageous behavior.

> I, thus neglecting worldly ends, all dedicated
> To closeness and the bettering of my mind
> With that, which, but by being so retir'd,
> O'er priz'd all popular rate, in my false brother
> Awak'd an evil nature.

He who is not aware that knowledge includes the responsibility for its application, or, to quote Bacon, its "power," has not fully learned the human lesson. Prospero as administrator of the island is trying to make up for what he had neglected when he was Duke of Milan. He, too, is now in an experimental situation, and the test he must pass is his ability to connect learning and doing.

The Utopian and the Caveman. Gonzalo understands and explains the role of learning on different levels, and counsels accordingly. He reminds us of Kent in *Lear,* who functions essentially as the rational norm by which the excesses, passions, and imbecilities of the others may be measured.

In the first scene of the first act, Gonzalo shows great respect for the social usefulness of manual skills. In addition, we learn later that it was Gonzalo who, when he had the distasteful assignment of shipping Prospero and his daughter into exile on a unseaworthy bark, had managed surreptitiously to provide them not only with the physical requirements of life but with some intellectual necessities as well. As Prospero reports it (I,2):

> Some food we had, and some fresh water that
> A noble Neapolitan, Gonzalo,
> Out of his charity,—who being then appointed
> Master of this design,—did give us; with
> Rich garments, linens, stuffs, and necessaries,
> Which since have steaded much; so, of his gentleness,
> Knowing I lov'd my books, he furnish'd me
> From mine own library with volumes that
> I prize above my dukedom.

On the island, Gonzalo proves himself by helping people who would not otherwise survive. His head and heart are instantly awake to situations that threaten life. It seems perfectly natural that Ariel should single him out to awaken Alonso to the Antonio-Sebastian conspiracy. In other words, Gonzalo displays that practical ability to apply his knowledge which Prospero has had to learn so painfully.

The Baconian doctrine that man fulfills his mission by functioning both as *ego cogitans* and *ego agens* is demonstrated in *The Tempest* by Gonzalo's draft of an Utopian "commonwealth." What Prospero, the unworldly philosopher, was driven by necessity to create, Gonzalo conjures up in a spirit of playful phantasy. To counter the melancholic apathy of the shipwrecked nobles, as well as his own, he volunteers a daydream of ideal life. This New Atlantis Gonzalo describes is not the dream of a scientific mind, as was Bacon's, but that of a critical moralist, who, like Cervantes, conceives the absence of domination as a condition for the fulfillment of the potentialities of the individual (II,1):

> I' the commonwealth I would by contraries
> Execute all things; for no kind of traffic
> Would I admit; no name of magistrate;
> Letters should not be known; riches, poverty,
> And use of service, none; contract, succession,
> Bourn, bound of land, tilth, vineyard, none;
> no use of metal, corn, or wine, or oil;
> No occupation; all men idle, all;
> And women, too, but innocent and pure;
> No sovereignty.[3]

In the play of his imagination, he bans not only institutionalized weapons for the domination of man over man, but also the technical instruments for the domination of man over nature:

> All things in common nature should produce
> Without sweat or endeavor: treason, felony,
> Sword, pike, knife, gun, or need of any engine,
> Would I not have; but nature should bring forth,
> Of its own kind, all foison, all abundance,
> To feed my innocent people.

White the feudal parasites can understand his dream only as an opportunity for Caliban-like behavior, whereby each of them "would be king" and everyone else "whores and knaves," what Gonzalo is really envisioning is shedding the privileges of his office in favor of a society in harmony with nature and in which the state has "withered away."

Caliban's phantasies, at the other extreme, may be looked upon as those of a man for whom the old order of life has lost its meaning, and who has not yet found his way in the new. He is like the eighteenth-century machine wreckers, who, ground down by history, blamed the machines for their misery rather than the factory system itself. When Caliban, plotting to imitate Antonio's perfidious plans, advises his two provisional masters—the drunken butler and the crude jester—to murder Prospero and dishonor Miranda, he advocates what three centuries later is to become a well-known practice:

> Why, as I told thee, 'tis a custom with him,
> I'the afternoon to sleep: there thou may'st brain him
> Having first seiz'd his books. (III,2)

And in order to make certain that the scoundrels have not missed the point, he repeats his advice in the middle of the same speech:

> Remember
> First to possess his books; for without them
> He's but a sot

And again:

> Burn but his books:
> He has brave utensils,—for so he calls them—
> Which, when he has a house, he'll deck withal.

Thus he advocates, so to speak, a pre-literate, indeed a prehistoric, stage of man.

Language

The dominant approach to language in the Middle Ages was that of scholastic realism, according to which concepts and existence were identical; both were regarded as manifestations of one and the same supernatural act of creation. During the Renaissance the emphasis shifted to the tenets of the nominalist school, that concepts denote things, physical as well as non-physical. Words now become the property of man—tools which help him to assume his responsibility in the human-centered world—and great literature begins to create the signposts by which man can recognize himself and his environment. Language becomes the instrument of self-identification, as well as of orientation. And, as we observed in our analysis of Cervantes' writings, the more firmly a person commands words, the higher is the degree of his self-realization.

The language of Caliban as well as that of Antonio and Sebastian is a kind of perverted scholastic realism. When they speak forthrightly, they curse. Enter Caliban; he enters cursing (I,2):

> As wicked dew as e'er my mother brush'd
> With raven's feather from unwholesome fen
> Drop on you both!

and thereafter he hardly opens his mouth without giving vent to similar barbarisms. The curses accomplish nothing, but like children the cursers attempt to give their objects the predetermined reality of names. Caliban, Antonio and Sebastian are remote from the world of human interaction; their curses are not viable in human affairs. What they accomplish is entirely negative: they limit the cursers to the confines of their underdeveloped and regressive personalities. When Prospero reminds Caliban (I.2):

> I endow'd thy purposes
> With words that made them known.

Caliban retorts

> You taught me language; and my profit on't
> Is, I know how to curse: the red plague rid you
> For learning me your language!

Prospero gives us the meaning of productive "nominalistic" language when he tells Caliban that while

> thou . . . wouldst gabble like
> a thing most brutish . . .

or has, in other words, only instinctual sounds at his disposal, he Prospero

> Took pains to make thee speak, . . .

so that he (Caliban) would

> Know thine own meaning.

The dynamic interconnection of work, learning, and language is apparent in the dispirited jesting among the lords that initiates the second act. The courtiers make conversation, but it is empty word play, a desperate dragging out of small talk and gossip to while away tedious hours and to conceal their fears. The artifice of their conversation has nothing of the deliberate decorative intent that we find in the courtly scenes of Shakespeare's early romantic and satirical comedies, in which the language is often as stiff and sometimes quite as silly. There, true enough, the ladies and gentlemen engage in a sterile type of repartee; they are not really making conversation with each other, but are tossing words back and forth as if engaged in a cunning boy's game.[4] But that is all convention and high artifice, whereas to call scoundrels such as Sebastian and Antonio "artificial" would be to compliment them. Antonio and Sebastian mock the very function of language. Their impertinent jokes constitute a play within a play—an anticipation of Restoration comedy to which the gentry came flocking in order to see the re-enactment of their depravity on the public stage. Until middle-class society finally consolidated its triumph over obsolete court cliques, the language of the latter continued to survive as a testimony to their parasitism.

Gonzalo's use of language is rational, affirmative, and humane. His age and profession have brought him a certain degree of stolidity and patience which permit him to repay insolence with solace; he tries to humor King Alonso, who thinks his son lost in the storm, by persuading him that after all there are still chances for survival; only wait, and the king will see Ferdinand alive again. But Gonzalo might have spared himself the trouble; as his king puts it (II,1):

> You cram these words into mine ears, against
> The stomach of my sense.

Nor does Gonzalo fail to chide Sebastian, the king's unsavory brother, for abusive language when the situation calls for words of comfort and hope. "Sir," Sebastian maliciously remarks, "you may thank yourself for this great loss"; naturally Alonso would prefer not to be thus reminded, and asks to be left alone, "prithee, peace." Sebastian will not leave him in peace; most certainly not:

> We have lost your son,
> I fear, for ever: Milan and Naples have
> More widows in them of this business' making
> Than we bring men to comfort them: the fault's
> Your own.

Gonzalo tries (in vain) to improve the situation by a lesson in humaneness:

> My lord Sebastian,
> The truth you speak doth lack some gentleness
> And time to speak it in; you rub the sore,
> When you should bring the plaster.

In short, Gonzalo is at pains to use language reasonably. For the rest, his task is to serve his king, more so than ever in a situation of emergency. He avows his loyalty—not ritualistically but sensibly, pragmatically even—whenever such avowals will do the king some good. Now, for example, he appeals to the king's own duty to bear up, lest his subjects, taking their cue from his own conduct, be cast down with him:

> It is foul weather in us all, good sir,
> When you are cloudy.

His Utopia oration (which comes next and which he designs to keep the king's mind off the loss of his son) has no effect. Gonzalo finally gives up with an inward shrug. His next-to-last lines very neatly, if somewhat self-disparagingly, sum up the whole scene:

> I do well believe your Highness; and did it [talked to his king]
> to minister occasion to these gentlemen, who are of such
> sensible and nimble lungs that they always use to laugh at nothing.

The function of language as a means of self-identification finds its most precise expression whenever a person is under stress. When Ferdinand, while looking for his father, meets Miranda this is how he tries to identify himself (I,2):

> My language! heavens!—
> I am the best of them that speak this speech,
> Were I but where 'tis spoken.

His opening speech reveals his essential qualities as surely as do Caliban's beginning lines. The one curses, the other appears musing in the wake of Ariel's ditty:

> Where should this music be? I' th' air, or th' earth?
> It sounds no more;—and sure, it waits upon
> Some god o' th' island . . .
> This music crept by me upon the waters,
> Allaying both their fury, and my passion,
> With its sweet air.

It should be noted that Ariel and Caliban both sing—Ariel lightly and continuously, Caliban once only and in a drunken stupor, when he stumbles over his own name:

'Ban, 'Ban, Ca-Caliban.

And it may be said in behalf of Caliban that he is not insensitive to beautiful sounds. Shakespeare endows him with one speech which might well be spoken by a worthier character. When Caliban (II,2) tries to persuade Stephano that there is nothing to be afraid of, he describes the charming noises on his island with a lyrical power as unexpected as Mercutio's Queen Mab recital.

Be not afeard: the isle is full of noises,
Sounds and sweet airs, that give delight, and hurt not.
Sometimes a thousand twangling instruments
Will hum about mine ears; and sometime voices,
That, if I then had wak'd after long sleep,
Will make me sleep again: and then, in dreaming,
The clouds methought would open and show riches
Ready to drop upon me; that, when I wak'd,
I cried to dream again.

Still the receptivity to music in itself tells us nothing of Caliban's humanity or lack of it. Caliban is receptive to lovely sounds, but then so are animals.[5]

Sleep

Sleep comprises one of the dominant metaphors in *The Tempest*. As we explore the extent to which the portrayal of this biological function varies with the social roles and personalities of the major figures in the play, it becomes apparent that even so extra-social a phenomenon as sleep is related to the image of man, to his potentialities for self-discovery, or for the loss of the self.

To put a character to sleep may be thought of as one means of reducing him to his essential nature, shorn of worldly prerogatives and unencumbered by extrinsic frailties. During sleep all social processes—work, learning, communication with the outside world—appear to have been suspended. Since the substances of the little sleeps which occur in *The Tempest* are not revealed, we may assume that in them all activity has ceased. The problem then, in the context of the metaphor, is to discover why a character falls asleep, the manner in which he falls asleep, and the manner in which he wakes up again.

They Fall Asleep. To begin with the situation as we find it in the first scene of the first act, we note that the crew of the ship, so ubiquitous in this scene, does not turn up again until the very end of the play; then a little reception committee, consisting of the master and the boatswain, expresses pleasure at finding the passengers safe and sound. In between, for five long acts, we are not once reminded of them. As it turns out, they have been asleep. They went to sleep almost immediately after the catastrophe, sung to their rest by the kind intercession of Ariel, who dutifully reports the event (I,2):

> The mariners all under hatches stow'd;
> Who, with a charm join'd to their suffer'd labour,
> I have left asleep.

This is a group of people who on a manual level have worked exceedingly hard, whose job is finished for the time being, and who are now rewarded for their physical strain with hours of well-merited rest. Shakespeare here has almost totally forsaken the anti-populism which frequently erupts in earlier plays, as in the great soliloquy of Henry V on the eve of Agincourt (Act IV, Scene 1).

Those who operate on a more complex level of rationality than do the skilled workers have different sleep habits. Theirs is the privilege of comfortable naps after intellectual exertion. Gonzalo has no difficulty in falling asleep once he has tried as well as he can to comfort Alonso. His sleep is as much an expression of inner peace as are the early afternoon naps of Prospero, the diligent scholar, who breaks up the strenuous mental labors of his day by a short after-dinner sleep.

It is during this respite from bookish pursuits that Prospero becomes more easily prey to Caliban's stratagems (III,2):

> Why, as I told thee, 'tis a custom with him
> I' th' afternoon to sleep: there thou may'st brain him.

In his primitive fashion, Caliban senses the connection between Prospero's scholarship and his resting habits. One might almost feel that the picture of Prospero asleep adds to Caliban's hatred; his outbursts gain momentum as he becomes emboldened by the thought of Prospero helpless:

> I'll yield him thee asleep,
> Where thou may'st knock a nail into his head.

Could it be, one might ask, that the serf experiences a kind of dread before the knowledgeable eyes of the intellectual—that he feels he can free himself from this dread only by putting out the "vile jelly" forever?

Now let us glance at Miranda as one who achieves, in the course of the play, a personal autonomy. Still between childlike innocence and full awakening to the experience of love, she falls asleep early, overpowered by the wealth of exciting information about the curious ways of humanity which her father has just given her (I,2). So much is "beating in my mind," she tells him, that she needs a pause before she can accept any more; for the time being she has absorbed all her consciousness can take. Her father gives his blessings:

> Here cease more questions;
> Thou art inclin'd to sleep; 'tis a good dullness,
> And give it way;—I know thou canst not choose.

And so too for Miranda sleep harmonizes with her personality, just as the sleep of the intellectual and the manual worker accords with theirs.

Two Who Stay Awake. The high lords, embodiments of anti-rational amorality and physical sloth, do not fall asleep easily. Alonso, who is not quite so abominable as are his brother and Antonio, has difficulty in getting rest but he succeeds eventually, though only after Gonzalo has already begun to snore. Sebastian and Antonio do not go to sleep at all.

We are aware again here of the essential unimportance of magic procedures in the play. True, Ariel has flown onstage, "invisible, playing solemn music," but the lullaby has different effects on different people—which after all must mean that the nature of the respective sleeps is determined not by the lullaby but by the sleepers. Gonzalo reacts to Ariel's singsong by slipping off to sleep immediately; Alonso finally drifts off after a period of moaning and jeering by turns; and Sebastian and Antonio, who no more deserve sleep than does Macbeth who "hath murdered sleep," are immune to Ariel's soporific ariettas. They remain very much awake indeed, hatching plots for their own benefit, which include a scheme to kill Alonso in his sleep.

The implication in their sleeplessness seems clear: their motives, their language, their type of reasoning, are directed toward goals the very opposite of those which are conducive to life-renewing sleep. Their solution to the dilemmas which face them is, like Caliban's, murder. While others sleep to restore their energies, which will be expended in rational and productive tasks, Sebastian and Antonio remain wide awake and, remaining awake, define themselves out of the human fold.

Waking Up. Awakening is described as the reintegration of the individual with his useful tasks. Miranda, having replenished the drained reservoir of her psychic strength after her father's protracted revelations, is prepared to encounter Ferdinand and to face the test of her maturity with which this meeting confronts her. Her father, guardian of her waking and her sleeping soul, recalls her to consciousness (I,2):

> Awake, dear heart, awake! thou hast slept well:
> Awake!

One may remember his earlier exhortations to Miranda to lend him an attentive ear: the young human being is in need of her mentor's repeated reminders to face the tasks of the day. It is a matter of sleeping soundly, waking energetically, listening diligently.

Gonzalo awakens the instant the plot against Alonso is about to be consummated. Antonio has given the signal, "then let us both be sudden"; and Gonzalo comes to life with his toast to the king's preservation. While Ariel has had a hand in Gonzalo's momentous awakening, the substance of this awakening consists of Gonzalo's spontaneous reactions, which are instantly directed toward life, his own and his king's.

Skipping over the better part of three acts, we find the mariners about to awaken. They come out of the deep slumber to which their mighty efforts have entitled them. Appropriately enough they are awakened by the noise of their own craft, the repair work which is being done on the ship by parties unknown (V,1):

> We were dead of sleep
> And,—how we know not,—all clapp'd under hatches,
> Where, but even now, with strange and several noises
> Of roaring, shrieking, howling, jingling chains,
> And more diversity of sounds, all horrible
> We were awak'd.

The good boatswain, hero of the wreck, is delighted with the expert job on the boat. He reports to Prospero that no sooner were they awake than

> we, in all her trim, freshly beheld
> Our royal, good and gallant ship; our master
> Capering to eye her.

The ship is the first thing they notice: as soon as they return to consciousness, they integrate themselves into their accustomed working situations, ready to take up the job where they left off before falling asleep.

Sex and Eros

Raping and Breeding. In Shakespeare, sex does not connote the immersion or relapse of the human species into an animal state; this would be non-creative, passive behavior. On the contrary, the closer man comes to the sexual, the more challenging is the need to penetrate the outer shell of *natura naturata* with rays of reason. The anarchy of nature must be transformed in the direction of felt and experienced harmony. In sex relations this task is most difficult because the ubiquitous force of the sex instinct, with its propensity to violence, makes greater demands on man's presence of mind than perhaps any other activity. Thus in a man's sexual behavior may be found an ultimate revelation of his humanity, precisely because of the challenge offered by the danger of reduction to the animal state.

Gratification of the sexual instinct does not seem to require any specifically human processes. It is therefore precisely here that the presence of rationality, of freely chosen and justifiable action, determines whether man is in control of himself or whether he is mere natural material, blindly surrendering to nonrational forces.

Here too, as always, behavior at the extreme poles is revealing. Caliban, Sebastian, Antonio, and Stephano, all of whom represent the lowest levels of human development,[6] display basically identical reactions. The slightest provocation or opportunity is sufficient to call forth—either in deed or phantasy—sexual desire; and it scarcely matters how or with whom their instincts are to be gratified. As Caliban describes Miranda's sexual attractiveness, Stephano lasciviously asks: "Is it so brave a lass?" Similarly, the only response Gonzalo's Utopian daydream evokes in Sebastian and Antonio is that of sexual promiscuity (II,1):

> *Sebastian:* No marrying 'mong his subjects?
> *Antonio:* None, man; all idle; whores and knaves.

Caliban at least wants offspring. Earlier, in his splenetic outburst against Prospero, when he is reminded of his attempt to rape Miranda in her father's cell, he says (I,2):

> O ho! Oh ho!
> Oh ho! Oh ho!—would it had been done!
> Thou didst prevent me; I had peopled else
> This isle with Calibans.

When he offers Miranda to Stephano he assumes the butler is thinking along the same lines (III,2):

> She will bring thee forth brave brood.

71

Here Caliban's very language suggests the pre-human level. Again he stands out as prime exemplar of the anti-rationalist, anti-individualist, pre-sensible brute.

Love: The Birth of the Individual. Ferdinand and Miranda, on the other hand, embody the truly human aspects of love. The two of them, meeting under the most primitive conditions, are completely unaware of each other's backgrounds or stations. They reenact, in a secularized world, the meeting in the Garden of Eden: a man alone and a woman alone are face to face for the first time. That is to say, they are essentially alone; Prospero in fact hovers near them, but the young people are unconscious of his presence. Their very first words as they become aware of each other set the tone: Miranda sees the young man as "a spirit . . . it carries a brave form"; for Ferdinand the young girl is "the Goddess on whom these airs tend" (I,2). There is no notion here of any reenactment of original sin, but rather a transfiguration of it. The substance of their relationship, germinally present before they have said a word to each other, is that of specific human qualities, which, in this particular case, find confirmation in their childlike delight at finding they speak the same language. They are two charming young Platonists.

What follows now in quick succession are stages of increasing awareness of the self and of the other. Prospero endeavors to impede the affair artificially; while he observes that "at the first sight . . . they are both in either's power," it still remains to be seen whether this is more than fleeting passion. He appeals to Miranda's childhood recollection of the days before their exile. The intention is to excite hostile emotions against the young prince from Naples, whom he labels an usurper and a spy bent on wresting the island from him. Miranda listens to all this quite unmoved[7]; the specific accusations Prospero makes she has neither the experience nor the factual information to deny. But she can scarcely believe that a young man of so noble a bearing is capable of such intentions. We encounter here, also, a Platonic facet of Renaissance ideology; the conviction that outer beauty and inner worth are intimately connected, that the beautiful is a manifestation of the good and the true:

> There's nothing ill can dwell in such a temple:
> If the ill spirit have so fair a house,
> Good things will strive to dwell with't.

Prospero, threatening absurd punishment for absurdly trumped-up charges, orders Ferdinand to follow him to a place of confinement. Ferdinand resists:

> No,
> I will resist such entertainment till
> Mine enemy has more power.

The young man whom Ariel reported as in a kind of stupor but a few moments ago

> cooling of the air with sighs
> In an odd angle of the isle and sitting
> His arms in this sad knot.

is now a very much composed and resolute person; and his refusal is actuated not only by the code of honor of a prince, but even more immediately by his desire to remain in the presence of his beloved. This extremely individualized type of conduct is taken up at once by Miranda:

> Oh dear father
> Make not too rash a trial of him, for
> He's gentle, and not fearful.

These words have, for their time, almost the same revolutionary connotation on the individual level that the boatswain's (I,1) words addressed to the feudal parasites—"work you, then!"—have on the social level. What Miranda expresses is the essence of the emancipatory process of an individual: freely chosen relationships have come to supersede tradition. She has made the first decision of her life, and has thus severed the original, unreflecting relationship with her father. She now follows the voice of her inner conviction. Mustering this new strength, she goes even further and attempts to prevent her father from striking Ferdinand with a sword. Prospero rudely brushes her aside: "Hang not on my garments!" Even her plea for pity—her childish "I'll be his surety"—is dismissed with a brusque "Silence!"

Prospero resorts to yet another of his testing devices: he challenges Miranda's perception of Ferdinand as a superior being:

> Thou think'st there is no more such shapes as he,
> Having seen but him and Caliban. Foolish wench!
> To the most of men this is a Caliban
> And they to him are angels.

The description assumes the authority of unchallengeable experience since it appeals to Miranda's ignorance in the matter of men; after all, she has no way of judging and discriminating, never having laid eyes on a young man before. For all she knows there really are yet more handsome men in the world than Ferdinand. But she replies:

> My affections
> Are then most humble; I have no ambition
> To see a goodlier man.

Her words are decisive, for they codify the essentials that make for the unique character of the individual. By choosing freely, against odds, in the teeth of tradition and outward command, Miranda has acted as an autonomous individual; she has created a new reality for herself. Her confession of love adds a new particle of reason, of self-created reality, to the world around her.

As we have seen in Cervantes, love appears as the key phenomenon in the autonomous development of the modern individual: it becomes almost identical with individuality itself. The point can hardly be over-stressed. Love, whatever else it may be, represents an inner decision. The giving and acceptance of love brings rationality into focus more clearly than anything else. True, one might say that the process of falling in love is completely accidental and arbitrary; there appears to be no firmly rational basis for an individual to make his choice among all pos-sibilities. But it is for precisely this reason that romantic love becomes the strongest expression of individuality. While it may be initially irrational, love creates its own situation, which, from the seemingly absurd moment of its acknowledgement, becomes a productive basis for a new rationality. A new situation, however isolated and unique, is introduced into human history once a person has *decided* that he has "no ambition to see a goodlier man" or woman.

Bonds entered into voluntarily do not create bondage, as do tradition, privilege, and subjection to extra-human powers; they are, rather, the content of freedom. Ferdinand no longer resists Prospero's command to follow him to his place of arbitrary punishment, once he knows where he stands with respect to Miranda. In his love is his freedom; compared to it (I,2):

> My father's loss, the weakness which I feel,
> The wrack of all my friends, or this man's threats
> To whom I am subdued, are but light to me.

The world of Ferdinand and Miranda beings with the experience that is their own and only their own:

> Might I but through my prison once a day
> Behold this maid: all corners else o' th' earth
> Let Liberty make use of; space enough
> Have I in such a prison.

With Ferdinand's speech we have retraced our steps to Don Quixote's scene with the Duchess. Man, Shakespeare tells us as Cervantes did, finds himself alone in a universe without moorings and without predictability; he has, nonetheless, the task of restoring sense to the chaos which the passing of the old order had left. And this sense, since it could no longer come from without, had to be achieved by individual acts of ordering and re-creation. Upon the individual devolved the burden of remaking his world. And his individuality was pressingly put to test when he was called upon to make intimate decisions concerning himself and those nearest him—those involving love.

Secularized Humility

Inherent in the play is the Baconian idea that man develops his humanity by acquiring and applying knowledge; knowledge begets the power to control nature. Nature is both in and around us, and the sciences are divided accordingly. The science of man rests on introspection and empathy; turned to the past, it becomes History. Prospero's story about his past, however, is not only information but also leads to the practice of Education. And when methods and findings of introspection and empathy are generalized, we enter the realm of Ethics. Thus in *The Tempest*, behavior may be observed as a basis for prediction of moral propensities: Prospero studies the development of Ferdinand and Miranda, as Ariel studies the repentance of the lords.

What, finally, has emerged from the experiment on the island? In terms of the five themes we have selected for study each member of the small, isolated society has acted out the potentialities of his own nature. The question remains: how should individual variations in human nature ultimately be explained? Why is Prospero essentially good and Antonio, to say nothing of Caliban, essentially evil? Theories of human nature from the Renaissance to the late eighteenth century leave this question unanswered; whether man is considered intrinsically good or intrinsically evil, the basic postulates do not allow us to deduce why some should be more successful than others in overcoming their original destructive bents or in maintaining their original innocence. *The Tempest,* at several places, comes close to formulating this dilemma. Prospero describes to Caliban the pains he has taken to give him a decent education, to teach him "with human care" how to work, how to think. In the end, despite labor and kindness, he has failed. Caliban has betrayed his mentor and his own humanity by trying to rape Miranda and by using language mainly for cursing. The only explanation Prospero can find for his failure is to take recourse to the key concept of the Renaissance intellectual—that arcanum of all secularized knowledge as well as ignorance: nature. He says (I,2):

> I endowed thy purposes
> With words that made them known: but thy vile race,
> Though thou did'st learn, had that in 't which good nature
> Could not abide with.

Similarly, Prospero can only account for his brother's behavior by concluding that Antonio's "ambition expell'd remorse and nature." A few lines later he calls Antonio "unnatural though thou art." (V,l)

The image of man which we get from *The Tempest* is that of a free agent, whose possibilities lie in several directions. If it does not say why some should choose one direction and others another, the play at least demonstrates the consequences of a variety of choices. Implicit is the belief that no formal and arbitrary code exists for self-discovery and that, in fact, the very process of self-discovery may lead to breaking certain rules otherwise taken for granted.

The Irrational Deviant: Caliban

In several instances in *The Tempest* people behave in a way that appears inconsistent with the portrayal of their characters. They do not behave as they might be expected to on the basis of what we know about their prior behavior and attitudes. Whereas in Cervantes deviations from the norm were discovered in figures marginal to the society at large, in *The Tempest* deviations occur by a reversal of previous patterns within the individual.

Again, two basically different types of reactions are displayed in inconsistent behavior, as they were in "normal" behavior. Caliban, the prototype farthest removed from self-control and creativity at one point seems to overcome his sullen, dumb, and blunted personality. To Stephano, who has initiated him into the delights of liquor, he voluntarily offers all the services that Prospero forces him to perform. He goes even further and volunteers to do many extra services (II,2):

> I'll show thee the best springs; I'll pluck thee berries;
> I'll fish for thee, and get thee wood enough.

Or:

> I prithee, let me bring thee where crabs grow;
> And I with my long nails will dig thee pig-nuts;
> Show thee a jay's nest and instruct thee how
> To snare the nimble marmoset; I'll bring thee
> To clust'ring filberts, and sometimes I'll get thee
> Young scamels from the rock.

Twice he asks Stephano for the privilege to "kiss thy feet." Twice the former specialist in cursing becomes inventive in similes, as if to emphasize the high respect in which he holds the person for whom he is willing to work. He implores to be permitted to "follow thee" and not only calls him a "wondrous man," but asks him to "be my God"; he introduces his speeches with a polite "I prithee." He follows up his dedication to Stephano by a grotesque rejection of Prospero:

> A plague upon the tyrant that I serve!
> I'll bear him no more sticks, but follow thee,
> Thou wondrous man.

Caliban presents himself suddenly as a superworker for whom no strain and exertion seems too much. But again his behavior is that of a pre-rational human being fixated in an infantile stage of development. He adapts himself to whatever seems to offer immediate satisfaction of bodily needs and desires, completely uninterested in consequences, like a baby or an animal grabbing a toy or a morsel of food. His words describe a Utopia in reverse—he voluntarily subjects himself to perpetual servitude and to an uninhibited exploitation of nature. He reminds us of the contemporary uprooted adolescent on the loose, in search of a leader and in need of compensating for his submission to authority by committing, under its protection, senseless acts of cruelty. Miranda as well as nature's flora and fauna are for Caliban nothing but opportunity for rape and violence. While in the humanistic Utopia of Gonzalo the exploitation of nature is limited to the irreducible minimum of providing for survival, the sadistic wish-dreams of Caliban are filled with senseless anticipations of cruel acts. He rejects Prospero's rational solutions for his plight—in fact, he experiences them only as threats. He now wants to eliminate the source of those solutions entirely, by bludgeoning the brain that devised them. The terror he feels as a result of his subjection to an overpowering leader, he can project and act out by an attack on the weak and defenseless.

The misery of Caliban—who is unable to comprehend that he is in the service of a decent master, and who equates liberation with humiliation and with alienation from humanity—reveals the possibilities for regression which the breakdown of feudalism had bared. His whole life is circumscribed by the necessity to follow commands, the rationality of which he is neither willing nor able to grasp. His sole motivation is mutiny against rationally functioning institutions of civilization.

Individual Fulfillment: Ferdinand, Miranda, and Gonzalo

At the other extreme, Miranda, Ferdinand, and Gonzalo seem to display deviations from their own standard of morality: they refuse to follow orders, or they break the word they have given. All three deviate, in their various ways, from the unconditional performance of duties they had originally accepted.

When Antonio, Prospero's brother, and his co-conspirators had set about to send Prospero and Miranda to certain death on "a rotten carcass of a boat," Gonzalo had been chosen to execute the plan. In violation of the usurper's orders, he had provided the rightful duke and his daughter with means of livelihood sufficient for them to survive Antonio's attempt to murder them.

Miranda, for her part, performs a whole series of acts that are in clear violation of her father's instructions and at variance with her heretofore child-like dependence upon him. She asks Ferdinand to loaf when her father is not present (III,1):

> My father
> Is hard at study; pray now, rest yourself:
> He's safe for these three hours.

Furthermore Prospero has expressly forbidden her to tell Ferdinand her name, but when he asks it, she answers without hesitation:

> Miranda.—Oh, my father!
> I have broke your best to say so.

Finally, as do many of Shakespeare's women in love, she reverses the mores of male-female relationships by offering herself in marriage and not waiting for the young man to ask the question.

> Hence, bashful cunning!
> And prompt me, plain and holy innocence!
> I am your wife, if you will marry me;
> If not, I'll die your maid: to be your fellow
> You may deny me; but I'll be your servant,
> Whether you will or no.

To this we should add Ferdinand's larceny in reverse; he obviously cheats himself in chess with Miranda (V,1):

> *Miranda:* Sweet lord, you play me false.
> *Ferdinand:* No, my dearest love,
> I would not for the world.
> *Miranda:* Yes, for a score of kingdoms you should wrangle,
> And I would call it fair play.

All three—Gonzalo, Miranda, and Ferdinand—deliberately engage, then, in actions which on first sight deviate from their general mode of conduct. Each case represents a decision in a direction that not only is unsolicited by other people, but is in violation of instructions or rules. At the same time, all three would have violated their own natures, the substance of their rationality and morality, if they had not committed these rebellious acts.

Gonzalo, in betraying his employers, acts, as Prospero formulates it, "out of charity." The preservation of human life is for him a higher value than obedience to an order that implies its destruction. It is not far-fetched to interpret Gonzalo's act as resistance against the arbitrariness of tyranny; he avails himself of the right of disobeying the sovereign if the sovereign violates the natural rights of men. He is here closely related to Don Quixote who, in his perspicacious craziness, detects such violations at every turn. In defying his masters, Gonzalo acknowledges a higher duty and realizes a higher truth.

Miranda's three acts of disobedience to her father display the development of an autonomous and free individual. For her, it is romantic love that is the touchstone of free and rational development. When she gives Ferdinand her name, she lives up to the implications of nominalist philosophy; her name denotes her individuality. It is also incompatible with reason that Ferdinand should slave to expiate a crime he never committed. Her bodily frailty is transformed by her moral strength when she endeavors to alleviate his forced labor. Finally, to hide her love would be a lie. No price is too high for the truth, even the violation of a parental order.

Ferdinand's setting aside of the rules is, of course, harmless, but it has its importance. When he obviously forfeits the advantage of chess moves which his less experienced opponent has made possible and which, in strict obedience to the rules, he ought to execute, he forfeits the supposed male superiority in intelligence within the charming context of a game. Miranda's awareness of his tricks and her understanding of his voluntary mistakes shows her, in fact, to be his equal in intelligence. The ideal relation between man and woman, in the imagery of the Elizabethan Renaissance, does not consist in the biological, naturalistic satisfaction of instincts, but in the recognition of one individual's reason by another, tempered by consideration of human limitations and by ensuing acts of indulgence.

The selection of chess as a motif in the love of Ferdinand and Miranda is an artful figure. No other game so completely shuts out the element of chance as does chess; called the game of kings and philosophers, and symbolizing the peak of humanly attainable reason, it is an appropriate token of ideal human behavior in a situation of leisure. The lovers who have found in each other a congenial spirit engage in the pleasures of reason even when alone and at play, and thus show an exemplary discipline under tempting conditions by playing the most intellectual of games.

Pity

Pity is for Shakespeare the one foundation for morality. Within a theological context, to be sure, pity had its rewards; man was credited for its exercise in the offices of heavenly bookkeeping, and his fate depended upon the entries. But such post-mortal expediency became weaker during the Renaissance, and the very decline in theological certainties created a challenge to the individual, forcing him to redefine his relation to others. Man now viewed pity as the outcome of self-awareness and of accepting personal responsibility for one's own and mankind's fate: pity—as it was now postulated—consists of insight into the limitations of finite reason and finite life, and compels acts of mercy. The exercise of mercy was the final maxim Don Quixote passed on to Sancho Panza in teaching him the rules of wisdom for statesmanship and judgment.

In *The Tempest*, pity is a dominant and recurrent element. Gonzalo pities Prospero and Miranda at the time he executes the brutal exile order; Prospero takes pity on Caliban and tries to teach him some of the techniques of civilization; Miranda pities Ferdinand when she sees him burdened with heavy work; Gonzalo takes pity on his mourning king; in a very delicate way Ferdinand pities Miranda for her shortcomings in chess; Ariel has pity on all the lordly passengers of the ship, including the criminals; and Prospero, listening to the voice of his conscience, realizes that wisdom should make him "kindlier moved" even than Ariel. In practically every major theme we have analyzed, pity is present: in work as demonstrated by Miranda, in learning as demonstrated by Prospero, in language as demonstrated by Gonzalo, and even in sleep, if we remember the careful way in which the tired seamen are put to rest.

The expression of pity as a consequence of the recognition of human frailty reaches two peaks as the play nears its end. When Prospero, at the beginning of the fifth act, finds in himself the strength of pity, he divests himself of his magic (V,l):

> But this rough magic
> I here abjure; and, when I have requir'd
> Some heavenly music,—which even now I do,—
> To work mine end upon their senses that
> This airy charm is for, I'll break my staff,
> Bury it certain fathoms in the earth,
> And deeper than did ever plummet sound
> I'll drown my book.

Now, without benefit of superhuman powers, he twice tells his brother that he forgives him. Thus, in a gesture of the kind we are familiar with in Gonzalo, he applies insight and theoretical knowledge to practice: having himself experienced the blessings of humanistic pity, he applies it now even to those who deserve it least.

A final expression of human sympathy is reached at the end of the play, when Prospero speaks an epilogue to the audience:

> Now my charms are all o'erthrown,
> And what strength I have's mine own;
> Which is most faint: now, 'tis true,
> I must be here confin'd by you,
> Or sent to Naples. Let me not.
> Since I have my dukedom got
> And pardon'd the deceiver, dwell

In this bare island by your spell;
But release from my bands
With the help of your good hands.
Gentle breath of yours my sails
Must fill, or else my project fails,
Which was to please. Now I want
Spirits to enforce, art to enchant,
And my ending is despair,
Unless I be reliev'd by prayer,
Which pierces so that it assaults
Mercy itself and frees all faults.
As you from crimes would pardon'd be,
Let your indulgence set me free.

In its most obvious reading, the speech is a conventional appeal by the chief actor of the play for applause. But the nature of its references to the play suggests another meaning, one that can sum up for us the situation of the individual at an early stage of modern history.

It reminds us of Don Quixote's speech about Dulcinea; the borderline between reality and illusion is fluid, and so are the status and location of the individual. There are no objective criteria for deciding whether it is Prospero, or an actor, or the poet himself, who is speaking; we do not know whether these words are still an integral part of the play or whether, as in *Don Quixote,* the poet views his creation as a part of himself about which he then reflects. The image is that of man removed from a specific setting and set of relationships, other than those he can create for himself. Divested of the tools of learning and technology, his magic "charms all o'erthrown," deserted even by his fellow actors, man appears as the modern individual in all his aloneness: "what strength I have is my own." In acknowledging individual existence he realizes, at the same time, the limitations of individual power, "which is most faint."

This, then, is the image of Elizabethan man, living in a world in which he develops his responsibilities to himself and his pity for others, anticipating that the future will fulfill his hopes. But in one important respect, the image of man will now change radically: with the advent of tighter social controls, the individual will never again feel himself so completely his own master.

Notes

1.   See Excursus A.
2.   It is difficult to imagine a Tudor poet acquiescing to any such doctrine as this. For a convenient summary of the theological view of learning we may go to *The Defense of Poetry.* Writing about 1582, Sidney, in a sentence often cited

by the anti-secular scholars, holds it axiomatic that "this purifying of wit, this enriching of memory, enabling of judgment, and enlarging of conceit, which commonly we call learning, under what name soever it come forth, or to what immediate end soever it be directed, the final end is, to lead and draw us to as high a perfection as our degenerate souls, made worse by their clay lodgings, can be capable of." (*Works,* ed. Feuillerat, Cambridge: Cambridge University Press, 1923, III, II). This theological formulation applies to learning in all its manifestations. But it applies to each separate branch and condition of learning. When, for example, Walter Raleigh, in his *History of the World,* written as late as 1614, tells us that "This cruel king, Richard III, Henry the Seventh cut off; and was therein . . . the immediate instrument of God's justice," he is really echoing Augustine's justification for the study of history as a means of getting to know the whys and wherefores of divine punishment. Nor must it be thought that such a view automatically implies an adherence to medieval and Catholic functions and schemata. It is perfectly consistent in a great pedagogue like Roger Ascham to propose, in the Dedication to *Toxophilus,* "the continual setting forth of God's word and His glory," and two pages later to grumble, "These books . . . were made the most part in abbeys and monasteries, a very likely and fit fruit of such an idle and blind kind of living." This is not to say, of course, that in 1603, upon the accession of James, Shakespeare decided to adopt a view of the world associated with the Jacobean reign and the name of Francis Bacon, and to discard his Elizabethan allegiances and an outlook which united him to Hooker, Sidney, Spenser, and Raleigh. The man who wrote *The Tempest* under James (or so we suppose) wrote (we are certain) *Henry V* under Elizabeth. Our contention here is that *The Tempest* bears witness to a view of learning far more akin to the Baconian than the Spenserian.

3. The passage presents some fairly difficult problems if we take it as seriously as, I think, it should be taken. How is such a political anarchism to be reconciled with the Renaissance view of order among its magistrates? The passage is directly indebted to Montaigne's "Of Cannibales," and has occasionally been interpreted as satirizing its source rather than as versifying it. This interpretation, by which Gonzalo would be made to spout nonsense, is, so far as I know, no longer regarded as viable. As has been said, Gonzalo is always skirting the edge of absurdity by reason of his age and Polonian mellifluence. The difficulty with him, as with quite a few of Shakespeare's old men, is always with how something is said, rather than with what is said. Gonzalo makes excellent sense, but one might wish—with the nobles—that he were not such a "spendthrift of his tongue."

4. For an astute analysis of Shakespeare's uses of the verbal conventions, see Wolfgang Clemens, *Shakespeares Bilder* (1935), transl. *Shakespeare's Imagery* (1951) and J. Dover Wilson's "Introduction" to the latter. The whole question of Shakespeare's dramatic verbal technique is brilliantly discussed in Moody Prior, *The Language of Tragedy* (1947), Ch. 2.

5. The notion that music exercises peculiarly seductive and dangerous powers over irrational and anti-rational minds is very old. A fairly recent disquisition on the toxic effects of song, with a prophetic political moral, is to be found in the chapter entitled "Politically Suspect" in Mann's *Magic Mountain.* We also recall the punch-drunk street songs of the brownshirts—Caliban's

political heirs. They, too, under the content analyst's magnifying glass (it needn't be a powerful one), reveal a decidedly high incidence of cursing.

6.   Of the four, the nobles Sebastian and Antonio represent the vilest of the vile, since the advantage of their station makes all the greater their fall. In this respect, one of Caliban's functions in the play may be said to be that of providing a yardstick by which to measure the depravity of these nobles.

7.   It is typical of Shakespeare's heroines that they are committed to one great love; love becomes so integral to their identity and their destiny that death alone can end it.

Excursus A

The Tempest, Act I, Scene 1

The storm and shipwreck that introduce *The Tempest* deserve intensive analysis. In this brief scene, Shakespeare confronts us with persons from widely separated social classes and places them in an extreme situation which enables him to study their essential characters. The analysis of the scene is presented both as a sample of close textual criticism and as background material helpful to an understanding of sociological implications in the rest of the play.

What may have appeared to Shakespeare's people as a matter-of-fact set of relationships is for us problematic. In interpreting them at all, there is the risk, of course, of making Shakespeare appear unduly aware sociologically. The purpose here, however, differs from textual literary criticism; the intent is not to burden Shakespeare's words with many meanings on different levels, but simply to listen carefully to the evidence implicit in the lines of the scene. In a sense, it is the evidence of that which was taken for granted in Shakespeare's day that is the objective of our search. Such an approach need not distort or overburden his meanings—at worst, it examines his characters, their roles, and their relationships, in the light of a larger picture of social change than he himself could possibly have known.

The shipwreck scene introduces us to the villainous and worthless characters of the play. Shakespeare is concerned, naturally enough, with furthering his plot, but he must first define the villains, and in this scene he carefully sets them off against the figures of Gonzalo and the boatswain. The princely usurpers and idlers are useless in the emergency at hand and behave stupidly, whereas Gonzalo acts and speaks in a reasonable way, and the boatswain works competently and industriously. If we bring to the scene what we learn from the rest of the play, it is apparent that Shakespeare uses the progressive ideas and moral concepts of his day to define his heroes, and leaves his villains in a reactionary, or at least non-progressive, torpor. In this light, we see in the villains the representatives of the declining noble class who are concerned only with enjoying the feudal prerogatives they have inherited. They have nothing in common with Prospero, Gonzalo or simple workmen, whose actions and ideas anticipate the qualities of middle-class individualism and industriousness.

The first persons we encounter in the play are working people, acting out their professional roles in a responsible way. The master calls "Boatswain," and the boatswain answers: "Here, master: what cheer?" The master continues:

> Good, speak to the mariners: fall to't yarely, or we run ourselves aground: bestir, bestir.

We are quickly introduced to a situation structured by the needs of expedient work under conditions of utmost stress. The speakers address each other by means of their functional names. The way in which they speak to each other is that of workers getting on about their business; it could also be the way of a senior and a junior engineer. The chief gives an order, the boatswain responds, and the whole mood is relaxed, friendly and factual despite their predicament. We can imagine that two skilled pilots might behave in the same way if their plane were in trouble.

The master expresses clearly and simply the need for speed. His words invite comparison with those of Alonso, king of Naples, when, a few seconds later, he enters the scene and commands the boatswain to "play the men." The attitude of the king is that of the feudal lord to the lowest of his subjects. He does not understand the situation, and his relationship to the crew members is that of imperium and domination, not of reason.

The words of the shipmaster, however, are strictly geared to the understanding that exists among the crewmen of the purposes of the work at hand. It is interesting to note that he never again appears on the scene. He has given the plan for overall strategy and his general directions to the boatswain, who will from now on know what to do. Authority is not something continuously visible as it was in feudal times; it is ingrained in the productive processes themselves, and the captain can, therefore, disappear. As a matter of fact, the sailors and the boatswain have a hard time trying to get the feudal lords out of their way, so convinced are the latter that their visible authority is needed, and so useless is it, actually, to the workmen. The working men are on the job, doing efficiently what has to be done without undue fear or impatience.

As the scene progresses, the crew members come on deck and the boatswain speaks to them as follows:

> Heigh, my hearts! Cheerly, cheerly, my hearts! Yare, yare! Take in the topsail! Tend to the master's whistle! Blow, till thou burst thy wind if room enough!

The boatswain reproduces the friendliness and simple efficiency of the master, although the tone is now somewhat more paternalistic. The distance between boatswain and sailors is patently greater than that between master and boatswain. Whereas the master has given general instructions about the main goal to the boatswain, the latter is more specific in his dealings with the less-skilled and less-educated group at his command. Nobody, however, uses harsh words except when the boatswain, in an ironical way, curses the elements. Here, as generally in modern literature, the irony expresses a feeling of limitation and constitutes an insight into the frailty of men; it is humility in nontheological clothing. What the boatswain is really saying is: We are doing all we can in our exchange with nature. We shall try to use nature for our purposes, but a wind can be stronger than a man's intelligence.

The feudal lords enter the scene at the very moment the boatswain has acknowledged the limitations of human power by shouting at the storm. Now, it is no longer merely man against nature, but man against man: Shakespeare pits the industrious professional and the workman against men who are in power. Among those who appear are Alonso, king of Naples, Antonio, usurper of the Dukedom of Milan, and Gonzalo, a minister of the state of Naples. (Ferdinand, the innocent young prince, who later will speak in a most human way, remains silent.) The king says,

> Good boatswain, have care. Where's the Master? Play the men.

The remarks are not unfriendly, but they are condescending. The king wants the master, nobody else will do. He can think only in terms of hierarchy. As we have seen, however, it is a hierarchy with which the master himself is little concerned; the entire crew from the master on down are interested merely in the matter at hand. The boatswain does not respond to the words of the king; he continues to behave rationally, and the only rationality possible at the moment is to keep the deck cleared of passengers so that the work of combatting the storm is not impeded.

Antonio interrupts brusquely and repeats Alonso's question:

> Where's the master, bos'n?

Shakespeare introduces this character by showing in this speech and, we may assume, in his gestures the relations between social usefulness and individual character. Antonio is a criminal and a socially useless, irrational person. Interestingly enough, the boatswain, who had nothing to say to the king, answers Antonio: "Do you not hear him?" He means, of course, the master. He then adds:

> You mar our labor; keep your cabins: you do assist the storm.

What Antonio is supposed to hear from the master is his whistle. We are given here an interesting juxtaposition of the old and the new societies. The master is invisible. He is the unseen supreme authority whose presence is mediated by the whistle, symbol of the rational ordering and structuring of reality. In the light of the new, the old order with its tradition, possession, and power—as these were built up in the Middle Ages—now appears ridiculous. The boatswain uses the key word that separates the two worlds when he speaks of "labor." Labor, along with its organization, is the leading principle of the new society; he who does not work, who has no useful function, is superfluous; he should disappear, he should go to the cabins. Antonio is, like the storm, a hindrance that must be overcome, made innocuous.

Gonzalo, the counsellor, takes no issue with the boatswain's orders and is only concerned to pour soothing oil on the human tempest that is brewing. "Nay, good," he says, "be patient." The boatswain's answer is in the same tone and appeals again to common sense: there can only be patience if the situation permits the crew to work patiently; because of "these roarers" there is unfortunately no time for lengthy explanation. But the boatswain goes a step further, and appeals, as it were, to the higher knowledge of the counsellor by saying:

> What cares these roarers for the name of king?

The boatswain now for the first time puts the issue quite straight. Nature is stronger than men of any kind and, by implication, he who knows how to master nature is superior to a man who does not, regardless of social titles. Ajain, as so often in Shakespeare, we encounter the stature and the inner dignity of the man of the new society coming into being in Elizabethan England; man is justified by his work, and his character is formed by his function in society. The feudal lords, impatient and useless, have nothing to do but act out their impatience in complete separation from the real situation.

Gonzalo agrees with the boatswain, but with a defensive note.

> Good, yet remember whom thou has aboard.

The answer of the boatswain,

> None that I more love than myself,

is one familiar enough in later statements of the egalitarian ethos: in our nature we are equal and are egotistic and altruistic at one and the same time; we all love ourselves but we overcome this self-love or raise it to a higher moral standing by useful work.

The boatswain then expresses the wisdom of the simple but experienced workman about the division of labor in society. He delineates the spheres of power and skill of those who work with their hands and those who work with their brains. "You are a counsellor," he says,

> If you can command these elements to silence and work the peace of the present, we will not hand a rope more; use your authority: if you cannot, give thanks you have lived so long, and make yourself ready in your cabin for the mischance of the hour, if it so hap.—Cheerly, good hearts!—Out of our way, I say.

The boatswain obviously takes Gonzalo seriously; as the scene develops it will become quite clear, in fact, that the two conceive of each other as colleagues of a sort. Neither is the source of authority; both are middlemen. They represent that middle station which the progressive forces of the new society are beginning to occupy. And not only professionally, but also in their basic character traits, they are removed from extremes. This motif of a middle station in life and in character is a theme that will come to the fore in subsequent literature, and will come increasingly to mirror the image that middle-class man has of himself.

It is interesting to note that in the boatswain's speech death appears in a completely non-theological meaning. The speech is related to the sentiments of Shakespeare's sonnet LXVI; both deal with love and death and in both death is viewed not as a fulfillment but as a terminal point. The entire scene is, indeed, secular, except for the recourse to prayer at the very end. During the emergency, no one claims to be in the hands of God; safety and security are viewed within the framework of the developing modernism of the Renaissance, and the generally shared belief is that we have security only to the extent that we have reason and experience. The boatswain, we may say, speaks as if he had read Montaigne, and Gonzalo answers as if he were Montaigne.

For a moment the boatswain leaves the scene to check up, we assume, on the work of the mariners. Gonzalo then delivers the following monologue:

> I have great comfort from this fellow: methinks he hath no drowning mark upon him; his complexion is perfect gallows. Stand fast, good Fate, to his hanging! Make the rope of his destiny our cable, for our own doth little advantage! If he be not born to be hanged, our case is miserable.

Gonzalo slanders the boatswain in *absentia;* his curses are ironical—he is simply using his urbane wit and language to give himself comfort.

The boatswain enters the now empty deck and after having given instructions to the mariners, says, upon hearing a cry from the cabin:

> A plague upon this howling! They are louder than weather, or our office.

We assume that he, like Gonzalo, is giving himself comfort with his words; he curses when those he insults are not present to hear him. The curses of both Gonzalo and the boatswain are in marked contrast to those of the reappearing feudal lords, who now include in their group Sebastian, the brother of the king of Naples. (King Alonso and his son Ferdinand do not reappear; they obviously heed the instructions of the boatswain.) Sebastian brings the swearing to new heights:

> A pox o' your throat, you bawling, blasphemous, incharitable dog!

We can infer that this powerless individual, who envies his brother in power, must live out in words his phantasies of domination (which later jell into a plan to murder his brother). In response to his cursing the boatswain says simply:

> Work you, then.

By his answer, the boatswain codifies the basic difference between the legitimate, well-organized rationale of ordered work and the parasitical, impotent, and decaying rationale of unprincipled domination. As if to prove the point, Antonio now joins in to call the boatswain a "cur," a "whoreson," an "insolent noisemaker," and in absurd fury indicts him as being more cowardly than themselves.

From now on, the lords abandon the scene, which the middlemen, Gonzalo and the boatswain, dominate. Gonzalo again acts as moderator, as a mediator who uses psychological methods to soften the shock for the despairing feudal lords and his king. The boatswain continues to give orders to the crew in accord with the changing situation of the ship, until the seamen enter shouting:

> All lost! To prayers, to prayers! All lost!

In a way, the mariners are still living on a cultural level different from that of the boatswain and Gonzalo; the latter no longer find solace in religion, but only in themselves.

At the end of the scene, Gonzalo says:

> Now would I give a thousand furlongs of sea for an acre of barren ground; long heath, brown furze, anything. The wills above be done! But I would fain die a dry death.

His speech is again urbane; even his invocation to the wills above seems ironic.

Throughout the scene it is apparent that the feudal lords are unaware of what is going on; they can only resort to vulgar behavior and direct personal abuse. Neither Sebastian nor Antonio realizes that the real issue is the relationship between skilled men and nature. Of course, the audience learns that the storm has been created by Prospero, but this does not alter their knowledge that the gentlemen lie and that the boatswain and his crew are neither incompetent nor drunk. The feudal lords emerge as stupid; they do not know what the relations of science, work, technology, and human skill really are. While the boat, so to speak, sails to the new world, the old lords are suffocating in an outmoded and completely senseless state of mind.

4

The Classical French Theater

So far, the emphasis of our study has been on the individual. In Cervantes and Shakespeare, organized society is present only as a conditioning background; the human being who emerges sees himself as the responsible creator, willingly or unwillingly, of important segments of his own reality. He seeks to overcome the vacuum left by the disappearance of the feudal order not so much by relating himself to the new society as by searching his own nature. Society as an experience is an almost accidental meeting with other individuals, and the literature records the successes and failures of these meetings. Man is limited, of course, by his experiences and contacts with others, but these do no jell for him into an image of society.

The relation of the individual to the world at large began to take on a new character. The seventeenth century in Europe saw the gradual emergence of a struggle of a new type. The victory over feudalism became final, and the new middle class started on its path of conquest with the spread of industry and trade and the growth of new urban cultural institutions. The political framework in which this class appeared, however, was still that of an absolute monarchy which continued to surround itself with an aristocratic coterie.

Against this background of politico-economic stabilization and struggle a new social consciousness arose. We find that the tensions displayed in literature are no longer merely those within the person; they are increasingly those of the self-conscious relation of man to his society. The long process of middle-class socialization had begun. The French theater in the seventeenth century admirably illustrates the various facets of this process. In Corneille's drama, man adapts himself by subordinating his personal desires and claims to the exigencies of the state; the subordination resolves his tensions and conflicts and becomes the true path of his self-realization. Racine's drama portrays, on the other hand, an irreconcilable conflict between the individual and the power apparatus, and his characters find no home in the absolute state. In Molière, the middle class emerges as a force in its own right; his characters feel their way into the new institutions and learn, although with reservations, to conform to the shared modes and values of middle-class life.

The theatre of Corneille is an exercise in political behavior accepting conditions of absolute monarchy. The tragedies of Racine are an exercise in middle-class behavior expressing intellectual and emotional resistance to the same social institution—the monarchy. The comedies of Molière are an exercise in behavior under conditions that demand conformity to a new social order. In Corneille the individual finds self-realization only after having adjusted to the state; in Racine, he finds it in resistance to the state; in Molière, he is again adjusted, this time into a pattern of conformism to the values of an emergent bourgeoisie. These characterizations are simplified and stand in need of qualification, but they can serve here to emphasize briefly three divergent approaches of European man to his social situation in the period of the rise of the middle class and before its final political victory.

In his studies of the final decades of the seventeenth century, Paul Hazard declared that "never was there a greater contrast, never a more sudden transition" than that from what people "held dear" in the seventeenth to what they believed in the eighteenth century.[1] This statement is largely true for philosophy, religious beliefs and political theory. If, however, we examine closely the great trio of French playwrights, we shall find this period of transition reflected in a decidedly less sudden way. We see not only the progressive shift of psychological views but also the gradual broadening of the social space within which the dramatic action takes place. In Corneille, the upper class is by itself, in Racine it is joined by the intellectuals—the professionals and educators—and in Molière we are faced for the first time with an almost homogeneous middle-class world.

Corneille, 1606–1684

"If he were alive once more, I would make him a prince." With these words Napoleon made Corneille a contemporary of a period when the political, legal, and economic institutions of middle-class society had achieved a definitive character. The words attest to basic social traits that had persisted over a time span of almost two hundred years. In both Corneille's and Napoleon's time, central government had to combat well-organized resistance. Strictly speaking, the similarity ends here; the government of Louis XIII set out to destroy the traditional prerogatives of the old nobility, whereas the Director and Empire of Napoleon, by dissolving the Committee of Public Safety, wrote *finis* to the tendencies toward political and economic radicalism of the French Revolution. However, while the historical situations differ, they harbor sociological similarities. When Corneille wrote *Cinna,* a play dealing with the suppression of a political conspiracy against Augustus, he was rewarded, if not with the post-hoc generosity of Napoleon, at least with Richelieu's permission to marry a titled lady. It thus would appear that ruling groups more than 150 years apart identified Corneille with something more than mere poetical whims; the question of the social relevance of his work has been answered by persons of far-reaching influence. And if Richelieu and Napoleon did not find that the *dramatis personae* of Corneille realistically typified the actions of their contemporaries, they at least wished this were the case.

Public Power and the Individual

At first sight the major works of Corneille appear to contain motivations and conflicts similar to those found in Shakespeare. The story of *Horace* reminds us of *Romeo and Juliet;* the story of *Cinna* is thematically and even chronologically very close to *Julius Caesar;* in *The Cid,* lovers whose fathers compete for honors from the crown remind us of *The Tempest's* Ferdinand and Miranda, whose fathers also were engaged in a struggle for political supremacy. However, all these similarities are more apparent than real. Shakespeare's people stand or fall with the development of their own essential being. It is not by chance that the monologue is an indispensable dramatic vehicle in almost all his plays; the actions of his characters are the outer manifestation of internal processes. Tragic endings neither condemn nor justify the social agencies that shatter the lives of Anthony or Romeo, but are the result of individually applied creative reason or its opposite: Verona stands for the foolishness of a Montague and a Capulet; Rome for the enlightened intellectuality and morality of Octavius Caesar. Even the dramatic histories of British kings make events contingent upon the individualities of the rulers, whose interactions with other individualities seem almost accidentally to create the social word. Unity, cohesion, or disorder in society proves to be nothing but unity, cohesion, or disorder in individuals, turned outward. Every event, every institution in Shakespearean drama is translatable into a psychic process of a particular individual.

But if in Shakespeare's work society reflects the individual, in Corneille's it is a reified individual who reflects society. The dynamic processes are reversed. Corneille's figures achieve stature only in institutional roles. The state gives them distinguishable contours and provides them with principles for organizing and structuring otherwise chaotic modes of reaction and behavior. Individuation is experienced—as it will tend to be in literature from now on—as socialization.

In Corneille's time, middle-class life had gained tremendous momentum, mainly as a result of the state's mercantilist policy supporting the development of industry and trade. For despite its aristocratic look, the prosperity of the absolute state depended upon the very economic gains which were bringing the middle class with its way of life and its ethos to the fore. Prior to Corneille, the problem facing the individual had been survival within an environment disrupted by the disintegration of the old order as well as by the appearance of the new. Now the problem changed radically; it was no longer one of self-orientation midway between a twilight of chaos and a dawning reconstruction, but of accommodation in one way or another to a flourishing absolute state with its rind of regal pomp and core of stable industriousness. Corneille's dramas are full of special pleading and rhetorical persuasions designed to demonstrate that acceptance of public power is both expedient and moral.

The unity and harmony of individual existence now emanates from social agencies. The process may be described in this way: the social agencies, specifically the state, force the individual to subordinate self-interest to public interest, and this public interest is ultimately experienced by him as eminently suited to his self-interest. The subtitle to *Cinna* is *The Mercy of Augustus.* The mercy of God transplanted into the psyche—an extreme consequence of Renaissance secularization— is now replanted into the state, for there is no doubt that in the play Augustus represents the state. Mercy is taken from the sphere of individual frailty and given to a trans-individual social agency with executive strength. The *raison d'état* begets its own acts of mercy whenever they serve its purpose; the individual is thus the recipient but not the source of mercy. He must learn how to internalize and reenforce these acts of the state, but the possibility of his initiating them is removed.

The State and Interpersonal Relations

Love—like mercy—is no longer in itself an ultimate creative act. Only insofar as it is compatible with and subordinate to the claims of the state, can love by a legitimate expression of the individual. The *raison d'état* must determine the consummation, or even the destruction, of intimate relationships; personal catastrophes or satisfactions amount to little as compared to the necessities of state. Thus in *Horace,* brothers, sisters, husbands, and wives, forfeit their happiness, and even life, when the state demands it. Corneille has Horace declaim:

> To die for the Fatherland is such a pleasant fate, that everyone yearns for it;
> But to sacrifice what one loves for the state, to enter into lists against one's other self,
> To fight the brother of one's wife, the betrothed of one's sister,
> To arm oneself for the fatherland against one for whose blood I'd give my life,
> That is a fate worthy of a Roman.[2]

At the end of the wars between the Albans and Romans, the only surviving protagonist is Horace, who has killed not only his brothers-in-law but also his wife; still the play does not become a tragedy of aloneness. On the contrary, he receives from the head of state these instructions:

> Live, Horace, live, great-hearted warrior.
> Your virtue will pale your fame about your deed.
> Your high-spirited ardor caused your monstrous crime.
> With so beautiful a cause one must take whatever result follows.
> Live to love your state.[3]

Don Roderick, the Cid, who has slain the father of his beloved Chimène, will be united in marriage with her after the bereaved daughter has observed a suitable period of mourning. While waiting, he will engage in patriotic deeds. The king addresses first Chimène and then Roderick:

> (*To Chimène:*)
> Take, if you will, a year to dry your tears.
> Meanwhile, let Roderick win new victories.
> (*To the Cid:*)
> You have destroyed the Moors upon our shores,
> Shattered their hopes, repulsed their wild assaults,
> Go now and bear the war to their own land,
> Command my army, pillage their domain.
> At the very name of Cid they quake with fear;
> They call you lord and they would make you king.
> But through all mighty deeds keep faith with her:
> Return if possible more worthy of her;
> And make yourself so prized for your exploits
> That pride will join with love to make her yours.[4]

There is no conflict, in the end, between duty to the state and one's own private happiness; the latter will be immensely increased, guaranteed and glorified if one behaves as a noble soldier.

The same system of values is displayed in *Cinna*. Augustus forgives Cinna, offers the former conspirator a responsible position and reunites him with his beloved Amelia—all for reasons of state. Amelia had forsworn her passion for Cinna because of his leaving the conspiracy of which she was a part; now when Augustus proposes to make Cinna her husband at the same time he nominates Cinna as Consul, Amelia responds to the offer and thus to the system of social values in these words:

> My hate is dying, that I believed immortal;
> Is dead, and in its place, a loyal heart.
> Henceforward, in stark horror of this hate,
> Ardor of service shall replace its fury.[5]

Her hatred had been directed against Augustus for exiling her father as a political enemy; it has also included Cinna when he withdrew from the anti-Augustan conspiracy. Prior to the denouement, Amelia is torn between loyalty to her father and love. Shakespeare's Miranda, finding herself in a similar situation, resolves her conflict through her own unique and unaided decision; there is no reference to any other moving force. Corneille's Amelia has her problem solved for her by the head of the state; her decision is simply to accept the imperial decree. By her submission, the general or social rationality represented by the decree brings order and meaning into her inconsistent and mutually exclusive desires. The superior *raison d'état* becomes her *raison d'être*; she "finds herself" by obedient identification with the political system, not by self-identification.

Prospero educates Miranda in order to make his educational efforts dispensable, and to help her achieve personal autonomy. The educational impact of organized society makes Amelia its pawn forever.

Honor and the State

The Renaissance image of mankind as a community of discrete individualities has given way to the concept of a social structure that is more than the sum total of individuals within it. The reality of the state replaces the individual dream. In Corneille's drama, the acceptance of governmental coercion is internalized and becomes a voluntary act which is glorified by the name "honor." However, it would be a sociological mistake to confuse Corneille's concept of honor with that of Calderon. For the Spanish dramatist, honor is the expression of the rigid value system of feudalism, of a society that has become obsolete; Calderon would dignify an outworn pattern as a defense against the present, but the France of Corneille is a progressive nation and his work reflects the distinction quite clearly. He is thus much closer to Calderon's predecessor Lope; both were poets of the new nationalism. But Corneille places the dynamics of secular power within the individual. Its acceptance becomes a purposive act through voluntary identification of the self with the state. His idea of honor points to the need for man to adopt the morality of the state. This becomes clear in the words of Augustus to Cinna:

> My favor makes your glory, out of that
> Your power grows; that only raised you up,
> And held you there, 'tis that the Romans honor,
> Not yourself. You have no rank or power
> Except I give it you, and for your fall
> There needs but the withdrawal of my hand,
> Which is your sole support.[6]

The words are echoed by Cinna to whom they are directed:

> Let but my duty, reborn in my heart,
> Pledge you a faith already basely broken,
> But now so firm, so far from wavering,
> The very fall of heaven could not shake it.[7]

The Cid is a particularly good example of the conflict between the new concept of honor and the old, offering a portrayal of the process of socialization called for by the absolutistic state. The first significant action of the play is a jealous outburst between the Cid's father, to whom the education of the crown prince is entrusted, and Chimène's father, who feels that he himself should have been given this distinguished task. The result is a duel between the Cid and Chimène's father; the latter is killed. The Cid has avenged his father's honor but has also embittered Chimène who now feels obliged to avenge the honor of her house. Honor at this stage reverts to the old feudal forms. It commands Chimène to avenge her father's death even in the choice of a husband, and the Cid to alienate the woman he loves. For three acts the Cid suffers this condition until he finally breaks out and declares to his father:

> Let me at least give voice to my despair;
> Which has too long been stifled by your words.
> I feel no mean regret for having served you;
> But give me back the joy this blow has cost me.
> My arm for you was raised against my love
> And by that stroke I lost my heart's desire.
> Tell me no more; I have lost all for you;
> That which I owed you, I have paid too well.[8]

Whereupon the father retorts:

> We have one honor only. Mistresses
> Are plentiful! Love is a pleasant toy,
> But honor is a master to be served.[9]

An impasse has been reached: Chimène cannot marry her beloved, the killer of her father; the son has to subordinate his personal wishes to the honor code of the feudal gentleman, and the father takes no interest whatsoever in the personal desires of his son. In the end, however, the play arrives at a complete reconciliation. When the principals are faced with the symbols, tasks and proclamations of the state represented by the king, a scaling down of personal interests satisfactory to all is achieved. Love, honor, and personal initiative are acceptable values—if subordinated to the state and "your king." These are the closing words of the play, directed to the Cid:

> *King:*   Rest hope upon your courage and my word,
> And since already you possess her heart,
> To still that honor which cries out against you
> Leave all to time, your valor, and your king.[10]

The State as the Ego

Corneille's moral beliefs might be likened to Cartesian metaphysics. For Descartes, the process of reason meant a cognitive progress by the individual toward ever more clear and distinct perceptions of himself; for Corneille, it meant the ever more clear and distinct perceptions by the individual of the state. *The Cid,* for example, starts with a confused semi-private, semi-official situation arising from the necessity to find a tutor for the crown prince; it ends with the problems of foreign politics and military might. So long as the *raison d'état* is perceived only in terms of private interests, rationality will fail and individuals will behave erratically in their official as well as in their private undertakings; once the superiority of the state is fully acknowledged, individuals and state act in unison, and reason triumphs. It is not without significance that the initial dramatic motif of *The Cid* is the education of a future ruler.

The location of Corneille's dramatic themes in the past, particularly in Roman antiquity, also reflects a Cartesian-like concern for safety, security, and reliability. When the data of history have been sifted again and again, the residuum assumes the qualities of unquestioned fact. Past events have become established knowledge: everyone is familiar with the early Roman wars, the conspiracy of Cinna and the fights of the Spaniards against the Moors. In addition, Roman and early Spanish history contain well-known examples of governmental practice; Corneille's models were safe and acceptable for presenting exemplary lessons on the socialization of the individual in a powerful state. Everything is accessible and articulate; nothing remains doubtful.

Thus while in Shakespeare there remains an eternal doubt as to whether Utopia will ever come about or even whether Prospero, once he has returned to Milan, will put his lessons into practice, the issue in Corneille is settled once and for all. We do not know whether the next generation of Montagues and Capulets will be more enlightened or be as big fools as their fathers, but we are certain that the Cid and Chimène will pass on to their offspring what they have learned and that the conflict of the play will be forever resolved. To the extent that Corneille's individual reconciles his private life with his social duties, he has fulfilled his potentialities; the rest is not silence, as in *Hamlet*, but articulate business in the service of an hierarchized "we" that endows the "I" with meaning.

Corneille's formula for a static harmony of the individual and society is, in its way, perfect. If the actualities of the state lived up to his idealization, all would be well, and we should no doubt have arrived at the end of drama. The individual, however, came to experience his position in the absolute monarchy as a kind of moral and social restraint that could not be resolved in the abstractions of pride and honor. Corneille's solutions came to exist only for a moment in time; history added the question mark he tried so hard to eradicate from his ideal representation on the stage.

Racine, 1639–1699

Racine, too, wrote 'classical' plays. They are worlds apart, however, from those of Corneille. If one changed the costumes of Corneille's characters to the contemporary garb of his time, most of them would be indistinguishable from French royalty and high military and civilian officials. Racine, too, wrote about kings and high persons, but they had no counterparts in the France of his day. There are no similarities between Louis XIV and the Nero of *Britannicus,* the Theseus of *Phaedra* or the Pyrrhus of *Andromache.*

A most significant change Racine effected in the *dramatis personae* is the introduction of a new type of man, the tutor; he is the unofficial intellectual, a person Corneille would not have tolerated. There are other differences. Although Racine, like Corneille, goes to antiquity for his themes, he avoids imperial Rome in favor of Greek times, and the legends he draws upon do not celebrate state power but individual passion. In addition, the titles of Racine's plays are significant, being almost invariably the names of women; and women certainly did not serve as spokesmen in the male-dominated society of seventeenth-century France.

Each of these differences serves to stake out the broad gulf between the two French dramatists. Racine's plays do not point to the state as the *raison d'être* of human existence. Kings rule over states that are close to unrest, sometimes even to chaos; educators moralize from a position detached from the state machinery; women, who have no political power, become the major spokesmen for ethical viewpoints; and the Greek locales underline the individualistic focus of the themes.

The State and Individual Self-Expression

In Corneille's drama the relations of the individual to society are shown as a successful reciprocity in a secularized world. In Racine, the relation breaks down; the state loses its sacred quality and becomes merely a worldly power. Moreover, it is often an obstacle to the self-realization of the individual who no longer accepts the state's hierarchy of values, and who can no longer reconcile his personal aspirations with those of the preordained system.

Both Corneille and Racine show us persons who rise in stature as a result of heightened self-awareness. In Corneille, however, the criterion for this awareness consists of deeds in the service of the state; his heroes become administrators or military leaders. In Racine, the touchstone is language. The heroes and heroines are encouraged by their tutors to speak out, to say what they feel. The tutors are spokesmen for freedom of expression. Social implications become apparent once the individual realizes that such free self-expression runs counter to the demands of the prevailing institutions. Racine's heroes and heroines do not live according to a superimposed morality—personal aspirations are acknowledged, and there is no ready solution to the conflict between individual and society. Phaedra, for example (as Racine himself says in a preface to the play), is neither entirely guilty nor entirely innocent, and individual passion is not *per se* a sin against God or man. In short, Racine's characters appear more sinned against by the social and political order, than sinning.

The Tutor as Intermediary

The role of the tutor serves a specific function in this reemergence of individual claims. Rarely do any of Racine's *dramatis personae* make such long speeches as does Burrus, Nero's tutor, or Theramenes, the tutor of Hippolytus, and what they have to say are not contributions to individual introspection as in the case of Shakespeare's Gonzalo. They are, directly or indirectly, bitter attacks on a social order that permits a ruler to destroy personal happiness.

Although political stratification at Racine's time closely resembles that at the time of Corneille, the moral perspective has shifted radically. This shift has the effect of revealing the instability of the social pyramid: the tutors (to whom we may add Phaedra's nurse, Oenone) help their wards to become aware of the moral inadequacy of the state and teach them to look to themselves for their true fulfillment.

The function of the tutors is not to try to impose their own values and motives upon those they advise, but to help them break their inner silence and put their wishes into words. (Leo Spitzer has aptly characterized them as "humanistic historiographers."[11]) When Phaedra tries to hide from herself her infatuation for Hippolytus, her nurse, Oenone, warns her:

> If you must blush,
> Blush at the silence that inflames your grief.[12]

Similarly, when Hippolytus tries to ignore his deep affection for Aricia, the royal prisoner of his father, his tutor Theramenes encourages him to speak his real feelings:

> What good to act a pride you do not feel?
> If you are changed, confess it![13]

The numerous confessions that appear in Racine's plays reveal an important change in the image of the self from the images in Cervantes and Shakespeare. Racine's people find out for themselves that they are tremendously complicated and that a person cannot be adequately described merely in terms of reason or the lack of it. If the Renaissance (to use Jacob Burckhardt's formulation) is the age of discovery of the individual, the seventeenth century in France witnessed the birth of his psychology. Racine's people begin to learn that the individual's encounters with his environment may activate the development of terrifying inner conflicts, but that the outer world will not in turn offer any solution for such tensions. The serene value system that posits a rational individual, whether he is autonomous as in Shakespeare or an obedient citizen as in Corneille, is now breaking down under the impact of heightened social pressures. This process leads to a great increase in knowledge of the self. The noblest of all men in Racine's dramas, the guiltless and loyal Hippolytus, pronounces the breakdown of an optimistic image of the rational individual when he confesses his love to Aricia. He tries to "find himself," as Shakespeare would have said, by introspection into his own nature, but the result is a negative one:

> The fruit
> Of all my sighs is only that I cannot
> Find my own self again.[14]

He can no longer find the naive calmness on which he relied before Theramnenes helped him to be true to himself, and he rejects his once optimistic belief that

> Reason did approve
> What Nature planted in me.[15]

Secularization and Love

Many writers have already dealt with the influence of Jansenism and Calvinism on Racine. They have pointed out that his people are, ultimately, helpless; the heroes and heroines are exposed to sinful passions and, presumably, dependent on divine grace. These critics may be correct in their estimate of the religious undercurrents in Racine's work, although it remains open to what extent his late biblical dramas were an intentional concession to the hostility of the clergy. Our interest here, however, lies in the extent to which the roots of Racine's drama emerge from the subsoil of the society of his time. From this standpoint, his characters are truly individuals who are unable or unwilling to control their passions through reason, but who nevertheless are precise observers of their inner states. Whatever the validity of religious interpretations of Racine's work, it remains possible to examine these self-observations against the social background in which they take place. The process of self-articulation becomes the basic content of the drama. The characters look in vain for a way of life that would free them from their misery, and during the genesis and the interplay of the symptoms of their condition they become increasingly aware of their inner conflicts.

Love is the most important theme in Racine's drama. It appears as the great libidinal motor force of the human being, and its range extends from mere instinctual infatuation to steadfast dedication beyond death. *Andromache* could almost stand as a textbook on the subject, including the intertwinement of love and hate. Racine uses the Greek legend to display the psychological effects of a series of unrequited loves. Orestes is in love with Hermione, daughter of the beautiful Helen of Troy. Hermione, however, is engaged to and in love with Pyrrhus, the king of Epirus, who is in love with Andromache, a prisoner from the late Trojan war and the widow of Hector. Orestes is being sent by the Greek states to Pyrrhus to ask for Andromache and her young son, who are the prisoners of Pyrrhus, in order to make sure that the survivors of the Trojan royal house will not become the core of a new Troy and therefore a danger to Greece. Before the journey, Orestes thought that his "passion had been turned to hatred"[16] but discovers when he sees Hermione that he had "never ceased to love her."[17] Pyrrhus, who loves Andromache but is spurned by her, says of his condition:

> I tell you that the heart that can no longer
> Love passionately, must with fury hate.[18]

Hermione, in her love for Pyrrhus, goes through a similar experience. When the nurse Cleone asks her:

> Have you not told me that you hated him?

Hermione answers:

> Hate him, Cleone? Could my pride do less,
> When he neglects my favor, given freely?
> The heart I learned to love was treacherous.
> He was too dear not to be hated now.[19]

Orestes, bent on winning Hermione, is even willing to accept hate as a messenger of love. When he berates Hermione for wasting her affection on Pyrrhus, she answers that there is no "need" to "envy him," "unless you crave that I should hate you." But Orestes replies:

> Yes,—
> For love might spring from such a strange beginning.
> I whom you wish to love,—I cannot please you,
> But if you wished to hate me, only love
> Would be obeyed, and I should have your heart.[20]

Hermiome interprets him, correctly, as meaning that her hate for Pyrrhus is prompted by her love. Her concentration on this theme through five acts of the play finally brings her to the psychological state of the *crime passionel* that culminates in the words:

> I will find
> Some way to bring me close beside my foe,
> To stab the heart I could not reach with love.[21]

The sentiment is remarkably similar to that of Phaedra when she is thrwarted in her passion for Hippolytus:

> My hands are ripe for murder,
> To spill the guiltless blood of innocence.[22]

Pyrrhus, Orestes, Hermione (and Phaedra) are all in love with those who do not love them and experience the counterforce of hate which the situation awakens in them. The only unambivalent lover is Andromache who is lost in the memory of Hector, a dead man.

Racine's people are aware of the relaxing of rational control that passion brings about. The tutor of Britannicus comments: "Love never waits for reason";[23] Orestes says at one point: "The voice of reason only wearies me";[24] and Phaedra declares: "Now you must serve my madness, not my reason." [25] Such examples—and they could be multiplied—do not represent a revival of the old Stoic view of the opposition of reason and passion; these qualities, rather than adding up to a formula, give rise to personal insight: psychic conflicts are raised to the level of awareness. Racine's people are shown making the kinds of discoveries about themselves which become increasingly typical in middle-class literature. When Phaedra is reminded by Hippolytus, who has spurned her love for him,

> That Theseus is my father and your husband, . . .

she answers:

> Why should you fancy I have lost remembrance
> And that I am regardless of my honor?

then adds almost immediately:

> I am not half so hateful to your sight
> As to myself.

The same self-awareness is as true for guilt as for love. Phaedra tells Hippolytus that he should not think:

> That in those moments when I love you most
> I do not feel my guilt.[26]

Later she reasserts, "I know my madness well,"[27] in much the same way as Aricia experiences her affection for Hippolytus, her political enemy, as "the maddening draught of love."[28] The very fact that madness and guilt become almost synonymous signifies the ascension of personal insight over a schematized system of absolute values. (Corneille would have had a neat solution to the love of Hippolytus for Aricia.) Theramenes, Hippolytus' tutor, asks him "Why should you fear a guiltless passion?"[29] and Hippolytus himself reflects that "surely innocence need never fear,"[30] and that "the gods are just."[31] But, in the end, his mental turmoil gives the lie to these comforting and reasonable words.

In his character portrayals Racine emerges as a depth psychologist. Besides the hate-love involvement, he shows us a number of more subtle effects which sadism and cruelty may have on love relationships. Nero, who is in love with Junia, the bride of his enemy Britannicus, makes her a prisoner in order to separate her from her lover and be close to her himself. He finds he loves

> The very tears that I had caused to flow.
> And sometimes, yet too late, I asked forgiveness,
> And often found my sighs would end in threats.
> And thus I have been nursing this new passion.[32]

Nero takes pleasure in observing the suffering Britannicus and tells his old tutor:

> I know quite well my rival has her heart.
> I'll have my joy in making him despair!
> How pleasant is his anguish to my fancy,—
> And I have seen him doubting if she loves him!

I'll follow her. My rival waits for you,
And he will vent his fury. Go, torment him
With new suspicions. Make him pay most dearly
For boons that he despises. I will witness
The tears she sheds for him![33]

Theramenes helps Hippolytus to understand that his love for Aricia is prodded by the very fact of his father's hate for the young princess. The tutor says to his master:

His hatred kindles you to burn, rebellious,
And only lends his enemy new charms.[34]

In *Britannicus* again, Racine, in another surprisingly modern touch, notes the extremes of ambivalence in the mother-son relationship when Nero's mother anticipates his latent murderous intent:

Deep in our secret heart I know you hate me.
You would be free from gratitude's hard yoke.[35]

Poet of Personal Rebellion

Racine is the poet of personal rebellion. His people begin to question the relationship between the *raison d'état* and their own legitimate concerns. The mood of their resistance to their social world is not such a far cry from the revolutionary temper of the eighteenth century as might at first appear. Even the theology, of the secular plays at least, is mainly negative. In passage after passage the gods are cursed; without them and their human counterparts in the state apparatus the individual might, we are made to feel, have a chance. While seventeenth-century man is of course not yet aware of a potential revolutionary situation, Racine's people herald this awareness in their efforts to arrive at a new understanding of themselves.

Public affairs mean little to Racine's characters. Pyrrhus is primarily interested in his own passion; his responsibility for the security of the state or toward his allies in Greece is comparatively irrelevant. He threatens to kill Andromache's son unless she reciprocates his love; if she yields, he will allow the boy, who is also the son of the old arch-enemy Hector, to live. Similarly, when Phaedra is made to believe that her husband has died and that the Athenians want her to reign in the name of her infant son, she uses this political event for personal ends, as a lure to win the love of Hippolytus (who had also been a candidate for the succession). She instructs Oenone:

> Go, and on my behalf, touch his ambition,—
> Dazzle his eyes with prospects of the crown. . . .
> He shall control both son and mother,—try him,—
> Try every means to move him, for your words
> Should meet more favor than my own could find.
> Urge him with groans and tears,—say Phaedra's dying,
> Nor blush to speak in pleading terms with him.
> My last hope is in you,—do what you will,
> I'll sanction it,—the issue is my fate![36]

All psychological tactics and all political means are permissible to reach a goal dictated by personal passion. Pyrrhus and Phaedra are extreme examples, but it seems equally clear that the goal for Britannicus is not Rome but Junia, for Hippolytus not Athens but Aricia, and for Orestes it is not the peace of Greek citizens but Hermione. Orestes, when he tries to forget his love for Hermione by taking on political missions, tells his friend Pylades:

> I hoped to find
> Freedom from other cares, in this new work,
> I hoped that, if my strength came back to me
> My heart would lose remembrance of its love.

But this act of submission to the state does no good, and he adds:

> But soon enough
> I found my lovely persecutor taking
> Her old place in my heart.[37]

In Corneille's dramas, when political responsibility falls on the shoulders of one of the heroes he rises to the occasion and eventually frees himself from his individual desires. But in Racine the morality of the state has ceased to be internalized. Phaedra says:

> I reign?—And shall I hold the rod of empire,
> When reason can no longer reign in me?
> When I have lost control of mine own senses?[38]

Another woman, Junia, in *Britannicus,* pronounces the estrangement of the state from genuine human morality in these words:

> Perhaps my frankness may not be discreet,
> But never have my lips belied my heart.
> Since I was not at courts, I had not thought
> That I had need to learn dissimulation![39]

Speaking to Britannicus she proclaims the need for finding a human home—a home for lovers outside organized society as it exists:

> Judge not his heart by yours, for you and he
> Pursue two different courses. I have known
> Nero and his court but one short day,
> Yet I have learned, if I dare speak of it,
> How different are their words from what they think;
> How little mouth and heart agree in them;
> How lightly they betray their promises.
> How strange a dwelling, this, for me and you.[40]

The Concept of Fate and the Indictment of the Gods

In the beginning of *Andromache,* Orestes, coming unexpectedly upon his friend Pylades, thanks his "fortune" for this good turn; but, soon after, he asks himself, "Who knows what fate is guiding me?"[41] Later he says, "I can never now what fate has ordered."[42] And, again, when giving a report of his adventures since he returned from Troy, he speaks of his "persecuting fates."[43] When Pyrrhus confesses his love to Andromache, he says of her and Hermione: "Fate brought you both alike into Epirus."[44] This idea of fate is quite different from that in Shakespeare, where fate dissolves into the actions of people and becomes human history. For Shakespeare the world is man's home, sometimes his hell, but "fate" is always a consequence of individual actions, moral or immoral, rational or irrational.

Racine's introduction of the idea of fate is not just a relapse into mythology, but reflects a comparatively open society in which people meet by chance and are brought into unpredictable situations by political, social, and economic mobility. Usually, fate appears in a context of governmental affairs; state business is full of traps that can spring on the individual; even the leaders sometimes become victims of these traps or at least react ambivalently to a social order that appears to impose insensible restraints. The person can only see himself as a victim of the blind chances of a system he did not create. When Pyrrhus, a ruling king, explains to Hermione his love for Andromache, he, paradoxically, becomes the spokesman for the individual caught between his own needs and the demands of the state:

> My heart accuses me. Its voice is strong.
> I cannot make a plea I know is false.
> I wed a Trojan woman. Yes, I own
> The faith I promise her was given you.
> I could remind you that our father made
> These ties at Troy; that we were never asked,
> Nor were we ever bound by any choice
> Or love, that was our own. But I submitted.
> It is enough for me.
>
> Until this day
> I thought my oath would hold in place of love.
> Yet love has won, and by a fatal turn,
> Andromache has gained a heart she hates.[45]

The gods as well as the exigencies of the state are blamed for such conflicts. When Phaedra reveals her love to Hippolytus she says:

> The gods will bear me witness,—
> They who have lit this fire within my veins,—
> The gods who take their barbarous delight
> In leading some poor mortal heart astray![46]

When Theseus finds that both his wife and son have killed themselves, he cries out:

> The gods are ruthless. They have served me well,
> And I am left to live a life of anguish
> And of great remorse.[47]

The dying words of Hippolytus to his tutor are: "The gods have robbed me of a guiltless life."[48] Similarly, Phaedra tells her husband with her last breath:

> The gods had lit a baleful fire in me,
> And vile Oenone's cunning did the rest.[49]

These unhappy people, having lived all their lives within what seemed to be a well-ordered external and spiritual world, are finally driven to realize that this world and its deities are not reliable. The cursing of the gods is, to be sure, ambiguous and does not differentiate between a rejection of social forces and the incapacity to solve one's own internal difficulties. This ambiguity suggests the intimate struggles of Racine and other intellectuals of his time, beset as they were by doubts about the stability of both their inner and outer worlds. This doubt is patently present when the gods are blamed for one's own passions, and it emerges unequivocally when they are held accountable not only for personal tragedy but for a bad state of society as such. In a most telling passage, Orestes sums up the state of the world in these words:

> When have the gods been so perverse before,
> Hunting the guiltless down, with crime unpunished?
> I turn my eyes, and everywhere I see
> Troubles and sorrows that condemn their justice.[50]

Corneille's positive theology of the state has given way to Racine's negation of theology by the individual. In the future man must look for other and newer forms of society. If the struggle of Racine's protagonists against power lacks the rationale of a planned campaign, it is nonetheless a declaration of war. Who remains alive when the drama comes to an end? Lonely kings whose wives, fiancées and children have died, and lonely innocent youths near insanity; on the one hand, the brutal Nero, the duped Theseus, the frustrated Pyrrhus—on the other, the heartbroken Aricia and Orestes. The glory of Corneille's empire does not find continuation in Racine, and only broken idols remain to take its place. The sadness of this dramatic configuration is the sadness of separation; historically it sets the tone of the prologue to the drama of emotional emancipation from an aging political structure. Racine gives us our first insight into the dynamics of the men who are about to write those enlightened treatises of the eighteenth century which will denounce the value system of the absolutistic monarchy.

Molière, 1622–1673

Dominant Motifs and Philosophical Assumptions

"Experience teaches me," Molière has one of his protagonists say with pride in *L'Avare*,[51] and we soon discover that the familiar adage has a very precise meaning. It is the advice often given to the young man to learn to adapt to the world for his own good; it is as well the motto of the tradesman learning how to get along with his customers. "Experience," we find, definitely means the outside world and particularly the social world; we are taught only by closely observing it, by keeping a watchful eye on its mores and demands. Inner experience appears to be excluded. In fact, Molière intends this exclusion; one who listens too well to his own reason or his own passion is precisely one who does not learn from "experience." The statement also implies a special definition of the world itself. The world one learns about from experience is an evolving structure; it is no longer a ready-made idea as in Corneille, and we can find out about it only by attending to its changing qualities. The expression, we begin to see, sums up an entire morality and way of life: in three words it gives us the rationale of conformism.

Earlier we related Corneille's moral beliefs to the rationalism of Descartes by equating the state with the Caresian ego. According to Corneille, the individual proceeds step by step to a position of secure knowledge by overcoming any uncertainties he may harbor about the rational essence of an absolutist society; the self-evidence of the rationality of the state is in effect a social extension of the self-evident rationality of Descartes' individual. For the philosophical counterpart of Molière we should have to look to empiricism, to a philosophy that found its ultimate certainty, not in innate ideas, but in sensation or the perception of discrete qualities, which have no guaranteed organization. The progress from Corneille to Molière indeed parallels closely the progress from rationalist metaphysics to empiricism then taking place. Corneille's protagonists take the state and the traditions of absolute monarchy for granted; a society thus grounded assumes an *a priori* and secure rationality. Molière's people, on the other hand, take nothing for granted but what they can observe and test. Experience is the teacher.

Molière for a time was a student of the philosopher Gassendi, an early forerunner of empiricism. In a famous philosophic exchange, Descartes sent to Gassendi, among others, his *Meditations* with a request for critical comments. Gassendi replied in a long letter that concludes with the following remarks:

> These, my good Sir, are the observations that occurred to me in connection with your *Meditations.* I repeat that you ought not to give yourself any thought about them, since my judgment is not of such moment as to deserve to have any weight with you. For as, when some food is pleasant to my palate, I do not defend my taste, which I see is offensive to others, as being more perfect than anyone else's; so, when my mind welcomes an opinion which does not please others, I am far from holding that I have hit upon the truer theory. I think

that the truth is rather this—that each enjoys his own opinion; and I hold that it is almost as unjust to wish everyone to have the same belief, as to want all people to be alike in the sense of taste; I say so, in order that you may hold yourself free to dismiss everything that I have said as not worth a straw, and to omit it altogether. It will be enough if you acknowledge my strong affection for you, and do not esteem as nought my admiration for your personal worth. Perhaps some matter has been advanced somewhat inconsiderately, as is only too likely to happen when one is expressing dissent. Any such passage which may occur, I wholly disavow and sacrifice; pray blot it out, and be assured, that I have desired nothing more than to deserve well of you and to keep my friendship with you quite intact.[52]

The passage is quoted at length because it is in many ways a very remarkable document. The philosophic exchanges of the time tended toward extraordinary bitterness; among them this letter is an astounding and exceptional example of tolerance. No adherent of Descartes, Spinoza, or Leibnitz could have written it. The remarks anticipate the concepts of common sense and of compromise in the era of liberalism, and they highlight an attitude that Molière was to take up and develop in his plays.

In his ethics, Gassendi considered the end of human existence to be a state of beatitude that results from a maximum of pleasure and a minimum of misery. Virtue consists of moderation, the absence of extremes, and is fostered by prudence, temperance, fortitude, and justice. Anyone familiar with Molière's plays will feel that these doctrines sound like abstracts of his work. The plays announce no absolute truth. Except for the Misanthrope, no one fights to the bitter end for principles. The dynamics consist of efforts to arrive at an equilibrium in human affairs. The pervading atmosphere is one of optimism and the equilibrium is usually achieved; some people get what they want most, and those who do not (omitting outright scoundrels and the Misanthrope) still are not left in misery at the end of the fifth act.

The analysis of Molière meets with a peculiar difficulty. In the works previously analyzed, it was relatively simple to categorize the value systems of the persons portrayed. But rigid yardsticks are lacking in Molière's people, who are remarkably mundane and who regulate their lives in an experimental, almost pragmatic way. Their orientation shifts as the situation demands it, and they have a multiplicity of motives generic to a pluralist society. What we see is a small aspect of individual behavior—a glimpse of the reality of a highly mobile society —observed through the artist's eyes for the one or two hours the action of the play requires.

The Comedy of Social Tensions

With the exception of the Misanthrope, there is not a single person in Molière's plays who claims the right and the responsibility to create the world in the image of his reason as did the figures of Shakespeare and Cervantes. A completely new tone is evident. Except for a light touch of ritualized deference, no major figure in Molière feels in any way motivated by affairs and ideologies of the state, and except for the Misanthrope no person goes into mourning and despair as a result of alienation from the established mores of society. The characters refer to their concrete experience with the world as a justification for their actions; they even play games that create a laboratory for empirical observation for those who need it, There are no longer such coercive or violent forces as in the literature we have previously discussed. Middle-class society is entering a period of common sense and adjustment.

But the adjustment is not easy. The middle-class individual learns his lessons painfully. Molière's protagonists find themselves in far more difficult social situations than do the heroes and heroines of Shakespeare, Corneille, and Racine. Since they lack any final principle of justification in themselves, they must learn the lessons their society has to offer and for which they have little prior guidance. Tragedy, we begin to see, is only possible if there is at least a potential choice between the ways of the world and the self. If adaptation is shown as difficult but necessary—its manner of achievement perhaps unknown but at the same time the only possible solution—we are in the realm of comedy. We are also in the realm of anxiety, wherein even suicide, as in Racine's *Phaedra,* would be no resolvement and would most often be merely ridiculous. For Molière's people even a noble defeat is out of the question.

The Intermediaries

The tutors and other intermediary persons in Molière's plays differ radically from their counterparts in Racine. In the latter, they serve as spokesmen who mediate between the protagonists and their own inner natures; they have no importance in their own right. In Molière's plays, the intermediaries are themselves protagonists and are the friends or close relatives of the persons they advise. Chrysalde is the friend of Arnolphe;[53] Cléante is the brother-in-law and adviser of Orgon;[54] Philinte is the friend of Alceste.[55] The advisers are never simply catalysts as in Racine; they give outright information and even interfere by direct action where they believe it is needed.

The intermediaries all talk like disciples of Gassendi. They preach moderation and a measured degree of hedonism; they are spokesmen of a reasonably regulated middle-class life, giving duty and pleasure each its due. These advisers are on good terms both with social reality and with the individuals to whom they are close, and by their good offices they bring their friends to similarly good terms. If they reject absolutes of virtue or vice, it is not because they have anything against these positions per se; they reject them merely as impediments to good-natured understanding and to the harmonious conformity of the social group. The intermediary figures might well be looked on as model personalities for Molière's time and as prototypes of the era he anticipates. They symbolize the Middle Way, mediation, and compromise, and they pronounce and practice social adaptation and adjustment as the highest virtues.

These mediating figures are central to Molière's work, and the manner in which they are portrayed is of considerable importance. They are never mere colorless bystanders and their behavior is never immoral. Their key motif is the avoidance of any extreme action. They are, in short, *bourgeois* in more than one sense of the word. Cléante warns Orgon, who is victimized by Tartuffe almost to the point of complete ruin:

> You exaggerate again! You never preserve moderation in anything. You never keep within reason's bounds; and always rush from one extreme to another![56]

Chrysalde warns the aging Arnolphe, who is making a fool of himself by trying to wed a young girl:

> To behave well under these difficulties, as in all else, a man must shun extremes.[57]

Philinte, the friend of the Misanthrope, tries to impress upon him that:

> Good sense avoids all extremes, and requires us to be soberly rational.[58]

These interventions sound, of course, like philistine righteousness, but to interpret their function as humourous would be to misconstrue the dramatic intent; it is not the interveners but the people they are trying to help who become objects of ridicule.

Individual Possibilities and Social Limitations

Molière's protagonists illustrate very specifically the social change that has taken place—the transition from a tradition-bound to an open society which does not prevent its members from engaging in the relatively free development of their idiosyncrasies. True, Molière's highly eccentric types emerge as caricatures and are ridiculed; nevertheless, these extreme cases of behavior are not suppressed by an absolute and universally accepted moral code. If he wants to make an interest in his own health the center of his life, no social agency prevents the Malade Imaginaire from doing so. The Miser can if he wishes focus his whole life on the accumulation of money. The Bourgeois Gentilhomme can spend his money aping the aristocratic style of life without interference from any authority. Finally, Tartuffe, the materialist hypocrite who cloaks his appetites with ascetic virtue, and Alceste, the obsessional moralist who tries to force his precepts on everyone in his environment, are headed for opposite poles of the individualist franchise.

But such apparent liberty is deceptive: if there is less institutionalized coercion, there is certainly no less social pressure. If these people are odd, it is because society sees them as odd or because they fail to understand social reality, and not because there is any individual principle that may be worthy or entirely natural in its own right. Alceste is a Don Quixote who tends to become ridiculous. Man is no longer alone; at the very moment he challenges the reality and reasonableness of the world around him, he condemns himself to passivity, to comic ineffectuality. The more the protagonists maximize their individuality and the farther they remove themselves from the common sense represented by the intermediaries, the farther removed they find themselves from the productive center of human affairs. The intermediaries, on the other hand, accept the normal vicissitudes of social life as the boundaries of a space within which they can develop themselves and fulfill their desires. The pseudoindividualists (since they are caricatures, it is hard to think of them as true individuals) do not meet with heroic failure, which was the fate of Don Quixote and which almost befell Prospero; they are not destroyed but are ignominiously cast aside, left to their own absurdities. Molière's "radicals" are not tragic heroes whose memory is kept alive as a symbol of an ideal or a, never-ending task; they are simply consigned to oblivion while the main stream of society goes on about its business. (The Misanthrope remains the special case.)

Moral Experimentalism

Certain basic trends in the relations of the individual to society remain constant: the world is not something given as in the Middle Ages but requires from man an act of continual production; the way in which man should behave is not prescribed by a set of inherited traditions but must be tried out by men themselves. However, these acts of creation and experiment are no longer conceived as the prerogative and responsibility of an unique individual, but as the efforts of socialized persons who act within a framework of consensus and whose behavior is intimately geared to the mechanism of social approval or disapproval.

When Molière uses the word *decorous* he is not referring simply to politeness and good manners; what he has in mind is, broadly, the individual's capacity for right conduct within the sphere of collective conduct. The decorous individual conforms sympathetically and successfully within the social pattern. This is not to say that the display of good form is not in itself of importance as the outward flourish of culture and breeding; but, more essentially, *décor* may be interpreted as the symptom and symbol for a new order in human affairs conceived of as the result of continuous consensus in behavior.

The world has become social practice. Orgon, the victim of Tartuffe, stops being his victim once he has decided to "judge by appearances."[59] True, as he speaks these words he is mistaken, since he believes his son and not Tartuffe to be the real villain; but, when his family helps him to witness a considerably larger piece of reality in observing his own wife's attempted seduction by Tartuffe, he is cured. We see the would- be gentleman of *Le Bourgeois Gentilhomme* being cheated by the worthless nobleman; if he were in the position of the audience to see it (or could be made to), he would be cured of his folly. There are no inner turmoils; everything is clear as day. We the audience have the answers the people on the stage would have if they knew as much as we, or if they looked at what was happening as realistically as we do. Molière gives *us* the reality, and whenever the protagonists appear ridiculous it is because they do not or cannot see it.

If they cannot see it for themselves, they are often made to see it in experimental situations. There is a considerable difference between the experiments of Shakespeare and Molière. In Shakespeare they are an arrangement for proving the individual and his responsibility to himself; interaction with others does not deny or weaken this autonomy. The truly important phenomena reside in the inner life, and outer events serve only to confirm them.

In Molière, experiment has a radically different connotation. As the reality of middle-class society is acted out in his plays, the experiments force this reality to the attention of his deluded protagonists. The world is seen as consisting of a rapid series of happenings that are as empirical as the middle-class world is in its daily practice, and the quick give-and-take of his people have made his comedies a pleasure for three hundred years. The extremist protagonists obtrude themselves from this background by their lack of ambience, and the experiments serve to show them their place. Perhaps rather than "experiments" one should say "tricks," since they are in the nature of jokes with, however, the serious purpose of helping the extremists to gain insight into the median reality of things. (The tricks are, in fact, often arranged by the intermediaries, who see more of the real from their central vantage point than the off-center, half-blinded protagonist can.) In every case, the trick tells us that if there is no absolute truth, there is always some pragmatic truth that can be found out empirically.

In *The High Brow Ladies* socially ambitious girls swoon at lackeys when the latter are dressed as aristocrats. Orgon is made to hide under the table and watch the scoundrel Tartuffe flirt with his wife. The faked theft of the Miser's cashbox proves that Harpagon is only too glad to trade the pleasures of love for the rewards of monetary possessions. All the tricks demonstrate that moral reality is pragmatic and observable and that the values of men are realized truly and exclusively by their actions. At the same time, the tricks have a very specific societal connotation: they are the result of joint decisions. In none of them do we find a Prospero or a Don Quixote who keep to themselves or find in themselves the reasons for their experimentation. In *The Miser* it is a plot of the children-in-law and their lovers; in *Tartuffe* the trick is the combined effort of Orgon's brother-in-law, the children, the wife, and the maid; in *The High-Brow Ladies* there is an agreement between the two lovers, with La Grange expressing the moral thus:

> We will play them such a trick as shall show them their folly and teach them to distinguish a little better the people they have to deal with.[60]

While the individual seems now to have a multitude of possible ways of behaving, society restrains and limits these possibilities. Molière's plays define these limits by asserting the virtues of discrimination, self- restraint, moderation, and common sense within a social structure that does not impose, so to speak, built-in limitations of its own. In marriage, for example, all combinations of persons seem to be possible. In *The Miser*, Harpagon, the tightwad, wants to marry Mariane who is in love with Cléante. Harpagon's son; Valère's father Anselme wants to marry Elise, the daughter of Harpagon, who is in love with Valère. Similar combinations occur in *Tartuffe* and to an almost absurd degree in *The Misanthrope*. But the resolution always sharply delimits these ambitions and is never absurd. The extremists are shown up as unrealists, the young people are united, and the intermediaries emerge as the true heroes who sometimes, as in *The Misanthrope*, gain personal advantage from their common sense.

The ability to adopt different social roles is also shown to be considerable; the people are able to change roles with astounding ease. The scoundrel Tartuffe appears as a preaching moralist; the upper-class Valère poses as a steward; the woodcutter Sganarelle in *The Physician in Spite of Himself* (*Le Médecin Malgré Lui*) pretends to be a physician; the bourgeois merchant Jourdan trains to become a gentleman of parts. Yet in the end everyone finds himself limited to the role which is appropriate for him in the context of social reality.

The King and the Bourgeois at Home

The comedies obviously presuppose an urban society. Role-playing, trick-playing, a diversity of social contacts, the interplay of the various strata of society—all these characteristics are possible only in cities. The miser, the hypochondriac, the hypocrite would have no field of action if it were not for the wide possibility of anonymous contacts. Scapin, in *Less Fourheries de Scapin*, can only hope to escape from the consequences of his frauds by fleeing to an anonymous crowd. The very possibility of translating the Misanthrope's moral programs into social action ends at the moment Alceste turns his back on the city and retires to the country.

The comedies show very specifically the exigencies of life in an open and mobile society. The aristocrats who come on the scene are shown in a realistic setting, and have hardly any social intercourse with the middle classes. The middle classes furnish the bulk of the protagonists and it is always their ethos that is by far the most influential. The servants, who are accepted partners in the tricks and games, display an astounding amount of middle-class knowledge. While the servants have no real life of their own, they bolster up the atmosphere of the plays and form part of the urban collectivity.

In none of the comedies does the monarch enter the scene. By and large, the people are left to their own affairs. Only when some business seems to get completely out of hand, as in *Tartuffe,* does a representative of high authority appear, but his intervention has no political meaning: Tartuffe turns out to be a criminal and it can be assumed that any high tribunal in France would have prevented his actually carrying out his fraud—while an executive act solves the dilemma of the play, still the king himself remains invisible. The absolute power of the state is no longer the dispenser of moral values as in Corneille, nor the stumbling block to individual development as in Racine. In Molière the image of the state is reduced to a mere means of keeping the affairs of men in manageable shape. In his comedies the bourgeois individual lives, emotionally if not institutionally, under a political order whose prime articles are the virtues of human interaction and the necessity of a middle course. The greatest praise the King's officer can bestow on the monarch is to endow him with middle-class qualities:

> Blessed with great discernment, his lofty soul looks clearly at things; it is never betrayed by exaggeration, and his sound reason falls into no excess.[61]

Molière's plays do not exalt the virtues of family life as the sermonizing novels of eighteenth-century England will in a succeeding generation, but they nonetheless contain the family morality in essence. There are many instances of marital upsets in the plays: Elmire has trouble with Orgon when he seems to be forsaking his family for Tartuffe; the wife of the would-be gentleman who is eager to acquire a titled mistress does not have an easy time of it; and, on a lower level, Sganarelle, the woodcutter, has spats with his wife Martine, and Jacqueline, the nurse, has trouble with her husband Lucas, the servant. But husband and wife are never locked in a tragic struggle, and the defects that do arise in marriages are remedied before the plays end. In fact, the last act usually brings the young couples together as the final happy solution to the troubles that have been depicted—in short, the happy ending, modern middle-class style, according to which the consummation of marriage leads to unqualified bliss.

Middle-Class Optimism

In the framework of Molière's comedies, death has no place. Such a solution, when it is ventured at all, becomes material only for a joke. As Mariane threatens suicide after her father announces his intention to force her into marriage with Tartuffe, her maid Dorine answers ironically:

> Very well. That is a resource I did not think of; you have only to die to get out of trouble. The remedy is doubtless admirable. It drives me mad to hear this sort of talk.[62]

The fool Orgon, in his devotion to Tartuffe, engages in such absurdities as saying to his brother-in-law:

> I could see brother, children, mother, and wife die, without troubling myself in the least about it.[63]

Not even the Misanthrope seriously considers suicide even though he is the only figure in all the plays who could come to a tragic end without appearing absurd.

We are at the height of middle-class optimism. Two hundred years later, an audience will feel self-conscious at the depiction of the sacrifices an individual must make on the altar of conformity, and will force Ibsen to change the ending of A Doll's House that had Nora close the door on her conformist husband. In the age of Molière, the Misanthrope's friends felt they should go after him and bring him back to his senses, bring him back from his "savage," "philosophical spleen" into the life of "ordinary customs" where we "torment ourselves a little less about the vices of our age" and are "a little more lenient to human nature."[64]

But even this attitude of optimism is not without its implications of difficulty and instability. The values of conformity contain their own limitations and are precariously dependent upon the social climate. Only in The Misanthrope did Molière come close to an explicit rendering of the less optimistic side of the relation of his individuals to the society around them. The issue of Alceste's struggle must have been pitifully ambiguous for Molière. At bottom, Alceste is made to appear quite right in laying bare social hypocrisy; on the other hand, he shows himself as something of a fool for trying so hard. To his creator as well as to the spectator, Alceste is the comic underdog who awakens sympathy. Molière seems to express the concern of the intellectual that as society tends toward the stabilization of its mores and institutions, it becomes increasingly difficult for the creative individual to express himself and defend his individual claims. Molière's problem can easily become, and without much shifting of the terms, one not of adaptation but of alienation.

It may seem odd that Molière should emerge as the poet of middle-class life when, after all, he was part of a flourishing absolutistic state. French monarchy had perhaps never seemed to secure, and European aristocracy still had a long history of political and social privileges ahead of it. Nonetheless the assumption that underlies the plays is the desirability of an integrated society of the middle-class type; more than that, Molière takes for granted that the value system of such a society is already an achieved reality. He takes us beneath the surface facts of political history and shows us the everyday ethos of his time, a reality that is not just an official pronouncement or an extraordinary event. Long before the middle class could think of asking for political power, it had laid a firm hold on the everyday reality of life. It might even be said that this class could more thoroughly go about the business of making everyday reality its own by not worrying about political power. Molière was the reporter of this time of "settling in." He stands at a social cross-road: he sprang from a past of Renaissance individualism; he saw this individualism sharply curtailed in his own time by new social controls; and he sounded a note of prediction for the time when the middle class was to make the world its own on all socially relevant levels.

Notes

1. See Paul Hazard, *The European Mind: The Critical Years* (1680–1715), (Yale: Yale University Press, 1953), p. xv.
2. *Horace*, Act II, Scene 3.
3. Ibid., Act V, Scene 3.
4. *The Cid*, Act V, Scene 7, in *Six Plays* by Corneille and Racine (New York: The Modern Library, 1931), p. 64. All the following quotations from Corneille and Racine are taken from this edition, by permission of Random House, Inc.
5. *Cinna*, Act V, Scene 2, p. 121.
6. *Cinna*, Act V, Scene 1, p. 115.
7. Ibid., Act V, Scene 3, p. 122.
8. *The Cid*, Act III, Scene 5, pp. 38–39.
9. Ibid., p. 39.
10. Ibid., Act V, Scene 7, p. 64.
11. Leo Spitzer, "The Récit de Thermanène," in *Linguistics and Literary History* (Princeton: Princeton University Press, 1948), p. 104.
12. *Phaedra*, Act I, p. 255.
13. Ibid., p. 253.
14. Ibid., Act II, p. 267. Cf. Gonzalo's last words in *The Tempest*, Act V, Scene 1.
15. Ibid., Act I, p. 251.

16. *Andromache*, Act I, p. 128.
17. Ibid., p. 130.
18. Ibid., p. 139.
19. Ibid., Act II, p. 141.
20. Ibid., p. 145.
21. Ibid., Act IV, p. 171.
22. *Phaedra*, Act IV, p. 291.
23. *Britannicus*, Act II, p. 201.
24. *Andromache*, Act III, p. 151.
25. *Phaedra*, Act III, p. 275.
26. Ibid., Act II, p. 271.
27. Ibid., Act III, p. 277.
28. Ibid., Act II, p. 263.
29. Ibid., Act I, p. 252.
30. Ibid., Act III, p. 282.
31. Ibid., Act V, p. 294.
32. *Britannicus*, Act II, p. 200.
33. Ibid., pp. 211–12.
34. *Phaedra*, Act I, p. 252.
35. *Britannicus*, Act V, p. 243.
36. *Phaedra*, Act III, pp. 275–76.
37. *Andromache*, Act I, p. 129.
38. *Phaedra*, Act III, p. 274.
39. *Britannicus*, Act II, p. 208.
40. Ibid., Act V, pp. 237–38.
41. *Andromache*, Act I, p. 127.
42. Ibid., p. 128.
43. Ibid., p. 129.
44. Ibid., p. 138.
45. *Andromache*, Act IV, pp. 172–73.
46. *Phaedra*, Act II, p. 271.
47. Ibid., Act V, p. 301.
48. Ibid.
49. Ibid., p. 303.
50. *Andromache*, Act III, p. 154.
51. *The Miser (L'Avare)*, Act I. Scene 1, *Plays* by Molière (New York: Modern Library), p. 286. All quotations from Molière are taken from this edition, by permission of Random House, Inc.
52. Pierre Gassendi, "Objection V to the Meditations," in: *The Philosophical Works of Descartes*, 2 vols. (New York: Dover, 1955), vol. 2, p. 203. The quotation is reprinted by permission of Dover Publications, Inc.
53. See *The School for Wives (L'École des Femmes)*.
54. See *Tartuffe*.
55. *See The Misanthrope*.
56. *Taruffe*, Act V, Scene 1, p. 161.
57. *The School for Wives*, Act IV, Scene 8, p. 87.
58. *The Misanthrope*, Act I, Scene 1, p. 180.
59. *Tartuffe*, Act IV, Scene 3, p. 151.

60. *The High-Brow Ladies,* Act I, Scene 1, p. 18.
61. *Tartuffe,* Act V, Scene 7, p. 171.
62. Ibid., Act II, Scene 3, p. 128.
63. Ibid., Act I, Scene 6, p. 116.
64. *The Misanthrope,* Act I, Scene 1, pp. 178–80.

5

From *Werther* to *Wilhelm Meister*

With Molière we have reached the threshold of contemporary history: from now on every authentic writer will face the problem of the integration of the individual into society. The keynote of this problem has already been sounded by Alceste; conformity, we see, involves severe limitation. We have come a long way from Cervantes and his Knight, to whom the very notion of conformity was alien as an ideal and as a norm of behavior. Molière's individual operates more or less unwittingly within a middle-class frame of reference and avails himself of middle-class metaphors; in short, what we looked for and found expressed in Molière was the manner in which he manages to codify man's relationship to modern civilization.

Individualism and the Middle Class

Molière to Goethe

Goethe admired Molière extravagantly and consistently. "I have known and loved Molière from my youth and have learned from him during my whole life," he told Eckermann. "I never fail to read some of his plays every year that I may keep up a constant intercourse with what is excellent."[1]

As late as 1828, as he approached his eightieth birthday, he commented once again on *Tartuffe* and *The Misanthrope* (a play which never ceased to astonish him) in two important book reviews.[2] His particular delight as a dramatist was the *Malade Imaginaire*.[3]

Goethe's own answer to the problem of man's socialization was not nearly so uniform as Molière's, if only because his career as a man of letters in a way served as a summation of all the social characteristics and tendencies which had waxed and waned in Europe since the end of the feudal period. Endowed with the urge to see himself as the "representative" of the world about him, he expressed this analogy between his own career and the growth of his country in a striking phrase: "I am glad," he once told his ubiquitous interlocutor, "when I was eighteen, Germany was in its teens also, and something could be done." However he added a sad comment on the increasing social pressures: "But now an incredible deal is demanded, and every avenue is barred."[4]

Goethe's position with respect to the individual's place in the social framework is more optimistic and more pessimistic than Molière's, depending on the stage at which he is writing. If again Molière's attitude is more consistent than Goethe's, it is only because Molière moved in a comparatively more setted society than the constantly changing, eventful social scene in the Germany between 1750 and 1830. Whereas Molière's reactions, for example his ambivalence, remain steady and predictable, Goethe spans the whole gamut of conflict with society.

Goethe agrees with Molière in one fundamental respect; he recognizes the existence of the middle class and its value system as a fait accompli. The nobility which snubs Werther is a nobility in the final stages of decay. For Goethe to have said, "I accept the middle class" would hve been rather like Margaret Fuller's "I accept the universe," to which Carlyle remarked that "she had damn well better." Goethe no more than Molière could ignore the conflicting claims of individual development on the one hand, and collective benefit and decorum, on the other. He inherited Molière's questions: What price individualism? What price conformity?

Goethe as a poet conceived of his artistic creation as "fragments of a great confession"; it was impossible for him to maintain the position of a calm, observant moderator which characterizes most of Molière's plays. In the various stages of his development, Goethe comes up with different solutions to the problem of the individual's relation to society. He tried ultimately to arrive at a synthesis which would take into account the kinds of social cooperation and integration which occupied Molière, while keeping in mind—as Molière did not always do—the claims of the individual. As a result, he not only recapitulates the history of the individual since the Renaissance; he preserves it.

Goethe: The Political Background

Goethe represents the culminating point in the long tradition which Cervantes began. His position in what was both a backward and a rapidly developing nation gave him a superior vantage point from which to view and connect past and present. If we think in terms of social development, the Germany of Goethe's youth antedated Molière's France; but in his eighty-three years he lived to witness a stage of society far more modern than that which Molière could have envisioned. By the time the middle class came to political power in Germany, the price of adaptation by the individual had become very high. To the end of his life. Goethe hoped for a reconciliation of an optimum growth of the individual and the optimum good of society as a whole, but he became increasingly aware of the dangers threatening such a reconciliation—dangers which later would provide the core of Ibsen's social drama.

It was in Goethe's lifetime, and particularly in the sixty-five years of his maturity (1767 to 1832) that German territories became once again—after almost two centuries of internal division and impotence—partners of some consequence in international political affairs. It was during his lifetime, too, that industrialization in Germany developed rapidly. Roughly in mid-century—with Kant, Lessing, Wieland, Klop-stock—German philosophers and writers entered the mainstream of European intellectual activity; only a decade or two later the German theatre became an important force in the national life. As the middle class extended its sway, Goethe witnessed the rise (as well as its tempo-rary fall in the reactionary era of Metternich) of constitutional govern-ment in a number of the petty monarchies. He was cognizant in his work of the several stages of the political development of Germany; at the same time he lived and wrote within a highly sophisticated European civilization. In the end he was able to claim for Germany honorable entrance into "world literature."

Only one significant post-Renaissance development was absent in Goethe's Germany. There is no trace of Corneilleian rationalism and patriotism in Goethe. In France, the national state represented by the Crown had brought a final end to the remnants of feudalism. To the French mind, the monarchy meant unification, peace, and internal progress. To the middle class specifically it meant at least the possibil-ity for expansion, if not for control. The trivial despotism of the many minuscule German states tended, on the contrary, to create an atmo-sphere of continual revolt, resistance, and depression. By the time the nation was finally unified, there was no longer any need for a symbol of centralization to combat a disorganized feudal structure. The middle classes by then already possessed real, if not nominal, power, and the monarch became increasingly an ally of their control.

Goethe belonged to the eighteenth-century German intellectuals who had little use for the kind of political obstructionism which was preva-lent before the middle class gained control. He was no revolutionary on any level; and he certainly was the very opposite of a patriot. But this outspoken lack of national allegiance in him is not really quite all of a piece. When, in *Werther,* he attacks the nominal ruling groups, he is being the young intellectual radical, very intimately in touch with the intellectual currents and sensibilities of his generation. When, in his old age, he grumbles sardonically about "our dear Germans," he is speaking rather more as Nietzsche was to speak fifty years later, from the viewpoint of the good European who is appalled by the perpetual provincialism of what is already a major power-state. The second, far more than the first, is the expression of an artist who feels himself increasingly isolated from the public.

Werther: The Dislocated Individual

The Novels Compared

This chapter is based on a brief examination of *Werther* and both of the *Wilhelm Meister* novels. Goethe's first novel was a product of his early manhood; the second, of his early middle age; the last, of his full artistic ripeness. The novel had by now become the specific art-form of the middle classes; it is no accident that it reached its highest development in the century of the middle class, the nineteenth. As an artistic medium for concerted social thought, the novel will eventually surpass all other genres.

Each of Goethe's novels[5] bears witness to its author's endorsement of the full participation of the individual in society; but the situations by which he enforces this thesis change radically between *Werther* and *Wilhelm Meister.* The first postulates a society which precludes intelligent participation; the second, a society which invites it. In the first, an unenlightened segment compounded of petty despots and antiquated snobs is held up to angry ridicule for its refusal to embrace a sensitive and potentially energetic human being. The tone here is hostile, rebellious, even splenetic; it is very much the work of a young man with an axe to grind. In the second novel, the individual is counselled to give to society the very best his talents have to offer and to abide by its mores.

Significantly, the society Goethe condemns in *Werther* is an outmoded group of small-time aristocrats; the society he celebrates in *Wilhelm Meister's Apprentice Years,* that pedagogic novel par excellence,[6] is the society of an increasingly democratized middle class. Hence it is that young Werther, even at his most passive, is always clearly the hero and sounding board of his tale, while *Wilhelm Meister* very strongly conveys the impression that Wilhelm, even at his most active and outspoken, is really less the novel's moving force than is the society which finally absorbs him. While Werther's personality influences and often actually dictates every incident in which he participates—whereby he becomes a prototype of his generation—Wilhelm Meister serves as a kind of blank sheet upon which the various educative forces to which he is exposed leave their impress. Werther acts as an agent while Wilhelm is reagent. Whereas *Werther* is rather narrowly autobiographical, *Wilhelm Meister* is broadly panoramic, cutting across all stratifications of labor and leisure. The difference between the middle class of *Werther* and the middle class treated in *Wilhelm Meister* is the difference between a class whose thoughts and feelings are accessible to the artist without its yet having attained political status and a class which has gained or is well on the way to gaining practical control of the state.

In *Wilhelm Meister's Travels,* the novel of Goethe's old age, sympathies are no longer with the individual in revolt, but with the society to which he is expected to submit. *Werther* argues the case of the dislocated human being; *The Apprentice Years* preaches individual exertion within the existing framework; the *Travels* counsels the subordination of individual claims, wherever these claims are in conflict with the pretensions of society at large (it will be recalled that the latter bears the subtitle *The Renunciants*).

But *The Renunciants* is not really Goethe's final answer, either; it seems more sensible to recognize it as merely another one of several possible solutions, as transitory an answer, in a way, as the answer given in *Werther.* In the long run, "renunciation" is only a relatively more admissible solution than rebellion. Goethe is reported to have said somewhere that "in the end the only thing that counts is progress," and his constant obsession with evolutionary theories, the continual onward-and-upward endeavors of Faust, and the critico-philosophical concept of "heightening" (*Steigerung*) all tend to reinforce the notion that to look for anything like an absolute answer is, to Goethe's way of thinking, to chase a will-o'-the wisp. It is all very well for the individual to "renounce" for the sake of the common good; but in the meantime society-at-large, the community, goes on making mistakes. The middle classes, once having achieved their triumphs, sit back to enjoy them, smoking their pipes and reading their newspapers, addictions which Goethe thoroughly abhorred. In time, they become complacent and frivolous, willing to accept frivolous entertainment complacently; and such a state of affairs threatens stagnation both to the artist and to his audience. Toward the end of his life, Goethe's utterances more and more come to reflect two (not necessarily incompatible) attitudes toward middle-class conformism: an affirmative and a critical one. The latter will be discussed briefly in a final section of the chapter, which touches upon the conflict between the serious artist and mass entertainment.

Let us look first at Werther.

Death of Werther

The Sorrows[7] *of Young Werther* all but closes with the notation that after the hero's suicide, it was discovered that Lessing's drama *Emilia Galotti* "lay open on his desk."[8] Goethe has frequently been berated for the "psychological" blunder involved in this: no young suicide, runs the argument, is likely to read himself to death with a stern bourgeois tragedy along austere English lines, when there are a thousand sentimental novels to be had for the asking. But Goethe's sociological instinct may have been a good deal sounder than the acumen of his literary interpreters. Werther is engaged in an act of identification: he recognizes in Emilia's catastrophe very much his own situation; both are the victims of an outdated and anachronistic group, the playthings of a decadent despotism. Lessing's play, refining upon his earlier *Miss Sara Sampson* and taking up where Lillo's *London Merchant* left off, provides us with an important clue for an understanding of Werther's motives and responses.

In contrast to the tradition of the French drama, which cloaked contemporary motives in ancient or exotic constumes (Greek in Racine, Roman in Corneille, Oriental in Voltaire), Lessing, in making use of a Roman story, put his characters in modern garb. The fable he adapted was the well-known and often-treated "Virginia" motif, the story of the girl whose father slays her in preference to surrendering her to the dishonorable schemes of a young tyrant. In Lessing's version the petty prince of a petty Italian principality tries to gain the favors of a middle-class patrician's daughter by having her abducted and her fiance murdered. In the end, father and daughter agree that death is her only way out of a life which is shameful and repugnant.

At first sight there seems to be little enough connection between Lessing's play and Goethe's novel. After all, Werther is in love with a decent middle-class girl who, having commitments elsewhere, simply rejects him. There is nothing of seduction or outraged honor here; Werther and Lotte gaze out the window together, watch the raindrops, and sympathetically invoke the name of their favorite poet. The situation is almost the reverse of the situation in *Emilia Galotti*. We have already suggested, in our remarks about Calderon's *Mayor of Zalamea*, that Lessing's theatre audience and readers were aware of the social implications of *Emilia Galotti*; it was the tyrant who by rights should have felt the dagger's thrust, and though Lessing chose the device of translating his setting from Germany to Italy, it was generally understood that he did so on the grounds of personal security (the same grounds which compelled Schiller to remove the scene of the yet more controversial *Robbers* from his native Wuertemberg a few years later). Emilia consents to her death because the arbitrary and cruel actions of the prince have destroyed all chances for personal happiness. Werther, on the other hand, ends his life because his beloved has become the wife of a solid middle-class citizen. Lessing's tragedy seems to be rooted in the violation of the respected social institution of marriage, while the tragedy of Goethe's hero springs from the maintenance of that very institution.

Since a well-read young man such as Werther could have chosen any number of fashionable fictions to epitomize his action, is the selection of Lessing's drama merely an arbitrary gesture on Goethe's part? We think not. In his introductory remarks to the novel, Werther's friend, writing in the *persona* of editor and literary executor, tells the reader:

> And you, good soul, who are laboring under the same distress as he, draw consolation from his sufferings and, if you should be prevented by fate or your own fault from finding one more intimate, let this little book be your friend.[9]

"By fate or your own fault." The words bring back the problem of Racine: the twofold pressures on the individual stemming from situations over which he has no control and from passions which he is unable to master. The individual's reason is overcome by the turmoil of his psychic life, and harsh social conditions offer no means of reconciling the inner combat. Under such circumstances man is prevented from integrating his capacities and putting them to the service of society. Racine's heroes and heroines must waste their richness and imaginativeness in self-destructive and introverted outbursts, because their social world precludes applying these potentialities to useful and personally gratifying tasks. If such antagonism between political absolutism and the individual can be detected in the restrained language of Racine's characters, hidden behind the garments of the myths he chose, how much more apparent is it in Goethe's stormy novel, which underlines the immediacy of the problem. The conflict between private and public concerns are as inextricably interwoven in *Werther* as they were in Racine. Goethe's device of having Werther read *Emilia Galotti* at the final moment of his life may not have been intended to guide the reader to the innermost meaning of the novel; but it serves to make clear that Werther is more than a pathological specimen of the rejected suitor, while it underscores as well certain societal aspects of the novel.

Werther's Sufferings: Dislocation and Rebellion

When Werther discovers his love for Charlotte (he knows already that she is pledged to another man), he quits her neighborhood to take a job in the service of a high-ranking official, an ambassador. But since the position becomes an impossible one, Werther returns to the region where Charlotte has settled with the man who is now her husband. There Werther lapses into the state of depression which ends with his suicide. During the period in which he is absent from his beloved, a good deal has happened to him; in fact, many of the elements which seem to be involved in his depressed state have nothing to do with Charlotte and are introduced while he is separated from her.

To begin with, Werther profoundly resents the boredom of working for the pedant the ambassador turns out to be. Further, he feels himself hopelessly circumscribed by the snobbery of the aristocratic circles in which he is forced to move. The feelings of anger and frustration at the "odious social conditions" which fetter him reach some kind of climax when, at a party given by a count (himself friendly and approachable), he finds himself snubbed, even insulted, by the "aristocratic company of ladies and gentlemen"[10] who join the party after Werther's private dinner with the host. That Werther chose to remain after dinner was a *faux pas* and one which led to his undoing. In the course of the evening he finds himself pleasantly chatting with a young titled lady. This agreeable moment is interrupted by the girl's spinster aunt, about whom Werther remarks that she has "neither a respectable fortune nor qualities of the mind" and who, in short, "has no support in her old age other than her ancestral tree."[11]

It becomes embarrassingly evident as the evening progresses that he is not accepted or wanted here; finally the host, as tactfully as possible under the circumstances, asks him to leave. The incident rankles; the slight assumes increasing intensity the more he broods on it. What especially aggravates the situation is his recognition, the following day, that he has become a target for gossip among the good middle-class people of the town. he writes:

> And now when I am pitied wherever I go, when I hear those who are jealous of me exclaiming triumphantly that one could see what happened to arrogant fellows who boasted of their modicum of intellect and thought it gave them a right to set themselves above all conventions, and that sort of twaddle—it is enough to make a man stick a knife in his heart.[12]

When again, a day later, he has a chance to talk to the young lady with the dessicated aunt, the girl expresses her sympathies with him and expatiates upon the idiotic customs of her class; she also makes the mistake of apprising him of the malicious gossip about him which is making the rounds among the nobility as well. Werther, in despair, writes now to his friend:

> To hear all this from her lips, Wilhelm, in a tone of sincerest sympathy—I was overcome, and am still raging inwardly. I wish someone would dare to cast it in my teeth, that I might thrust his sword through his body! If I were to see blood I should feel much better.
>
> Oh! I have taken up a knife a hundred times to let air into my suffocating heart. It is related of a noble species of horses that, when they are frightfully heated and at their last gasp, they instinctively bite open a vein to help them to breathe. I often feel like that. I would like to open a vein and achieve eternal freedom.[13]

And it is this very same state of mind which the fictitious editor reports near the end of the book:

> He could not forget the rebuff at the embassy. He rarely mentioned it, but one could feel imperceptibly that he considered his honor irretrievably outraged, and that the episode had inspired him with a dislike for a profession or political activity. He therefore resigned himself totally to the odd emotional and mental idiosyncrasies with which we are acquainted from his letters, and to a bottomless passion which was bound to cause the eventual extinction of all his vital energies.[14]

Thus we see that the idea of suicide does not occur to Werther for the first time toward the end of the novel, nor is it inspired exclusively by motives of romantic frustration. On the contrary, his first impulse in that direction is explicitly linked to the rebuff at the embassy. The personal tragedy is rooted in a social tragedy no less than *Emilia Galotti:* the tragedy of a young and spontaneous individual kept from identifying himself productively with those social instincts and social institutions to which he might apply his "stormy spirit."[15] In his frustrations Werther stands as an example of a whole class, the young German intellectuals and professionals who would like to work in the political order, but are prevented from doing so by its obsolete structure. If Werther were really a precursor of the latter-day bohemian (as literary historians and critics have often interpreted him), the chances are that he would never even have got to the point where it becomes possible for him to be inspired "with a dislike for a profession of political activity"; he would never to begin with have considered a profession of political activity in the sense of a broadly useful administrative job.

An interpretation of *Werther* as an early species of *épater le bourgeois* has been favored largely by Goethe's somewhat caustic treatment of Werther's successful rival-in-love. In point of fact, the society which Werther castigates at every turn is not the middle-class society of Charlotte and her fiancé, for which Werther is actually full of sympathy, but rather the one at whose hands he suffers continual humiliation. His venom is expended on the pedantry and uselessness of his official position and on the shameful slights to which he is exposed when in the company of silly dowager-aristocrats. His letters report in detail the means by which the nobility manage to keep his potential social usefulness and social freedom in check. Werther's problem is not one of having been born maladjusted but of having maladjustment thrust upon him. He is forced by his profession into the company of the nobility; he is rejected by them as an undesirable. At the same time, the middle classes sneer at him for being a careerist (and not a successful one at that). He finds no milieu in which he can assert himself productively. In a later period Balzac's Rastignac might have enjoyed such a milieu; but in Werther's time, social action and social decor are still determined by the nobility.

As a consequence of social rejection, Werther is thrown back onto an institution with which he should not have come into conflict, the family. In fact, Werther is profoundly and instinctively drawn to family mores and ideals. Whenever Goethe shows him to us within the tableau of family life, the picture is of the utmost charm (and incidentally, Goethe was an enthusiastic admirer of Goldsmith's *The Vicar of Wakefield*[16]). Any number of passages in the novel attest to Werther's dedication to the family ideal; he is full of admiration for its structure and for the substance which it lends to the lives of both sexes and of various generations. To him the family is the backbone of middle-class life; it supports and provides a refuge for the individual when all else has failed.

If Werther had not been rejected by an antiquated social group filled with clannish prejudices and invoking senseless privileges, and if the state bureaucracy had not made it impossible for him to put his abilities to constructive use, there would have been no tragedy in the first place. Werther's suicide articulates the same protest which the death of Emilia Galotti articulates—in each case a decidedly social one: a protest against the mores and nostrums of a tyrannical, petty, useless, and superseded society.

Wilhelm Meister: The Integrated Individual

Germany's Theatrical Mission

That Goethe's hero in his final moments reads a play (rather than some other literary form) is probably more than accidental. For the drama was the one available public platform for the German middle class in the eighteenth century. Unlike England with her highly developed industrial and commercial economy and her copious literary outlets, and unlike France whose progressive aristocratic and middle-class intellectuals tended to make common cause to their mutual benefit, Germany permitted her middle class virtually no voice in either practical or intellectual matters. The theatre provided the conspicuous exception. One could almost write a social history of the eighteenth-century German middle classes by tracing their various attempts to create permanent theatrical organizations (Lessings' early effort to make the Hamburg theatre a national institution is perhaps the most notable of these efforts).

The theatre provides an excellent medium for the display of interacting social forces. By definition a drama presents a pluralistic world; it is hardly ever limited to a single person and seldom to a single institution, and usually ranges over many individualities and the social meanings of which they are the bearers. Further, the final act with its aura of human continuity lacks the inflexible finality and definition which the ending of an epic poem or a novel tends to convey. The play, by its very nature an imitative representation of life, can more easily be connected with reality itself; there is, in short, more "carry-over." Great dramatists from Corneille and Racine to Lessing and Goethe were well aware of this. They agreed that the moral message of drama may be continued in the life process of the audience, whose catharsis results from the reenactment of conflicts between the individual and society. The dramas of the Storm-and-Stress period—which so often portrayed a character broken but not destroyed, bloody but unbowed, in a hostile political and social climate—were eloquent statements on behalf of the individual's interest; and in reading *Emilia Galotti*, Werther speaks symbolically for a generation of Werthers.

Wilhelm's Apprenticeship: Integration and Assent

The first volume of *Wilhelm Meister,* the novel on which Goethe began work after completing *Werther,* bore in its original version the title *Wilhelm Meister's Theatrical Mission.* The version which found its way into print was published as *Wilhelm Meister's Apprenticeship,* and it is centered in the theatre both as an institution and as a way of life. The book is largely concerned with extensive interpretations of plays, above all those of Shakespeare, especially *Hamlet.* Werther merely reads a play preparatory to dying; Wilhelm is educated in the theatre, helps to produce plays, stage them, act in them, elucidate them. Wilhelm Meister's apprenticeship to the theatre is his apprenticeship to life.

The literary artist deals with the individual's development of his inner capacities. In the Germany of the 1780's, one solution to the problem of self-realization was to act out, in the theatrical meaning of the term, one's personality. In our time, psychologists have often helped disturbed persons by having them act out, mainly in the form of playlets, their anxieties and concerns; the result has frequently been a vast increase in self-awareness, even self-confidence. We might say that the German theatre of 150 years ago was the psychodrama of the healthy middle class, who resorted to this means of awakening to the decay of their political and social environment, which had become as obsolete as the seventeenth-century Spanish monarchy had been in its time. In *Wilhelm Meister's Apprenticeship,* Goethe describes this experience in a variety of ways. Particularly interesting are the double aspects which the experience tends to assume. On the one hand, the individual uses the theatre as refuge from obsolete political and social tyranny; on the other, the theatre portrays a burgeoning civilization that cannot be prevented from coming to full fruition.

At one point in the *Apprenticeship,* Goethe describes the staging of a play in which a peasant and a miner argue the comparative merits of their respective occupations, and the necessity for their productive cooperation is portrayed. After the performance, Wilhelm (himself the son of a well-to-do businessman with widely ramified commercial interests) and his friends (most of them professional actors) discuss the play, and Wilhelm suggests that responsible government officials as well as the population-at-large might well look upon the theatre as an experimental situation of instruction.

Referring to the discussion between the miner and the peasant, Wilhelm asserts:

> In this little dialogue we have a lively proof how useful the theatre might be to all ranks; what advantage even the state might procure from it, if the occupations, trades, and undertakings of men were brought upon the stage, and presented on their praiseworthy side, in that point of view in which the state itself should honor and protect them. As matters stand, we exhibit only the ridiculous side of men: the comic poet is, as it were, but a spiteful tax-gatherer, who keeps a watchful eye over the errors of his fellow-subjects, and seems gratified when he can fix any charge upon them. Might it not be a worthy and pleasing task for a statesman to survey the natural and reciprocal influence of all classes on each other, and to guide some poet, gifted with sufficient humor, in such labors as these? In this way, I am persuaded, many very entertaining, both agreeable and useful, pieces might be executed.[17]

Wilhelm Meister stands on the borderline between conformity and individual protest; it is this medial position which makes the novel a particularly important document for us. Despite the bustle of artistic and theatrical activities, one senses both the urge and the capacity to turn to the serious business of the real world. Goethe is constantly reminding us that the theatre is all very well, very useful, a handy reflector of larger issues, but that the issues themselves lie elsewhere, in the real activities of men, in society itself.

That is one side of the ledger. The other is expressed by Wilhelm himself. His friend Werner has just complimented him by letter on his increasing understanding of how to handle the affairs of the world side by side with his growing acquisition of statistical, technological, and rural knowledge. Wilhelm protests. As a true member of modern society, he recognizes only one goal: the perfection of his individuality. The rest are trappings, embellishment, ways of filling out the "well-rounded personality."

> To speak it in a word, the cultivation of my individual self, here as I am, has from my youth upwards been constantly though dimly my wish and my purpose. The same intention I still cherish, but the means of realizing it are now grown somewhat clearer.[18]

To a degree not hitherto encountered in our studies, the artist-hero self-consciously interprets his dilemma in terms of social conditions. What Werther blurted out in a highly emotional manner is now formulated by Wilhelm as a dignified and discriminating credo:

> Being a simple burgher, I must take a path of my own; and I fear it may be difficult to make thee understand me. I know not how it is in foreign countries, but in Germany, a universal, and, if I may say so, personal, cultivation is beyond the reach of anyone except a nobleman. A burgher may acquire merit; by excessive efforts he may even educate his mind; but his personal qualities (*Persoenlichkeit*) are lost, or worse than lost, let him struggle as he will.[19]

In Molière's plays the development of individuality is discussed solely in terms of the middle class, imitation of the aristocracy being shown as absurd (e.g., *Les Précieuses Ridicules, Le Bourgeois Gentilhomme*) and aristocratic characters tending to become conspicuously vapid; in this respect, Molière appears to represent a rather more advanced stage of society than does Goethe, if one is to judge by the foregoing words of Wilhelm. Later, Wilhelm goes on to explain:

> Perhaps the reason of this difference [between burgher and nobleman] is not the usurpation of the nobles, and the submission of the burghers, but the constitution of society itself. Whether it will ever alter, and how, is to me of small importance: my present business is to meet my own case, as matters actually stand; to consider by what means I may save myself, and reach the object which I cannot live in peace without.[20]

As a modern individual trying to "find himself" he is not content with a statement of the facts involved but is oriented rather toward the specific ways open to him for overcoming the obstacles of his society. This assertion of his individuality is thus to him the very essence of middle-class existence:

> This harmonious cultivation of my nature, which has been denied me by birth, is exactly what I most long for . . . My inclination to become a public person, and to please and influence in a larger circle, is daily growing more insuperable.[21]

Well, what is left for somebody who wants to be a "public person" and at the same time is interested in "poetry and all that is related to it"? The answer is a foregone conclusion and is given by the very context in which the question is put: it is the theatre. In the theatre alone a person may be able to find all the modes of expression which he craves and which society otherwise prevents him from realizing:

> Thou seest well, that for me all this is nowhere to be met with except upon the stage; that in this element alone can I effect and cultivate myself according to my wishes. On the boards a polished man appears in his splendor with personal accomplishments, just as he does so in the upper class of society; body and spirit must advance with equal steps in all his studies; and there I shall have it in my power at once to be and seem as well as anywhere.[22]

Dependence on Society

All these protestations notwithstanding, Goethe's version of individualism is a far cry from that espoused by the Renaissance. In *Wilhelm Meister's Apprenticeship* it is apparent that the complaints of Goethe's people include a heavy admixture of the urge to "belong." The theatre itself is a collaborative enterprise, in which the individual can display his creative strength only by joining himself to other people in idea and in practice. Goethe reiterates the basic post-medieval theme which asserts the re-creation of the world out of man's activity. One of the revered figures in Goethe's novel serenely defines man's task as that of structuring and restructuring reality for himself:

> Life lies before us, as a huge quarry lies before the architect: he deserves not the name of architect, except when, out of this fortuitous mass, he can combine, with the greatest economy and fitness and durability, some form, the pattern of which originated in his spirit. All things without us, nay, I may add, all things on us, are mere elements; but deep within us lies the creative force, which out of these can produce what they were meant to be, and which leaves us neither sleep nor rest, till, in one way or another, without us or on us, that same have been produced.[23]

Elsewhere this statement is extended to show that the creative personality is constituted in and through the social task. Wilhelm is advised by another one of his preceptors:

> It is all men that make up mankind, all powers taken together that make up the world. These are frequently at variance; and, as they endeavor to destroy each other, Nature holds them together, and again produces them . . . Every gift is valuable, and ought to be unfolded. When one encourages the beautiful alone, and another encourges the useful alone, it takes them both to form a man.[24]

In the continuation of the *Apprenticeship* which Goethe wrote in his old age under the title *Wilhelm Meister's Travels,* it is made even more clear that the individual becomes worthy of the name only through useful production and successful integration into society. He must find his way by limiting his desires and adjusting them to the needs of society; and Goethe could not have given expression to this law more succinctly than he did in subtitling the novel *The Renunciants.* It is only at this point that Wilhelm ceases to be the *Lehrling* and becomes truly the *Meister* of reality.

In Goethe's time, the fulfillment of the individual by his reconciliation to society is the prevailing motif. It will take fifty more years for the less optimistic aspects of the individual's social integration to become fully apparent. A plot analysis would show that in every drama of Geothe (and of Schiller as well) the conflicts premised in the first act find in the final act a resolution within the greater whole of society, whether in a real or an idealized form. This is as true of *Faust,* in which the aging philosopher experiences his greatest happiness in cultivating fallow soil for the good of mankind, as it is of *Don Carlos,* in which the attempted assassination of the tyrant anticipates, in imagination, the idea of the people freed from the yoke of absolutistic arbitrariness. Behind all the sadness which pervades the drama of German classicism is hidden a deep confidence in commonly shared virtues and values. The Marquis Posa demands "freedom of thought"; Iphigenia wants "friendship," "friendliness"; and in their context these are both middle-class articulations, the one avowedly political, the other communal and humane.

World Literature and Popular Culture

Artistic Integrity

To a very considerable degree, the idea of "world literature" (the phrase is Goethe's) was for him and his fellow intellectuals an ideal of a community of creative minds. Goethe's intimate knowledge of Moliére in particular helped him to arrive at a concept of intellectual and professional continuity. Such identification with past writers, and above all past dramatists, was facilitated by the theatre, which—as we have noted earlier—functioned as a particularly suitable intellectual middle-class institution in Germany.

Goethe was inclined to identify the personal circumstances of the literary artists of the past with his own as a professional man of letters. In an earlier period Cervantes experienced acute difficulties in trying to confer an appearance of respectability upon the role of the artist as a useful member of society, and Racine and Molière in their private life had considerable trouble with the Court and the Church. Goethe—ignoring the role of patronage by the Court and the nobility—thought of Molière primarily as a success in a commercialized economy. In a conversation with Eckermann he referred to both Shakespeare and Molière approvingly as professionals who by their literary activities had made a living. In this respect he was disposed to share Dr. Johnson's impatience with writers who condemned an interest in earning money as a slur upon their artistic integrity. Goethe went on to speak of Shakespeare and Molière as useful and successful members of a social order, and he referred to them as principal witnesses for his own social philosophy which he espoused in *Wilhelm Meister's Travels.* Speaking of the problem of patronage for the theatre, he commented:

> For if a theatre is not only to pay its expenses, but is besides to make and save money, everything about it must be excellent. It must have the best management at its head; the actors must be of the best; and good pieces must continually be performed, that the attractive power required to draw a full house every evening may never cease. . . . Even Shakespeare and Molière had no other view. Both of them wished, above all things, to make money by their theatres. In order to attain this, their principal aim, they strove that everything should be as good as possible, and that besides good old plays there should be some clever novelty to please and attract. The prohibition of *Tartuffe* was a thunderbolt to Molière; but not so much for the poet as for the director Molière, who had to consider the welfare of an important troupe and to find bread for himself and his actors. [25]

Goethe was particularly fond of Alceste, Molière's Misanthrope. In a book review written late in life he describes Alceste "as the genuine human being." [26] Not without significance, Goethe used almost the same expression to describe Molière: "a genuine man; that is the proper term." [27] In the same year in which his review of *The Misanthrope* appeared, he wrote to his friend Zelter:

> The French themselves are not quite clear about the Misanthrope; now Molière is said to have modeled him on a certain rough courtier; now to have described his own person. To be sure, he had to wrench all that out of his own bosom; he had to describe his own relations to the world; but what relations! The most general imaginable. I'll wager that you've caught yourself in the act in more than one place. And are you not playing the same role against your contemporaries?[28]

143

As Molière had left it indefinite whether he personally championed the rebel Alceste or the level-headed conformist Philinte, Goethe, too, in taking up and explicitly developing Molière's formulation of the moral dilemma of the intellectual, left unanswered whether the cultivated individual could entirely "find himself" by becoming a useful contributor to society. At the same time as Wilhelm Meister becomes a symbolic figure of responsibility on the model of the industrious burgher, he voices concern lest the individual's gifts be leveled off by the social threats of compromise. Alceste was for Goethe a symbol of this social tension which he had found in "world literature":

> Earnestly contemplate *The Misanthrope* and ask yourself whether a poet has ever represented his internal being more completely and gracefully. We would fain call the substance and treatment of the play tragic; such, at least, has been the impression it has ever left upon us; for what is here brought to our view and our intelligence is just what often drives us, like him, from the world. [29]

And again:

> Here is represented the genuine human being who, having attained to considerable education, has yet remained natural and would like nothing better than to remain as true to and thorough with himself as with others; we see him, however, in conflict with the social world, in which one cannot get along without dissimulation and superficiality. Compared with him, Timon is no more than a comic subject.[30]

It is no longer a Werther that Goethe is thinking about fifty years later, when writing still, as in his youth, about "the genuine human being . . . in conflict with the social world." The motivation has now been reversed: Werther was driven to despair because society was closed to him; in the oncoming expanding and expansive nineteenth century, society opened its doors to all energetic Werthers. In this situation the artist begins to recognize that the price of identification with society can be as high as that of resistance; in fact, it may constitute an even graver, because more subtly precarious, danger to his individuality. Against a rotten society or social class, the artist is free to inveigh with a clear conscience. But what about a society which works to all appearances for the benefit of all its members and yet manages, by subtle influences, to poison the artist's work, to pit against a fine craftsman its own criteria of excellence, and thus to compel his consent and his conformism, precisely because the social milieu seems favorable to artistic autonomy? Onto Molière's Alceste, Goethe projects these difficulties—the difficulties of the avant-garde artist—and his concept of Alceste anticipates the nonconformist of later generations whose moral, artistic, or political convictions remove him to the garret, the ivory tower, or the barricade.

Also, in the conversation with Eckermann, in which Goethe characterized Molière as "a genuine human being," he indicated that the time had come when the artist would no longer be listened to as the principal intellectual spokesman for his generation. His remarks point to a condition we have since learned to live with, the defensive position of the arts under the impact of marketable products of popular culture. Goethe speaks bitterly of "the weak, sentimental, gloomy character of modern productions"; more specifically he observes:

> There is nothing distorted about him [Molière]. He ruled the manners of his day; while, on the contrary, our Iffland and Kotzebue allowed themselves to be ruled by theirs, and were limited and confined in them. Molière chastised men by drawing them just as they were.[31]

The writers alluded to here were mass producers of sentimental tragedies which enjoyed a tremendous vogue among theatre-going audiences all over the country. In contrasting these facile fabricators of popular entertainment with Molière, Goethe nostalgically formulates a problem which is central to a sociology of literature. Mass production comes into being as an easy propitiation of mass taste. But only insofar as the literary artist "rules" the manners of his day—that is, only insofar as he expresses the legitimate concerns of the individual in his encounters with the world—will he remain a reliable source for the understanding of a period. The moment he allows himself to be ruled by the fashionable manners, the exemplary role of his art will be in constant danger of being relegated to the margins of society. Hereafter the alternatives are whittled down to the two extreme types: *l'art pour l'art* for the élite; railroad literature (as John Ruskin would have called it) for the rest.

Threats from Below: "The Prelude on the Stage"

The gravity with which Goethe viewed the problem raised by encroaching mass entertainment is reflected in the superficially amusing but essentially serious "Prelude on the Stage" to *Faust*. The prelude deals with the question as to whether and to what extent an artist might make concessions to the taste of the populace and to its predilection for mere entertainment and passive relaxation. The piece is presented in the form of a dialogue between the theatre Manager, a cynical and caustic fellow, and the Poet, a slightly sardonic, though sympathetic, caricature of the eternal malcontent. The issue is the character of the works to be presented to the public. The Manager, who is interested only in box office receipts, has some definite ideas about "art," as managers always have. For him the secret of success is quite simple: "a hash, a stew—easy to invent" will do the trick. The public, he observes with a cynical shrug of the shoulder, is quite stupid, and its favor is won easily enough by the simple expedient of "sheer diffuseness":

> Only by mass you touch the mass; for any
> Will finally, himself, his bit select.

When the Poet objects that "such a trade debases," and that to produce "botching work" is inconsistent with the artist's pride and love of truth, the Manager invokes the age-old principle that the end justifies the means, that form and content must be adjusted to the audience:

> A man who some result intends
> Must use the tools that best are fitting.[32]

The poet is compelled to cater to popular taste, says the Manager. People come to the theatre bored, exhausted, or, worst of all, "fresh from reading the daily papers." They come "as to a masquerade": their sole motive is curiosity, or, in the case of the ladies, to display their finery. He invites the poet to take a look at his patrons' faces: "The half are coarse, the half are cold."

> Why should you rack, poor, foolish bards,
> For ends like these, the gracious Muses?
> I tell you, give but more—more, ever more. [33]

The dialogue reveals a deep-seated change from earlier discussions concerning the cleavage between art and entertainment—from the justification of the one in terms of the other, which had been the court of final appeal to every artist after Horace. To writers such as Montaigne and Pascal, for example, it was axiomatic that entertainment furnish a means of satisfying the need to escape from inner suffering—a need to be gratified (on a high artistic plane), according to Montaigne, or to be denied gratification in favor of spiritual pursuits, according to Pascal. Here in *Faust* we find the discussion divested of its moral and religious overtones, and new components are introduced: a consciousness of the manipulative factors inherent in entertainment; the role of the business intermediary between artist and public, whose criterion is success and whose goal is merely economic; and a sense of conflict between the needs of the true artist and the fickle wishes of a mass audience. The Manager as much as says that the audience can be made to swallow anything, so long as they get quantity and variety, and he attempts to convince the Poet that the audience is so much putty in his hands. At the same time, the Manager does not advise the Poet to give his audience variety on the grounds of a Montaigne—that it is psychologically wholesome—but because by providing something for everyone, variety insures financial success. Similarly, when the Poet resists the Manager's exhortations, he does not do so in the name of Pascalian, transcendental values, but in terms of the specific mission of an artist.

Goethe on His Audience

Goethe foreshadows modern criticism of organized entertainment when he complains of the restlessness, the continuous desire for change, novelty, and sensationalism which characterized his contemporary audience. "The theatre," he says, "like the world in general, is plagued by powerful fashions," and fashions (we would call them fads) consist in pursuing an object with abandon one minute, only to "ban it later forever."[34]

Not only the theatre, full of the plays of Iffland and Kotzebue, reflects this absurd restlessness; it is evident, too, in the newspaper craze for which Goethe reserves his special venom.

> We have newspapers for all hours of the day. A clever head could still add a few more. This way everything—whatever everybody does, wants, writes, even what he plans, is publicly exposed. One can only enjoy oneself, or suffer, for the entertainment of others, and in the greatest rush this news is communicated from house to house, from town to town, from empire to empire, and at last from continent to continent.[35]

This restless urge for novelty would not have disturbed Goethe so much if it did not effectively prevent the kind of ripening which is essential to the creative process; in the constant reading of newspapers, one "wastes the days and lives from hand to mouth, without creating anything."[36] The artist abhors distraction on principle; and the newspapers constitute a particularly vicious form of distraction, because the sheer number of trivia which the reader is asked to assimilate day after day spells death to the synthesizing and generalizing faculties of the mind. Goethe congratulates himself on lacking all curiosity concerning these literally fruitless and stagnant miscellanies; he reports somewhere that he has just glanced through a five-year-old volume of newspapers, and is struck again by the total essential vacuity inherent in so much idle plenitude. "I have time only for the most excellent,"[37] he remarks in another place, to explain why he has stopped reading Sir Walter Scott.

Another trait which Goethe noticed in the modern audience was its complete passivity. The audience, as he put it, is "soft wood given for splitting." They want to be given their money's worth of pleasure, but as for the message of a play, they have no real interest in that at all. Instead, they "throng into the theatre unprepared, they demand what they can enjoy directly. They want to see something, to wonder at something, to laugh, to cry"[38]

And finally Goethe objects to the degree of conformism which he notices everywhere. He hints at the conformist urge of the public in his ironical remarks on the fashion display of theatre-goers, and he anticipates Tocqueville and other social critics (Toennies in Germany, Ward and Cooley in America, and above all, Karl Kraus in Austria) in his comments on the role of the newspapers as promoters of social conformism, rather than as outlets for truth: the so-called free press, he remarks frequently, is in fact contemptuous of the public; everything is acceptable except dissenting opinion.

> Come let us print it all
> And be busy everywhere;
> But no one should stir
> Who does not think like we.[39]

The art which appealed to the public's appetite for distraction was for Goethe not generically different from esoteric art, but merely "botching work." His characterizations of such esthetically inferior products anticipate another of the many elements of the modern critic's description of the popular art, produced for the mass media. Inferior art, he suggests, aims only at entertainment. Thus he makes a distinction not between types of art, but a distinction on the basis of audience effect. He wrote to Schiller:

> The public in a big city . . . lives in a perpetual turmoil of acquisition and consumption. . . . All pleasures, even the theatre, are only supposed to distract, and the strong affinity of the reading public to periodicals and novels arises out of the very reason that the former always and the latter usually bring distraction into distraction.[40]

He was not unsympathetic with the desires of the audience to be entertained, but he condemned those who capitalized on such desires by offering cheap wares. Although "everyone who fools the public by swimming with the current can count on his success,"[41] he felt nevertheless that the bad taste of the public was to some degree the producer's fault. Supplied only with shoddy art, or what passes for art, the public might finally be reduced to shoddy thought as well.

The several stages of the issue of individualism versus conformism are reflected in Goethe's writings. At the outset of his career as a man of letters, in his *Werther* period, we find Goethe looking backward to the petty despot who stifles the individual's crative energy; this is the Storm-and-Stress Goethe, holding up to his generation the creative individual kept in check by a ruling group for whom the German intellectuals never had much use to begin with. During his middle years, in *Wilhelm Meister's Apprenticeship,* Goethe, to be sure, straddles the fence; if the individual is no longer the rebel, the reasons are largely that the grounds for rebellion are waning. During his entire career Wilhelm Meister proves to be the very suitable paradigm of the middle classes by professing his chief ambition to be the "cultivation of my individual self"; he is indeed an appropriate spokesman of his social group during a period of transition in the acknowledgment that this cultivation "is nowhere to be met with except upon the stage," as long as other public platforms are not yet available. As Goethe grows old and as the political, social, and cultural predominance of the middle classes becomes clearly established, he grows more and more suspicious of all personal exertion which is not rooted in the desire to benefit the commonweal; wherever individual action threatens to be in conflict with social action, it is the individual's duty to renounce. It has been said that "renunciation" is Goethe's life-long theme, as "freedom" is Schiller's, but "renunciation" may, after all, take an infinite number of forms; and the renunciants of *Wilhelm Meister's Travels* specifically subdue their private desires to the public welfare.

Yet this adulation of the commonweal was not Goethe's final word. He felt more and more uneasy about the climate of complacency which had set in. What earlier had been productive energy and creative ability had become an incessant urge to be amused, distracted, titillated. And once more Goethe's voice is heard, this time against the prevailing disposition to conform—to conform with what by now threatened to become cheap and suspect, devoid of intellectual content. Now the laws of decorum have been tossed to the winds of fashionable doctrine;

and every fresh production bears the impress of its own mortality. The Philistine had entered, and in his old age Goethe pointed the way to the critical position that was to become Matthew Arnold's: "Culture works differently." If he became increasingly humane, Goethe also became increasingly exasperated, and to the facile conformists of his day he might have flung back Alceste's haughty phrase:

> I like to be distinguished; and, to cut the matter short, the friend of all mankind is no friend of mine.[42]

Notes

1. Eckermann. *Conversations of Goethe* (New York: Everyman's Library, 1827), p. 180. (Quotations from this translation by John Oxenford are reprinted by permission of E. P. Dutton & Co., Inc.) The same adulation is expressed everywhere; see e. g., *Tag- und Jahreshefte* [*Diaries*], 1805 (*Werke*, Grossherzogin Sophie edition, V. 35, p. 189); also Goethe, *Briefe* [*Correspondence*], ed. Philipp Stein (Berlin, 1905), vol. 8, pp. 235–36 (July 26/27, 1828). (All translations from the German text of Goethe's writings, unless otherwise noted, are by Edgar Rosenberg.)
2. See his reviews of "Histoire de la vie et des ouvrages de Molière" and of "Richelieu ou la journée des dupes," *Werke,* vol. 41, 2, pp. 335–38.
3. See Eckermann, *Conversations,* p. 180.
4. Eckermann, *Conversations,* pp. 38–39 (Feb. 15, 1824).
5. We might, to be sure, have included a fourth and last novel, the *Elective Affinities,* in our discussion, if only by way of anticipating some of the motifs which recur in the dramas of Ibsen, treated in the next chapter. But it seemed advisable to confine our remarks to the conflict in its widest application, between individualism and conformity, a conflict not really basic to the *Elective Affinities* except as it relates specifically to the problems of marital and extra-marital relationships.
6. The reader who is interested in both the dynamics and the mechanics of this literary genre is referred to Lionel Trilling's excellent essay on Henry James' "Princess Casamassima" in *The Liberal Imagination* (New York, 1950), pp. 58–92.
7. Literally "The Sufferings." The title has been consistently mistranslated and the error, alas, if fundamental. Werther is not conspicuously addicted to *Sorgen,* but very much to *Leiden.*
8. Goethe, "Werther," in *Great German Short Stories,* Modern Library, p. 99. (Quotations from this translation are reprinted by permission of William Rose.) Goethe's friend Kestner reported that a copy of this drama was found on the desk of Karl Wilhelm Jerusalem, a young civil servant with strong philosophical and literary interests, whose unhappy life, ending in suicide, inspired Goethe's novel.
9. Ibid., p. 3.
10. Ibid., pp. 54, 58.
11. Ibid., p. 55.

12. Ibid., p. 60.
13. Ibid., p. 61.
14. Ibid., p. 80.
15. Ibid., p. 6.
16. To Zelter, on December 25, 1829, Goethe wrote, "It is not be be described what effect Goldsmith's *Vicar* had upon me just at the critical moment of my mental development. That lofty and benevolent irony, that fair and indulgent view of all infirmities and faults, that meekness under all calamities, that equanimity under all changes and chances, and the whole train of kindred virtues, whatever names they bear, proved my best education: and in the end these are the thoughts and feelings which have reclaimed us from all the errors of life." (Goethe, *Briefe*, p. 287).
17. Goethe, *Wilhelm Meister's Apprenticeship and Travels*, 2 vols. Translated by Thomas Carlyle (New York: Burt), vol. 1, p. 91 ("Apprenticeship").
18. Ibid., vol. 1, p. 261.
19. Ibid.
20. Ibid., vol. 1, p. 262.
21. Ibid., vol. 1, pp. 262–63.
22. Ibid., vol. 1, p. 263.
23. Ibid., vol. 1, p. 359.
24. Ibid., vol. 2, p. 50.
25. Eckermann, *Conversations*, p. 108 (May 1, 1825).
26. Goethe, *Werke*, p. 335.
27. Eckermann, *Conversations*, p. 127 (January 29, 1826).
28. Goethe, *Briefe*, p. 236 (July 26/27, 1828).
29. Goethe, *Werke*, p. 334.
30. Ibid., p. 335.
31. Eckermann, *Conversations*, p. 127 (January 29, 1826).
32. Goethe, *Faust*, (New York: Modern Library), p. 5.
33. *Loc. cit.*
34. Goethe, "Weimarisches Hoftheater," in *Sämtliche Werke* (Stuttgart and Berlin: Jubiläumsausgabe), vol. 36, pp. 193–94.
35. Goethe, *Maximen und Reflektionen* (*Maxims and Reflexions*), 1829.
36. Ibid.
37. Goethe in a conversation with Chancellor von Müller, October 12, 1823, in *Gespräche und Zeugnisse*, ed. Ernst Beutler (Zürich, 1950), vol. 2, p. 311.
38. Goethe, "Weimarisches Hoftheater," pp. 191–92.
39. Goethe, *Zahme Xenien. Sämtliche Werke*, vol. 4, pp. 46–47.
40. *Der Briefwechsel zwischen Schiller und Goethe* (*The Correspondence between Schiller and Goethe*), 3 vols. (Leipzig, 1922), vol. 1, pp, 370–71 (August 9, 1797).
41. Ibid., vol. 2, p. 5 (January 3, 1798).
42. Molière, *The Misanthrope*, p. 177.

6

Henrik Ibsen, 1828–1906

In the latter half of the nineteenth century, the institutions as well as the mores of society have come completely under the control of the middle class, and its ethos is challenged only by a handful of European artists and intellectuals. English utilitarianism now states this ethos of unmitigated progress in the most optimistic form conceivable: the good of the individual is identical with the good of society.

Ibsen is a true liberal. Nonetheless he emerges as one of the most severe critics of his age. He followed Lessing's advice to make the theatre a moral testing ground, but while Lessing had used his esthetic precepts to advocate social conditions which would permit the freer development of the individual, Ibsen, a century later, used the same principles to question whether these conditions had been met. The stage becomes a tribunal in which society is defended by its ideology and prosecuted by its reality. The characters (dynamic often to the point of self-contradication) try by every available means to achieve the success and happiness that liberalism has promised them. The outcome of the trial is unequivocal: the sentence is to be found in the social meanings of the defeats the protagonists suffer.

This indictment and trial was intentional. Ibsen wrote in one of his letters:

> A man shares the responsibility and the guilt of the society to which he belongs.... To *write* is to summon one's self, and play the judge's part.[1]

The concern of writers with the relation of the individual to society had for some time been deliberately invoked as a weapon—first of defense, and then of attack—against the aristocracy and reactionary monarchies which at least until 1848 remained a threat in Europe. But now this social consciousness is used to examine and judge the middle-class world itself.

Private Life and Social Forces

Liberalism conceives of society as a more or less elastic system whose function is to make possible the individual's pursuit of happiness. Ibsen appears to share this attitude. He does not write "social drama." Specific social, political or economic questions are touched upon only occasionally, as in *An Enemy of the People*, or *Pillars of Society*. Hardly ever does a policeman, soldier or other public official appear. The state seems to be reduced to the role of a night watchman. Official institutions appear only in such incidental business as the report of the prison sentence of old Borkman in *John Gabriel Borkman*, or as the threats of Dr. Wangel to call in the authorities against the Stranger in *The Lady from the Sea*. The scenes of Ibsen's plays are usually laid in the home, and the dialogue tends to be limited to the problems of the private person.

Here, however, we find the key to Ibsen's social concepts. He indicts society in the area of its strongest claims by allowing the prevailing social philosophy every opportunity, especially in the field likely to be most conducive to a favorable judgment: in the sphere of private life where the individual can reveal himself freely. And this revelation shows man as the focal point for contradictions that originate in the society.

Public and private interests of the protagonists are portrayed as being inevitably irreconcilable. Energies available for use in public affairs deteriorate as soon as private needs and desires come into play. Solness, the Master Builder of churches and settlement houses, finds his only happiness in friendship with a young girl, whereupon he becomes completely lost in his dreams. The sculptor Rubek confesses to an emotional crisis when

> all the talk about the artist's vocation and the artist's mission and so forth began to strike me as being very empty, and hollow, and meaningless at bottom. . . . Yes, is not life in sunshine and in beauty a hundred times better?[2]

Allmers (in *Little Eyolf*) abandons his book, his great calling, to dedicate himself to the education of his son, little Eyolf, in order to "perfect all the rich possibilities that are dawning in his childish soul."[3] These either- or attitudes are products of the isolation of the spheres of life. Not only does the pursuit of happiness in one realm require neglect of human obligations in every other, but even voluntary withdrawal from society cheats the individual of the happiness he seeks. The Master Builder never erects his dream castle but falls to his death from a real tower. The sculptor Rubek's (in *When We Dead Awaken)* original zest for life and art is lost in the tedium of a banal marriage. Eyolf's father is tortured by his unproductive existence, as well as by the jealousy of his wife and finally by the death of his child. Whether man turns to private or public life, as soon as he begins to develop his potentialities in one he runs into conflicts and frustrations in the other.

Ibsen's portrayals thus follow a pattern. A person starts out with the expectation of fulfillment. Then he finds himself involved in a series of conflicts and troubles which almost always bring ruin to him and force him to injure others. The result is solitude, death, or worse still, the announcement of social programs that have been thoroughly discredited by what has gone on before. Mankind is trapped in a cycle of unattainable hopes and real suffering.

Ibsen's dramas display a virtual catalogue of failure—in daily life, in the professions, in the arts, in marriage, in friendship, and in communication between the generations. Either the person cannot make an adjustment to these relationships, or he develops some of his powers at the expense of certain others or at the expense of his fellows. The discrepancy between the apparent wealth of potentialities and the narrow range of their fulfillment is a steadily recurrent motif.

The Competitive Personality

For Ibsen, Molière's advice—that the road to happiness lay in observation, adjustment, and moderation—would have been irrelevant, if not absurd. Goethe had foreseen that the individual would come to feel increasingly the limitations caused by adjustment to social conditions, but he had not anticipated the frustrations demonstrated by Ibsen. The individual can no longer merely renounce certain claims in order to preserve others. He must, to adjust, develop certain sides of his being to a point where the whole man ceases to exist. Competition has now entered a new field, private life. In *Pillars of Society,* Consul Bernick can conduct his financial transactions successfully only at the price of slandering his brother-in-law and suppressing his love for his future sister-in-law. The merchant Borkman sacrifices the love and happiness of two women to his ambition to expand his industrial enterprises. Solness pays for the success of his real-estate development with the inner peace of his wife and the lives of his children. Rubek drives a woman crazy in order to complete his masterpiece.

In claiming the right of individuality for themselves, the characters often justify the damage they cause to those near them by claiming that they have created happiness, instead, for the many.

Borkman:	I have loved power.... The power to create human happiness in wide, wide circles around me!
Mrs. Borkman:	You had once the power to make me happy. Have you used it to that end?
Borkman:	Some one must generally go down in a shipwreck.[4]
Solness:	That I might build homes for others, I had to forego . . . the home that might have been my own. I mean home for a troop of children—and for father and mother, too . . . But her [Solness' wife's] vocation has had to be stunted, and crushed, and shattered—in order that mine might force its way to—to a sort of great victory.[5]

Competition turns out to be not only a struggle for social and economic success among various individuals; it is also an inner struggle in which the individual must drastically curtail certain sides of his own being, his personality, in order to realize his particular ambitions. There arises a sequence of guilt and retribution. Bernick's projects lead him to the verge of collapse; Borkman ends in economic and social ruin; the Master Builder's plans are surpassed by those of younger men; the sculptor's creative power is exhausted. The Consul Bernick's lies do not, however, save him from melancholia; Borkman pays for his ambition with bitter misanthropy; the Master Builder succumbs to his guilt; Rubek flounders in discontent bordering on despair.[6]

Ibsen formulates the predicament of the modern individual: he is fated to become a specialized, one-sided being no matter what he chooses to do. The very concept of adaptation has acquired a new meaning from the one Goethe implied—to say nothing of Molière. What once was a bearable degree of anxiety about fitting oneself to new conditions has become veritable anguish; life becomes a game that one hopes to win by achieving success, only to find that the specialization and exertion required for this success add up, after all, to failure.

Marriage and the Family

Failure manifests itself right in the very center of private life, in marriage. For the eighteenth-century novelists the home was a stabilizing force in a mobile world. For Molière, marriage was the happy end, whatever the conflict. It was the impossibility of marriage that occasioned the suicide of Werther. Ibsen's plays, however, do not stop at the threshold of family life; on the contrary, it is precisely there that they begin.

In almost every case, the characters or interests of the partners are at variance and bring marriage to defeat or frustration. Weak husbands such as Tesman, Alving, Hellmer, or Allmers fail their wives and drive them to distraction.[7] Ibsen is not partial to either of the sexes; weak wives like Aline Solness, Irene Rubek, or Gina Ekdal have a similar effect.[8] Marriages may be ruined by the love for a third person (*Hedda Gabler* and *Master Builder*), by an unbridgeable rift between parents and children (*John Gabriel Borkman*) or between the parents on account of the children (*Little Eyolf*), and by increasing boredom (in nearly every play).

Consul Bernick and Borkman marry women whom they do not love, and the insincerity of the relationships brings feelings of guilt to the husbands and of inadequacy to their wives. Rubek marries a woman inferior to him as a personality and pays with nervous restlessness; she in turn, to avenge herself, deserts him. Ellida, in *The Lady from the Sea*, seems fated to stagnate in a marriage she had contracted merely to escape from an unbearable environment. Nora, in *A Doll's House*, breaks off a relationship in which husband and wife could educate neither each other nor the children to live together equably. In *Little Eyolf* the husband conveys to his wife his decision to concentrate on the education of his son; the ensuing dialogue illustrates vividly the manner in which the law of competition operates within the intimacy of the family.

Rita:	Now you have given yourself up to something worse.
Allmers:	Worse! Do you call our child something worse?
Rita:	Yes, I do . . .
Allmers:	I am often almost afraid of you, Rita.
Rita:	I am often afraid of myself. And for that very reason you must not awake the evil in me.
Allmers:	Why, good heavens, do I do that?
Rita:	Yes, you do—when you tear to shreds the holiest bonds between us.
Allmers:	It is of no use demanding anything. Everything must be freely given. . . . I must divide myself between Eyolf and you.
Rita:	But if Eyolf had never been born? What then?
Allmers:	Oh, that would be another matter. Then I should have only you to care for.
Rita:	Then I wish he had never been born. . . . I will live my life—together with you—wholly with you. I cannot go on being only Eyolf's mother. . . . I will not, I tell you! I cannot! I will be all in all to you. To you, Alfred![9]

The family does not live up to the function of being a sanctuary where the hurt suffered in public life can be healed. Even the relationship between the two generations is one of interference, not of help. The death of the Allmers' child terminates the father's interest in education, which from the beginning was not rooted in generic sympathy for the younger generation. This is, briefly, the life of the Allmers family: incompatibility between public and private life, neglect of the wife because of the husband's preoccupation with the child, dull pressure on the husband's life from lack of confidence in his productivity, general spiritual disorder.

The atmosphere in Consul Bernick's house is similarly unpleasant. Bernick tries to justify his social and personal machinations with the claim that he is seeking to provide his son with a life work.[10] His eventual self-reproach disavows his previous life and program which had brought about a hypocritical mentality in himself, an inner impoverishment of his wife, and a guilt-ridden relationship toward his son.

Ibsen's characters voice dubious educational doctrines which actually conceal antagonism and competition. When John Gabriel Borkman's proposal that he and his grown son should build a new life together is coldly rejected, he has earned the same fate as Bernick and for similar reasons. The aging Master Builder is bitter against the younger generation:

> Some one or other will take it into his head to say: Give me a chance. And then all the rest will come clamouring after him, and shake their fists at me and shout: Make room—make room . . . presently the younger generation will come knocking at my door. . . . Then there's an end of Halvard Solness.[11]

It is left uncertain how heavily the death of Solness's children lay on his conscience. Ideally, the long experience and the mature wisdom of an aging man should invest him with a higher humanity, the benefits of which he could pass on to the younger generation. Instead, the sheer biological difference in age becomes a source of hostility. Biology itself is incorporated into a category of property, and the limitations of old age appear as a loss of property, a loss that has no compensations.

Social Nature of Personal Conflicts

Social relationships intimately permeate the personal disasters Ibsen portrays. In all the plays someone stands in the way of another's needs or the protagonist frustrates his own needs by the nature of the activity he has selected. The characters themselves explain these conflicts on the grounds of inner necessity: they cannot change their natures.[12]

This explanation, however, leaves out of account the social connections which are clearly established. Ellida, the Lady from the Sea, finds life unbearable after she recognizes that her marriage actually rests on a sales transaction, and the tawdry yet expedient middle-class career marriages of Bernick, Tesman, Allmers, and Borkman signify that we are concerned with something else than innate human nature. In other instances human problems develop which seemingly do not have any connection with material questions or broader social relationships, yet they are described in almost the same language as that which is used to describe instances of business and professional competition.

> Oh, it all seems to me so foolish. . . . Not to be able to grasp at your own happiness—at your own life! Merely because some one you know happens to stand in the way![13]

Indeed, this remark from Hilda, the Master Builder's friend, is close to the Master Builder's own language when he feels threatened by his competitors. The professional pattern in which the success of one means the failure of another has penetrated intimate relationships. The aggressiveness of the Master Builder is matched by that of Hedda Gabler. Rubek must use the same force and drive to succeed in the art world that Borkman or Solness uses in the world of business and industry.

Acclimatization and Specialization

Like Cervantes and Shakespeare, Ibsen often puts truths into the mouths of marginal figures. Ballested, jack-of-all-trades and master of none in *The Lady from the Sea*, declares that man can and must "acclimatize" himself, that he must adapt himself to the "facts."

The men in Ibsen always respect the facts of their world: eliminating competitors, cheating partners, playing ball with public authorities—these are realistic and profitable activities. If these people seem to be crushed by a blind fate, it is because they live their social roles in their private lives but fail to see them for what they are, namely, as the struggle to succeed, to obtain more, and to treat all things in an acquisitive manner. The protagonists may prefer one lover to another, one generation to another, or one side of their own nature to another, but in every case the choice is pursued with a restlessness and tenacity identical to that by which they forward their careers. As their social roles are extended to private relations, they almost inevitably miss happiness in the very act of energetically pursuing it. The schema of utilitarianism backfires.

An outstanding characteristic of almost all of Ibsen's persons is that they are, in one form or another, specialists. Only a few escape the isolation resulting from a high degree of specialization, and even those who do pay a heavy penalty. The good-for-nothing Ballested is a painter, actor, decorator, hairdresser, dancing master, and music teacher all in one; he is, of course, a failure. The identity of self-interest and social interest proves to be a misstatement of reality. Selective, self-centered activity is the requirement for effective social participation; the alternative is to become an ineffectual jack-of-all-trades. It is true irony that advice to conform should be put into the mouth of a man who fails to conform.

The social trait of specialization afflicts Ibsen's people in their private lives. The position of husband, wife, friend, father, or mother is seen as a form of existence at odds with the prerogatives of the individual himself as well as with those of the other members of his family. Hedda, who has managed for a while to assert her integrity in spite of a banal environment, tells a friend about the disappointments of her honeymoon, which have become the leitmotif of her marriage. She says:

> Tesman is a specialist . . . and specialists are not at all amusing to travel with. Not in the long run, at any rate.[14]

When the friend asks, "not even the specialist one happens to love?" she makes a bitter reply.[15] The episode is particularly significant because Tesman is not unattractive to women and his profession (he is a scholar) is hardly repelling. Far removed as he may seem from the average pattern of commercial activity, he still remains caught in a web of narrow specialization

Gunhild Borkman's hatred of her husband is a reaction to his view of life which centers its emphasis on the sound business reputation of the family. Aline Solness's tolerance of her husband and his friend Hilda is not born of a limitless feminine capacity for love but only of the naive, dutiful desire to assist her husband's business and to maintain a conventional family life. The asceticism of Pastor Manders has more to do with his own bigotry than with morality. Hellmer's ethical pretensions spring from his anxiety to retain directorship of the bank rather than from conscience and remorse.

Although Ibsen slates in various forms the view of Dr. Stockmann that he who stands alone is most powerful, nevertheless his dramatic work illustrates again and again that the enforced self-dependence of man leds to solitude and loss of vitality. The pursuit of special self-interest spells ruin, and not fulfillment. Such is the fate not only of his less engaging characters, for instance the overbearing merchants Bernick and Borkman, but also of the likeable ones. The latter—like Helen Alving, Hedda Gabler, Rosmer, and Rubek—finally go to pieces in the complete isolation into which they have been driven; the pressure of outside interests pursues them even when they seek to withdraw into themselves.

The Dilemma of Freedom and Necessity

Love and Anxiety

Men face each other as strangers. When Ibsen's characters speak of love they often tremble—a phenomenon which proves on examination to be historical and social in its origins. The division of the individual into a professional self and a private self frightens the wife lest her beloved turn out to be someone vastly different from the man she knows; he may even be different from the man he thinks he is. The man who binds himself for life to a woman—to a member of the sex which, in Ibsen's day, society still confined to an existence within conventional marriage—may also expect disappointment. An order of life in which husbands and wives are specialized beings intensifies the anxiety that in any case goes with love.

When his wife asks him what his first sensation had been upon meeting her. Allmers replies quite frankly: "Dread."[16] Wangel admits that "the terrible" plays a dominant role in his relationship with his wife.[17] Madly in love with the childish Hilda, Solness sees his world full of devils: "If only you could always tell whether it is the light or dark ones that have got hold of you!"[18] Ellida indicates what is problematic in her love in these words:

> Oh, there are times, you may be sure, when I feel as though there would be safety and peace in clinging close to you, and trying to defy all the powers that frighten and fascinate me. But I cannot do it No no,—I cannot do it![19]

Personal relationships are more fearful than comforting. "She must bear it all alone."[20] Love cannot efface this insecurity, and Allmers, who has tried to break away from public life completely, finds no peace.

Allmers:	There is something horrible in being alone. The thought of it runs like ice through my blood—
Asta:	O, but Alfred, you are not alone.
Allmers:	There may be something horrible in that too, Asta.[21]

Several of Ibsen's plays seem to suggest that he nonetheless believed in the possibility of realizing a genuine human relationship within and despite the prevailing social aura. But while there are glimmers here and there of such hope, by and large, where true love seems about to be realized, it is only at the point of death. Solness, Hedda Gabler, Rubek, and Irene die at the very moment overpowering emotion tears these people from their self-preoccupation. Solness, we are told, is too frightened to mount a scaffold, but he clambers to the top of a new house the first time he feels truly and warmly human, and jumps off. Accustomed to a soft life, Rubek climbs the most forbidding mountains when he meets the mate who stands beyond all conventional conceptions of life, whereupon an avalanche buries them both. Hedda Gabler, tied down by a wealthy marriage, exults in the suicide of her friend as an expression of freedom and the beauty of life, and she confesses that she feels alive for the first time just before she shoots herself. Death climaxes the will to life of all these people. It stands in somber contrast to the complacent self-confidence of Molière, for whom suicide was absurd and ridiculous. The disparity between Molière's and Ibsen's resolutions illustrates the decline of the curve of the middle-class optimism.

The Imagination and Art

Ibsen is obsessed by the dilemma of how to maintain the integrity of the individual under the impact of the prevailing social atmosphere:

> The fault lies in that all mankind has failed. If a man claims to live and to develop in a human way, it is megalomania.[22]

> So to conduct one's life as to realize one's self—this seems to me the highest attainment possible to a human being. It is the task of one and all of us, but most of us bungle it.[23]

The sum total is mostly negative. Face to face with the injury he has done to himself and to others, Solness condemns his professional accomplishments:

> See, that is the upshot of the whole affair, however far back I look. Nothing really built . . . Nothing, nothing! The whole is nothing![24]

What remains is loneliness without hope.

Even individual phantasy and artistic imagination—which ordinarily we would think of as the last strongholds against the inroads of the world—do not transcend social reality but merely reflect it. Wishdreams, for example, without ever being translated into action, are consummated in events that injure and kill. Solness wants his old house to burn; when his wish comes true, the fire destroys his children. Rebecca West (in *Rosmersholm*) desires the love of the married pastor, only to feel eventually that her innermost wishes were responsible for the death of his wife. Rita Allmers confesses her jealousy of her child and would rather it had never been born than that it detract from her husband's love for herself; the child dies.

Art, too, is engulfed by this process. At the beginning of the liberal era, music sang triumphantly of joy and solidarity; in Ibsen's work the tune has changed to one of suffering and isolation. Hedda Gabler plays the piano in a moment of supreme distress, and she draws out, according to stage direction, notes of despair. In *When We Dead Awaken* Ibsen introduces the plastic arts. A comparison with the Greek legend might help to point up the character of Rubek, the sculptor. The ancient story tells how Pygmalion fell in love with his statue of a young girl, how then a goddess endowed her with life, and how finally Pygmalion married the product of his own creation. In this tale, inanimate material is released for the development of a human being, but Ibsen's drama displays a reverse process: the artist sees in his wife only the model. The egoism of the artist, on a special plane to be sure, is as boundless as the egotism of the business and professional man. He transforms human relations and men themselves into objects to be used for his own purposes; they have value for him only when they serve his ambitions.

Idealism Disenchanted

For the Wilhelm Meisters, the language in which idealism set forth its values—truth, freedom, responsibility, and duty—was a meaningful part of the emancipation of the middle classes. Now, however, when these same words are pronounced by a Rubek, who is imprisoned in his egoism, or by a Bernick, whose whole life has been based on the deception and repression of his fellow men, or by an Allmers, whose weak soul can escape conventional norms only at rare moments, they have ceased to provide a genuine motivation for creative acts.

Two parallel themes run throughout Ibsen's works: the one shows an effort to live up to established social values and ideals only to meet with defeat, and the other shows the defeat of those who reject these values and have nothing to put in their place. Ulrik Brendel, a vagabond and down-at-the-heel writer, is a spokesman for such pointless disillusionment. The first time he visits his former pupil, Rosmer, to arrange for lectures on human freedom, he begs for some cast-off clothes. The plan for the lectures is abandoned when he becomes aware of the apathy and cynicism in the town. He visits Rosmer once more before leaving, and this time begs for "one or two cast-off ideals."[25] He announces cynically that life can be mastered only by men like Mortensgard, an unscrupulous climber "capable of living his life without ideals." "And that," he adds, "is just . . . the sum of the whole world's wisdom."[26] Again a marginal figure has formulated a basic feature of society. A world of ideals is invoked to dignify the relentless pursuit of material advantage, and they dissolve as soon as their consequences are considered; man's life runs its course between the pursuit of material goods and the worship of powerless ideas.

Of the values implicit in the categorical imperative, duty had struck a particularly militant note; the equal commitment of all men to duty aimed at the elimination of hereditary privilege. In Ibsen's drama, however, this concept becomes self-defeating. Pastor Manders life is governed by wholesale acceptance of moral and sexual conventions, and his every action and world are confounded by the mirror of truth that Helen Alving holds up to him. Yet this man, wallowing in the comforts gained by submitting to conformity, preaches duty to Helen Alving when she confesses her unhappiness:

> What right have we human beings to happiness? We have simply to do our duty, Mrs. Alving! And your duty was to hold firmly to the man you had once chosen, and to whom you were bound by the holiest ties.[27]

He says to this woman whose life has been wretched and whom he had humiliated when she revealed her love for him:

> And what a blessing has it not proved to you, all the days of your life, that I induced you to resume the yoke of duty and obedience![28]

When the curtain has fallen and the audience strikes a balance, it is found that "duty" has brought Chamberlain Alving and his son to a terrible end, shattered the life of Mrs. Alving, brought about the degradation of her husband's illegitimate daughter, helped establish a sailor's brothel, and destroyed an orphanage. This is the reality. The pastor's sermon is an insipid moral recipe.

Aline Solness, too, is a victim of official morality. Ruled by a domineering and unreliable husband, robbed of her children by a terrible accident, restricted to a narrow circle of gossipy companions, she clings to the doctrine that all that matters is duty. All she gets for her faith in this moral dictum is mockery from her successful rival, the Master Builder's young friend:

> *Hilda:*   She said that she would go out and buy something for me, because it was her duty. Oh I can't bear that ugly, horrid word!
> *Solness:*   Why not?
> *Hilda:*   It sounds so cold, and sharp, and stinging. Duty—duty—duty. Don't you think so, too? Doesn't it seem to sting you?[29]

Time and again Ibsen's people sacrifice themselves and do what they believe to be their duty, only to achieve negative results. Sacrifice of human lives becomes absurd, unless it is linked with a value that transcends those lives. It is a sheer perversion of the idea of self-sacrifice when sickly and childish Hedwig Ekdahl commits suicide to satisfy the pathological ideas of Gregor Werle and the inner instability of the man she believes to be her father. When Rebecca West joins Rosmer in death to satisfy the feeling of guilt he has projected upon her, the result is only the heaping of human destruction upon destruction. Even Nora's renunciation of her home has something of the sadness of a futile sacrifice.

The Role of Women

Ibsen once wrote to his friend Georg Brandes:

> What will be the outcome of this mortal combat between two epochs, I do not know; but anything rather than the existing state of affairs—so say I.[30]

The standards for a life superior to the "existing state" are set by women in Ibsen's plays. Although for them it is not hunger and other material privations that indict society, their frustrations are allied nonetheless to the present "epoch." Ibsen occasionally links the situation of women in his time to that of the workers. He insists on the nobility of character as superior to the privileges which come with property, and adds:

> This nobility . . . will come to us from two sources . . . from our women and from our workingmen.

The reshaping of social conditions which is now under way out there in Europe is concerned chiefly with the future position of the workingman and of woman.

That it is which I hope for and wait for; and it is that that I will work for, and shall work for my whole life so far as I am able.[31]

Ibsen again turns to a minor character for the formulation of an important problem. In *The Lady from the Sea*, Boletta, an elderly, dry, prosy woman, asks the sculptor Lyngstrad, who is declaiming that the wife must accommodate herself to her husband:

Has it never occurred to you that perhaps a husband might be absorbed in the same way into his wife? Might come to resemble her, I mean. . . . But why not the one as well as the other?[32]

Women fare badly in a society where economic and social functions are almost exclusively male prerogatives. They represent, in a sense, incomplete men. They must not only suffer from the pressures of society, they must also serve and seek the approval of the men. Or, as Ibsen himself says:

A woman cannot be herself in the society of the present day, which is an exclusively masculine society, with laws framed by men and a judicial system that judges feminine conduct from a masculine point of view.[33]

Modern society is not a human society; it is only a society of males.[34]

But the disenfranchisement of women has positive as well as negative results. Thanks to the fact that public life is ruled by men, women retain traces of another kind of existence; they are at least capable of expressing true human traits. Their greater distance from public life does not free them entirely from social pressures (the latter are, as we have seen, too omnipresent for that), but it does allow them at times to transcend these limitations.

Insofar as women have any business life in Ibsen's plays, they are helpless, falterirg and of poor judgment—with the exception of essentially innocuous characters like Gina Ekdahl, who does have some practical ability. Nora forges a note with almost touching clumsiness and carelessness. Helen Alving is persuaded by Pastor Manders' spurious arguments not to insure her orphanage. But this removal of women from men's work serves in the end to protect them from complete surrender to social and economic pressures.

The unique human quality women retain is the steadfastness with which they cling to the truth as an absolute value. It is man, ready to combat others for his own success, who preaches the ideals of progress, humanity, duty—the ideals that are undermined by the conduct of his life. Ibsen's male protagonists almost never live up to what they preach, and they never admit the one principle by which they in fact do live, the materialism of personal profit. Women are also materialistic, but their materialism is significantly different and outspoken. It is dramatic irony that egoists preach morality and moralists egoism; Ibsen's women often say that desire for personal happiness is their only true goal, but, in fact, they love to the point of self-sacrifice. Not once does Ibsen honor a man by allowing him to come forth as a witness to the humanly desirable. Only women such as Ellida, Hedda, Nora, Irene, Mrs. Rentheim, and Rita Allmers defend that faith. Ibsen remarks of his own wife that she never succumbed to the temptation of inertia in the present society.[35]

The clash between the self-seeking world of men, and love and humanity, represented by women, is crucial in Ibsen's drama. Rubek, perhaps the most talented character in Ibsen's works, abounds in creative ability, passion and a feeling for nuance. His wife. Irene, has neither the intellectual superiority of a Helen Alving, the zest of a Hedda Gabler nor the healthy directness of a Hilda. In this instance, the husband towers above the male average, while the wife fails to reach the level of several other women in Ibsen's dramas. It is in this relationship, however, that the mutually exclusive principles become most clear: adjustment to the "fact" on the one hand, and unconditional love on the other. Rubek, as a youthful sculptor, pursued the ideal of symbolizing, in the form of a young woman, the awakening of mankind from its present state. Later, having "learned worldly wisdom in the years that followed," he placed this single figure far in the background and transformed the central theme of the work into an allegory of life with "men and women with dimly-suggested animal faces." Irene tells him: "There you uttered your own doom."[36] The sculptor has betrayed the promise of his youth; he has achieved material success by turning out works that did not come sincerely from his own humanity; and because of his guilt he represents himself in his sculpture as a penitent who indeed has forfeited his life. On the other side, Irene's steadfast love for Rubek signifies a humanity which any number of shocks and depressions could not weaken; it holds out against every difficulty, disappointment and convention. For Hilda, no outside world—neither reputation nor family—exists when she wants to erect her castle with the Master Builder. Hedda Gabler goes to her death without giving up her faith in beauty as the only worthy aim of life.

In male idealism, truth becomes mere talk. In feminine egoism, on the other hand, there is an element of truth, for desires are consciously recognized and defended. Helen Alving opposes the sermonizing call to duty by men with the idea of "joy." She says to her son:

> A little while ago you spoke of the joy of life; and at that word a new light burst for me over my life and everything connected with it.[37]

In the same vein, Irene's love casts light on Rubek's confusion, just as Hilda's need of happiness exposes the Master Builder's disorganized existence. Hedda Gabler's contempt for the world of the specialist shows the abyss between the latter and a total human existence.

By their intransigence, Ibsen's women uncover the rationalizations of men: the architectural ambitions of Solness, the artist's egoism of Rubek, the conceited scholarship of Tesman, and the pomposity of Bernick and Borkman. In fact, the relation between men and women can be compared to that of the neurotic and the psychoanalyst. The men say everything that comes into their heads; they express guilt feelings, justifications and accusations. In contrast women represent the ego-ideal of a structured, realistically grounded existence. As in the analytic session, everything is restricted to the field of conversation and there is no lecturing. But the comparison ends here. True, Ibsen studies the psychological effects of society upon the individual, but his work does not proclaim that the mere understanding of psychological difficulties will cure the social ills which are at the bottom of personal misery.

Ibsen's women are not judged by specific "good" actions as opposed to "bad" ones, but rather, by the good faith they bring to their acts. Their attitude toward sex illuminates their struggle for happiness. The men generally declare sensual pleasure inferior to more ideal varieties. Those of the women who are endowed with the greatest critical clarity and energy are also the most sensual, and they admit it themselves. Against weaklings like Rosmer, or the vacillating Allmers, the colorless Tesman, or cowards like Manders, or the thoroughly beaten Rubek, all of whom flee from women in the pursuit of their "ideals," Ibsen opposes women who admit their demand for sexual happiness with the same candor as that with which they berate compromises demanded by the world. True, Rosmer, Rubeck, and Allmers have traces of the rebel, but their ideals express dissatisfaction only with certain facets of prevailing society. Their female partners, however, say "no" to the claims and pressures of society as a whole, and hence to the weak principles of their men.

The Role of the Artist

The naturalistic school, of which Ibsen was a leading figure, expressed an increasing conviction that esthetic purism—art for art's sake—must give way to the artist's concern with the concrete problems of men. Ibsen's critique of the ideals of modern society did not derive from a philosophy of relativism but from a desire to relate these ideals to the social struggle. He expressed the idea that the subdivision and independent existence of different spheres of life—the seemingly unconnected separatism into economics, politics, and culture—are transitory and once wrote:

> I believe that the time will soon come when political and social conceptions will cease to exist in their present forms. . . I believe that poetry, philosophy, and religion will be merged in a new category and become a new vital force.[38]

In challenging the purely esthetic approach, Ibsen tried to avoid specialization and isolation, which he had stigmatized in his dramas as a danger to human development. While traveling in Italy, he wrote to Björnson:

> If I were asked to tell you at this moment what has been the chief result of my stay abroad, I should say that it consisted in my having driven out of myself the aestheticism which had a great power over me—an isolated aestheticism with a claim to independent existence. Aestheticism of this kind seems to me now as great a curse to poetry as theology to religion. . . . Is it not an inexpressibly great gift of fortune to be able to write? But it brings with it great responsibility; and I am now sufficiently serious to realize this and to be very severe with myself.[39]

Yet, much as he tried to throw off the limitations set upon him by his milieu—by sharing "the responsibility and the guilt of the society" to which he belonged—he nevertheless displayed traits characteristic of the society he criticized.[40] Although his female protagonists speak of freedom and joy as goals that are incompatible with prevailing conditions, still the manner in which they express their desires is often reminiscent in terms and tones of the austere language of the professed idealism of the male; it remains part and parcel of the value system they themselves protest.

Austerity lives closely with misanthropy and arrogance. Dr. Stockmann, the enemy of the people, rejects the world in a pronunciamento of truculent self-sufficiency. Rubek imperiously lashes the mob for its lack of appreciation. Rosmer prefers to take his program for nobility to the grave rather than make it public. Ibsen himself possessed traces of the misanthropy displayed by these characters. He wrote in a letter to Georg Brandes:

> What I chiefly desire for you is a genuine, full-blooded egoism, which shall force you for a time to regard what concerns you yourself as the only thing of any consequence, and everything else as non-existent. . . . I have never really had any very firm belief in solidarity; in fact, I have only accepted it as a kind of traditional dogma. If one had the courage to throw it overboard altogether, it is possible that one would be rid of the ballast which weighs down one's personality most heavily.[41]

Suggestions of pessimism also may be found in the use of dumbness in his plays. He could have said with Goethe: "Silence befits the man who does not feel himself to be fully rounded. Silence also befits the lover who cannot hope to be happy."[42] In any case silence is the answer whenever men are giving up the confidence that they can lead their lives, as Wilhelm Meister had hoped for, in the direction of "a harmonious cultivation" of their nature. Silence comes over many of Ibsen's persons when they find they do not know how to break through the hard shell of their environment. Ellida, the Lady from the Sea, cannot communicate what she calls the "incomprehensible" in her life. Similarly, Hedda Gabler engages in an abruptly muted conversation:

> *Brack:* Why should you not, too, find some sort of vocation in life, Mrs. Hedda?
> *Hedda:* A vocation—that should attract me?
> *Brack:* If possible, of course.
> *Hedda:* Heaven knows what sort of vocation that could be. I often wonder whether—(breaking off). But that would never do either.[43]

Irene confesses that in her youth she had hated Rubek but loved his work, and had kept quiet on the subject. Silent hatred and silent love, the aging woman's recollection of her earlier dumbness, these are signs of actual human isolation.

In Ibsen's plays the societal concept of man reaches a climax: his inner life appears at once as a reaction to social forces and a reflection of them; social forces continue to live inside the individual, and thus to control him. In this context, nature as the symbol of freedom becomes a significant issue: many of his figures dream of natural space as a counter-image to society. Ellida longs for the great open sea, Rubek and Irene have faith in the redemptive power of the mountains, the parents of Little Eyolf turn to the peaks and the stars. Even Oswald Alving's longing for Paris ("light and sunshine and glorious air") and the ecstasy of Solness and Hilda over their air castles imply a renunciation of the possibility of human fulfillment in society, and a surrender to the demiurge of nature.

Such generous hope for the salvation of the individual's integrity is destroyed—as we shall try to show—by Hamsun's image of nature.

Notes

1. Letters of Henrik Ibsen, tr. by J. N. Laurvik and Mary Morison (New York, 1905), p. 334 (June 16, 1980). All quotations from Ibsen's plays and drafts of plays are taken from the William Archer edition of *The Works of Henrik Ibsen* (New York: Viking, 1911–12), 12 Vols., by permission of Charles Scribner's Sons.
2. *When We Dead Awaken, Act II*, vol. 11, p. 429.
3. *Little Eyolf*, Act I, vol. 11, p. 49.
4. *John Gabriel Borkman*, Act III, vol. 11, pp. 296–97.
5. *The Master Builder*, Act II, Vol. 20, pp. 350–53.
6. The plays referred to are *Pillars of Society, John Gabriel Borkman, The Master Builder*, and *When We Dead Awaken*, respectively.
7. We refer to *Hedda Gabler, Ghosts, The Wild Duck*, and *Little Eyolf*, respectively.
8. See *The Master Builder, When We Dead Awaken*, and *The Wild Duck*, respectively.
9. *Little Eyolf*. Act I, vol. 11, pp. 61–63.
10. See *Pillars of Society*, Act IV, vol. 6, p. 457.
11. *The Master Builder*, Act I, vol. 10, p. 284.
12. See, for example, *The Master Builder*, Act I, vol. 10, p. 258; *When We Dead Awaken*, Act II, Vol. 11, p. 450; *Little Eyolf*, Act II, vol. 11, p. 117.
13. *The Master Builder*, Act III, vol. 10, p. 402.
14. *Hedda Gabler*, Act II, vol. 10, p. 92.
15. Ibid., pp. 92–93.
16. *Little Eyolf*, Act II, vol. 11, p. 117.
17. *The Lady from the Sea*, Act IV, vol. 9, p. 368.
18. *The Master Builder*, Act II, vol. 10, p. 367.
19. *The Lady from the Sea*, Act V, vol. 4, p. 380.
20. "Notes for a Modern Tragedy" (Draft of *A Doll's House*), vol. 12, pp. 91–92.
21. *Little Eyolf*, Act III, vol. 11, pp. 140–41.
22. Draft for *Ghosts*, vol. 12, p. 186.
23. *Letters*, p. 359 (August 8, 1882).
24. *The Master Builder*, Act III, vol. 10, p. 426.

25. *Rosmersholm,* Act IV, vol. 9, p. 183.
26. Ibid., pp. 184–85.
27. *Ghosts,* Act I, vol. 7, p. 255.
28. Ibid., p. 256.
29. *The Master Builder,* Act II, vol. 10, p. 335.
30. *Letters,* p. 234 (April 4, 1872).
31. "Speech to the Workingmen of Trondhjem" (June 14, 1885). In: *Speeches and New Letters,* tr. by Arne Kildal (Boston, 1910), p. 54.
32. *The Lady from the Sea,* Act IV, vol. 9, p. 334.
33. Draft for *A Doll's House,* vol. 12, p. 91.
34. Ibsen, *Nachgelassene Schriften,* ed. by J. Elias and H. Koht (Berlin, 1909), vol. 1, p. 206.
35. See *Letters,* p. 199 (October 28, 1870).
36. *When We Dead Awaken,* Act II, vol. 11, pp. 447–49.
37. *Ghosts,* Act III (Vol. VII, p. 336).
38. "Speech at the Banquet in Stockholm," (September 24, 1887) *Speeches,* pp. 56–57.
39. *Letters,* p. 86 (September 12, 1865).
40. See his letter of June 16, 1880.
41. *Letters,* p. 218 (September 24, 1871).
42. Goethe, *Der Sammler und die Seinigen. Sämtliche Werke,* vol. 33, p. 182.
43. *Hedda Gabler,* Act II, vol. 10, p. 105.

Excursus B

Note on August Strindberg

With the report on August Strindberg by his second wife, yet another volume has been added to his "autobiographies." Even though this recent publication stems only in part from his own pen—the letters that are included in the text—Frida Strindberg constructed her memoir in such a way that it can be considered the work of one of Strindberg's students, if not, indeed, a minor accomplishment of the writer himself. This is why the book reads, like all of his autobiographies do, as though Strindberg were defending his own position under a different name.

Goethe's statement that all of his works are merely fragments of a grand confession, captures one of the decisive motives of every writer in bourgeois society: the presentation of the solitary and isolated individual. Yet the melancholic undertone barely audible in Goethe's formulation is fully brought to light only with Strindberg. The autobiographic character of all his works contains the real secret of his extraordinary existence as an artist as well as of his extraordinary effect. In the epoch in which he lives as a mature man and in which his works continued to have an effect even after his death, faith in the possibility of improving the prevailing social order had been already considerably shaken. Precisely this breakdown is mirrored in the specific form of Strindberg's autobiographic works. He does not share the confidence of that literature which seeks to exalt liberal society either in its existing state or in taking for granted inherent possibilities for reform. Precisely those writers of the preceding liberal epoch who had a critical relationship to liberalism were convinced that the literary characters they created—who continued, as they themselves admitted, their own life and blood—showed people whose own development would help each other individual in his search for well-being—providing by means of literary representation either a warning or an incentive. For them, the autobiographical component in their writings was only the symbol for the possibility of genuine cooperation between individuals in the real world. The autonomy of these invented figures, who might or might not correspond closely to the self-concept of the writer, was supported by the not always conscious Kantian conviction that the desires and values of an autonomous subject derived, in the last analysis, from a generally binding and generally accessible sphere which regulates, or at least influences and corrects, human behavior.

During the transition from the liberal to the monopolistic phase of capitalism, wide sections of the bourgeoisie lose their sense of the harmonious relationship between the life of the individual and the overall order. This loss finds its overt expression only later, when masses of people who are under authoritarian rule blindly abdicate to the crudest and most simplistic irrationalities. But in Strindberg's life as well as in his writings, this collapse of liberal faith and confidence announced itself ideologically much earlier. His autobiographies, which include even works that he himself would not explicitly group in this category, no longer exude the spirit of an autonomy which conjures up an ultimately successful harmony of single individuals and universally binding values, but they express inexorable loneliness. His frequent use of monologues express the monadic nature of bourgeois existence, which had been present from its very beginning but only now begins to show its depressive aspects.

The pride of the individual who had been conscious of his productivity contributing to the social whole now turns into the rage and the defiance of the lonely individual, wanting no connection with the social whole that he experiences only as negative and abusive. Strindberg marks the beginning in literature of modernity as far as it contains the individualist's enraged universal indictment. A monotonous tone now concomitantly enters literature. Because the complaints and accusations do not emerge in relation to distinctive groups engaged in social contexts but instead express the misfortune of a single individual, their artistic rendering becomes stereotyped. In Strindberg's art, repetition is an index of a weakness that has its social foundations. True, Ibsen almost continuously repeats the scenary of an average bourgeois household in his plays, while Strindberg's props roam about Indian and Christian mythology, about all of world history, including the worldliness of Paris and the remoteness of a skerry.

Nevertheless, each of Ibsen's plays has a new and unique thematic structure, while almost every one of Strindberg's works features the tortured and lamenting autobiographer at the center. Ibsen's plays are not simply guided by his confidence in the educatability of the contemporary human being for a more humane social order, they are also illuminated by a glow of lavishness, abundance, and splendor that was associated with the fertile periods of the bourgeoisie. These plays truly are works of poetry; even some of their titles conjure an atmosphere of beauty, a picturesque atmosphere, an artistic promise which the plays themselves fulfill. The common conception that Ibsen's characters are only the incarnation of slogans is actually a criticism that is much more appropriate for Strindberg's theatre. Think in particular of his continuous efforts to persuade us of people's meanness, people for whom no one can, in the end, feel sorry—above all for the artist himself.

The harsh analysis and critique of society, which certainly included a moment of self-criticism, has by now been followed by the indefatigableness of hate derived from impotent loneliness. Strindberg is the classic literary witness for resentment. He turns the imperfection of social conditions, which the individual cannot even touch, into a world that is absolutely evil and which only deserves malicious responses. Strindberg's bohemian characteristics ought be seen in this context. The bohemian represents the most exaggerated case of bourgeois autonomy: he seeks to extend his self-sufficiency to the external conditions of his life. In the middle of the nineteenth century, the bohemian represented a progressive counterimage to the philistine, but in the course of development, this type is transformed into its opposite. The critical attitude toward traditional bourgeois evaluation and values turns into a blindness toward all human values in general, an instability that is without principles and which therefore ultimately can become venal.

In the bohemian occupants of attics, the future power holders of totalitarian states found a breed of ideologists who turned out to be quite useful for paving the march to power. And Strindberg stands exactly in the middle of this road that leads from the radical bohemian to the mercenary of ideas. At the same time, he also stands on the road that leads from bohemia to the philistine and his resentment is characteristic of the later phase of bourgeois development just as satiety was in an earlier phase. The life stories of basically nonconformist personages of this historic epoch lack the aura of sensational details, unless one wants to include persecution, police intimidation and material misery to which they are often exposed. On the other hand, more spicy biographies of artists who identified with the classical bohemian world have lastly an affinity to the average population satisfying a moment of wish fulfillment for fantasies denied them in the real world. Even the most banal person can find some fun in learning about Strindberg's unstable and bizarre day-to-day existence. But the morality in Ibsen's dramas cannot be assuaged by a bad social conscience.

Upon reading Mrs. Strindberg's memoirs and her husband's letters, the affinity between bohemia, resentment and conformity becomes apparent. Those who nourish an image of an artist as has him leading an inconsiderate and shocking life, will be rewarded by this book. Strindberg's work habits, his travels, the people he meets, the things he renounces and those which he pursues relentlessly, his attitude and behavior—all of it is completely unpredictable. This solitary individual renders himself even more lonely through the arrangements of his daily life, which are usually conditioned or at least justified by annoyance. In two respects, however, the writer makes his peace with the world; and the matters involved are the most indispensable of bourgeois life: money and virtue.

"It is money, always money," Mrs. Strindberg once exclaims in despair (p. 269). The lack of money never leaves the writer and his close family. One might expect that the tenaciousness with which Strindberg usually holds onto moments that he experiences as negative and seeks to uncover their origins, would be activated with respect to the phenomenon of money as well. Indeed, one might even expect that the anger and resentment of his individualism would give him access to the relationship between the arbitrary character of private property and the necessity of its unequal distribution. He could have learned a great deal about this from his predecessors, the naturalists. But in his writings, he transforms their critical concept of "nature" (human and extrahuman) into a negative and reified state. If the authority and power of the male really does have its social roots in his economic superiority, then Strindberg's own economic insufficiency becomes for him a matter of guilt. "What right do I have to call you my wife if I cannot support you and am almost at the point of having to allow you to provide for me?" he writes to his wife (p. 273). Once, when he is suffering extreme poverty, he is indignant about his wife's intention to send him some money that she had come by: "what you write about the money you plan to send is incomprehensible to me. Are you responsible for feeding me?" (p. 257). When he describes himself in his unsteady, monadic manner as a "man of the future," who is so masculine a male that he has to do his utmost to hide it (p. 296), his relationship to money is playing a trick on him: that which is considered typically male today, namely, a reified self-consciousness of the economically ruling gender, has been exposed.

If one considers abstractly and without any content this contradiction between the happy-go-lucky bohemian and the conforming average bourgeois, then it appears as a coincidental, pathologically explainable biographic event. When seen as a social phenomenon, however, it becomes explicable once one sees this very same bohemian, not ignoring so-called universally accepted values but subjecting himself to this convention.

Even more surprising than Strindberg's concern with money is his tendency to puritan virtuousness, which emerges from these memoirs. Close scrutiny reveals considerable material that will put an end to the literary legend about Wedekind's extremely strong dependence on Strindberg. Wedekind, too, is a moralist, but his conception of morality is characterized by an anticonformist moment: he proclaims the moral character of lust and desire, indeed, of immediate and sensuous desire. For Strindberg, the man who had three wives, exponent of the bohemian scene in Paris and Berlin, guest of the most extravagant bars and social circles, desire is never an articulated concern. On the contrary: the impotence of disappointed loneliness returns via resentment, to the conventionality of virtue of abstinence, of strict morality in marriage, of a traditional legitimation of exclusive sexual relations by an alliance of formalistic legality and a socially approved emotional apparatus. Strindberg cannot forgive himself or his wife for their curious interest in an event that transpires, in their presence, in a Parisian cafe: "Why do you want to study the artificial preparations for intercourse? This study only is good for a cocotte. You don't need it. Do understand: everything that you perceive you in fact also experience" (p. 489).

If there is still any doubt whether Strindberg's prudishness was really sincere, we have only to read the verdict he pronounced on his wife's social behavior: "A married woman, who has dates and rendezvous with unmarried men, is no longer a respectable woman. . . . You do not notice your wrong-doing because you live according to instinct and do not distinguish good from evil" (p. 506). What is good, in other words, is the conventional norm, what is evil is its violation. It is actually quite ironic: Strindberg's individualist accusation against the world subverts its own raison d'être: not only does he fail to deduce this right to individual happiness from the continuous violation by the outside world, but he actually slanders the very claim to happiness.

Strindberg's most conscious insults are not directed against the existing state of affairs and the holders of power, but against women. For him, they are the natural and immutable expression of those miserable conditions from which he suffers but fails to attack directly. Whatever his contribution might have been to increasing our psychological understanding of the specific role of woman disenfranchised in this society, he ultimately confuses cause and effect and turns the effect into an untrue caricature. When he describes women as people who "distort, torment, humiliate," when he talks about their veneration of swindle and mediocrity (p. 420), one might expect that he is referring to economic reality out there rather than to the private existence of women. When he claims that one can never rely on a loving woman (p. 439), when he reproaches his wife for wishing that he should love his child, "his rival," as he calls it (p. 501), he captures something of the animosity and competition that is inherent in the existing order, which permeates even the most private relationships. But he never comes close to understanding the status quo itself. Strindberg lives—without being aware of it—a private life that is constrained by competition; and it was Ibsen who showed clearly the tragedy of this inescapable fate.

Strindberg shares with the entire bourgeois epoch an ideological ascetic opposition to complete joy; but, in addition, he builds a bridge between this posture and certain other traits which only come to full fruition in the heroic nationalism of our time. His dislike of Rubens— "too much flesh and fleshiness" (p. 68)—only brings to consciousness the resentment that he shares with every philistine, even if the latter would not be willing to admit his dislike of the great masters for whom he has been taught to have respect. When in one of Strindberg's dreams of a "new kind of human existence . . . the blessed . . . are released from the animalistic, from carnal and sensual existence" (p. 69), then the dream is a psychological projection of the enforced denial demanded by society. But the religious sanctification with which he endows this imagined new species anticipates the mythology of blood, before which all claims to individuality must be silenced. He knows it better than "the general opinion": He "does not believe in the pains" of birth. "He believes that giving birth is part of the bliss of the fall of man" (p. 388). He does not mind sprucing up his little home together with his wife, and when this work is finished, he exclaims: "It is magnificent, now we can welcome the child" (p. 384). These activities and opinions seem almost to be a vignette of totalitarian population politics. They show a painful proximity to that ideology which seeks to veil the fact that people are cheated of happiness by conceding to them only one legitimate happiness: their contribution to the succession of generations connected by blood ties.

This biography makes much of Strindberg's doubtful "scientific endeavors"—of his efforts to create gold, to prove that sulphur is not an atom, to refute that air contains nitrogen. His naturalization of human beings has tempted him to search for the key to all existence in the science of nature. But all that is left of the scientific spirit of the liberal bourgeois is a distorted image and dilettanteism. Strindberg's own positivistic creed, that "laws of nature can usually be applied to the psychic life of human beings as well" (p. 444), a creed which he tries to support with simplistic generalizations, represents not so much an ideological pattern of upwardly mobile strata that subjugates nature to its own social and individual purposes; rather, it is part of a rising human type who has learned so little from history that he is willing to accept the most stagnant phrases, the naked lie of power.

Strindberg plays a decisive role in the history of the decline of the originally humane motives of the naturalistic school which tried to demonstrate by critical analysis that the individual became increasingly corrupt in competitive society. Thus what was imposed on the individual by society was judged to be not only negative but changeable. But the transfiguration of this bad, socially grounded "naturalism" of the human being into the very essence of humanity, the interpretation of man as nothing but naked nature, the forsaking of any image of another transcendental or secular world—this reductionist change from history to nature is implicitly present in Strindberg's works. Where man is comprehended as the embodiment of bodily reactions, the road is cleared for a legitimation of his existence by criteria of blood and race.

In this context I am not concerned with Strindberg's art per se. Instead, I want to show the effect of the reception of such a book in our time (1938). It illustrates how even a highly sophisticated intellectual becomes a harbinger for a new mode of behavior patterns which by now have taken hold of broad strata. In his own time, Strindberg was conceived as a critic, but ultimately his critique turned into conformity—not that of liberal but of authoritarian society. In the work of one of his less-talented followers, Knut Hamsun, such transition from autonomy into isolation, from critique into resentment, from bohemia into philistinism, from positivistic intellectualism into pure glorification of power—has become completely clear.

Note
On the occasion of the publication of Frida Strindberg *Lieb, Leid und Zeit* (Hamburg/Leipzig: H. Goverts, 1936).

7

Knut Hamsun, 1860–1952

In the periods studied so far, literary artists expressed through their characters the conviction that the activities of the individual are rooted in universally binding values and that therefore these fictional life histories could serve as a parable or a stimulus to others. By the end of the nineteenth century, however, the artist ceases to reflect this ideal of the ethical unity of men.

At his best the modern writer, like all writers, keeps alive the hopes of the individual and the ideal of his self-realization in society; even the defeats he portrays are meaningful within this context. At his worst, however, he can fall victim to an irrational escape into the arms of authoritarianism. Knut Hamsun was this kind of writer. In the twenties and thirties his work not only enjoyed an excellent international literary reputation but also was regarded—even by liberals and socialists—as politically above reproach. However, in his act of joining Quisling's party during the Second World War, he expressed in practice the authoritarian themes and moods that had long been implicit in his novels: the pagan awe of unlimited and unintelligible forces of nature, the mystique of blood and race, hatred of the working class and of clerks, the blind submission to authority, the abrogation of individual responsibility, antiintellectualism, and spiteful distrust of urban middle-class life in general.[1]

Nature

In Ibsen, the hymn to nature as a last gesture of hope comes at the end of his final play, *When We Dead Awaken*. Man has found, in the social realm, not true freedom but only a mirage. By contrast with its pressures and restrictions, nature appears as a realm of freedom and a source of happiness and consolation. In enjoyment of the countryside, nothing seems to remain of the perpetual toil and responsibility, competition and even hostility. Communion with nature holds out a new image of man, one that will counter the image of himself as a victim.

The meaning of nature in almost every age is inseparable from social considerations. In the Renaissance, nature meant at once a scene of man's activities, a field for conquest, and an inspiration; it formed the *mise-en-scène* of men's lives. To be sure, even then there was an element of protest—the idyls of natural life in the works of Cervantes and Shakespeare implied a rejection of the contemporary "unnatural" society. Nevertheless the concept of nature as a counter-ideal to society strengthened the optimistic belief in progress, since it provided men with a yardstick against which shortcomings could be more clearly seen and evaluated. In the history of Western European drama from Shakespeare to Ibsen, and of poetry from Petrarch to Hölderlin, the path to nature was not a flight but a stroll toward liberation.

However, with the coming of doubt and even despair about personal fulfillment within society, the image of nature was no longer a basis for a new perspective, but became an alternative. Nature was increasingly envisaged as the ultimate surcease of social pressure. In this context, man could submit to nature and feel at peace—at least in phantasy. His soul, inviolable in ideology yet outraged in reality, could find solace in such a submission; frustrated in his attempt to participate autonomously in the societal world, he could join the world of nature. He could become a "thing," like the tree or the brook, and find more pleasure in this surrender than in a hopeless struggle against man-made forces. This is the most significant change in man's imagery of his environment to take place in the closing decades of the nineteenth century in Europe. The novels of Knut Hamsun portray this antinomy of society and nature in an extreme form.

Sentimentalism and Brutality

The image of nature in Hamsun's novels has little in common with earlier conceptions of nature as a source of directives for human conduct. It lacks the critical element that made Rousseau's naturalism, for example, a progressive political and cultural force in the eighteenth century. Since the Renaissance man had seen himself able, at least potentially, to conquer some of nature's forces. This attitude reflected his faith in the unlimited potential of reason and, specifically, his hope for political and social reconstruction.

In Hamsun, submission to nature functions as an escape from the burden of social responsibility. This passive attitude in part explains why Hamsun's heroes are able to profess sentimental pity for the unsheltered animal, the tree in the wind, or for the withering foliage. In the fate of nature's children, they see a reflection of their own helplessness. To be a victim in the world of men is a threat to dignity. There is a certain solace, on the other hand, in being a victim of majestic natural forces for which man cannot be expected to be personally accountable.

Paradoxically, this new type of submission to nature is closely related to political submission. The yearning for surrender to nature as it appears in Hamsun's novels not only glorifies the awareness of individual weakness but at the same time exalts reverence for superior power in general. In our time we have seen in Europe's totalitarian movements the apotheosis of unshakable political authority—unshakable, in part, because one cannot fathom it. The timelessness and magnificence of nature reinforces the finality of the political power under which man lives. The yearning at once for stability and for glory is a trait of fascist ideologies (Hitler's "thousand years of history") that appears alongside this new type of nature worship.

The home, in the Victorian period particularly, was a refuge from the harshness of business and professional life. In Ibsen, we saw the idyl of the home devoured by the monster of competition, and nature appeared on the horizon as the Utopian realm of hope. In Hamsun, flight to nature as protest becomes flight to nature as idolatry, and communion with nature is transformed from sentiment into sentimentality, and then into brutality.

Implicit in this change is an element of anti-intellectualism. The use of reason, in whatever form, is indissolubly bound up with the responsibility of the thinker. Thus the flight to nature for the sake of abdication of human responsibility soon comes to be rationalized in thought that abhors thinking. This anti-intellectualism must be distinguished from vitalist and pragmatist philosophies earlier in this century. Bergson, Dilthey, and certain American philosophers rebelled against rationalist rigidity, to be sure, but their works were nonetheless responsible theoretical enterprises oriented toward the goal of higher individual development. Vitalism (*Lebensphilosophie*) as it was taken up by the ideological spokesmen of fascism looked rather to the submergence of the individual; reason was rejected in favor of overpowering mythical forces, blood and race.

This submergence of reason accompanied a glorification of the peasant, an integral part of anti-liberal undercurrents. The peasant is seen as not alienated from his work; unlike the industrial worker, he does not seem to violate nature but follows, so to speak, its true rhythm. Since his work is hard, healthy, meaningful, and in harmony with natural processes, it is set forth as the model of true manliness, dignified and silent. In the analysis that follows, an effort will be made to show that the sentimental conceptions of nature and peasant in Hamsun's novels anticipate an intrinsic part of those political ideologies that forge the concepts of leader, social coercion and soil into a tool of brutality.

Flight into Nature

At first slight, Hamsun does not seem qualified to represent the emergence of a typically modern European authoritarian ethos. (It is noteworthy, however, that it was in Germany that Hamsun obtained his greatest response from the very beginning.) Coming from a small country that, unlike the larger nations, has primary economic interests in agriculture and fishing, Hamsun might be expected to portray themes different from those of writers in highly industrialized nations. But, in fact, it is just this disparity between Norwegian conditions and the situation of the larger and industrially more advanced countries that makes Hamsun's picture of his society so reassuring at first glance and so foreboding upon closer analysis.[2]

Hamsun's first novel, *Hunger,* written in autobiographical form and published in 1890, states the themes that are almost endlessly repeated in the later novels: abandonment of any participation in public life, submission to the stream of incomprehensible and incalculable forces, distrust of the intellect, flight from the city and escape to nature.

The opening sentence of *Hunger* evokes the fate of the average city dweller:

> It was during the time I wandered about and starved in Christiania; Christiania, this singular city, from which no man departs without carrying away the traces of his sojourn there.[3]

The theme of the city is set at once. The fate of the hero is not comprehensible in terms of any conditions specific to him (he is, in this case, luckless and starving), but only in terms of the most general fact, the city. When he has finally had his fill and leaves as a newly hired sailor, the novel ends on the same note with which it began:

> Out in the fjord I dragged myself up once, wet with fever and exhaustion, and gazed landwards, and bade farewell for the present to the town—to Christiania, where the windows gleamed so brightly in all the homes.[4]

One of Hamsun's figures once replied to an apologist for the city:

> You have your home in the city, it is true, and you have decorated it with trinkets and pictures and books; but you have a wife and a maid and hundreds of expenses. In waking and sleeping you must struggle with things, and you never have peace. I have peace. Keep your spiritual goods and the books and art and newspapers, keep your coffee houses and your whiskey which always makes me sick. Here I can roam about the woods, and I feel fine. If you put intellectual problems to me and try to drive me into a corner, I merely reply that God is the source, and that men are in truth only specks and threads in the universe. Even you have gone no further.[5]

The motif of peace is rare in Hamsun's writing;[6] its use here as the key to the blessings of rustic life could perhaps be interpreted as a legitimate protest against urban conditions. When, however, a protest in the name of a seemingly higher idea becomes a wholesale condemnation of civilization, when it does not discriminate between marketplace manipulation and family life, between the newspaper and artistic creations, between anxious restlessness and emotional pleasure, between the futility of mere distraction and the earnestness of serious reading—all of which Hamsun spurns with equal rancor—then we are not dealing with alert social criticism, but with anti-intellectual resentment. Hamsun in the same breath ridicules the cheap pictures on the wall and jeers at the intellect. The final outcome of such impotent resentment is the surrender to brute power.

But first we must trace the steps of this process. What did Hamsun's heroes seek and what did they find in their flight to nature?

Solitude

When Hamsun speaks of man's solitude in nature, he seems at first glance merely to advocate liberation from the pressures of society:

> And there is another thing with which I am never finished, namely, retreating and sitting in the solitude of the woods, surrounded by beauty and darkness. That is the final joy.[7]

Nature appears to hold forth the promise of fulfilling the desire for relationships in which gratitude, joy, and rest can come to fruition:

> Thanks for the lonely night, for the hills, the rush of the darkness and the sea through my heart! Thanks for my life, for my breath, for the boon of being alive to-night; thanks from my heart for these! . . . By my immortal soul, I am full of thanks that it is I who am sitting here![8]

But on closer inspection, it becomes clear that a new approach is in the making, according to which nature is more than a soothing balm:

> You must not believe that nothing happens here . . . I could send significant tales from here, but I don't do it. I have sought the woods for solitude and for the sake of my great irons. I have a few great irons within me, and they are getting red hot.[9]

These passages do not conjure up an idyllic and peaceful image of nature, but introduce a note of boastful resentment. A few pages later in the novel, the hero, thinking of the reindeer, ponders the secrets of his existence:

> I think all these things.
>
> And you? Have you compared your two newspapers, and do you know now what is the public opinion in Norway today about old age insurance?[10]

Hamsun anticipates his imagined antagonist's retort, and with considerable resentment:

> Here you will certainly help yourself and make sport of me; you can say many droll things about the tree stump and me. But deep down you know that I am superior to you in this as in everything else, once I admit that I do not have as much city knowledge and that I was no student, ha ha. You can teach me nothing about wood and fields, for there I feel what no man has felt.[11]

The idea of a private kingdom to which man stubbornly clings (we have only to think of the dreams of fulfillment with which Ibsen endows his women) is transferred by Hamsun to the solitude of nature. This nature, however, is not merely an extra-human place where one can go and from which one can return; it is a substitute for human society. Nature is the seat of magical qualities of a new kind. In the old fairy tales, men learn to speak the language of animals; in order to be lords of all creation, they seek to overcome the barriers of nature by bringing the animal world into the human through the medium of speech. Hamsun's hero, however, seeks to draw from nature the meaning which he can no longer deduce from history. What he "overhears" (the tales he could tell but does not) is not meant to increase man's knowledge of his world and himself; if the tales were told, they would report only his own resentment and contempt.

Identity

The philosophy of liberalism did not encompass the idea that the whole world had come within man's power. Subject and object were opposed in the forms of active man and conquerable nature. Nature was raw material and man the unrealized potential; man realized himself in its conquest. Social relationships were implicit in this interaction; the knowledge of nature was won through communication of man with man, and nature was transformed by organized societal enterprise. The relationship toward which Hamsun's ideas tend is of a totally different kind. Nature is no longer looked upon as an object for scientific and practical control; instead Hamsun's hero consecrates his life in rapt surrender to nature and even in mystical identification:

> We are in the midst of an omnipresence. That is truly God. That is truly we ourselves as parts of the whole.[12]

To Hamsun, nature means peace, but a peace which has lost its spontaneity and its will to know and to control. It is a peace based on submission to every arbitrary power, a pantheism which offers an escape from the gloomy framework of history. Nature comes to mean the solace of the unchangeable and the all-pervasive:

> He lost himself, was carried away and wrapt in the frenzy of sunshine. . . . He was in a mysterious state, filled with psychic pleasure; every nerve in him was awake; he had music in his blood, felt akin to all nature, to the sun and the mountains and everything else, felt surrounded by a whisper of his own ego-sense from trees and tufts and blades of grass.[13]

The hero avoids asking any embarrassing questions about the rest of mankind. He shows concern only for his own fate. There is even a hint that nature is his private property and that his enjoyment of it is a kind of personal possession. Paragraph after paragraph of exalted description communicates neither observation nor knowledge, but only a desire for personal omnipotence and for pantheistic possession of the world by emotional immersion:

> The sky all open and clean; I stared into that clear sea, and it seemed as if I were lying face to face with the uttermost depth of the world; my heart beating tensely against it, and at home there.[14]

The timelessness of such pantheism gives the illusion of an immediate, complete possession of the entire world, a possession that at the same time cuts off historical progress. Gone is the optimistic dualism of liberalistic philosophy which always maintained close contact with history, considered the transitoriness of the human situation, and often gave birth to a conception of the future, Utopian to be sure, in which a final stasis of perfection might be reached.

Hamsun's identification with the whole of nature can be consummated with no exertion and with no fear of disillusionment. What the Utopians had envisioned as a potential unity of man and nature comes to be proclaimed as already realized: the meaning of man's life is to be found in natural factors such as blood and soil. When such a myth is consciously used in the interests of a power apparatus, as it was under fascism, men are told that their inevitable and irrevocable share of nature is their "race" and their nation.

Fury

The shift to an authoritarian concept of nature is apparent also in the changed imagery of the fury of the elements. Compare Hamsun's descriptions with similar ones in earlier literature. Hamsun writes:

> Lightning flashes, and soon thereafter the thunder rolls like an immense avalanche far beyond, between the mountains . . . Lightning again, and the thunder is closer at hand; it also begins to rain, a driving rain, the echo is very powerful, all nature is in an uproar, a chaos. I want to enfeeble the night by yelling at it, otherwise it will deprive me mysteriously of all my strength and will power. . . . More lightning and thunder and more driving rain, it is as if I were whipped by the echo nearby.[15]

Kant, too, once wrote about the power of nature:

> Bold, overhanging, and, as it were, threatening rocks, thunderclouds piled up to the vault of heaven, borne along with flashes and peals, volcanoes in all their violence of destruction, hurricanes leaving desolation in their track, the boundless ocean rising with rebellious force, the high waterfall of some mighty river.[16]

At first sight there appears to be no essential difference between the two passages. For Kant, however, the sublimity of nature and the experience of man's helplessness before it are counterbalanced by the concept of nature as subordinate in the face of humanity. It is man's own knowledge and imagination which creates the conception of the grandiosity in nature that dwarfs him. In the end, the rational faculties of man are of a higher order than the elemental force of nature, and they allow him to see it as sublime, instead of simply terrifying:

> We readily call these objects sublime, because they raise the forces of the soul above the height of vulgar commonplace, and discover within us a power of resistance of quite another kind, which gives us courage to be able to measure ourselves against the seeming omnipotence of nature.[17]

Thus for Kant, nature is not to console man for frustrations, but to stimulate his moral and intellectual development.

In Hamsun, the relation of man to nature takes on an entirely different cast.

> I stood in the shelter of an overhanging rock, thinking many things; my soul was tense. Heaven knows, I thought to myself, what it is I am watching here, and why the sea should open before my eyes. Maybe I am seeing now the inner brain of earth, how things are at work there, boiling and foaming.[18]

The locus of knowledge has become nature itself, mysterious and beyond man's capacities to know. Hamsun's questions are framed so they cannot be answered; his tired individuals seek to silence themselves as quickly as possible. They really have nothing to say, and they welcome the storm that can roar loudly enough to drown out their own silence. The relationship of man to nature as seen by Kant is reversed; for Hamsun the storm serves as an occasion for increasing the individual's awareness of his own insignificance.

> When a moment of sadness and realization of my own nothingness in the face of all the surrounding powers comes over me. I lament and think: Which man am I now, or am I perhaps lost, am I perhaps no longer existent! And I speak aloud and call my name, in order to hear whether he is still present.[19]

Anxiety enters as a component of Hamsun's pantheism. Kant's pride in human autonomy is replaced by a sentimental uneasiness that is announced in every thunderstorm and that is subsequently ramified as a jumble of mawkish sympathies for both natural objects and spiritual difficulties.[20] Hamsun's nature world fore-shadows the affinity of brutality and sentimentality, a well-known phenomenon in Nazi Germany.

Rhythm

When Hamsun speaks of nature, it is generally the forest and the sea. In the world of the forest, the law of rhythm, another significant element in Hamsun's imagery of nature, emerges:

> There is nothing more glorious than the soughing of the woods. It is like swinging, rocking—a madness: Uganda, Antananarivo, Honolulu, Atacama, Venezuela.[21]

The countries and cities have no concrete significance: what is essential is the sound of their names, which serves only to evoke and echo the order of natural motion. The rhythmic cycle of the seasons is also incessantly noted in the novels, where hypnotic prose again seems to imitate the phenomeon itself:

> Then came the autumn, then came the winter.[22]
>
> But the road leads on, summer follows spring in the world.[23]
>
> The days passed, time passed.[24]

Innumerable sentences of this kind sometimes take the form of a linguistic leitmotif, such as the ruthlessness of life, the procession of the seasons, the march of time, the men who go over the field or walk along the road, the measured steps of life, and so forth.[25] Elsewhere we find the seasonal and the daily rhythms unified:

> It is the autumn season now, a silence in the woods all round; the hills are there, the sun is there, and at evening the moon and the stars will come; all regular and certain, full of kindness, an embrace.[26]

The rhythmic principle can also take on a normative character. What is wrong with certain people is that

> they won't keep pace with life . . . but there's none should rage against life.[27]

Even man's sexual relationships are oriented to the regularity of nature. The shepherdess will walk past the hunter's cabin in the autumn just as infallibly as she comes to him in the spring:

> The autumn, the winter, had laid hold of her too: her senses drowsed.[28]

Uniformity of rhythm and tempo is sought in both the natural and human spheres; the passage of time brings recurrence, and not change.

Nature's timetable replaces the timetable of history. This tendency displays the same simplification that is found in Hamsun's selection of landscapes. Whoever senses and accepts these rhythmic patterns as fundamental has full knowledge immediately and without rational effort. At the same time, the endless reproduction of natural phenomena, the cyclic order of nature, as opposed to the apparent disorder and happenstance of all individual and historical facts, testifies to the powerlessness of man. It is the extreme opposite of human self-assurance before nature. In this new ideology, which seeks to transfigure helplessness and subjection, the individual in seemingly free volition lays down his arms before a mythical power. Once, nature was held to be "autonomous" only insofar as it was not yet recreated as the product of human activity. Now, however, man must expect a life without meaning unless he obediently accepts as his own what may be called the law of nature. And the social counterpart to the law of natural rhythm is blind discipline.

Hero Worship

When Hamsun speaks of the forces of nature to which man should subject himself, it is, as we have noted, mostly of the woods and the sea. But when he speaks of man himself, as he should be, he leaves these unspoiled provinces behind and speaks foremost of farming. Hamsun's emphasis is not upon the social conditions of the farm; rather, he is again involved in constructing the myth which demands the necessity of man's submission to nature. The peasant tunes himself to forces stronger than himself, and that is supposed to be the lesson he can teach us. In addition vigorous youth and women are portrayed as truly obedient to nature's forces. Hamsun gives us, in fact, a gallery of unheroic heroes, whose qualities are primarily those of subjection and discipline.

The Peasant

Hamsun's peasants are not individuals; they are aspects of nature, and his apparent admiration of them is not a love of man, but a reverence for the domination of nature over its inhabitants.

> His [the peasant's] life was spent in this work and that, according to the season; from the fields to the woods, and back to the fields again.[29]

This sentence is typical. The peasant himself is not charcterized; he is presented only as a natural phenomenon that comes and goes like the blossoming and withering of the leaves in the forest. That is precisely the identity which Hamsun seeks, an identity established by nature, not by man:

> ... looking up at blue peaks every day of your lives; no newfangled inventions about that, but field and rocky peaks, rooted deep in the past— but you've them for companionship. There you are. living in touch with heaven and earth, one with them, one with all these wide, deep-rooted things.[30]

The course of history is reversed: "Man and nature don't bombard each other."[31] In Hamsun, natue has no place for the individual as such; his irrelevancy is not only described but glorified in the person of the peasant who is reduced to a biological speck in the rhythm of life.

> 'Tis you that maintain life. Generation to generation, breeding ever anew; and when you die, the new stock goes on. That's the meaning of eternal life.[32]

Daniel is the name of this peasant, but any other peasant could serve as well. "Daniel was the same today as yesterday."[33] And the elements in nature with which the peasant deals are always the same, too.

> Wherever there was a tiny patch of fertile ground, there hay or potatoes or barley grew; in summer the cattle were out in the pasture, in winter they stood in their stalls—it was all so eternal and so changeless.[34]

In the course of the flight to nature, Hamsun's individual is stripped of his singular human qualities and subjected to "eternal" naturalness. "'Tis the land I'm here for."[35] Service to nature is the real law of peasant life, and happiness means only that he has fulfilled his naturalistic destiny. Only submission to the laws of nature that dictate, for example, the cultivation of grain makes man an admirable figure:

> Growth of the soil was something different, a thing to be procured at any cost; the only source, the origin of all.[36]

> For generations back, into forgotten time, his fathers before him had sowed corn; solemnly on a still, calm evening ... Corn was nothing less than bread; corn or no corn meant life or death.[37]

192

The products of cities are devaluated or totally ignored, in a kind of travesty of the theories of the physiocrats:

> "There isn't a human being anywhere in the world who can live on banks and industries. Not a single human being in the world."
> "Ho! What do they live on, then?"
> "On three things and nothing else," replies Ezra. "On the grain of the fields, the fish of the sea and the birds and beasts of the forest. On those three things. I've thought it all out."
> "There's quite a few that live on their money—"
> "No," said Ezra. "Not a single soul!"[38]

As contrasted with the emptiness of urban existence, the concreteness of the peasant's world seems to comprise the meaning of life itself:

> He did not feel poor and forlorn, as he really was; why, all the stones he had cleared looked just like a crowd of people around him, he was personally related to every stone, they were acquaintances every one, he had conquered them and got them out of the ground.[39]

The authoritarian state did not have to invent the idea of man's roots as being in blood and soil, nor devise the manipulation of this slogan as a solace for want. "We will not be any happier if we eat more bacon," says Hamsun's peasant in defending life on Norwegian soil against a life outside that might mean greater material success; the worst fate is

> to be torn up by the roots from our own barren soil and transplanted into richer . . . [40]

If we accept this belief, we do not scorn the hardest labor,[41] for we know "where we really do belong."[42]

> It is a good thing to belong to one's class, otherwise one becomes an upstart and gets one's originality frittered away.[43]

A good thing if you are a peasant, that is. Hamsun's eulogy of the peasant, apparently undertaken in the spirit of social critique, ends up as a sermon on temperance, humility, privation. The message is to keep one's roots where they are, even though the soil may be very poor indeed.

As we might expect, Hamsun combines his cult of the hero and that of the natural forces with praise for the vigor of youth per se. In comparison with this vigor, the restrained wisdom of maturity counts for little; the demand of youth for power is natural obedience to the "law of life."

> Old age should not be revered for its own sake, for it merely restricts and hinders the progress of mankind. Even primitive peoples despise old age,[44] and they emancipate themselves from it and its hindrances without further ado.[45]

He applies to human beings the lessons of biology—more precisely, of botany—thus:

> And what have you learned from the woods? But what did I learn in the woods? That there are young trees there.
>
> Now the young stand behind me, ridiculed shamelessly and barbarously by every fool, simply because they are young.[46]

This resentful yet sentimental sermon is tied to an attack on leaders who are old enough to have learned from experience.

> One should not rely too much on the leaders; the country's youth should be our hope. No; a leader is apt to prove a broken reed. It is an old law that whenever a leader reaches a certain age he pauses—yes, he even turns right about face and pushes the other way. Then it is up to the young to march on, to drive him ahead or trample him down.[47]

Hamsun's heroes do not often speak with such harsh frankness. He lends exultation to the rough tone of the young male in order to glorify manliness in general. He is happy that the peasant, reverent and serene as he is, knows how to bring his wife to her senses: "To think that a man's hard grip could work such wonders!"[48] The myth of manliness is created out of "natural" qualities of superior force.

The Vagabond

Along with the peasant, the vagabond receives affectionate treatment in every period of Hamsun's career. August, his favorite, longs "to shoot the knife out of the hand of a man who was trying to make off with his wallet" because that would be a thrill for the "children of the age" in their dreary existence.[49] As a matter of fact, Hamsun seems fascinated by such brutal mischief:

> And steal a bag of gold and silver plate from the market, and hide it in the mountains, so that a blue flame can float over the spot on autumn evenings. But don't come to me with three pairs of mittens and a side of bacon.[50]

In this pseudo-romantic flirting with a nuisance crime, he ridicules the "unheroic" spirit of urban efficiency ("no thunderbolt ever falls");[51] he cries for "gigantic demi-gods" and blunders into a political program of violence:

> The great terrorist is greatest, the dimension, the immense lever which can raise worlds.[52]

The peasant with his roots in the soil and the bohemian vagabond with no ties to anything may seem mutually exclusive idols. Still, Hamsun's ability to sympathize with such apparently opposite types has a certain logic; their common denominator is the rejection of organized urban culture, in favor of the application of raw, unmediated "natural" force. Incidentally, it was the socially uprooted literati (the "armed bohemians," as they have been called) who performed the spadework of German fascism, playing up the cult of the hero and the maintenance of one's roots in the soil.

In Hamsun, the function of such marginal figures as the vagabond is emphatically different from that in the literature thus far discussed. From Cervantes through Ibsen, marginal characters have stood outside society and criticized it in the name of freedom and self-determination. In Hamsun, however, such figures serve as coquettish expression of his veneration of brutality and power.

The Relation of the Sexes

The endorsement of violence and mischief seems to be a far cry from the theme of passive surrender to nature. But the connection between violence and passivity becomes unequivocal in Hamsun's treatment of the relation between the sexes. In his novels there is a conspicuous absence of genuine yearning for love. When one of his characters is seized by a strong passion, it is quickly transformed into sado-masochistic torment of himself or of the partner. This is as true of the desperate ecstasy of the hero in *Hunger,* or of the literally speechless and unexpressed affair between the main characters in *Victoria,* as of the mutual hatred of the partners in

Pan. The hero of *Mysteries* enjoys telling his beloved the most frightening and brutal stories;[53] the hero of *Pan* shoots his dog and sends the corpse as a farewell gift to the beloved from whom he has become estranged.[54]

What passes for love is closer to hostility:

> Does she then love a dead man to the point of hatred and cruelty and is she still trying to hurt him? Or is Glahn still alive and does she want to continue her torture?[55]

In general, however, sadism is much less developed than masochism. People seem to find happiness only when subjected to strength, power, and authority. On occasion one can readily observe the shift from sadism to masochism:

> Eva answers: "It was cruel of her to laugh at you."
> "No, it was not cruel of her," I cry . . . "it was only right that she should laugh at me. Be quiet, devil take you, and leave me in peace—do you hear?"
> And Eva, terrified, leaves me in peace. I look at her, and repent my harsh words at once; I fall down before her; wringing my hands. "Go home, Eva. It is you I love most. . . . It was only a jest; it is you I love."[56]

In one of his earliest novels as well as in one of his last, a lover asks for harsh treatment:

> Only you torture me too much with your forbearance; how can you put up with my having more than one eye? You ought to take the other, you ought to take both; you shouldn't allow me to walk along the street in peace and have a roof over my head.[57]

> Hurt me in return! Do you hear! Otherwise you'll go off and believe I've been ruined by some one, but that isn't true.[58]

Satisfaction in love seems possible only in the sexual sphere, and even then it is not because sensual pleasure signifies any feelings of affection and identification, but on the contrary springs from malice and disdain, particularly for women:

> "Come and show where there's cloudberries," said Gustaf . . . And how could a woman say no? Inger ran into her little room and was both earnest and religious for several minutes; but there was Gustaf standing waiting outside, the world was at her heels, and

all she did was to tidy her hair, look at herself carefully in the glass, and out again. And what if she did? Who would not have done the same? Oh, woman cannot tell one man from another; not always—not often.[59]

This spiteful eulogy of lust brings Hamsun back to his point of departure: the definition of man as mere nature. In an early novel promiscuity seems to thrive in gaiety and freedom:

"Iselin, I saw what you did," he says again; "I saw you."

And then her rich, glad laughter rings through the wood, and she goes off with him, full of rejoicing from top to toe. And whither does she go? To the next mortal man; to a huntsman in the woods.[60]

But even this cavalier concession to pleasure and satisfaction describes only another form of isolation, for there is complete lack of interest in the happiness of one's partner. Sexual relations are ruled by the laws of nature which men and women instinctively obey.

There she goes, a human being like the rest of us, a wanderer in the earth, a little girl, ah me! a life gone astray, a flying seed. She was fairly undejected in her walk. . . . She had the packet of papers under her arm, she knew what awaited her at the barn, and there she went. Some call it free will.[61]

He broke through all rules of propriety and was very friendly, picked the hay from her bosom, brushed it from her knees, stroked, patted, threw his arms around her. Some call it free will.[62]

Whatever is distinctly human and spiritual is forgotten. Love, which for Cervantes and Shakespeare appeared as the key phenomenon in the autonomous development of modern man, becomes reduced in Hamsun to a bawdy jeer at free will.

Women

Hamsun belittles Ibsen's women, and thumbs his nose at Ibsen himself for his description of Nora (in *A Doll's House*):

I know a sage, and he wrote of woman. Wrote of woman, in thirty volumes of uniform theatre poetry: I counted the volumes once in a big bookcase. And at last he wrote of the woman who left her own children to go in search of—the wonderful! But what, then, were the children? Oh, it was comical: a wanderer laughs at anything so comical.[63]

Woman attains fulfillment of her destiny when she limits her functions to those of a housewife and a mother. This enshrinement of biological function leads Hamsun to bitter hatred for any emancipation, intellectuality, or political reforms that women might desire[64] and finally, in an attack on actresses, to utter contempt for the "modern woman":

> You ladies pretend to look down on domestic life, pretend to be indifferent to the scanty personal respect you enjoy; you are either not mothers at all, or very bad ones, either incapable of bringing up children or pitifully incompetent at it—every day of your lives you sink into deeper shame on account of this impotence. That is the truth.[65]

The ideal peasant woman, wife of the ideal peasant in *Growth of the Soil,* unpleasant in appearance and not always faithful, has a meaningful existence as a housewife and mother: A "good nature, a clever nature,"[66]

> the Margravine . . . is indoors preparing the meal. Tall and stately, as she moves about her house, a Vestal tending the fire of a kitchen stove. Inger has made her stormy voyage, 'tis true, has lived in a city a while, but now she is home.[67]

This theme is constantly reiterated: woman receives her true consecration as a mother. Of the tragic ruin of a woman who sought to run away from an unsatisfying marriage only this is said:

> She had no occupation, but had three maidservants to her house; she had no children, but she had a piano. But she had no children.[68]

It is another woman, a paragon of mediocrity, who receives the accolade:

> A mother many times, realizing life—it was worthy of a great reward.[69]

In such idealization of fertility, biology takes precedence over the conventions of middle-class morality; as in the case of Inger, sexual vicissitudes are blinked at—indeed are condoned—provided the end or denouement is that of producing children. This was also a stock in trade of the Nazi ideology, which reduced womanhood to a biological function. Hamsun's language becomes almost epic when he speaks of woman as the bearer of progeny: she becomes a fertility-heroine:

> A real girl shall marry, shall become the wife of a man, shall become a mother, shall become a blessing to herself.[70]

Urban Society

The idolatry of nature is set up against "a world where cheating goes on in the dark"[71] The composition of this rejected world is quite apparent. It is, in brief, an inventory of modern urban society that Hamsun condemns—industry,[72] public officials,[73] the natural sciences,[74] the teaching profession,[75] the coffee house,[76] the corporation,[77] and countries under liberal governments—as well as the city, the intellectuals, the workers and platforms of social reform; these are all surveyed in the novels and dismissed as hateful. Significant, for example, are his contemptuous remarks on Gladstone,[78] and his rejection of "the modern type, a man of our time," who believes "all the Jew and the Yankee have taught him."[79] He has warm words of praise for Sweden because she is oriented toward Germany, not toward Switzerland.[80] and he tells the English that they "will someday be whipped to death by the healthy destiny of Germany."[81]

Numerous are his attacks on Switzerland—not just coincidentally the model of democratic experimentation. In one of his novels, a man plans to build a comfortable home for his family in the "Swiss fashion." He is taken to task by Hamsun for believing he can learn something

> from a miserable little people up in the Alps, a people that throughout its history has never been or done anything worth speaking of.[82]

These attacks are typical of a romanticizing primitivism anticipating in literature the sneering propaganda of the middle-European authoritarian parties against "effeminacy" and the "morass" of the big cities. When Hamsun assumes the posture of social critic, he focuses his attention only on superficial, secondary aspects of industrial society. Everything the inquiring mind finds of interest and of crucial importance—including consideration for mutual help—is flattened out, or swept away with an imperious gesture. Not accidentally, a chief butt of his ridicule are the manufacturers of consumer goods, whom he epitomizes in those who seem most readily to lend themselves to caricature, such as producers of canned goods, candies and herring-meal.[83] "Butter?" he asks:

> One did not churn butter any more—one went to the store and bought margarine. Storehouse and shed full of meat, pork and fish? One would have died of laughter at anybody who kept salt meat . . . wasn't there food to he had in tins—tinned food? It was ready cooked, it was chewed too, it was ready to put into a cloth to make a child's sucker of for all mankind. . . . What did mouths want with teeth anymore? Weren't there false teeth hanging on a string in the toothmaker's shop? And as for the tinned foods . . . it dealt gently with people who had already got stomach-trouble from eating it.[84]

Middle Class

For Hamsun, intellectuals and public officials exemplify middle-class triviality. The work of the journalist, the teacher and the historian find no favor in his eyes.[85] Scientists are represented as having wrought a permanent injury against man; science is an empty mechanism, an incomprehensible hodge-podge of data.[86]

The brunt of the attack is on civil servants[87] and clerks in general:

> Officials—believe me, they are a miserable tribe. . . . Nothing but mediocre abilities and stunted energies; the triumph of the commonplace.[88]

In the midst of a hymn to nature ("I am never done with grass and stones"), Hamsun plunges into an attack on the "sons of clerks," the "official residence," and the "garden of the commonplace" where everything is decided "on account of age, length of service, and school learning."[89]

> With such useless hands as theirs, which they could turn to no manual labor, they could only sit in an office writing . . . such servile work as writing the letters of the alphabet. . . . The most that can befall them is to fail in an examination. . . . I pity them . . . bent over a table so long that they are round-shouldered; they are helpless with their hands; they generally wear glasses—a sign that as learning poured into their brains, it sucked the sight from their eyes.[90]

Now—as we see the clerk, the bureaucrat, the intellectual portrayed as sickly, decadent, impotent—there emerges by implication the counter-image of the self-assured, vigorous, tough Nordic hero. Those who do not display these virtues are summarily disqualified.

Working Class

Contempt for factory workers and for workers' movements permeates Hamsun's novels. It first appears in the disguise of his romanticizing naturalism:

> What was more, I liked to be among field and forest, not with lumbermen and proletariat.[91]

But soon in the same novel the disguise falls away and resentment comes to the fore:

> These gentlemen of the proletariat think a good deal of themselves; they look down on farm workers, and will have nothing to do with them. . . . Then, too, they are more popular among the girls. It is the same with men working on roads or railways, with all factory hands . . .[92]

This contemptuous sarcasm remains a key motif. In one of his last novels we read:

> The moment that Alex had found himself with a job and with money in his pocket, food in his belly and clothes on his back, he had crawled to his feet and begun stalking around like a man, had even applied for membership in the trade union, to which he pointed with considerable pride.[93]

The competitive interwovenness of urban lower strata appears as a threat to the "heroic" status quo—life on the soil.

> The others, the workingmen, businessmen, the day-labourers, go about showing their teeth at one another and fighting. That is life. They are really fighting over the old landowner, they are fighting over his possessions.[94]

For Hamsun the struggle for an increase in material welfare is merely vulgar. Whatever rational justifications such claims may have is no concern of his. He engages in a variety of attacks on "the proletariat's strong and blind craving for food,"[95] on "the roar of the masses," who unfortunately have learned from "mechanical reading and writing" how beautiful it is to "live by others' labor."[96] But worst of all are the destructive tendencies that are bound up with the workingman's "worldly greed."

> They [the masses] want to roar and turn things upside down, and when it comes to a pinch even their own leaders can't hold them in. The whole thing's crashing, let it crash![97]

Here indeed we are face to face with the nihilistic furor of the authoritarian mentality.

Nihilism

Antiintellectualism

At the peak of liberalist optimism, popular manifestations of confidence in scientific progress made the coffee houses and beer halls the layman's university, with natural science, medicine, and politics the favorite subjects in the curriculum. True, these flourishing ideas were without influence, not only in the groves of Academe, but in society at large; still, the constant critical concern with the affairs of science and public life served to perpetuate a confidence in the efficacy of each member of society.

The incomprehensibility and inexorability of the social process has increasingly given rise to pseudophilosophies and pseudosociologies which claim to possess superior wisdom, keys to the mystery of human relationships, recipes for the best and quickest possible solution to man's dilemmas. The attraction, in recent decades, of innumerable panaceas for curing the ills of the world through programs which promise to discover the meaning of life in nature illustrates this trend. Nudism, astrology, dietary and breathing fads are cases in point. Man seeks to draw from nature the meaning he cannot find in society.

At the same time, the results of science and education are often not experienced by broad strata of the population as aids to progress. What was actually to be gained from the work of the natural scientists, from the apparatus of schools and other cultural institutions?—so people asked. To the extent that these activities seemed unrelated to universal improvement in material welfare, an impression grew that learning was an empty program, busywork, or pointless pastime. Antiintellectualism is intimately linked with disillusionment in the credo of progress among broad social strata in Europe. To them, the intellect appeared either as an instrument of domination or as an abstract conglomeration of phrases and slogans having no reference to their own concerns.

This loss of faith by Europeans in their rationalistic daydreams, wherein their power had seemed to grow without bonds, was given respectability by the anti-liberal literati's devaluation of reason. Hamsun's antiintellectualism soon became apparent in his attacks on earlier nineteenth-century writers. One of his heroes calls Maupassant "crude and soulless."[98] Tolstoi "a fool in philosophy" who talks "twaddle,"[99] and Ibsen a "little writing oddity"[100] who has brought shame upon his country, a land which has engendered nothing but "peace conferences, the skiing spirit, and Ibsen so far."[101] In 1892, Hamsun already contributed to the authoritarian *Führer* cult—which jeers at the moral anxieties and compulsions of the intellectual, while arrogantly exalting the morally insensate body-beautiful ideal of the racial hero—when he joined his contempt for one of Ibsen's more remarkable sayings with an alleged physical weakness of the playwright:

> The great poet produces a pursed-lips expression, braces his chicken breast to the utmost, and delivers himself of the following words: "To make poetry is to summon oneself to the Day of Judgment."[102]

Philosophy of Life

Hamsun's heroes are querulous in posing the problem of their destiny. The hungry one asks:

> Was the hand of the Lord turned against me? But why just against me? Why, for that matter, not just as well against a man in South America?[103]

The journalist Lynge never finds an answer to his question:

> Why could not everything be good, and why could not men be happy in life?[104]

A lover poses the problem:

> The other he loved as a slave, as a madman and a beggar. Why? Ask the dust of the road and the leaves that fall, ask the mysterious God of life, for there is no other that knows such things.[105]

When August, the vagabond, meets with misfortune, the question is raised:

> Possibly somewhere away out in a universe there was a great eye which was watching him, a power which in some way or another had learned of his labours in the desperate service of nothing at all.[106]

In the end, the answer to all these questions of suffering humanity is invariably surrender—surrender to a sphere of power existing before and beyond all individual existence. Man is not capable of changing it in any way, nor is he entitled to do so. "What is life's? All! But what is yours?"[107] And the answer demonstrates once more the worthlessness of the individual. "Life could afford to waste her, to throw her away."[108] That is true of every floundering human being—and every human being is going under. "Life is a loan. . . . I know no one who has not fared as badly as myself.[109] Hamsun again and again gives expression to the passivity and obedience which such inexorability of life requires. While life itself "has thrust me away into something hostile to myself," there is no court which must answer the question, "why should Life do that?"[110] There is only one law here: "Life can afford to waste."[111]

Hamsun's philosophy of life has a twofold social function. On the one hand, it offers the socially less successful the consolation that their insignificant role in the economic process can be compensated for by the acceptance of the greater, metaphysical context of the omnipotence of life:

> And so it is: the mere grace that we are given life at all is generous payment in advance for all the miseries of life—for every one of them. No, do not think we have the right to more sweetmeats than we get.[112]

The individual is to become reconciled to his condition in society by perceiving himself as a necessary sacrifice to a natural process, a sacrifice not merely mechanical but full of meaning.

On the other hand, this mythology offers no tangible expectations for alleviating deprivation and disillusionment. The consolation turns against those consoled. They must accept life as it is, and that means the existing relations of domination and subordination, of command and serve.

The Image of Man

Hamsun's mythology throws new light on his misanthropic contempt. His exalted picture of life stands side by side with the image of crawling and creeping man, in the same way that authoritarian propaganda later combined ostensibly lofty notions with expressions of vulgar misanthropy. A metaphysics of the miserableness of man is mobilized against the idea of human progress. Every desire for a more rational organization of society becomes incongruous.

It is significant that Hamsun uses the analogy of the ant hill, so popular in liberal reformist literature as a model of constructive social order, as an image of planlessness:

> ... but that made no difference to the town, the town remained the little crawling ant-hill it was, and this in itself must have been a proof that life itself went its way in spite of all theories.[113]

> Oh, that little anthill! All its inhabitants are occupied with their own affairs, they cross each other's paths, push each other aside, sometimes they trample each other under foot. It cannot be otherwise, sometimes they trample each other under foot.[114]

We have returned with the ants to the starting point, the myth of nature. Every recollection of historical existence has now been obliterated. We are left with an apotheosis of the merely natural—of force without reason. The exodus from social reality is complete.

Behind Hamsun's bitter responses to contemporary civilization lies the cold and nihilistic negation of the very image of man on the road to freedom. His characters are not truly individuals but irrelevant particles in an ahuman process forever beyond their control. Both as an artist and as a political partisan, he was unequal to the challenge of the great heritage of libertarian thought in the West. Cervantes and Shakespeare, Racine and Molière, Goethe and Ibsen, had this in common: all embraced the struggle of the individual with his social and natural environment; all refused to place limits on human imagination and achievement; all, with fervor and tenderness, served human liberty.

Hamsun promotes the feeling of the nullity of the individual with specific stylistic means. Frequently, he assumes a larmoyant tone. But above all, his use of repetition must be stressed again in this context. For once, we find an endless recurrence of linguistic leitmotifs such as the mercilessness of life, the change of seasons, the steady passing of time, the people who are forever crossing the fields or walking along their street,[115] the rhythm of life, and so on. The alleged immutability of human fate is demonstrated with these stereotyped literary clichés reminiscent of the propaganda devices of political authoritarianism aimed at "reeducating" people to accept the preordained fate that has been imposed upon them from above. The stylistic means of repetition are commandeered for the purpose of reining in humanity. In addition, repetition enters into the very construction of the novels. It is always the same pattern: in the early period, where the know-it-all hero has bohemian characteristics and always articulates exactly that which frightens average people, new stories could actually be constructed from the elements of the novellas *Hunger, Mysteries. New Earth, Editor Lynge* without any significant change. The later novels like *The Women at the Well, Vagabonds, August Sail-Around-The-World, After a Year and a Day* always have the same topics: the contented peasant; the person who is always out for the "main chance" the vagabond and the solidly rooted man; herring fishing; lust and love which is in truth never authentic. All major nineteenth century literature—novels as well as dramas, beginning with Balzac, indeed, with Goethe, up to the naturalists—represents concern with the fate of a specific individual whose life unfolds potentialities or is damaged under the pressures of society. This literature enlists the entire quantitative and qualitative wealth of culture to bring to artistic life the foil and the substance of an individual's fate.

Hamsun's world, on the other hand, is extremely impoverished; indeed, it is difficult to recall decisive connections or very many particulars in the life course of even the most important of his protagonists, though some of them make an appearance in several of his works. And those of his readers and critics who see in this meagerness of cultural inventory and in the vague and shadowlike characters created by him a sign of special purity, of mature acerbity, a pious awe for life and "epic greatness" express in their eulogy of this writer tired resignation and social defeatism.[116]

Reception

This is not the place to offer a complete history of the reception of Hamsun's works and to demonstrate, on hand of voluminous documentation, the extent to which literary criticism was aware of Hamsun's worldview as an important stepping stone on the road from bourgeois liberal consciousness to the slogans of the authoritarian state.[117] But at least I shall try to suggest with the help of a necessarily very limited documentation an internal connection between the reception of Hamsun's writing and structural changes in society.

Only one book about Hamsun was published in Germany after World War I. In his monograph, Berendsohn expresses the peculiarity of Hamsun's worldview as satisfying bourgeois ideals at the same time that it reconciles these ideologically satiated strata with the ruling authorities. He writes: "[Hamsun] regards every deed as the free expresssion of everyone's will. He rejects sociological analyses, which try to demonstrate man's dependence on the moral conditions of the social whole. It is true, he touches on social questions in his personal circle as well as in his workshop, but his thought process remains, at the core, individualistic. In a letter to the editor of the publication *Klassenkampf,* who had asked Hamsun for a contribution, the writer had only to propose his slogan 'More Cultivation of Land!' as the cure for all evils. Hamsun cautions against the overestimation of reading and writing, he supports the king as a symbol which casts a bit of splendor over the grey country, he declares war to be a necessity, and equates disarmament with making one's home defenseless. As always, Hamsun writes in opposition to the city and in favor of the countryside. The industrial worker, according to him, 'creates nothing and only transforms.'"[118] But when Berendsohn declares that "no one would ever think of evaluating Hamsun's work from a political standpoint,"[119] he seriously misjudges this writer. It is true, Hamsun's works do not contain political expositions and he only makes occasional insipid comments about current conditions and institutions.[120] Nevertheless, they contain, like that letter, key words which should warn all those readers whose social situation, character and level of understanding, leads them to oppose an authoritarian social system, not to assume a naive attitude toward Hamsun.

The fact that it is still possible for such a progressive literary historian as Berendsohn—who does not conceal the author's reactionary political slogans—to advocate a purely hermeneutic interpretation of Hamsun's works in the most recent past, immediately before the collapse of Weimar's German democracy, shows that very deep-seated sociopsychological interests are at play in the reception of Hamsun's work by bourgeois readers. Their naivete suggests resignation. Only one generation earlier, when the bourgeois intelligentsia still judged the world with eyes that had been enlightened by naturalism, another expert of literature had clearly seen the gap between current social questions on the one hand, and the individual plight of Hamsun's characters on the other. Leo Berg's verdict regarding the "final flight of the modern soul to the heart of nature"—this was his interpretation of *Pan*[121]—a verdict that can certainly be understood as an expression of social-reformist optimism, is very reserved. Berg, an important spokesman of modernity and naturalism around 1900, also criticizes the protagonist of *Mysteries,* describing him as a "modern man of suffering, who has no real reason to suffer because he is well-off—a Jesus-character without the moral strength."[122] He still has the progressive instinct of an alert liberal who notes the inner affinity between Hamsun—that "martyr of pantheism, who derives untiring bliss from his humiliation"[123]—and Dostoevski. In his cautiously formulated judgment Berg reveals that he senses the threat surging from this masochistic pantheism—which is inexplicable to him—to progressive bourgeois life.

The most surprising documentation, however, is not found in liberal but in social-democratic literary criticism. In the commentaries on Hamsun which appeared in the leading theoretical publication of German social democracy, the *Die Neue Zeit* in the 1890s (a time when some of these literary pieces were written by the later leader of social reformism Eduard Bernstein, who at that time still entertained an unmitigated Marxist posture) there is a clear position: Hamsun's novels should be rejected because they do not create real, live characters, but conjure moods that have nothing in common with those trends that are truly oriented toward social change. In a discussion of *Hunger,* he writes:

> We do not have the right to reproach the author for the selection of his material;[124] but the evaluation of *Mysteries* already attests according to Bernstein that "Hamsun . . . shows a strong inclination towards distortion and a tendency to make fun of the reader. . . . And if the fragmentation of conversation, of scenes, of the entire plot of the novel—in so far as we can even talk about a plot—are not a product of the writer's own blase attitude or of nervousness, they are certainly suited to make the reader nervous and blase.[125]

This is "a story which becomes less and less important to us as we read it," a hero, who becomes "a pure automaton of moods," a book that is "at the most of pathological interest."

Two years later the evaluation of the writer, who is judged as having even the external appearance of one who is a carrier of resentment ("the bristly mustache is jealous of the head of hair and the straight nose carries a dreamy pince-nez") is even more explicit: "This juxtaposition is not intended to prove Hamsun's affinity with Shakespeare. On the contrary! It is intended to show that even if two people do the same thing, it is not at all the same thing. It is intended to show what a difference there is between a W. Shakespeare and a Knut Hamsun! Knut Hamsun sews with crude twine, and what he sews is not silk. . . . Thoughts are not relevant . . . characters are not permitted to exist."[126] The same criteria of judgment are sustained throughout the entire epoch: "*Hunger* is not a social novel" "*Editor Lynge* leaves the reader totally uncontent: . . . does he [Hamsun] begin yawning and lose interest in the entire story?"[127]

Georgij Plekhanov, the most significant theoretician of Russian socialism also around 1900, has an even clearer conception of Hamsun; he analyses the writer's resistance to, indeed, his hatred for the proletariat by pointing at a character in one of his plays. Plekhanov points out that the class antagonism of the bourgeoisie toward the worker had never found such clear expression before Hamsun. At the same time, Plekhanov recognizes the insincerity of the "revolutionary" aspects in Hamsun's writings: "Revolutionary feelings are often a distinct characteristic of a conservative attitude," and he points out that this is even more apparent in Hamsun than in French romanticism.[128]

But if one begins to look at the volumes of *Die Neue Zeit* published during and after World War I, one finds hymnic descriptions of the same writer who was unequivocally rejected twenty years earlier. What was then judged as "empty mood" and "mere nerve-irritation" has now become "gripping images of life and soul, in which the plentiful reality with all of its light and all of its shade is condensed to become the symbol of innermost life."[129] The same writer who appeared to earlier critics "as an infatuated exclamation mark [seated] in a melancholic easy chair,"[130] has now grown "into that solitary greatness,"[131] which cannot be compared to others without doing him injustice. That which appeared in his earlier novels to be "transitory as a mood"[132] has now become a "parable of the eternal."[133]

After the war, the spokesmen of liberalism are united with the proletariat which Hamsun hated so much in their hymn of praise for this writer. Berendsohn and *Die Neue Zeit* belong to the same social constellation: they both represent political resignation and ideological seduction of broad strata in central Europe today.

There is one final and valid proof for this sordid and sorry alliance, as it were. In one of the most influential books of the authoritarian propaganda apparatus, in which the great literature of the nineteenth century is rejected almost without exception, we read:

> No other living writer has more profoundly expressed the mystic-natural, the willful features than Knut Hamsun. . . . *The Blessing of the Earth* is today's great epic work of the nordic will in its eternal archetype, heroic even behind the wooden plow, fertile in every movement, straight and unwavering to the unknown end. But just as inexplicable and yet as self-evident art Benoni, the merchant Mack, Baronness Edvarda, the hunter Glan. Each character has an inner law, which is breathed into him from the very beginning. And each acts accordingly. . . . In contrast to the lawfulness of Isak, whose nature is immersed in the soil, the vagabonds make their appearance. With this same medium, Hamsun describes in a mysterious and natural manner the laws of the universe and of the soul. . . . They move, restlessly, from place to place, they change their activities and their loves!

Because the roots have been torn from the strength-giving earth, the blossoms also die. So they live, the Edevart, August, Lovise Margarete, and they know not why and for what purpose. They are the decline, at best they are the transition. Experimental pieces of humanity, they exist in order that new forms and types can be attained, so that new values can be created, and new honors can be won. They live the way the writer has presented them, naturally and mysteriously. Seen from this standpoint, a Hauptmann, even an Ibsen, recede far into the background. In Hamsun, however, the world was conquered once again.[134]

The function of the ideology of transcending irreconcilable antagonisms through through the semblance of harmony is apparent in the unison of the voices of social-democratic, liberal and nationalistic critics. During the period of transition from the freely competitive economy to monopoly capitalism, liberalist ideology, whose real foundation disappears, falls victim to an increasing disorientation. Finally it becomes—mostly in contrast to the conscious intentions of its carriers—a victim of a broadening authoritarian mentality. When the new holders of power no longer need the ideological apparatus as a weapon in their struggle to secure their social position, then fascist reality puts an end to postliberal fantasies. The calmness of nature, into which the bourgeois readers want to doze along with Hamsun himself, is mere appearance; its core reveals itself as the industrial and military noise of authoritarian domination.

Notes

1. In its original form the following study was written some time before the political sympathies of Hamsun for the Hitler movement became public knowledge. It is presented here not only as a case of sociological prediction but as a documentation of the authoritarian character and his ideology. See *Zeitschrift für Sozialforschung*, ed. by Max Horkheimer, vol. 6 (1937), pp 295–345.

2. We may remind the reader of our analysis of Spanish literature—another case of social marginality illuminating traits of social typicality.

3. *Hunger*, tr. by George Egerton (New York: Knopf, 1920), p. 1, Whenever possible we have quoted from the American editions of Hamsun. Where these have been unavailable. German translations have been used as a basis for quotations. Quotations from American translations are reprinted by permission of Alfred A. Knopf. Inc.

4. Ibid., p. 266.

5. *The Last Joy* (*Die letzte Freude*), *Gesammelte Werke*, 12 vols., German tr. ed. by J. Sandmeier (Munich: Albert Langen, n.d.), vol. 5, p. 291.

6. In connection with one of his eulogies of the natural strength of youth, Hamsun criticizes the aged who "have mollycoddled it [youth] with hymns and rot about peace eternal. . . . If some one smites it on one cheek it turns

the other accommodatingly, and keeps its fists in its pockets with admirable self-control." *Shallow Soil,* tr. by C C. Hyllested, (New York: Knopf, 1914), p. 120. Brutal resentment is much more apparent here than in the sentimental dress of the quotation in the text.

7. *The Last Joy,* p. 376.
8. *Pan,* tr. by W. W. Worster (New York: Knopf, 1921), p. 130.
9. *The Last Joy,* p. 289.
10. Ibid., p. 293.
11. Ibid., pp. 301–2.
12. Ibid., p. 376.
13. *Mysteries,* tr. by A. G. Chater (New York: Knopf, 1927), p. 67. See also, *Pan,* p. 130: "This silence murmuring in my ears is the blood of all Nature seething; it is God weaving through the world and me."
14. *Pan,* p. 15.
15. *The Last Joy,* p. 310.
16. Kant, *Critique of Aesthetic Judgment,* tr. by J. D. Meredith (Oxford: Oxford University Press, 1911), p. 110. Kantian idealism, it should be remarked, received its most winning, and perhaps most profound, application to public affairs in the teachings of Thoreau and other New England Transcendentalists, who in turn, of course, influenced Tolstoi and Gandhi.
17. Kant, pp. 110–11
18. *Pan,* pp. 10–11.
19. *The Last Jay,* p. 311.
20. See, for example, *Pan,* pp. 23–24: "I pick up a little dry twig and hold it in my hand and sit looking at it, and think my own thoughts; the twig is almost rotten, its poor bark touches me, pity fills my heart. And when I get up again, I do not throw the twig far away, but lay it down, and stand liking it; at least I look at it once more with wet eyes before I go away and leave it there."
21. *Wanderers,* tr. by W. W. Worster (New York: Knopf, 1922), p. 320.
22. *The Road Leads On,* tr. by Eugene Gay-Tifft (New York: Coward-McCann, 1934), p. 46.
23. *The Ring is Closed,* tr. by Eugene Gay-Tifft (New York: Coward-McCann, 1937), p. 152.
24. *Vagabonds,* tr. by Eugene Gay-Tifft (New York: Coward-McCann, 1930), p. 448.
25. Cf. *Growth of the Soil,* tr. by W. W. Worster, 2 vols. (New York: Knopf, 1921), vol. 1, p. 7; vol. 2, p. 120; *Vagabonds,* p. 47.
26. *Growth of the Soil,* vol. 2, p. 120.
27. Ibid., vol. 2, p. 246; also cf. *Rosa,* tr. by A. G. Chater (New York: Knopf, 1926), p. 18: "'What are you sitting here for?' 'Ah, young man,' he said, holding up the palm of his hand. 'What am I sitting here for? I sit here keeping pace with my existence. Ay, that's what I'm doing.'"
28. *Pan,* p. 164
29. *Growth of the Soil,* vol. 1, p. 99.
30. Ibid., vol. 2, pp. 243–44.
31. Ibid.
32. Ibid.
33. *Chapter the Last,* tr. by A. G. Chater (New York: Knopf, 1929), pp. 266–67.
34. *Vagabonds,* p. 47.

35.   *Growth of the Soil,* vol. 1, p. 122.
36.   Ibid., vol. 2, p. 179.
37.   Ibid., vol. 1, p. 42.
38.   *August,* tr. by Eugene Gay-Tifft (New York: Coward-McCann, 1931), p. 149.
39.   *Chapter the Last,* p. 4.
40.   *Vagabonds,* p. 540.
41.   See ibid., pp. 537–38.
42.   Ibid., p. 539.
43.   *The Women at the Pump,* tr. by A. G. Chater (New York: Knopf, 1928), p. 316.
44.   Hamsun is factually mistaken here. Primitive people often revere old age.
      The elders frequently enjoy the highest status in their societies.
45.   *The Last Joy,* p. 351.
46.   Ibid., p. 318.
47.   *Shallow Soil,* p. 74.
48.   *Growth of the Soil,* vol. 1. p. 211.
49.   *The Road Leads On,* p. 409.
50.   *The Last Joy,* p. 298.
51.   *Children of the Age,* tr. by J. S. Scott (New York: Knopf, 1924), p. 82.
52.   *Mysteries,* p. 51.
53.   See *Mysteries,* p. 121.
54.   See *Pan,* p. 169.
55.   *Rosa,* p. 55.
56.   *Pan,* p. 132.
57.   *Mysteries,* p. 276.
58.   *The Ring is Closed,* p. 254.
59.   *Growth of the Soil,* vol. 2, p. 92.
60.   *Pan,* p. 34.
61.   *Chapter the Last.* p. 177.
62.   Ibid., p. 102.
63.   *Wanderers,* p. 317.
64.   Cf. *Chapter the Last,* pp. 105–7.
65.   *Segelfoss Town,* tr. by J. S. Scott (New York: Knopf. 1925). p. 299.
66.   *Growth of the Soil,* vol. 2, p. 220.
67.   Ibid., p. 253.
68.   *Wanderers,* p. 312.
69.   *Growth of the Soil,* vol. 2, p. 9.
70.   *The Last Joy,* p. 344. It is consistent with his concept of women that "the
      greatest thing" in which Hamsun participated was his struggle against the
      lenient treatment of infanticide. ("Barnemord" [Infanticide], Morgenbladet
      for March 6th, 1916, cited from Walter A. Berendsohn, *Knut Hamsun,*
      [Munich: Albert Langen, 1929], p. 104.)
71.   *Vagabonds,* p. 143.
72.   See, for example, *Segelfoss Town,* p. 27: *The Women at the Pump,* pp. 193–94;
      August, p. 342.
73.   See *Children of the Age,* pp. 81–82, 216; *Segelfoss Town,* pp. 166–68, 314–15:
      August, p. 230; *The Road Leads On,* p. 167.
74.   Cf. his contempt for positivism in *Mysteries,* p. 157: "I am a fact!" See also
      The Last Joy, p. 329; *The Women at the Pump,* p. 120.
75.   See *Chapter the Last,* pp. 80–81, 107.

76. See, for example, *The Last Joy*, p. 291.
77. See *Mysteries*, p. 66; *Chapter the Last*, p. 15.
78. See *Mysteries*, pp. 89–90.
79. *Growth of the Soil*, vol. 2, p. 245.
80. See *The Last Joy*, p. 337.
81. Ibid., p. 328.
82. *Wanderers*, p. 207.
83. *August*, p. 351.
84. *Segelfoss Town*, p. 27.
85. See *The Last Joy*, p. 362.
86. See *Mysteries*, p. 157; *The Last Joy*, p. 329; *The Women at the Pump*.
87. See references in note 72, above.
88. *Children of the Age*, pp. 81–82.
89. Ibid., pp. 82–83.
90. *Segelfoss Town*, pp. 167–68.
91. *Wanderers*, p. 189.
92. Ibid., p. 215.
93. *The Ring is Closed*, p. 191.
94. *Children of the Age*, pp. 79–80.
95. *Segelfoss Town*, p. 337.
96. *The Women at the Pump*, pp, 144–45.
97. Ibid., p. 147; cf. *Segelfoss Town*, pp. 10, 21.
98. *Mysteries*, p. 200.
99. Ibid., pp. 187, 201.
100. Ibid., p. 201.
101. *The Last Joy*, p. 337.
102. *Mysteries*, p. 49.
103. *Hunger*, p. 22.
104. *Redakteur Lynge*, German tr. ed. by J. Sandmeier (Munich: Albert Langen, 1922), p. 31.
105. *Pan*, p. 157.
106. *August*, p. 342.
107. *Wanderers*, p. 314.
108. Ibid., p. 291.
109. *The Last Joy*, p. 317.
110. *Rosa*, p. 99.
111. *Wanderers*, p. 312.
112. Ibid., p. 314.
113. *The Women at the Pump*, p. 138.
114. Ibid., p. 5.
115. See, for example, *Growth of the Soil*, passim.
116. With technical rigor, the same tendency can be noted in Jan Sibelius' symphonies which belong, in quality as well as effect, in Hamsun's category. Think, for example, of the Pan-like atmosphere of nature which is vague and regressive in its coloristic means, but also of the compositional process itself. This symphonic knows of no musical development. It is built from indiscriminate and incidental repetition of a basic theme which is trivial. The semblance of originality that derives from this can only be attributed to the senselessness with which these themes are moved together, their

connectedness guaranteed by nothing except the abstract passing of time. The darkness, product of technical awkwardness, feigns profoundness which does not really exist. The structurally opaque repetitions claim an eternal rhythm of nature, which is also expressed by the lack of symphonic time-consciousness. The nullity of the melodic monad which is carried into unarticulated sounds corresponds to the contempt of humanity, which delivers Hamsun's individuals to all-powerful nature. Sibelius as well as Hamsun are different from impressionistic tendencies, however, because all-powerful nature is constructed from petrified remnants of traditional bourgeois art and does not originate from the vantage point of the original protesting subjectivity. (Th.W. Adorno)

117. A list of Hamsun literature in German translation that has appeared up to 1930 which consists almost exclusively of articles that appeared in newspapers and journals can be found in *Hamsun Bibliographie,* ed. by Fritz Meyen, (Braunschweig. 1931).
118. Walter Berendsohn, p. 105.
119. Ibid., p. 149.
120. See this essay, part III.
121. Leo Berg, *Zwischen zwei Jahrhunderten. Gesammelte Essays,* (Frankfurt a.M., 1896). p. 129.
122. Ibid., p. 117.
123. Ibid., p. 125.
124. *Die Neue Zeit,* 1890–91, vol.1 (Stuttgart. 1891), p. 803.
125. Ibid., 1893–94, vol. 2, p. 376.
126. Ibid., 1895–96, vol. 1, p. 538 (anonymous critique).
127. Ibid., 1898–99, vol. 1, pp. 249–50 (Eduard Bernstein).
128. See Georgij Plekhanov, *Art and Society* (New York, 1937), pp. 66f. (Plekhanov wrote this work almost eighty years ago.)
129. *Die Neue Zeit,* 1919, vol. 1, p. 356 (Edgar Steiger).
130. See ibid., 1895–96, vol. 1, p. 538.
131. Ibid., 1919, vol. 1, p. 190 (Edgar Steiger).
132. Ibid., 1895–96, vol. 1, p. 538.
133. Ibid., 1919, vol. 1, p. 190.
134. Alfred Rosenberg, *Der Mythos des 20, Jahrhunderts.* (Munich, 1933), p. 438.

Part II

Studies on the German Novel in the Nineteenth Century

8

Romanticism: Revolution Repressed

One commonly associates the word *reaction* with the word *romanticism*. Arnold Ruge once said, "I call those writers Romantics who use the means of our education to oppose the age of enlightenment and revolution, those who reject and combat the principle of self-contented and self-contained humanity in the field of science, of art, and of ethics."[1] This condemnative judgment, which comes from a "Young German" philosopher who himself emerged from the Romantic movement suggests the first of many paradox relations that characterize romanticism. August von Platen, Heinrich Heine, Nikolaus Lenau, and with them a number of other writers, share Ruge's attitude; even if their opposition to romanticism is not conscious, objectively, their writing shows them to be in an adversary posture. All of these writers belong to the bourgeoisie, and this is often involved as evidence for the thesis that romanticism is a bourgeois movement. In this context, we shall recall the critical question posed by Friedrich Schlegel: "Could it be that the harmonious development of aristocrats and artists is nothing but a harmonious figment of the imagination?"[2] This question almost appears to be a critical annotation to Goethe's veneration of allegedly harmonious aristocratic life style.

The supposition that romanticism is a bourgeois movement is reinforced when we take a closer look at the romantic poets themselves. Granted, we find among them a number of aristocratic names like Achim von Arnim, Joseph von Eichendorff and Novalis, but even these men belong to a stratum of intellectuals and artists who pursue free occupations and cultivate a bourgeois lifestyle. While the prototypical intellectual Gotthold Ephraim Lessing was an exception during his time, by the turn of the century an entire occupational group of freelance writers has emerged. They owe their existence to a growing aristocratic and bourgeois audience which reads books and subscribes to magazines.

The most progressive elements from this audience—among whom the socially emancipated Jews played a special role—amplify the social resonance of this literary occupational group in their salons. At the same time, classical poetry and writing continues to be supported by the patronage system—consider Goethe, Schiller, Christoph Martin Wieland, but also Johann Gottfried Herder, Friedrich Gottlieb Klopstock and again, Lessing. For a writer, professional activity that is independent from the noble court corresponds to the lifestyle of the French thinkers of the Enlightenment. Here, then, we have another paradox: the same movement that turns away from the Enlightenment actually takes over the social forms of its adversaries. The novelty of this occupational group of independent writers and artists in Germany is portrayed in a passage from the story of "The upright Kasperl and the lovely Annerl" by Clemens Brentano; the narrator considers at great length how he might best explain to the traditional peasantwoman what a writer is:

> I did not know how I might explain to her that I am a writer. To say that I was an "educated man" would have been a lie. It is strange that a German is always slightly ashamed to admit that he is a writer, and one likes to say it the least to people of the lower estates because they usually think of the scribes and the pharisees from the bible. The expression "writer" is not as commonly used as is "homme des lettres" among the French, who, as writers tend to be more guild-like and have more of a tradition of rules in their works; indeed, they are asked "Ou avez-vous fait votre philosophie? Where have you arrived at your philosophy?" just as the Frenchman himself tends to have the qualities of one who has "arrived." But it is not this un-German custom alone which makes it difficult to say the word "writer" for one who is asked about his character at the city gate; it is a certain inner shame that holds us back, a feeling which descends on everyone who deals with goods of the free and spiritual realm, with the unmediated gifts from heaven. Educated men need not feel as much shame as poets, because they usually have paid a tuition, they work in state offices, split crude blocks of wood, or work in shafts where much rough water must be pumped dry. . . . All human beings who do not earn their bread by the sweat of their brow must feel a certain shame, and one who has not completely hit rock bottom knows this. Thus, all kinds of thoughts passed through my mind as I deliberated what I should say to the old woman.[3]

The writer apparently feels uncomfortable when he has to account for his occupation. His long-winded and roundabout reflections seem like the expression of a guilty conscience. Indeed, the existing corporate system of estates in which each occupies a position from which he cannot move is so embedded in the poet's consciousness that a deviation from the norm appears to him almost as a sacrilege.[4] Granted, a bourgeois element also appears in the passage, especially in the reference to France. But the quoted passage shows clearly that his bourgeois generation of writers in Germany has not come to terms with its social position yet: it defines the difference between the German and the Frenchman in folkloristic terms rather than in connection with a specific situation. Furthermore, it is characteristic for the romantic writer that he automatically refers to writing as "composing poetry." The idea that writing could have contents other than "free and spiritual matters"—that is, essentially lyrical contents—does not occur to him. The irrelevance thereby attributed to subject matter stands in fundamental opposition to the "philosophy" of French writing.

Actually, the writings of eighteenth-century France which Brentano had in mind are concerned with society and include such concern even in their concept of nature. In Brentano's consideration of the "lower estates," one might see a certain identification, or at least a recognition, of socially oppressed strata, but his glorification of work, which one is to carry out "in the sweat of one's brow," diffuses this aspect into a harmonizing contemplation of the world. It is no less significant of romantic literature that the lifestyle of the upper estates, who are able to devote themselves to the pursuit of cultural goods precisely because they are able to dispense with tedious labor, does not even enter the field of vision as it did with Goethe. The concrete social situation does not make its way into the consciousness of the romantic; it is repressed, "overlooked" or used—as are the concepts "Germany," "France," and the "lower estates"—merely as elements of poetic folklore.

Certainly, romanticism includes more than these poetic aspects and clearly takes on a political content which manifests itself in three ways. To begin, the term "political romanticism" refers to the national independence movement as expressed in the appeal "to my people" of the Prussian king Friedrich Wilhelm III (March 17, 1813) which displayed self-confident German national individuality to French politics. The self-consciousness of the individual is joined with the self-confidence of the group, the nation. But on German soil this national self-consciousness remains purely formal; indeed, it becomes a label appropriated by the interests of the existing absolutist powers. Because it is not supported by a broad bourgeois revolution, this political movement bears no fruit; or better, after the defeat of Napoleon, no German state is any longer interested in preserving the vitality of such a movement.

A second strand of romantic politics is represented as a critical progress movement tied to the names of Freiherr von Stein, Wilhelm von Humboldt and Ernst Moritz Arndt. These thinkers cast their criticism of absolutist rule by the nobility in "nonpolitical" terms: this type of domination is rejected as unnatural, as inorganic, as arbitrarily imposed onto the original life of the people. They find their ideal of a humanly appropriate social order in the late Middle Ages. These men, however, are not clear about how their social ideals might be put into practice, and contradictory political notions such as corporate estates, constitutional monarchy, and republic are promulgated side by side as political demands in a rather unmediated fashion.

If this critical progress movement can be described as "ideological," then that description is even more true for the third strand of Romantic politics, which lasted the longest and was the most influential. I am referring to the romanticism of the later Friedrich Schlegel and Friedrich von Gentz—that reactionary accompaniment to Metternich's politics which sanctifies this reactionary postrevolutionary status quo as a product of history, and thereby legitimates the absolutist state.

The other side of the coin, however, is romantic artistic literature which actually has little in common with any of these political trends. A true understanding of romanticism must clearly differentiate between progressive bourgeois and regressive feudal-absolutist interests. For political romanticism, the existing state of affairs is sacrosanct; here lies the focus of its interest. Bourgeois poetic romanticism, on the other hand, simply disregards the existing order; bourgeois consciousness which represents this literature sees no possibility of its own unfolding within that order. All the same, artistic romanticism contains dialectical moments which transcend social resignation, as we will try to demonstrate below.

Among the forefathers claimed by romantic poetry are Herder and, curiously, Lessing. Friedrich Schlegel even dedicated a treatise to the latter:

> Given the general lack of appreciation for moral education and moral greatness, the fashionable, non-discriminating contempt of aesthetes for everything which claims to be—or actually is—moral; given the feeble laxity, the obstinate arbitrariness, the oppressive pettiness and consistent irrationality of the conventional morality which actually prevails in society on the one hand, and the narrow-mindedness of abstract and literal virtue-pedants and maximalists on the other, there is not likely to be any discussion of *Lessing's character*, of the

worthy male principles he represents, of his *great, free lifestyle,* which might possibly be the best practical instruction on the vocation of scholars; of the audacious self-reliance, of the coarse strength of his whole manner, of his noble and refined cynicism; of his holy open-mindedness; of that honest warmth which this man—not usually sensitive—felt towards everything having to do with duty towards children, loyalty of brothers, love of fatherland and generally towards everything that relates to the primary bonds of nature and the closest relationships of society; all of them feelings which are occasionally expressed—attractive and touching in their very rarity—in works which otherwise appear to be composed by reason alone; of virtuous hate of half-truths and lies, of the slavish and power-hungry sluggishness of mind; of the aversion to even the slightest infringement of the rights and liberties of every independent thinker; of his warm and active respect for everything which he deemed to be a means for broadening knowledge and therefore considered to be the common property of humanity; of his pure enthusiasm for efforts which he himself knew would come—in the opinion of all—to naught, which, however, undertaken as they were in this spirit, are more worthy than any purpose; of the divine restlessness which always and everywhere must act—not merely do—from an instinct of greatness, and which affects everything which it touches—inadvertently and without knowing or wanting this—in the direction of the good and the beautiful.[5]

We will later encounter a similar hymn to Lessing in Gottfried Keller's writings. He, as well as Schlegel, attributes all kinds of positive qualities to Lessing, provided that these correspond to his own intellectual orientation; the true meaning inherent in Lessing's work, however, is never mentioned. How characteristic of Schlegel that he emphazises the paradoxical, the witty, the "cynical" aspects of Lessing, but not the bourgeois morality, not the humane tolerance which culminates in a historic sketch of the education of mankind. Schlegel transforms Lessing into an individualist figure by rejecting the Enlightenment aspects of his work; his falsification of Lessing's writing is substantiated precisely because he ties his condemnation of the enlightenment as an intellectual movement to his eulogy of one of its most prominent representatives. While in the Enlightenment and therefore in Lessing, the horizons of genuine issues, of "reality," become increasingly clear, at least in intention, with romanticism they once again recede into the obscurity of uncertainty.

Increasing confusion also characterizes the romantic biographies themselves: Friedrich Schlegel, author of the frivolous and liberal *Lucinde,* who raves about the philosopher Johann Gottfried Fichte's atheism and supports a democratic republic, finally hurls himself into the arms of Catholic mysticism and lends his journalistic services to reactionary absolutism. Novalis, who was a pantheist in his youth and full of hope regarding the possibility of a universal republic, saying at one time that "true popularity is the highest goal of man,"[6] later sees the king as an earthly fatum and glorifies the Pope and the Jesuits. The Protestant theologican and philosopher Friedrich Schleiermacher, too, is initially a pantheist and writes the candid *Letters on Lucinde,* but in his age he renounces them and becomes an orthodox Protestant zealot. Brentano starts out as a rebel and ends in unfortunate enthusiasm for a "visionary" by the name of Katharina Emmerich. The young Johann Ludwig Tieck lives among Christoph Friedrich Nicolai's enlightenment circle in Berlin; the old Tieck accepts honors from the utmost conservative Prussian king Friedrich Wilhelm IV. E.T.A. Hoffmann's existence fades until it disappears into obscurity.

Again we are confronted with a contradictory fact: all of these writers share what might be called progressive beginnings and end either in political reaction or psychic regression. And this peculiarity is underscored by the fact that the generations of the Young Germans and of the Hegelian Left, both of which emerged from the romantic movement, situate themselves in direct opposition to the aging romantic intellectuals in their manner of living.

Not only are their biographies marked by inconsistency; at the turn of the century, the entire epoch is characterized by it. Bourgeois development trends already exist but they are inhibited by a governmental superstructure consisting of 300 sovereign rulers (if one were to count barons that number would increase to over 1500). Nobles still enjoy privileges, the judical system is not yet democratized, the development of the bourgeois entrepreneurial spirit is restricted by paternalistic traditions. The bourgeoisie typically found three solutions to dealing with this situation: all three amount to political acquiescence. Lessing actually pursues the most radical course in his representation of the conflict situation on stage; Goethe harmonizes the conflicting life interests by overemphasizing patriarchal leadership. Romanticism shifts the contradictions from the concrete situation, the praxis of daily life, into the realm of beautiful appearances, a sort of indirect construction of ideology.

The basic schema of works of romantic artistic literature looks as follows: the immediately given reality that is ordered in time and space has no existential significance; only the past, which is conceived of as a congealed and fixed state that is closed to the possibility of dynamic transformation in the future, is seen as significant. The average world of the adult is rejected; one returns to early childlike stages of human existence and attempts to give artistic expression to them: they alone are regarded as happy, as fulfilled, and as worthy of human existence. In this sense, the enthusiasm of the romantics for the Middle Ages agrees with their enthusiasm for fairytales. Both, things historical and prehistorical in character, help avoid the harsh reality of the immediate surroundings; both draw people out of a reality which is characterized by relationships of tension, opposing interests, layers of conflict, and contradiction between what is and what ought to be. Even the fascination with mining is relevant in this context.

Art is the medium which accomplishes this regression to childish stages of human life. It is the medium which transforms these stages into essential reality. In fact, the only function that romanticism still attributes to the immediate environment is that of being able somehow to point the way, through the medium of art, to a higher and essential reality. To quote from Brentano's story:

> I said to her: "ah, old woman, you have
>   become quite sprightly," and she replied:
> "Sprightly, sprightly,
> always brightly,
> always more round,
> he stood on the mound,
> now came down lightly,
> it shouldn't astound!"[7]

The banal comment of the narrator triggers verses in the old woman who has already begun to become childlike again, and this gives poetically legitimated significance to the whole situation. The continual discovery of the essential world through art converts the world itself into something spiritual, or at least into something that is spiritually mediated in all of its aspects. Even though the everyday world resists the intellectual grasp of the bourgeoisie, it nonetheless becomes the spiritual property of the new social stratum in a higher sense: in the philosophic systems and in the great poetic works of romanticism, the bourgeoisie "appropriates" the world ideologically.

The mark of the individual is the third feature of the romantic schema; it exists alongside the "essential" world and its spiritual constituents. While no path actually leads out of the romantic world into the future of everyday reality, this world remains nonetheless forever unfinished, organic, in the process of development, in short: alive. Though the fate of the bourgeois class remains rigid and hopelessly standardized before and after the Wars of Liberation, in the imaginative, at times even fantastic world of appearances it appears as multifaceted and richly nuanced. And this realm of appearances contains, much like a cocoon, the political liberalism of later years: a space which grants the possibility of unfettered development to the citizen is created artificially, that is, artistically, before it opens up in actuality.

The individualist spirit makes poetry its highest priority. And if it is true that art is a medium of the essential reality, then it is true that poetry actually constitutes a part of this reality. This is clearly apparent in the case of the fairy tale, but in the romantic view it is also true of the Middle Ages, for that epoch of *Minnesaenger,* of Heinrich von Ofterdingen, and even of Hans Sachs. When Schlegel says, "Poetry is a Republican speech: a speech which is a law and a purpose unto itself, in which all parties are free citizens and may participate,"[8] the very terminology he uses suggests liberal bourgeois contents, even if in this context, those contents are referring to that "higher reality."

Individualism is, moreover, expressed in the poetic form of the fragment. Even the romantic novel is clearly fragmentary. Schlegel once refers to it as "an encyclopedia of the entire intellectual and spiritual life of an individual gifted with genius."[9] This definition of the novel stands in contradiction to all preceding and all subsequent practice. In Goethe's educational novels, the hero—who is by no means a genius, but remains a rather normal individual in spite of his special gifts—is called upon to fit himself into society. And the novel of the nineteenth century does not derive its "encyclopedic character" from specific individuals, but from social reality. Romanticism, however, subordinates fiction entirely to an enchanted "reality" which is completely individualized. Novalis has said of Goethe's *Wilhelm Meister's Apprenticeship,* "*Wilhelm Meister's Apprenticeship* is, in a certain respect, a thoroughly prosaic and modern book. In it, Romanticism perishes, and with it dies the poetry of nature, the element of the miraculous. This book deals only with common human occurrences and things—nature and mysticism are completely forgotten. It is a poeticized bourgeois and domestic story. And it explicitly treats the miraculous as mere poetry and rapture."[10] These words demonstrate clearly that the basic romantic schema includes an individualist-fragmentary as well as a spiritualist and reality-transcending element. A third element joins these two characteristics of poetic romanticism: that of irony. According to Schlegel, "Irony is the form of the paradoxical. Paradox is everything which is at the same time good and great."[11] Romanticism thus praises reality most highly when it is contradictory; indeed, contradiction is the very essence of romantic reality. One might recall the end of the second part of *Heinrich von Ofterdingen*:

> The epic period must become a historic drama, even if the scenes are connected by narration.
>
> Heinrich's speech in iambics. The love of a young distinguished man from Pisa for a Florentine woman.
>
> Heinrich attacks the hostile city with a lot of fugitives. All elements of war in poetic colors.
>
> A great war, like a duel—definitely generous—philosophic—human. The spirit of old chivalry. The joust. The spirit of bacchanalian nostalgia. The people must kill each other—that is more noble than death by fate. Honor, fame, etc. is the desire and the life of the warrior.
>
> The warrior lives in death and as a shadow.
>
> The wish to die is the spirit of the warrior.
>
> Romantic life of the warrior.
>
> *War* is at home on earth, war must exist on earth.[12]

All individuals lie in confrontation with each other, and this reciprocal competition of individuals—a global tournament—constitutes the very meaning of life. The opposing interests of those groups and individuals struggling with one another find their appropriate poetic expression in the form of a drama. It is no coincidence, of course, that Novalis did not execute his project for the ending of the second part of *Ofterdingen*. It leads one to believe that the fragmentary intimation most accurately fulfills the poet's intention; the fragmentary and the sketchy, which is conveyed even by the cut-up sentence structure, emphasizes the impression of liveliness, of incompleteness, of contradiction.

Sociologically speaking, this means that, given its interests, the bourgeoisie exists in radical but seemingly inescapable contradiction to the feudal structure of authority. The real contradictions of daily life are unambiguously presented. But the fundamentally contradictory situation of everyday reality is not taken seriously; it is—psychologically speaking—actually repressed. The romantic reality, which is by means of irony rendered paradoxical, ambiguous, and contradictory, appears as the product of this repression. This is an example of the indirect creation of ideology. The real contradictions of life are harmonized because the very reality of that life is denied; another "reality"—which contains contradictions of its own—is substituted for it. The contradictory character of this other reality, however, appears as legitimate because it corresponds to the interests of those who have control over it. The "infamy of the existent" (to use Georg Lukács' expression) seems to be disempowered by this process. Actual reality loses the character of the real, and the world of fantasy becomes the secret home of bourgeois consciousness. In this vein we might interpret Novalis' famous phrase, "Where are we going? Always home."[13]

This is the collective side of romantic ideology; an individualist side can be identified as well. It is, after all, precisely because bourgeois individuals do not come to a consciousness of their collective interests that their class situation appears to be so hopeless in the historical epoch of romanticism. We have already mentioned that the individual falls into regression when he returns, childlike, to a fairytale world. This same process is at work in the surrender to nature in romantic literature. In the concept *Waldeinsamkeit*—solitude in and of the woods—formulated by Tieck, there is contained a sense of the return to the philogenetic childhood of humanity. The turning away from "culture" is a flight from the world of adults who refuse to grant space to the individual. Mediated by an ideological process, a virtue is made of this emergency state: the forced isolation of the bourgeois individual is transformed into the fantasy of desired isolation.

A similar process is at work in the romantic enthusiasm for the Middle Ages—with the difference that here, the individual assumes the fictitious position of the father rather than the fictitious position of the child. Because the real "fathers"—the feudal classes—resist any encroachments, their abdication is accomplished in an unconscious and roundabout manner—by identifying with earlier generations of fathers and thereby imagining oneself into a position that is superior to the real holders of power.

Romantic ideology contains dialetic moments which transcend the apparently hopeless situation of the bourgeoisie. One might think, for example, of the support given to the historical sciences. The study of primary sources first undertaken by German philology and the political historiography of romanticism become progressive methodological tools in the nineteenth century: tools that are used, not only for the justification of the victory of the bourgeois class, but also in the service of Marxism. It is true that the romantics were not able to develop an appropriate relationship to the natural sciences. In their preoccupation with mining (think of Novalis) or with medicine (consider the following excerpt from Brentano's story: "I have taken possession of her soul through certain medical remedies which have magical qualities."[14]) they do not strive to demystify the secrets of nature in order to control its powers. Here, too, the romantic attempts, like a child, to surrender to a large meaningful whole. It will take the self-conscious and self-confident bourgeoisie to support the eventual rise of the natural sciences.

And, like historicism, individualism also contains a dialectical moment. Tieck writes in the novel *William Lowell:* "All subjects itself to my arbitrariness. I can name every appearance, every action as I wish; the animate and inanimate world hangs on chains that are ruled by my mind. My entire life is only a dream whose various characters are shaped according to my will. I *myself* am the only law in all of nature; everything obeys this law."[15]

Certainly, these sentences bend Fichte's notion of the "I"—which produces the external world as the material of its duty—in the direction of the Romantic fantasy world. Nevertheless, this unconditional individualism contains not only resources to prevent one's life from dissolving into a cranky, resigned and hopeless humdrum existence, but if individuals actually came to consciousness about the oppression of their "I" and recognized their power, such individualism could stir the fires of a bourgeois revolution.

Indeed, the dissatisfaction with the existing state of affairs distinguishes the romantic literary arts from political romanticism. Even if this is ideologically veiled by the repression of reality from consciousness, the very fact of repression constitutes a fundamental critique, an attack, a rejection. True, this is not a theoretically founded social critique, but such a critique would not be irreconcilable with the romantic spirit. A comparison of the opening lines of Goethe's *Wilhelm Meister's Apprenticeship* and Novalis' *Heinrich von Ofterdingen* serves as an illustration of this. Goethe writes, "The theater play lasted for a very long time"; Novalis, "The parents were already asleep." For Goethe, the theater is one among many elements of social reality; Novalis, on the other hand, makes this reality disappear symbolically into sleep, into nothingness, into insignificance at the very outset. Both novels are descriptions of an artist's life. To be sure, Goethe treats the artist as a special kind of human being; however, for romanticism the artist is the essential, the most precious human being. The dialectic aspects of romanticism lie precisely in this dissolution of the causal and the rational-scientific into artistic creation, and in the uncompromising rejection of all reality which is not the product of a specific individual.

Incapable of political critique, even more incapable of political action, romanticism substitutes instead an exaggeration of the esthetic principle and of the artist. From a sociological perspective, this amounts to a declaration of war on the status quo. Eichendorff explicitly preaches "war to the philistines"; and Schlegel says about his heroine in *Lucinde:*

> She, too, was one of those who do not live in the common world, but in a self-made and imagined reality. Only that which she loved and honored with all her heart was real for her, nothing else; and she knew what was valuable. She, too, had courageously abdicated all responsibilities and severed all ties and she lived completely free and independently.[16]

In his *Theory of the Novel,* Lukács speaks of the "renunciation of all social conditions"; precisely this is essentially romantic: to serve notice to the existing reactionary order.

Let us take a final look at Brentano's short story *The upright Kasperl and the lovely Annerl* in order to clarify how discontent with the existing is always simultaneously present and repressed. In comparing this story to Goethe's *Werther,* we find two common elements: the importance of the notion of honor and the occurrence of a suicide. But while Werther is offended by the social disregard he experiences in the arrogant aristocratic society, Kapserl does not know such ill feelings. He derives his notion of honor from the sphere of petit-bourgeois religiosity, which is closely tied to a naively accepted soldierly conception of honor. In the hands of the romantic writer, a poetic, socially critical element becomes a historical folkloristic characteristic. Society's rejection of Werther contributes substantially to his suicide; after Kasperl's suicide, however, the grandmother says to the narrator:

> "An order was issued to all the courts, that only those who committed suicide because of melancholy should be buried honorably, all those who acted out of despair are to be sent to the anatomy department; and the court official has told me that he would have to send Kasperl to anatomy, because he himself had admitted his despair." I said: "This is a

very peculiar law because one would have to undertake an investigation for each suicide to determine whether it was a result of melancholia or despair, and such an investigation would take so much time that in the end judges and lawyers themselves could fall into melancholy and despair and would all have to be dispatched to anatomy."[17]

The following interpretation suggests itself: melancholy is a disease and those who are destroyed by it have suffered a random fate. Despair, on the other hand, is a psychological state which attacks the entire system in which an individual person is involved. Thus, despair is a social disease—it is a condition which stigmatizes the social situation as deadly for the individual. Thus we understand why Lessing's *Emilia Galotti* lies opened on Werther's table. With the romantic writer Brentano this option of an implicitly political attitude is suppressed in favor of a simple historical statement. A poetic image with which the young Goethe could stir a whole generation appears here simply as "strange."

In a merely schematic review of the story, one's sense of justice will be violated since two innocent people perish. But the fate of secular suffering, with which this story is concerned, is, so to speak, desecularized; the old woman nurses no doubts about secular justice itself, but is sensitive to the concept of justice only in the sphere of religion.[18] Only the "pardon" granted by the state is at home on earth, and the story closes with the arbitrary compassion of the sovereign: the Duke erects a celebrating justice and pardon on the graveside of the wretched poor, to whom Brentano refers—in a characteristic romantic denial of reality—as "unhappy victims of honor."[19] As long as an act of grace by the sovereign is given the last word in this novel, misery and suffering in the real world are not indicated, but actually transfigured.

The romantic persona contain what might be called a dynamic consolation. To the extent that they have a "real" position in the social world, in other words, to the extent that they are not merely "romantic" figures such as the so-called miners and merchants in *Heinrich von Ofterdingen*, they are all people who will be passed over by social developments and who have no option besides becoming extinct. In this context, think of Eichendorff's wandering journeymen, or of Hoffmann's figures, almost all of whom belong to the small-state bureaucracy. When this imaginary world perishes, the veil with which Romantic poetry has covered reality will also be removed: the Young Germany and early realist writers signify the literary beginnings of the history of the class consciousness of the bourgeoisie.

Notes

1. Arnold Ruge, *Gesammelte Schriften,* vol. 1. (Mannheim, 1846), p. 11.
2. Friedrich Schlegel, *Kritische Ausgabe,* ed. von Ernst Behler, Jean-Jacques Anstett, and Hans Eichner. Munich; and Schlegel. *Charakteristiken und Kritiken I* (Zurich, 1967), p. 161.
3. Clemens Brentano, *Werke,* vol. 2. ed. Friedhelm Kemp (Munich, 1963), p. 781ff.
4. Proof of the German bourgeois ambivalence regarding the literary artist can be found in a later epoch: "We are not, after all, gypsies travelling in a green wagon, but respectable people, Consul Kroeger, family Kroeger . . ." muses young Tonio as his conscience troubles him slightly. Quoted from Thomas Mann, *Tonio Kroeger,* Novellen, vol. 2 (Frankfurt, 1922). Reprinted in *Werke,* 12 vols. (Frankfurt, 1967), "Erzaehlungen I," p. 208.
5. Schlegel, p. 105.
6. Novalis, *Schriften,* ed. Paul Kluckhohn, Richard Samuel, Hans Joachim Maehl, and Gerhard Schulz, vol. 2: *Das philosophische Werk I,* (Stuttgart, 1965), pp. 432, 433.
7. Brentano, p. 778.
8. Schlegel, p. 155.
9. Ibid., p. 156.
10. Novalis, *Schriften,* vol. 3: *"Das philosophische Werk II"* (Stuttgart, 1968), p. 638.
11. Schlegel, p. 153.
12. Novalis, *Schriften,* vol. 1: *"Das dichterische Werk"* (Stuttgart, 1960), p. 346.
13. Ibid., p. 325.
14. Brentano, vol. 1, p. 806.
15. Ludwig Tieck, *Schriften.* vol. 6 (Berlin, 1828), p. 179.
16. Schlegel, *Kritische Ausgaben,* vol. 5: "Dichtungen," p. 53.
17. Brentano, pp. 793ff.
18. Brentano, p. 798.
19. Ibid., p. 806.

9

"Young Germany": Prehistory of Bourgeois Consciousness

The July Revolution of 1830 smashed the Bourbon reign, which had been restored after Napoleon, and led to the institutionalization of the bourgeois king. With this event, the French bourgeoisie gained ultimate political hegemony. While the upheaval had its effects on the German bourgeoisie as well, the efforts made by that class to topple its own crowned tyrants remained unsuccessful. A series of political riots in the years 1832, 1833, and 1937 only led to an increase in reactionary administrative measures. But the German bourgeoisie actually showed relatively little interest in politics during the fairly stable period between 1815 and 1848, and this disinterest prevailed until the founding of the Reich. While a process of gradual democratiziation occurred in the former states of the *Rheinbund,* in Northern Germany the political and economic demands of the bourgeoisie were by and large met by the Customs Union *(Zollverein)* of 1834, and with the constitutional concessions that were instituted between 1847 and 1849. These demands were met to such an extent, in fact, that between 1849 and 1859 even industrialists and bankers, who were increasingly gaining economic power, practiced political abstinence.

The Young Germany was a radical bourgeois movement which mirrored the influence of the July Revolution as well as the conditions prevailing in Germany thereafter. It was a particularly sensitive instrument for measuring the intellectual problematics because the stratum of freelance writers was specifically affected by the continued existence of the outdated political forms of absolutism and the remnants of feudalism. In contrast to France, where an ever-expanding group of literary intellectuals had developed without interruption since the Enlightenment, the politically backward Germany offered no such possibilities. Democratization proceeded slowly, as did industrialization; bourgeois consciousness developed even more slowly, and therefore the preconditions for the formation of a literary audience were not propitious. Initially, the Young Germany polemically used political and social issues to draw attention to the conditions of its own literary existence. But in wielding their pens in the service of timely subjects, the writers emancipated themselves from a romantic position; and in reflecting on the bases of their own social existence, they laid the foundation for a more general reflection of social conditions. The Young Germany welcomed for the first time the social question as a topic for literature.

This movement had its precursors; these include Platen, Christian Dietrich Grabbe, Lenau and Franz Grillparzer. While all four belong to the generation of late romanticism, they lived and worked as artists already in an atmosphere of the new reality-oriented world of professionally oriented writers. Thus, one might remember that Lenau is not satisfied with a romanticized glorification of history in his "Schlussgesang" ("Closing Song") of the *Albigenser.* Instead, in direct reference to the present, he talks of the "fragmentation of our times" and of the "freedom" which beckons as the goal of future generations. Thereby, he demonstrates an attitude that stands in contrast to the elimination of the future prevailing in the Romantic movement.[1] One might further recollect how Grillparzer surprises his audience in *Der Traum ein Leben* (*The Dream a Life*) when he reveals that the romantic gaiety of the action leads the mere shadow-existence of a dream, and that the protagonist Rustan is happy when he finds that he does not have to continue his sleep. In the fourth act Rustan says:

> and I stretch and shake,
> morning breeze touches my forehead.
> When the day arrives, all is clear.[2]

One might also think of Platen, who riles against the idiocy of readers encouraged by potboilers and the low quality novels of Heinrich Clauren, Christian August Vulpius or Johann Zschokke; he condemns the bombastic and pessimistic "literature of fate" (*Schicksalsdichtung*) of Adolf Muellner, Zacharies Werner or Ernst Raupach. Platen is the enemy of all pseudoprofundity; that is, of any attempt to veil the real situation in which he and his contemporaries live by whatever devices.

His rejection of Goethe becomes understandable in the context of his bourgeois enlightenment attitude and specifically of his feelings of responsibility regarding the mission of the literary artist to identify reality as it is, to call everything by its appropriate name, For him. Goethe is too harmless when he loses himself in the contemplation of natural objects. He sees Goethe as spinning himself into "a cocoon in the world of plants," while he, Platen, feels deeply moved by the "unfolding complexity of human fate."[3]

Therefore, the classicism of Platen's poetic form has nothing to do with the classical measure of the later Goethe and Schiller—at least in the context of a sociological interpretation. Rather, it is linked with his animosity toward romanticism's fragmentation and its selective omissions of reality. Platen's classicism is an expression of bourgeois discipline, which reveals itself even in gesture and outward countenance. Although Platen, like Goethe, visited Italy, he did not go there in search of antiquity or the baroque, but rather in order to live among people fighting for their political freedom. And finally, think of Grabbe's critical attitude toward Shakespeare, about whose historic dramas he remarks:

> It is true that all of his strengths and talents are apparent in them [the dramas]; here, where he is unique, Goethe can hardly compete with him (for example, in *Egmont*), and Schiller can do so even less. But from a poet who undertakes to dramatize history, I expect a *dramatic, concentric treatment of history which also reproduces the idea of history.* This is what Schiller strove for and his healthy German sense guided him. None of his historic plays are without a dramatic center and without a concentric idea. Even if you allow that Shakespeare is more objective than Schiller, his historic dramas . . . are nothing more than poetically decorated chronicles. No center . . . no final goal is visible in most of them.[4]

Platen spoke under the impression of the July Revolution which Goethe dismissed with a gesture, only to proceed talking to Johann Peter Eckermann about Leopold Cuvier and Saint Hilare. In Grabbe, the legitimation of poetry through politics is expressed even more explicitly. It is peculiar, however, that Shakespeare serves as his negative star witness when he proves his point. Since the middle of the eighteenth century, there is little for which Shakespeare has not invoked as a reference point. Wieland translates him as a writer of enlightened courtliness; for Lessing and Herder, who were moved by their incipient bourgeois perception of the world, he is the great example of authenticity; he serves the romantics as the enchanter who transforms harsh reality into a sweet world of semblances. And he is criticized by an early bourgeois realist.

Grabbe's criticism has the same roots as Platen's, Lenau's and Grillparzer's: dissatisfaction with reality. We sensed this same atttude in romanticism, but now this negative mood is no longer repressed and converted into poetry, but instead finds its conscious and direct expression in a critique of the social facts and issues which are on the contemporary agenda. The Young Germans and to a lesser extent their literary predecessors were the first intellectual generation of bourgeois enlightenment in Germany.

Not until the 1820s and 1830s do economic and social conditions prevail which resemble those that existed in France in the 1770s and 1780s. But the conditions were similar rather than identical, because the pace of economic development of the Western European powers pushed Germany into a defensive position. At the same time, however, the proletariat was of great significance in Germany during this period than it was in eighteenth century France, and we encounter proletarian poets like Ferdinand Freiligrath, Georg Herwegh, and Georg Weerth at this time. It is probably no coincidence that they were poets rather than playwrights. At this time, no theory of society dealing with the social role of the proletariat and no proletarian class consciousness had been developed; poetry was, for the time being, the available resource to give nonconformism a voice. No play exists in which the proletariat might become visible as a factor in history, and there is no novel that includes the proletariat as acting personnel. Things are different for the bourgeoisie. Grabbe precisely expresses the desire for a social theory which would define the position of the individual historically and endow his political activity with a direction and a goal. The fact that Grabbe undertakes to improve Shakespeare, not with plays but with novels, is very characteristic for the historic situation of the bourgeoisie during the generation of the Young Germany.

Theodor Mundt, himself a spokesman for the Young Germany, once said. "Gendarmes are positioned in front of the theater to guard the play. The novella flees to the drawing room where there are no gendarmes. In the privacy of his own home, the German believes in liberty and in a higher national life. There he looks almost as though history might be able to make use of him one day."

This established the possibilities and the limits of the Young Germany. The movement did not change and transform society and it did not set out to do so. Its strength lay in its diagnosis of the times, in its "taking inventory" of society, and also in its protest against the status quo. But a firm belief in a final hegemony of the bourgeoisie or any conception of how this goal might be achieved was missing. By and large, the literati of this movement could not translate such a concept of social change into the dialectical form of the drama as harbinger of conflict solution.

Karl Gutzkow is the most significant narrative representative of the Young Germany. Even in his personality, he is more independent than Heinrich Laube, Mundt or Ludolf Wienbarg. Heine and Ludwig Boerne, the creators of the feuilleton—the art form of independent writing—had a strong influence on him. Heine's statement, "journals are our fortifications," had an eminent political significance. The Young Germany led the struggle for what might be called an intellectual customs union—extending the ideology of free competition into the intellectual realm. (Incidently, the Young Germany was never a conscious union of particular poets and writers, rather, this nomenclature was a creation of the police.) An actual union was almost realized, but in 1835, the German Bundestag, at the instigation of the reactionary informer on literature Wolfgang Menzel, issued a prohibition of the literary journal *Deutsche Revue*, which was in the planning. Simultaneously, a more general prohibition of all future literary publications of the Young Germany was ordered. As a result, the movement dissolved and most of its members turn into reactionaries. And so a stratum of bourgeois ideologues crumbles because its audience does not exist yet.

Gutzkow himself felt increasingly isolated in the midst of the rising literary philistinism, and his material situation also became exceedingly difficult. Together with Friedrich Hebbel, he was one of the first poets of proletarian origin, He was born on March 17, 1811 in Berlin; his father was the royal "breaker-in" of horses and the young poet grew up in the milieu of proletarians who were loyal to the throne. As a nineteen- year-old, he witnessed the July Revolution, which inspired him with enthusiasm; he abandoned his study of theology and turned to writing. He left Berlin at the age of twenty, and this marked the beginning of his turbulent life as a writer.

At first, he was successful as a playwright and in the 1840s he was the reigning figure in the German theather. He toyed with the idea of carrying on a project begun by Lessing—the editing of Hermann Samuel Reimarus's philosophical writings, but the publisher rejected the proposal. In 1850, his novel *Die Ritter vom Geiste* (*The Spiritual Knights*) is published, followed by *Der Zauberer von Rom* (*The Magician of the Land*), published between 1851 and 1861. Because he lacked material means, he was also forced to write pieces without literary significance. He died on December 16, 1878. Gutzkow's story *Wally die Zweiflerin*

(*Wally the Sceptic*) was the reason for the notorious Bundestag's decree of 1835 against Young German writers.[5]

The novella was declared indecent because it includes a scene in which a woman shows herself nude to another man with whom she is in love on the eve of her wedding, a scene which is modeled on the medieval poetry of Sigune and Schionatulander. The real reason for the general censorship of this book, however, must be sought somewhere else. The instinct of the reactionary powers was superb; it was not this episode of nudity but the story as a whole which accomplished what the Bundestag decree took to be the intention of the Young German Movement, namely, "the discrediting of existing social conditions."[6] Although an occasion for the censorship can also be found in the realm of writing and literary criticism out of which the Young Germany originally developed—in this case, it was provided by Wolfgang Menzel who feared the competition—the political significance of the prohibition extends far beyond the boundaries of the literary community into the open sea of social critique. The very title, which includes the word "sceptic" reveals clearly the critical attitude of the story.

The novella actually had personal origins: Gutzkow's experience of Charlotte Stieglitz's suicide. Her death was intended to shake her husband, a literary artist, out of his dull and narrow-minded attitude. The Young Germans did not treat this woman's fate as the romantics would have done, whose adoration of woman was based on the belief that she is a unique and special being possessing strong irrational powers. Charlotte Stieglitz, on the other hand, wanted to tear the bourgeoisie from the confines of philistine comfort and victorian (*Biedermeier*) resignation and bring it into a conscious and active life. As an intellectual product of this suicide, *Wally* is a piece of consciously tendentious literature.

In a preface to a new edition of *Wally*, Gutzkow wrote late in 1851:

> This is how one thinks of everything in literature that does not follow the straight path which everyone wants to follow. Poets are like solitary couriers who imprint the snow-covered roads with the first footprints early in the winter morning, when the roosters have hardly begun to crow. It is easy for you to promenade down these same roads at noontime: Think of those who had to search—somewhere between field and forest and pond, beneath an indeterminable snowy expanse (for who can determine the realm of premonition!)—for that road at dawn; those who had no lead other than the smoke from the almost invisible white chimneys, [searching] at a time when the comfortable sleeper is awakening to hot coffee.[7]

In these words, the artist's attitude, which counterposes itself to romanticism, becomes apparent. Certainly, the artist continues to think of himself as someone special; certainly, he attributes a greater significance to his task; certainly, he does not—as Gustav Freytag and Friedrich Spielhagen do in later years—include the activity of writing as just another profession in the general catalogue of bourgeois occupations. But while the romantic writer still finds a great measure of happiness in his productivity, for Gutzkow being a writer has a bitter flavor. The artist exists in opposition to society, not because his world exists apart from everyday reality, but on the contrary, because it is his duty to face everyday reality. A romantic would lose himself in the dusk and enter, as Novalis did, into the secrets of the night. But the Young German poet tears himself away from such complacency, which appears to him as dull and philistine; he strides into the advancing day, into the future. He moves in exactly the opposite direction as the romantic: the everyday world and the bourgeois home.

Gutzkow himself was aware of the fact that this new attitude of the writer was related to the situation of the bourgeoisie which had been undergoing gradual changes since the 1830s. As Spielhagen was to do sometime later, Gutzkow touches on the connection between literature and society. Indeed in the preface cited above he goes so far as to explicate his story, written twenty years earlier, in reference to the social and political conditions which then prevailed. Regarding the present, the 1850s, he sees the possibility that, because of the diminishing reactionary politics, new issues might be raised by the writers. He says:

> The rumbling, which was not absent 16 to 20 years ago, even though it was not very audible, spread into the realm of art and literature and went on to rumble in those creations which are referred to as tendentious literature. . . . The era between 1830 and 1848 was full of parliamentary proceedings, censorship decisions, imprisonments, expulsions from all German states, but under this imposed ice-cover of laws and legislation, the sea roared and rushed, moved by the breath of eternal spring. Quiet love towards all kinds of humanistic ideals had moved everyone, giving this epoch a dreamy and impractical air, especially in consideration of the fact that in a country without a public sphere and with a censored press, a population easily comes to lead a drawing-room existence as it is still the case today in Russia. . . . This much is certain: the less we allow ourselves to exist as German monks, the more certainly we can avoid similarly tangled paths of thought and imagination. Censorship was the most dangerous closure. . . . The public realm, the freedom of political life, great ideas in general will become regulators for our world, it is just like with the theater, where the visualization audience educates the playwright.[8]

Gutzkow thus addresses the connection between the romantic movement and the Young Germans: indeed, both of them contained "rumblings." But in romanticism, the significance of this rumbling was never made conscious. The Young Germans, on the other hand, treated at least the symptoms, if not the cause of the rumblings in their literature. Gutzkow is aware that the generalizing and diffused direction of the romantics and the Young Germans is an ideological product of their inability to play a constructive role in public affairs. Lessing's comment at the end of the *Hamburgische Dramaturgie* comes to mind: "one cannot create a national theater for the Germans as long as the Germans are not a nation."[9] Similar to Lessing, who touches on the interconnections between the political and social situation of an epoch on the one hand and its intellectual phenomena on the other, Gutzkow establishes a relationship between the "audience" and the "drama." In fact, Gutzkow is following Lessing's conception of the theater as a mouthpiece for the rising bourgeoisie:

> A national body which has enough room for all of its movements, which does not have its arms tied and its feet hound, will bear a healthy and clear national soul. Well! Do not droop your wings, but fly towards the sun! For us Germans, it is contained in the one statement: A great, undivided nation with the strong organs of a natural and free movement.[10]

Bourgeois class consciousness proclaims itself under the title of the "national." This merely follows the pattern of the French Revolution and the German Storm and Stress (*Sturm und Drang*) movement, and will turn up again in Gustav Freytag. In contrast to the absolutist police state, whose despotism in lawmaking, administration, foreign and domestic policy only serves the interests of a very small group, the nation appears as the real chance for unbridled business activity. No longer is the individual the hero of Gutzkow's story, but society itself. Gutzkow chooses the rising propertied bourgeoisie, merchants as well as intellectuals, for his subjects. He himself explains in his preface that Charlotte Stieglitz's death was merely the occasion for the story and that he did not write the novel "simply for the sake of a psychological problem."[11]

Yet psychology itself (as will be shown) is actually a progressive element in the writings of Eduard Mörike as well as Gutzkow. Psychology serves as the vehicle by which sociology and even the natural sciences—all scientific endeavors oriented toward ordering and controlling the social and natural environment—enter into bourgeois consciousness. But Gutzkow wants to avert any suspicion that he is concerned only with an individual—even if it be a highly gifted individual—the way the romantics were. On the contrary, as Gutzkow states, "This novel, motivated by Charlotte Stieglitz's death, is an attempt to depict an interest in ideas as well as a personal and purely emotional matter in the context of everyday existence."[12]

When he says "ideas," Gutzkow means the public sphere in the broadest sense, the social forces of his time. In exact opposition to romanticism, immediate everyday reality is to become the guiding methodological canon of literary representation.

And the most immediate aspect of everyday social reality is its disintegration. Bourgeois society is sick and the writer diagnoses this disease. The presence of doctors, sanatoriums and health spas in the story is not coincidental. The pathology of society is actually the theme. Gutzkow no longer conceals the collective disease which has befallen the social "organism" by pushing it into the realm of fairy tales or dreams, he makes this conscious. One could actually say that a very specific disease is the decisive theme of the story: nervousness. Almost all the characters in *Wally*, especially the heroine and Caesar, are nervous creatures: fidgety, playful, dreamy, without a desire to work; satiated, insomniac, unfit for life—they appear, as it were, faded. Perhaps the description of Caesar's character will clarify the significance of this phenomenon:

> Caesar was in his mid-twenties. Around his nose and mouth twisted furrows into which the early seed of knowledge had fallen, those lines that could mount from the friendliest of impressions to a level of demonic sinisterness. Caesar's education was complete. Whatever he absorbed now could only serve to strengthen, but not to change, what already existed within him. He had climbed the first ladder of the idealistic rapture that our age has allowed to penetrate young minds. He had behind him an entire cemetary of dead thoughts, glorious ideas in which he had once believed: he no longer fell prostrate before himself and let his past embrace his future and pray to it: holy future, glowing Moloch, when shall I cease to sacrifice myself to myself? He no longer buried the dead; the silent ideas lay so far from him that his movements could not crush them any more. He was ripe, only a follower of forms, only a skeptic; he dealt with the shadows of concepts, with an enthusiasm now past. His schooling was completed, and his only recourse was to action; whatever his meaningless ideas made of him, he possessed a strong character. Unhappy youth! You are still cut off from the field of activity, your soul is so sated with knowledge that it cannot be born anew in the stream of events; you can only smile, sigh, ridicule, and if you love, make the ladies unhappy![13]

We are introduced to a wealthy young man from bourgeois circles, a man whom the writer says is full of urgency for activity. Objectively, however, there are no possibilities for realizing this urge for action.

We thus come face to face with the conflict between bourgeois interests and a diametrically opposed life situation. At this point, there is still no clarity as to the origins of these contradictions, there is no clarity about how these stirring powers might be developed. But the directions toward the future, the "holy future," has definitely been taken. The generation of the 1830s is no longer satisfied with the imminent resignation of romanticism; indeed, the abdication of romanticism actually enters consciousness:

> Still, everything turned out better than expected. The gradual waning of romanticism is relaxing the hitherto tense nerves of the various nations. There were enough Germans there who were suffering from Hoffmann's death, enough Frenchmen who sensed the bad consequences of Victor Hugo's inactive pen. They all sought pleasure. The Spanish crisis had struck the vitals of many and had given rise to a hypochondria of sorts. Iron water spas are to be highly recommended.[14]

In relation to literature and society, liberal currents in Southern Europe appeared as an appropriate stimulus for the intellectual and spiritual movement of the bourgeoisie. After all, the category of "enticement" refers to nothing else than change. And the necessity of change no longer appears in the romantic cloak, but is uncovered as discontentment. Upon careful scrutiny, we see that its form of expression is nervousness. No analysis of style is necessary in order to recognize nervousness as the mental symptom of the contradictory situation of the 1830s; Gutzkow himself actually undertakes the depiction of a collective disease.

The application of this sociological interpretation of nervousness reveals the inversion of the romantic method. We saw how Brentano transmuted and transformed realistic situations into the romantic world of appearances. Conversely, Gutzkow takes situations which could serve as appropriate entries into the romantic realm, rids these of illusions, and dissolves them in a realistic manner. This is evident in the scene in which Wally cannot sleep:

> One evening Wally had gone to bed late and in a bad mood. The lamp was still burning on her table, but she could not sleep. Her blood was in a fever of excitement. She tossed back and forth, but her body simply could not relax.

> Suddenly she jumped up, sat down at the table and began to try all the methods which people recommend for calming the blood. She counted the twelve strokes of the steeple clock, did the multiplication

tables backwards and forwards, and recited the one poem which she, with her bad memory, knew by heart: "A little bee flits from flower to flower, And sucks quite busily by the hour." Nothing helped. Then her eye lit upon the table and the articles which she had recently gotten out to write to her friend. She seized the pen and wrote.[15]

Here, night does not appear embellished with its natural and supernatural secrets; no one descends into a magic intermediary realm of soulful or cosmic dusk; instead, the nervous Wally uses customary means to find sleep.

One might also think of Wally's reaction when Caesar tells her the story of the wife of the trumpet player, who was plagued by a bad conscience. Caesar describes her so vividly that in the end he jestingly pretends that the foolish woman is actually standing before them at that very moment:

> "Where?" screamed Wally.
> Caesar laughed. It was meant in jest, but she did not take it that way and bitterly gave vent to her feelings about his jokes and fantastic tales.
> "Go on with your drums and trumpets! What crazy things you get involved in," she snapped peevishly, took her leave, and went back alone to the Kaisersaal."[16]

Wally is ashamed that she did not immediately think of "weakness of nerves," of "drum addiction," and similar psychopathic symptoms of the woman the way that Caesar did, instead of allowing herself to be infected by the situation of which he spoke.

We can see that every mythic or folkloristic secret which romanticism would love is destroyed. This secularization, or better, this realistic-scientific fragmentation of favorite romantic configurations is most pronounced in the treatment of religion. At one point it is said about Wally that she suffers from a "religious tick, a disease which expressed itself in nervous irritability rather than in long and drawn out pain,"[17] because she so loved her deceased mother. Her religiosity is actually a phenomenon that can be explained psychologically, and this fact is also demonstrated in the following passage taken from a conversation she has with one of her husband's brothers:

> "Forget philosophy, Wally! In the bosom of God you once wore the same yellow slippers your foot now cocquettishly toys with."
>
> Yellow slippers. They are shoes, my dear sir! Wally responded, angry over this humor. She could not stand blasphemy. Then she always thought of her deceased mother.[18]

Even though Gutzkow does not assume an unequivocal position on religion, his psychological reduction of religious affects is far removed from the romantic veneration of religiosity. From this individual-psychological explanation of religion, it is not a long distance to a socio-psychological one. Gutzkow himself took a few steps in that direction. Indeed, the fact that Gutzkow's novel treats religion as one of several manifestations of the general syndrome of nervous irritability afflicting bourgeois society constitutes such a sociopsychological element.

At this point, the disillusionment still has an essentially negative character. If one is permitted to say that romanticism holds to the ideal of the childlike, while later realist writing, in full possession of bourgeois self-confidence, has the adult as its ideal, one should like to select the half-grown, *Weltschmerz* adolescent as the generational symbol of the Young Germany. While romanticism devalues reality by ignoring it, this story, much like other Young German works, does not really take it seriously at all. Rather, reality becomes material for playful activity. The curtains have been drawn away, the feudal world order is no longer impressive. Class forces are active enough that they do not suffocate in the hopelessness which is so often implied in romantic writings. But still, political reaction is in power and liberal society is unable to unfold. The playful individualism which is expressed in *Wally* is the immediate precursor of a liberalism which takes reality quite seriously, as Gustav Freytag will demonstrate. Playful dissolution, depreciation, and shredding of reality is best accomplished by the heroine of the story:

> But one type of conversation is inexhaustible, one kind of play-acting untiring. That is coquetry. Wally had her hands full of this. Artificial and natural moods were the numbers of which she constructed her examples of deportment. Wally let the whole world dance around like elastic toy figures on the sounding-board of her sudden inspirations. For all these movements which made her laugh she played capricious melodies. What else would she possibly want? She did not even want the reputation of being able to juggle the tastes of her surroundings so excellently. She did it all witliout pride, without design, without consciousness. She was bewitching![19]

Inconsistency and instability are necessary aspects of this nervous attitude. But contradictoriness is no longer ideologically mystified as the essence of reality, as it was with the romantics. Instead, a playfulness that borders on cynicism exists side by side with a diffuse humanitarianism as unconnected manifestation of this reality. The erotic element, which led to disillusionment when it was played out, becomes the object of pantheistic rapture.

> She allowed Caesar to embrace her, not because she loved him or out of egotism or of pride at having conquered a man, but because she felt herself the weak link in the great chain of being which God had created, because she knew that she was indeed quite naked and exposed and pitiable in the face of truth and nature, and finally because she believed that the burning kisses which Caesar was pressing on her lips were for all the millions beneath the firmament.

> Behold here a scene that could not have happened in earlier times! Here all is artful, contrived, born from the inner disharmony of our times—and what is the truth of Romeo and Juliet when compared to this lie! What is selfish sexual love compared with this enthusiasm of ideas which can hurl two souls into the most wretched of confusions! I tremble before a century that is so tragic in its errors and yet worthy of adoration even in its accursedness![20]

So far we have selected material which permits a general understanding of the social situation of the Young German poets. But this story also contains very specific bourgeois elements.

First of all we find a keen, differentiated psychology. Consider for example, how differently disposed Wally and Caesar seem to be toward suicide. A kind of instinctual disposition for greater or lesser susceptibility is assumed by Gutzkow. He writes: "Suicide, in all of its various forms was all around her, and the consequence of madness stretched out—like bony, suffocating arms—towards those who were at all accessible to them. Ceasar warded them off, Wally was less able to do so."[21] When considered from a psychological standpoint, the way in which Wally forgets herself when the unloved husband leaves her bedroom is observed even more realistically:

> She wiped her face where he had touched it. She aired the bed to cleanse it of the lewd words which had fallen into it, for it was turned down. For the first time she grasped the situation in which she found herself: that for the last four months she had been married to a man whom she did not know. Soundlessly the words rose up in her: She had to flee! Not until she had considered the means by which she could accomplish this foolishness did she go to sleep.[22]

Here, Gutzkow assumes conscious and unconscious psychic reactions. Even the phenomenon of repression appears when Wally falls asleep precisely when she should be thinking about concrete possibilities for the realization of her fantasies. We also encounter the possibility of interpretation of expressions. The presentation of such psychologized details, of minute events, is reminiscent of Stendhal's statement: "*il n'y a que les détails*." The predecessors of this psychological literature can be found in the French Enlightenment. Then as now, applied psychology is a necessary precondition for the development of capitalist society; one must know one's partner and understand with whom one is dealing in business transactions. In liberal economy, contractual freedom of movement has replaced the secure boundaries of the estates, a rigidly regulated economic system. The producer or the merchant confronts other producers, merchants or consumers who have not become familiar with each other through a network of tradition. He must know the motives of others, he must understand their psychological makeup in minute details better than they know him or themselves.

This brings us to a second aspect of bourgeois specificity. Conversation is the measure of psychological knowledge of freely competing subjects. He who is better, more agile and adept at this, who has rational superiority due to his knowledge of the reactions of his conversation partner, will secure a victory. A history of the dialogue could show how the verbal exchange developed—and was, indeed, forced to develop—from a rigid and fairly safe tradition to become a "casual," an inventive conversation technique of bourgeois society. In this context, one might think of the rhetorically bound mode of expression in Johann von Saatz's *Ackermann aus Boehmen* at the middle of the 15th century and of the endlessly varied conversation deluge in Spielhagen's fictional world three hundred years later. Gutzkow's story may very well represent the first example of a modern converation in bourgeois society. Selected excerpts from such a conversation are cited below:

> Caesar said nothing. Her last answer was too serious. He looked at the five rings which he wore over his gloves and asked: "Are you going to the spa?"
> "In a week."
> "You'll see the Rhine?"
> "From Mainz to Cologne."
> "From Mainz to Düsseldorf. You can't miss visiting Immermann and the painters. If Düsseldorf were in Thuringia it would be a second Weimar."

"Are the river banks really so charming?"

"They are pleasant, and beautiful at the spots where you allow some
sentiment to enter your observation."

"I don't understand."

"The beautiful, Wally, is always synonymous with the surprising."

"What you're trying to say is that nature will speak to us only according
to how our eyes and hearts see her."

"Once I was standing in the Cologne cathedral. You are aware of
the disruptive principle of our times, that of assuming nothing
as right which is proclaimed by people who oppose us, even if it
might be right."

"The Rhine steamers go too fast."

"They go too slowly and tire your eyes. The idea of a fiery turtle
creeping across the water is part of our imagination, and we
have simply become accustomed to considering the creeping
slow."

"That's a strange image! I wonder what my aunt is laughing about
so loudly. . . ."

"Your aunt is a spider creeping over the ocean."

"What makes you say that?"

"She's speculating in stocks."

"She's talking politics. It's all beyond me."

"If it were within your grasp, you'd resemble a butterfly which had
strayed into the gas-lit confusion of a drawing-room."

"Butterflies have been overused as analogies."

"Like immortality itself."[23]

Certainly, this conversation still contains elements of playfulness
and witticisms as ends in themselves. But in moving from weighty to
small matters and back again, interspersing emotions with business
matters, it contains all the necessary elements of a successful modern
conversation.

When Wally and Caesar speak of the "discovery of gunpowder, of
the law of gravity, of the compass and the magnetic needle," when it
is said of Wally that she enjoys using "physical analogies,"[24] we are
touching again on the bourgeois content of the story: the positive
elements of the Enlightenment. First of all, conversation turns to the
natural sciences, whose significance for bourgeois society had been
mentioned already;[25] but the topic of economic life is not absent either.
It is no coincidence that a great part of the story takes place in Paris;
in the 1830s, France was the most progressive bourgeois nation; Italy
no longer held that position and England did not occupy it yet. During the era of the July Monarchy, industrial capital develops next to

more archaic forms of commercial capital. Gutzkow confirms these developments:

> To the two old aristocratic elements of Parisian society, the Bourbons and the Bonapartes, the most recent revolution had added a third aristocracy, that of the banker. Since the emergence of this class, with whom it was difficult to compete financially, money had become the social lever more than ever before. Because the Parisians do not hoard money but rather amass it as a dowry and then let it be tossed about by the wind, every manifestation of life is ultimately swept along by the metallic current. This raging river causes the most hideous devastations in morality and friendship. Its ebbing and flowing determine life and death. It does not flow underground, but discharges itself freely, openly, before the eyes of all. Its goldfrothing billows roll through stately halls and the poorest hovels. In Paris one is always close to money, not so much the money one has as that of which one cannot get enough, and which one desperately tries to acquire. Out of this problem arise most of the tragic and comic conflicts in Parisian society.[26]

Here, Gutzkow is reminiscent of Balzac. He establishes not only money as social reality, but also the potential and social position of the capitalists, and he tries to show all social phenomena as determined by capital. Granted, his attitude toward this state of affairs is critical and his reservations might even appear to be petit bourgeois, especially if one considers the following excerpt:

> She was an energetic confederate in that great campaign against nature, truth, virtue, and universal freedom, which almost always coincides with the lives of the great, a campaign, however, whose danger is outweighed by the joys of its petty victories.[27]

Here, Wally appears as a member of the newly developing bourgeoisie, a class which is presented only in its negative aspects and only in the realm of ideologies. But this criticism grows out of essentially realistic considerations and, furthermore, is an expression of the German bourgeoisie's insecurity about its own interests.

Directly connected to this is the greatest defect in Gutzkow's sociological analysis. His analysis knows no theory; it does not arrive at a comprehensive image of society and it finally loses itself in mere details with which it had started out. His analysis amounts to a pathology of society, but it is a pathology of symptoms rather than one that might actually lead to diagnosis and therapy. In fact, it is much the same pathology as that portrayed by Balzac. With the character Luigi, Gutzkow created a figure that could have come out of one of Balzac's novels:

> Luigi knew that his brother would come to Paris. When he saw what an impression Wally made on Jeronimo he realized that he had a method to use against him and did not shy away from it. What did Wally mean to him? What pleasure had she ever bestowed upon him? Yet he was not so base that he actually intended to sell her to his brother. He was more evil than mean, marked more by European wickedness than Italian vulgarity. He wanted to hold Jeronimo's desire in check and in that way to assure his own profit. His avaricious side saw with horror how his brother's fortune would drain into the thirsty sands of Parisian pleasures and extravagances. He could already visualize a thousand open arms, a thousand caresses laid as traps; he trembled in the face of this wide ocean whose depths must soon swallow up Jeronimo's inheritance. He wanted to rescue it. He wanted to absorb it first, as he thought, in order to protect it, and then, in order never to release it again. Wally had to serve his purpose. Her coquetry had to captivate Jeronimo and make him unhappy. Luigi worked methodically to upset the mind of his brother.[28]

Such a nervous and criminal character creates the impression that the Young Germany feared its own courage. The bourgeois class situation becomes conscious, but it does so in a way as to appear abnormal. The question whether the proletariat, which is already growing in spite of the underdeveloped German condition, plays a role at this time—as it was to do later in Spielhagen's work—remains open. Suffering is relativized because its cause is regarded as a disease which is, in principle, curable. Gutzkow imagines a way out from social changes in the following terms:

> The impoverishment of society is a great wrong, but the distribution of wealth would not alleviate it. Because who can give wealth together with the ability to preserve it? It would not be long before diligence would once again be way ahead of laziness. But something has to be done. We must awaken a consciousness of kindness or even reverence towards nature. We must mobilize the urge to sacrifice in our feelings; we must attain at least this: that no one who lives in a palace admist poverty that has not even rags with which to cover itself can sleep easily at night; we must reach this goal: that money is no longer drawn out of circulation, out of agriculture and industry by the stock and bond market. The egoism and the coldness of our contemporaries is hidden in countless separate ways and bifurcations. What means do we have for our campaign?

None other than those of the world, none more convincing than those of poetry. . . . My novel—in so far as it indeed has a particular tendency—is written in this sense. It is the tendency to give the Christian mentality a new direction, to bring it into harmony with the morals and the needs of this time, to make it the foundation of a new movement. In my first novel, I attempted to develop liberalism into a religious matter and to characterize all progress of the spirit and of truth as a significant moment of Christian ideas. If later I tore myself away from the theological one-sidedness and pursued a negative course on the road to achieveing my goal, [I did so] because I had become a prisoner of art—it is rare that the artistic creator is fortunate enough to hit upon just the right thing. I wanted to portray the picture of a sad restlessness of the soul, for which our egoistic time offers countless examples, and I wanted to depict an end to the violence of which would constitute a warning that would encourage us to contemplate our hearts and the decisions we make."[29]

He says himself that these statements, which he directs to the critics of his novel *Wally* in 1835 as the "last words in a literary debate,"[30] capture precisely the tendency of his novel. His first priority is warding off communism which is, for him, Saint Simonism. He does not intend to identify with the interests of the proletariat, but he is not willing to take the side of the bourgeoisie, either. Instead, he paints the picture of a "capitalist mentality," thereby becoming, in the last analysis, a representative of petit bourgeois resentment in spite of his other tendencies which were mentioned before. He knows no solution for the contradictions of bourgeois society besides his general idealist analysis which he labels, incorrectly, as liberalism.

Gutzkow could not have found better evidence for what he writes in his preface of 1851, that the literature of the 1830s had "a preeminently dreamy and impractical character."[31] For a particular sphere, he accomplishes a brilliant description of the propertied bourgeoisie *via* the sociological introduction of nervousness. But the reactionary forces are still powerful enough that nothing besides idealist generalities can appear as solutions. And this ideological conception—that the world will change if a more decent mentality develops—shows his relationship with the romantic spiritualization of reality. In Gutzkow's conception of religious improvement, the illusion that a social order can be transformed without a change of its material basis lingers on. Indeed, he only had ridicule for the notion of change when he seriously considered it. In 1835, he already had an alibi that distanced him from any revolutionary theory, and sixteen years later he repeated his protest against the socialists:

> The human spirit wanders as in a desert; taking a small oasis such as Saint-Simonism as a newly discovered green island of salvation; accepting communism as real—with smoking chimneys, tasty meals, and all conceivable comfortable amenities—for which one had to pay nothing, only to furnish simple proof of being human. All of them were fata morganas.[32]

In Gutzkow's works, the ideologization of social conflict, which appears as alienated in romanticism, becomes consciously aware of itself.

Notes

1. Nikolaus Lenau, *Die Albigenser* (Leipzig, 1965), pp. 117ff.
2. Franz Grillparzer, *Saemtliche Werke*, "Ausgewaehlte Briefe, Gespraeche, Berichte," ed. Peter Frank and Karl Poernbacher, vol. 2 (Munich, 1961), p. 166.
3. Cited from Rudolf Schloesser, *August Graf Platen*, vol. 2 (Regensburg, 1913), p. 418.
4. Christian Dietrich Grabbe, "Ueber die Shakespeare-Manie," *Werke und Briefe. Historischkritische Gesamtausgabe*, ed. Alfred Bergmann, vol. 4 (Akademie der Wissenschaften in Goettingen, Emsdetten, 1966), p. 41.
5. George Brandes refers to this book, which he describes as an "extremely weak novel," as the "most momentous literary book of the time." (*Hauptstroemungen der Literatur des 19. Jahrhunderts*, vol. 3 [Berlin, 1924], p. 470.) In a similar vein, Henrich Hubert Houben writes in his preface to the Gutzkow edition published by Max Hesse in Leipzig: "Wally must be seen as an expression of the mood of the times much as Goethe's Werther had been half a century before, even if its poetic form is rather poor." (Vol. 1, p. 46). This is why I prefer the historic-sociological analysis of this work to the *Ritter vom Geiste*.
6. Quoted from Heinrich Hubert Houben, *Jungdeutscher Sturm und Drang* (Leipzig, 1911), p. 63. Also in *Das Junge Deutschland. Texte und Dokumente*, ed. Jost Hermand (Stuttgart, 1967), p. 331.
7. Karl Gutzkow, preface to *Wally die Zweiflerin*, in *Ausgewaehlte Werke*, ed. Heinrich Hubert Houben, vol. 5 (Leipzig, 1908), p. 89.
8. Ibid., pp. 77ff.
9. Gotthold Ephraim Lessing, *Hamburgische Dramaturgie*. "Hundert und erstes, zweites, drittes und viertes Stueck" (Stuttgart, 1963), p. 392.
10. Gutzkow, p. 89.
11. Ibid., p. 83.
12. Ibid., p. 81.
13. Gutzkow, *Wally the Sceptic*. Trans. Ruth Ellen Boetcher-Joeres (Frankfurt, 1974), pp. 30–31.
14. Ibid., p. 41.

15. Ibid., p. 55.
16. Ibid., p. 46.
17. Ibid., p. 53.
18. Ibid., p. 70.
19. Ibid., p. 58.
20. Ibid., p. 50.
21. *Wally* (German ed.), p. 161.
22. *Wally* (English ed.), p. 68.
23. Ibid., pp. 39, 40.
24. *Wally* (German ed.), p. 130.
25. Ibid., p. 133.
26. *Wally* (English ed.), p. 65.
27. Ibid.
28. Ibid., p. 74.
29. Gutzkow, *Appellation an den gesunden Menschenverstand,* in *Ausgewaehlte Werke,* pp. 2l3ff.
30. This was not really his last word in the "Wally scandal." When the novella was published in a new edition in 1851, it contained a long preface, from which we have already quoted.
31. *Appellation,* p. 79.
32. Ibid., p. 78.

10

Eduard Mörike: Troubled Embourgeoisement

Eduard Mörike's work belongs primarily in the period of the Vormaerz, a time when German particularism is still identical with a reactionary domestic policy that enormously hinders the development of a free economy. Between 1815 and 1830, there exists no body of literature which is directly oriented toward the social problematic. All we have is a romantic enchantment of secular life.

If romanticism constitutes a revolution in a type of reality that exists only on the other side of social life, then the Young Germany is a movement which for the first time represents a new literary form expressing the new bourgeois consciousness which energetically moves towards the problems of present day life.

Mörike occupies a special position in the Vormaerz period. This becomes obvious as soon as one begins to look for references to him in literary history, He is treated in a section that deals with the Swabian Literary School; another time, he is said to introduce the beginning of realism; elsewhere, he belongs to late Romanticism; or one finds him under the heading of "marginal figures" or "Biedermeier." We will select two of these strangely different attempts to label him.

Georg Brandes, the voice of progressive liberalism, writes: "There were spirits who aspired upwards, real poets who stood apart from the common paths of literature in those years. These were men such as the excellent poet from the southern part of Germany, Eduard Mörike (b. in 1804), the final offspring of the Swabian Literary School who burst the bounds of the School and who was, as a poet, more a descendent of Goethe's: a writer genuinely gifted with genius, the idyllic, rogueish, sad singer of the life of the soul."[1] Alfred Kleinberg (a right-wing Social Democrat) describes the younger romantics, with whom he explicitly groups Mörike, in the following words: "it was the task of the Romantics to transfigure the day which they helped to bring on, or to escape from its grey drudgery into golden dreams. The conquering trend abdicated once and for all; the clarity of intellect, which had hitherto united itself with the forward rushing imagination on equal terms, slipped away; the dreamy poet had the word."[2]

In much the same sense, the radical socialist and later communist Franz Mehring also places Mörike in the Swabian Literary School, which represented, in his estimation, the reactionary or certainly the philistine tradition of the 1830s and 1840s.[3] The matter becomes even more interesting, when one discovers that Brandes discussed Mörike in a chapter entitled "the revolutionary literature," while Kleinberg treats him under titles such as "romantic reaction" and "Dreamworld."

These seemingly contradictory judgments about Mörike are not, however, mutually exclusive. Indeed, Mörike presents a dialectical phenomenon; he is a transitional figure. On the one hand, he entirely shares the romantic attitude toward life, which essentially dismisses the world, finds no constructive possibilities in it, and certainly refuses those that do exist. Evidence of this attitude can be found in Schleiermacher, for whom the reality of the bourgeois world is the "common and the unworthy" which according to him Schlegel justifiably omitted in Lucinde.[4] On the other hand, in contrast to a true romantic, Mörike does not embellish or transfigure this lacking contact with reality poetically or philosophically, but certainly experiences it in his life and his work as something quite pathological.

Mörike's writings contain a primordial impetus to conquer the world. The instrument with which he probes the secular and daily reality is psychology—sensititized to even the smallest detail. Instead of regarding Mörike as "nature" as a naive writer in Schiller's sense of the word, as the prevailing interpretations tend to do, one should consider him as "neurasthenic." This world causes him suffering; he hates it because the prevailing social conditions force him to lead the life of a philistine. Psychologically, this hate develops into melancholy. He despises the life tasks which confront him, and he withdraws from them into his interior. He hides in sadness from a social order which is still quite feudal. Nevertheless, his melancholic regression proved to be extremely fruitful: he discovered in his own person essential subtleties and details of emotional life and this enabled him to arrive at new insights or at least it prepared the ground for their discovery. Another result was the enrichment of the German language.

Mörike was born in Ludwigsburg in 1804. In terms of his generation and his background he belongs as an older contemporary to those who realize a consciously bourgeois, realistic breakthrough into the present in the area of public criticism; the names Friedrich Strauss, Friedrich Theodor Vischer and Ludwig Feuerbach will make clear what is meant. Much like it did for Strauss and Vischer, Mörike's education at a Latin school and at the gymnasium brought him—through the medium of the study of antiquity—into contact with questions of public and social life, and with the notion that individuals have a right and a duty to participation.

By 1817, he was already a half-orphan and was never quite able to leave the rather impoverished conditions into which his father's death put him. He visited the gymnasium of Stuttgart in order to prepare for the least expensive career that is available to a petit-bourgeois man: the ministry. Perhaps unconscious rebellion is the reason why he did not pass the exam. In 1818, we find him at the monastery school in Urach. There, he had his first intensive contact with literature, and it is characteristic that Mörike's selection of books already reveals his split attitude: he read revolutionary works of enlightened cosmopolitanism represented for him by Calderon and Shakespeare, as well as the romantics Novalis and E.T.A. Hoffmann.

Finally, in 1822, he entered the Tuebingen seminary. His first and final disappointement with a love relationship, from which he was never able to free himself completely, occurred during this time. Secretly, the hope of seeing again the girl he had felt forced to leave because of external reasons, continued to haunt him. This disappointment, together with the intolerable time at school and the loss of his father, the grounds for his regression, which his aversion to theology only served to deepen. Mörike forgets the real world; instead, Orplid is the land of his longing, and his early writing is conceived under its sign.

At last, in 1826, he finished his studies and began leading the pitiful existence of a vicar in different rural villages in the southeastern region of Germany. After two years, he decided to change his profession; after working as a private tutor in Munich, he tried his hand at journalism, only to become a vicar once again. He carried out his work, however, in an indolent and careless manner. Attempts at playwrighting during this time fail. His contact with the external world was simply too limited, and all the real tensions with individual people or groups that a playwright must have in order to be productive were closed to him. A hopeless sadness also colored his marriage with Luise Rau, a minister's daughter (1829).

Beginning in 1834, he earned a modest livelihood as a pastor in Cleversulzbach, but the vocation still remained alien to him. When his mother died in 1841, his sister Clara reigned in the household. After Mörike was dismissed from his post with a small pension in 1843, he lived, in constant poor health, in Schwaebisch Hall and Mergentheim. Not even his marriage to Margarethe von Speeth brought him real happiness, because the childlike man, always surrounded by women, could not assume control of his domestic life, and this led to constant friction between wife and sister.

In 1851, he began work as a teacher of literature at a girls' school in Stuttgart. Gradually, he became famous, and honors finally came his way. In 1852, an honorary doctorate was conferred to him; he became professor in 1856, and eventually received a stipend from the Schiller-foundation. He died on July 4, 1875.

In Gutzkow's story *Wally, die Zweiflerin,* we encountered nervousness as a sociological phenomenon, namely, as the mass illness of the socially and politically unsatisfied bourgeoisie. Mörike is himself a particularly notable example of this phenomenon. He was, as one would say in his homeland, a *Bossler,* a "fix-it" man; he could turn on a lathe, he could shape vases, he carved his mother's burial epitaph. But all of these activities are only symptoms of a general inactivity, of constitutional laziness and childlikeness; the result of his constrained bourgeois existence in the era of political reaction.

Mörike's entire life and his work constitute a search for reality, which he never attained. The impossibility of attaining and the longing for Orplid comprise the themes of his poetry. He himself once queried: "Is art something other than the attempt to compensate for all that reality denies to us?" His prose, however, is different; here, the desire to attain is the basic theme, and he actually wants to grasp the world in his prose writing. Granted, he was not successful in the sense of grasping the struggles of individuals and groups in any way. As a reflection of the social world, his prose is quite opaque; indeed it even projects into the world of the fairytale. Social classes are without clear contours; only the peasantry, that class with almost no history, appears with some preciseness.

> You wanted to overwhelm me
> neither with happiness
> nor with sorrow!
> Since blessed modesty
> lies in between.

These lines from "The Prayer"[5] are not just the expression of a philistine soul which, wandering in the dressing gown of Biedermeier, strives only for comfort. Their meaning also captures the classical-antique ideal of a calm, solid center of life. Mörike's inclination toward antiquity finds its expression in poetry, as it will sometime later with Platen. It is true, Mörike's prayer was not granted. He was not overwhelmed by life and he hardly found solid ground in it. For average middle class people, the social order of his time granted a realm of freedom only to the soul. The soul becomes the dream-playground of Mörike's life, and this becomes visible in his poetry. Even if he did not succeed in describing social reality, the outlines of his fictitious characters are socially correct. For Mörike, psychology becomes a guide into real social relations. The fairytale is actually only a detour. Spirits, elves and nymphs remain romantic configurations in his prose, but they do not constitute its meaning. He desires, as his friend Vischer said of him later, "a serene clarity."

This can be demonstrated most clearly in his main work, *The Painter Nolten,* written in 1832. The plot is strangely entangled and simple at the same time. Nolten has separated from Agnes, his seemingly unfaithful fiancée. In reality, the gypsy Elsbeth, who was moved by jealousy, had convinced Agnes that she was not the right woman for Nolten. When he enters the circle of the royal court, he falls in love with the countess Constance. His friend Larkens, however, who wants to save the old engagement, continues to correspond with Agnes in Nolten's stead and finally reveals all to him. In spite of the fact that Nolten reestablishes his old relationship with Agnes, the story ends with a triple death and suicide. When Larkens, who is a pathological skeptic, takes his own life, Nolten reveals the entire story to Agnes. She, in turn, despairs over Nolten's unfaithfulness and dies, and the painter himself dies shortly thereafter upon having an encounter with the gypsy.

In an analysis of this work, three aspects appear important: psychology, morality, and death. In relation to the psychological aspect, it is interesting to consider the words of F.Th. Vischer, taken from a speech he gave at the unveiling of a Mörike statue: "You know the world of fear, the abysses of the soul, and the chasms of life. You know terror and horror and you knew that something sinister hovers about the world of crime, of unfaithfulness, of murder, of desperation. But you never became engulfed in this horror; always, the beautiful equanimity of the pure soul emerged victorious."[6]

For Mörike, psychology was not yet a social phenomenon. For him, society discloses itself in a very mediated way through the individual analysis of the human soul, therefore his point of departure is very simple. Discord has appeared between the bride and the bridegroom, which finally seems to make it impossible for the man to even consider continuing to live with the girl. Because the narrator depicts bourgeois relations in fairytale-like simplifications, one human predicament after another naturally—or let us say, mythologically—follows from this situation. The disappointed groom seeks solace in new relationships, the abandoned bride vacillates between female influence suggesting a new liaison and the transactions of the friend who seeks to reestablish the old union. All relationships that can conceivably exist between five people develop, or they are at least hinted at to such an extent that *The Painter Nolten* can be seen as the embodiment of all possible conscious and unconscious relationships. Two examples must suffice to illustrate this. When Nolten meets the beautiful countess Constance after the painful renunciation of the bride, the poet tells us:

> Theodor, too, was secretly drawn to her, and during the one and a half months in which he was permitted to spend three evenings a week in her presence, this gay pleasure turned into a stronger measure of affection than he might admit to himself . . . and when his intellect, when the most cursory glance at the external circumstances suppressed his every distant wish, on the other side he nevertheless mulled over a good many small clues of her special favour with indefatigable self persuasion, never forgetting for a moment, of course, that in the person of the Duke, he must fear a brilliant rival.
>
> By the by, he certainly had reason to mystify himself as much as possible about his growing affection, because a relationship which he had entered into earlier still issued claims on his heart even though he had begun, with some persuasion of his conscience, to reject these.[7]

In fact, Mörike applies progressive psychological theories in this description of his protagonist's interior world without using any scientific terminology—he is, after all, a poet. He describes the struggle between wish and claim to reality so objectively that the fundamental insolubility of the conflict, which seems to constitute all human existence familiar to us, appears before us. The continual dialectical movement from one dilemma of the soul to the next, and the incomplete ability to master matters of practical life grows out of human instinct and desire, and this human conflict confers the searched-for coherence and constitutes the theory of human action in society.

This dualistic basic structure of human beings also determines our second example, which concerns Nolten's friend the actor Larkens. From the outset, he is convinced of Agnes's innocence and he undertakes to make both happy by proving this. After his unfortunate end, we are told, "A few years later, we heard from acquaintances of the painter the rumor that the actor was driven to the desparate decision (Larkens' suicide) by a secret passion for the fiancée of his friend."[8]

The narrator himself rejects this interpretation—to which a comment by Nolten allegedly gave rise[9]—due to lack of proof. But still, in spite of his precautions, he does not make it completely implausible that Larkens' death grew out of his ambivalent attitude toward the friend and his bride. In his portrayal of Agnes' reaction when she attempts to reconcile herself to her fate by following the gypsy's advice and renounce Nolten, Mörike shows the artificiality that is inherent in any attempt to interpret one's inner life as a clearly rational and unequivocally constructed unity:

> It happens that changes transpire in our soul, about which we do not give account to ourselves and which we cannot resist, we make the transition from waking to sleeping without consciousness and are incapable of describing it afterwards. Similarly, the knowledge of the irreconcilability of her own and Nolten's fate gradually was implanted in Agnes, without her actually knowing when or why this thought had assumed an irresistible power for her. Her basic feeling was one of compassion with a loved and honored man, to whose intellect she deferred, whom she feared to make unhappy because ultimately it could not remain hidden from him how little she would be able to satisfy him as a wife.[10]

The problem of Nolten's morality is the second aspect of sociological relevance for this novel. In a certain way, *The Painter Nolten* is an "educational novel," a *Bildungsroman*. But even though the protagonist is a painter, the problem of the artist per se is not given preferential attention, as in the pertinent works of Goethe and especially of the romantics. Here, the subject is the education of a human being, who just happens to be an artist. In this respect, too. Mörike reveals himself to be a transitional figure. Without having romantic intentions, he chooses the artist as an object for pedagogical treatment, and this puts him in the romantic tradition. Even though this choice of the protagonist as well as the unfinished, fragmentary form, the interruption of the narrative flow by songs and dramatic intermezzos may sound romantic, the work as a whole certainly does not participate in the individualist cult of personality, but instead rests on the foundation of a strict social morality.

Because the participating individuals do not always speak the truth or make sure of that truth, because they themselves do not reject half-baked resolutions, life seeks revenge. Their demise is justice. Mörike constructs—often in the language of loving irony—characters who ultimately conceive of themselves as moral neurasthenics of life, and the writer is thus following his own existential experience.

What remains, finally, as the major impression of the work is the theme of death, which is touched upon three times in the novel. In the story "Mozarts Reise nach Prag" (Mozart's voyage to Prague), the thinking about death strikes like thunder. But as it were, Mörike falls behind Mozart, the enlightened freemason who depicts the powers of life and death as having distinct social referents in "Don Giovanni." Herein lies what constitutes perhaps the most realistic access to the sociological relevance in Mörike's works: again and again, he sensed the bourgeois striving for life which was condemned to death in the age of reaction, and he did not even lose this feeling after 1870. His life and his death represent ultimately the tragedy of Biedermeier—of the social status of the middle classes that, although prerevolutionary, is ultimately destined to become the ruling social stratum.

Notes

1. Georg Brandes, Hauptströmungen der Literatur des 19. Jahrhunderts, vol. 3 (Berlin, 1924). p. 562.
2. Alfred Kleinberg, Die deutsche Dichtung, in ihren sozialen, zeit- und geistesgeschichtlichen Bedingungen (Berlin, 1927), p. 247.
3. Franz Mehring, *Gesammelte Schriften und Aufsätze*, ed. von Eduard Fuchs, vol. 1: *Zur Literaturgeschichte* (Berlin, 1929), p. 310; Jetzt, *Gesammelte Schriften*. ed. von Thomas Höhle, Hans Koch, and Josef Schleifstein, vol. 10 (Berlin, 1961). p. 378.
4. Friedrich E. D. Schleiermacher, Vertraute Briefe über Schlegels Lucinde, *Sämtliche Werke*, III, Abteilung, vol. 1: *Zur Philosophie* (Berlin, 1846), pp. 432f., 504.
5. Eduard Mörike, *Sämtliche Werke*, ed. H. Göpfert (Munich, 1964), p. 127.
6. Friedrich Theodor Vischer, *Kritische Gänge*, vol. 6, ed. Robert Vischer (Munich, 1922), pp. 556f.
7. Mörike, ibid., pp 439f.
8. Ibid., p. 735.
9. Ibid.
10. Ibid., pp. 468f.

11

Gustav Freytag:
Bourgeois Materialism

Mörike is a transition figure. Half romantic, half realist, he seeks to capture that life which is unattainable to the bourgeoisie of the 1840s and ultimately becomes the victim of neurosis, the bourgeois disease described by Gutzkow. His writing, which still contains romantic elements in the sullen and dark realism of folkish culture, is progressive in its search for coherence, and especially in its efforts to establish an explanatory psychology. But the overall mood of Freytag's writing is colored by the theme of death—the social symbol of bourgeois existence in the time of Biedermeier.

The literature which precedes Mörike—the writings of romanticism and of the Young Germany—are expression of lost social battles. Romanticism was a reaction to the bourgeois fate in the era of absolute monarchy, when antiquated forms of feudal life still existed and poet and audience created for themselves the ethereal reality of a spiritual realm. But because this flight contained a dissatisfaction with the existing state of affairs, it harbored an imminent critique of it. The Young Germany which followed romanticism expressed this general and abstract social and political discontent explicitly without, however, arriving at a theory of society which could have explained prevailing conditions and thereby make them changeable. Immermann, for one, whom we only mention here without any further analysis, suceeds in capturing the figure of the bourgeois in *Oberhof.* But the composition of the work is romantic and therefore, Immermann's embryonically present bourgeois class consciousness is bent into a nonhistorical, romanticizing construction of the bourgeois in the countryside. Stifter's idyllic world is still a poetically wonderful transfiguration of patriarchal relations that were actually already disappearing during his time; it is the illusionary history of a bourgeoisie which is unable to capture the dynamic element that can lie in resignation. In any case, Mörike is the last significant representative of the repressed bourgeois class feeling that prevailed in Germany between the wars of liberation and the revolution of 1848.

Friedrich Theodor Vischer made the following statement about Mörike: "Life, real life, needs still other forces, prudent, indefatigable ones, even the realm of the Muses needs forces that are different still from yours."[1] Certainly, this statement no longer applies to Gustav Freytag, but only because in the meantime, fundamental changes have transpired in society. The writer of the generation between 1850 and 1870 no longer lives in an era of political and social reaction, but under the auspices of a victorious liberal bourgeoisie and this victory is reflected in Spielhagen's writings as well as in Freytag's.

Essentially, the development of the liberal German bourgeoisie proceeds in two phases and an intermezzo. During the first ten years after the revolution of 1848–49, this class more or less turned away from politics and was absorbed with the development of its economic position. One of the most important political demands of the bourgeoisie was largely met in 1843 with the creation of the Prussian Customs Union, which established unified economic laws and one customs area, thereby permitting increased exchange and, consequently, production. We must remember that the failure of the revolution has two sides for the German bourgeoisie. Granted, the liberal, unified, small German state with a parliament was left a dream. At the same time, however, at the end of the revolution all radical attempts at revolution by artisans, small farmers and proletarians had collapsed—thanks to the established police authorities. As a result, the bourgeoisie was not pushed into a defensive position and was not forced to defend its very economic foundation.

The years from 1859 to 1866 and 1870 were, at least for northern Germany, an interlude. The pacifist interests in further expansion of export relations appeared to the liberals to be threatened by Bismarck's armament policies. Therefore, in their struggle against Bismarck's ministerial absolutism, Liberals attempted to carry out a dry revolution with tax strikes and parliamentary obstructionism.

In the second phase of the formation of bourgeois society—the first years of the heyday of capitalism—the bourgeoisie was once again able to make peace with Bismarck. This is the period that Spielhagen presents in his work; Gustav Freytag's writings mirror the former phase. Therefore, a few more general characteristics of this first phase should be mentioned here.

One might call the period from 1848 to 1870 a capitalism with limited means. Production was still restricted primarily to textile and metal industry, to spinning mills, mining and metallurgy, and to a few engineering factories; wholesale trade and business developed separately from this, and gradually a modern banking system grew. A mere glance at Frankfurt, the banking capital in the 1850s, shows how underdeveloped the current account and credit business still was. Each day, numerous freightwagons laden with silver pulled in and out, and one of the main responsibilities of retainers was to carry bags filled with coins back and forth. The size of firms was still limited. During this time, the single entrepreneur dominated; the stock company only moved to the forefront of economic activity after 1870, when the Deutsche Bank is founded. Firm names like Krupp, Borsig, Siemens, and Rothschild give testimony to the single-entepreneur origin of the businesses of that time.

If one were undertaking an analysis of the class situation in Germany since the mid-nineteenth century, one would begin by looking at the bourgeoisie and consider its relationship to other classes as characteristic of the transformation which occurred in social relations. In the generation of older and younger romantic writers, this was different; here, the appropriate sociological orientation has to begin with the aristocracy. In the first phase of the liberal middle class, only the feudal class—those large landowners and officers who are not easily forced out of social and bureaucratic positions that have been sanctified over the centuries—can be considered a class enemy of the bourgeoisie. In comparison, the newly emerging proletariat completely diminished in significance. Of course, there were few opportunities for social mobility; at best, one could have risen within the specific and limited stratum into which one is born. A great deal of conceptual fetishism actually lies in the often mentioned transformation from estate to class. The lowest class did not move from its place when the patriarchal-feudal-absolutist society transformed itself into the capitalist one. The proletariat became more important as a conscious class with antibourgeois interests in the 1860s and 1870s, during the period of the large-scale railway construction. (Allegorically, too, the railway is the symbol of the heyday of capitalism: it is symptomatic that of the 359 stocks traded in 1870 at the Berlin stock exchange, 177—almost half—were railway stocks, while the remainder, except for nine industrial stocks and bonds, were government bonds and securities.)

The goals articulated by this bourgeoisie between 1850 and 1870 were transparently captured in the slogan "liberalism." Politically, one wants a parliament as the leading organ of the state. This parliament, however, is not thought of as an expression of competing interest groups that are represented in parties, but rather, as an auditorium in which eminent personnages know the right things to say in each situation. Even in the ideal of life-conduct, it is the capable fellow—the business-man who is thrifty, industrious, reliable, farsighted and prudent, the old-style entrepreneur who developed in Western Europe, especially in England, during the eighteenth century—who rules. In relation to his subordinates, this ideal entrepreneur takes the view of "live and let live," where the "let live" amounts to an attitude which turns the employee into a mere assistant. Therefore, it is an irony of history when today the capitalist-oriented employee associations refer to this notion of assistant: thereby they are implicitly accepting that entrepreneurial ideology which maintains that an employee can never be more than one who merely renders assistance and support.

Freytag was unromantic even in his appearance, and his life passed in a rather commonplace fashion. He was born in 1816 in the small town of Kreuzberg in Silesia. He sprang from a bourgeois milieu. The area where he grew up was the seat of the early capitalist textile industry and metal-lurgy. His father was a doctor and then became the mayor of the town; he harbored a conflict: he was in a middle class profession, but by conviction he belonged with Prussian feudalism. Granted, the Prussian atmosphere in Freytag's home was not very monarchical, and was oriented more toward the nation and the state (after all, it lies in the conquered bound-ary territory of Silesia) and this was probably not without later influence.

Freytag studied German philology with Hoffmann von Fallersleben and Lachmann in Breslau and Berlin, and he appears to have chosen the educational path of the romantics possibly to follow the tracks of the Grimm brothers. But, as becomes apparent later, Freytag sought to grasp real history, not fairytales and myths, when he studied Germanic languages and literature. Together with Julian Schmidt, he was an editor of the *Grenzboten* between 1848 and 1861, and again from 1867 to 1870. Heine's already cited statement "journals are our fortresses"—a radical and critical bourgeois proclamation—surely no longer applies to the *Grenzboten*. This journal was not a fortress but rather a castle. It was the political literary magazine of the solid, educated, liberal bourgeoi-sie. *Nation* and *freedom* are its slogans, and assistance to the respected Prussian National Union of 1859 constitutes its political involvement.

For a time, Freytag also lived in Leipzig, and it is in Breslau, Berlin and Leipzig—centers of German trade at that time—that he received the object lesson of his life. When he began to feel uneasy in Prussia because of his liberal mentality, he went to live at the court of the Duke of Gotha, who aspired to the throne of a German emperor and believed that this might be attained via Frankfurt-style liberalism. Freytag was taken in by such dynastic cleverness a second time when he moved in the circle of Crown Prince Friedrich, the subsequent Emperior Friedrich III. Once he recognized Friedrich's truly antibourgeois sentiments, however, Freytag unmasked him in a piece that he wrote, and a long time passed before he was forgiven for this. Even in these courtly surroundings, Freytag consciously gave his life a bourgeois shape; he accepted nothing and threatened to renounce his friendship with the Count of Gotha when the latter wanted to knight him. After 1879, he passed the summers on an estate and the winters in Wiesbaden, where he died in 1895.

To gain an initial understanding of Freytag, one must consider his self-conception as a writer because this is significant for his work. For the romantic, an artist is a special human being. Not even the Young German writers are able to avoid such romantic exaggerations completely because in their eyes, too, the writer has a special mission which he can only carry out in ascetic selfdenial. Freytag, however wanted to be nothing more than an industrious and capable citizen, even as a poet and writer. In contrast to Flaubert, who seriously suffered as a result of the embourgeoisement of the artist. Freytag felt comfortable about the fact that the literary artist did not represent something special but was merely pursuing one vocation among others in his society. The feeling that bourgeois society is good as it is and everything in history was only preparation for this society captures the real meaning of Freytag's life. Two literary life tasks follow from this: the analysis of the bourgeois present and the investigation of the preparation for this society in the past.

Freytag's most important works are the novels *Debit and Credit* and *The Lost Handwriting,* and the cycle of novels, *The Ancestors.* He also wrote two plays. *Die Fabier* and *The Journalists.* Of his historical works, we will only touch upon *Pictures of the German Past.*

This last work in particular, which was written in the years 1859 to 1862, was not read as a scholarly contribution, but as a novel. The reference point for these historic portraits and descriptions is the German bourgeoisie of Freytag's time and specifically the way in which it relates itself to the state. It is the German bourgeois state that matters to him, not so much the "Victories of the Hohenzollern."[2] Throughout his historical portrayals, Freytag wants to show the gradual development of those good bourgeois qualities which are fully realized in his own epoch. This book is the first widely read great unromantic, historical-philosophic rendition of history which refers to and is interested in the present, and which scrutinizes history for the sake of the present.

The introduction is characteristic of this. Freytag begins his survey of the epochs of German history—or better, of the epochs of German lifestyle—with the year 1560. He consciously omits the Middle Ages, apparently in order to forestall the impression that he intends to engage in romantic constructions or historic exaltations. In the introduction he speaks frequently about the aristocratic landowner between 1560 and 1760 because, in terms of numbers, the incipient bourgeois stratum tends to recruit itself from this social background. Freytag's literary tone seems to say: "how awful were things for you aristocrats in the past and what bad people you were in comparison to the bourgeois of today!" "In vain the German searches for the good old days." This is how the introduction to *Pictures of the German Past* begins.[3]

In other words, this history is not a book of enchantment or edification, but a manual of education. With his writing, Fretag wants to teach us "some of the sound lessons which can be gleaned from the stream of history and applied to the future."[4] Given this educational intention, history cannot be an intuitive overview of manners and characters; it is, in principle, of interest only to the extent that it can be captured scientifically. Precisely that which made the Middle Ages attractive for romanticism—these years were unfamiliar and unexplored and therefore they constituted something transcendent of everyday reality—made Freytag suspicious and especially careful in his depiction of this epoch:

> For these ancient times, reports containing details of daily life are very scanty, our knowledge of the most important life forms is uncertain, there is a large body of literature and almost every sentence of the old historians gives rise to the controversies of our science.[5]

For Freytag, being scientific meant being in fundamental agreement with the most progressive modern theories of the natural and social sciences; it meant describing phenomena as governed by laws.

> If we selected a whole range of evidence for all cultures, it might be possible to observe the peculiarities of culture and mentality in its becoming, being and passing in a way similar to that by which we understand [the] lawful changes of tree and blossom.[6]

Granted, in Freytag's comparison of social processes with organic nature one finds transfigured interpretation and the harmonization which characterizes all organicist social theories. But here lies a dialectical moment: in relation to Ranke, who wanted only to know "how everything really was," Freytag represents progress because he wanted to understand how and why everything became as it did.

In his literary execution of his conception of history, Freytag represents the standpoint of his class. He casts a malicious sidelong glance at the aristocrat: "Even the conservative landowner who struggles with established powers for the privileges and rights of his estate" would, if he were placed "in one of the previous centuries [feel] first amazement, then fright"[7] in his surroundings. The depiction following this statement shows how the lifestyle of this class gradually ascends, from ethical, scientific, cultural, political and economic primitiveness, to the highest level—the bourgeois society of the present. Thereby, the law of history is revealed: the further we go back into the past, the more the individual lives as a communal creature whose entire existence transpires within forms that are assigned or imitated, forms which leave him dependent.[8] The individual develops only slowly, and the free, understanding human being, who wrests himself from the constraints of compelling and confining social forms only gradually appears in history:

> Millions live in such a way that the content of their existence quietly and unnoticeably merges with the great stream. But in all directions, personalities who have greater influence on the development of the whole, develop and emerge from the mass. Occasionally, an individual with enormous human power rises and dominates the superhuman life of the people in a large area for a time, [thereby] imprinting an entire epoch with a single spirit. At such times, the collective spirit which also passes through our heads and our heart, becomes familiar to our eyes as the soul of an individual human being; then all the strength of the people appears to be in the service of one person for a few years; they obey him like a master. These are the great periods in the formation of a people.[9]

It is the individual who counts in history, and the closer we approach the bourgeois epoch, the more frequently and distinctly this single individual tends to constitute himself as leader of the nation. This individual is actually nothing more than the ideal liberal citizen, who seeks to find the meaning of life in the unfettered development of his own personality.

In his cycle of novels *The Ancestors*, Freytag adds a poetic dimension to his scholarly history of the bourgeoisie as the pinnacle of social existence. Here, the history of a single family is depicted, beginning with the times of the Teutons and ending with the year 1848. The author's bourgeois standpoint becomes even more apparent in this work than in *Pictures:* "This work . . . will . . . gradually be continued to the last grandchild, a lively journeyman who still now strolls along under the German sun without caring much about the deeds and the suffering of his ancestors."[10] Freytag's Germanomanic and nationalist remark contains a social core. As the very title of one novel of this sequence, *Markus Koenig,* indicates, the ancestors of this family are kings, while the descendents are bourgeois. These bourgeois citizens are not inferior to their forefathers. For one, we are immediately struck by the fact that the aristocrat and the bourgeois are of common descent. So, for simple historical reasons, every middle class citizen has the right to feel equal to the King of Prussia. Moreover, the ancestors of this particular bourgeois family are historically relevant only because they were more industrious than others; this is why their descendents attained middle-class status—that lifestyle which Freytag saw as combining the best qualities of a strong and purposeful life. He himself gave expression to this feeling of bourgeois confidence in a letter which he wrote after the celebration of his seventieth birthday:

> I have never felt towards the sovereigns of the earth the fierce loyalty and devotion which even highly gifted men often feel towards the gentlemen to whom they devote their strength and their life [he meant the princes], and when such feelings overcame me at certain moments. I at once dismissed them as untrue, exactly as I had done when I was only a schoolboy: then I left, a cornet filled with sweets in my hand, from a prayer in dissatisfaction. The warmest sentiment which I could muster for them was a cheerful humour. The brittleness of my nature, or, to phrase it very proudly, this independence granted by poetic talent, was always noted by my distinguished friends. I never belonged to them completely, instead of feeling completely at ease with them, I always felt more as a guest.[11]

The *Lost Handwriting* (1864) is a cultural-political novel which does not, in contrast to the two works just discussed, analyze the past as the preliminary stage of bourgeois society; instead, it analyzes the present itself. Over against the particularist principality stands the Pan-Germanic orientation under antiabsolutist auspices. A strong wind blows from the bourgeois world into the sweetly mendacious air of the noble court. Freytag's class standpoint becomes most clearly apparent when characters who embody middle class competence are depicted in the city as well as the countryside. The princely court is painted black in black, but life in the countryside is no longer transfigured romantically as it had been for Immermann's pseudobourgeois citizens. In the marriage of the urban professor and the rural estate daughter the class solidarity of the various bourgeois class strata is celebrated. Romanticim would have sought to find the old handwriting in this deed, or would have made its loss the subject of the tragic muse. But the realistic, self-assured bourgeois man, Gustav Freytag, is completely uninterested in making an antique, scholarly discovery when higher interests, namely the founding of a bourgeois family, are at stake.

Gustav Freytag was not a great dramatist. The theater was probably the most significant art form of a class engaged in an struggle for domination. The drama depicts polarized power groups among which a conflict develops, and the writer shows one, the only possible way out. Thus, the theater belongs to a particular situation of class struggle, in which the writer, as a representative of his social group, is discontent. The drama preceedes the actual bourgeois seizure of power, but the novel is the great inventory where stock is taken of the goods which one already possesses.

Still, Freytag's dramatic attempts are solidly rooted in liberalism. The play *The Fabier* (1859), which depicts the tendency for patricians and populace to unify, transparently makes reference to the bourgeois class solidarity of the present. In the contemporary play *The Journalists* (1854), an election campaign is the backdrop to the characters' action, and a luster of transfiguration falls onto this specifically bourgeois political institution from the very outset. Even the characters show definite sympathy with the liberal bourgeoisie: the figures of the dying patriciate, hot-headed cononel Borg and the good Ollendorf, are obscured in relation to the magnificent philistine Piepenbrink, whose talents as winemaker are matched by his capability as elector; they diminish in comparison to the daring and good-natured Bolz, who demonstrates what a pleasure it is to be a bourgeois journalist.

Gustav Freytag's best-known novel is *Debit and Credit* (1855). With this work, the writer reaches his artistic and ideological peak. It is definitely a tendentious work. Only the bourgeoisie appears as productive, constructive and agreeable in its mastery of individual existence and the general life process. All other social groups are subjected to criticism, regardless of whether they fancy themselves superior to the bourgeois sphere or live at a lower level. Of the nobility and the "rabble"—the two enemies of the bourgeoisie—the one deserves to perish and the other deserves nothing more than a servile position in the social totality. The worst possible social constellation materializes when nobility and rabble unify. Freytag saw this occurring in the Polish uprising, in the alliance between bankrupt Polish Junkers and unscrupulous, usurous Jews, of whom he makes a caricature.

This novel is the least idealistic and the least romantic book of the nineteenth century. But it is by no means a dull or a dry book; on the contrary, the characterization which we have applied to *The Ancestors* and the *Pictures* is quite appropriate here as well: *Credit and Debit* is a hymn of praise for the bourgeois businessman. Not only does God's blessing lie on the firm O.T. Schroeter's sacks of coffeebeans, the poet also transfigures them, because these sacks are full, manifold and eminently marketable. Where it is a matter of elucidating for the reader the practical order of the profitable enterprise, Freytag's realistic language assumes the most subtle nuances, even employing turns of phrases which evoke a waft of dreamy romanticism:

> Mr. Jordan did his best to initiate the apprentice into the secrets of the world of merchandise. The hour at which Anton first entered the warehouse of the firm and learned the names of hundreds of different fabrics and strange products became, for his receptive mind, the source of a peculiar poetry, which was worth at least as much as so many other poetic feelings that emerge out of the fantastic fascination which the strange and exotic brings forth in the human soul.[12]

One can read for oneself what a wondrous spell the sight of bast mats, dyewood, coffee and palmoil is able to cast over the soul. In comparison to this, the blue flower of romanticism wilts.

Essentially, the novel deals with three social groups. On one side, we find the businessmen; self-assured, strong, capable characters who are reliable in their knowledge of merchandise, in their morals and love of fatherland, and in their self-confident manner of handling employees and account books. They are invested with all the positive qualities that an entrepreneur could possibly have, and are fully entitled to their well-being. Usurers and nobles are described as caricatures of the true and vigorous businessman. They make use of a style of life and economic practices that might have had their place in the Middle Ages or during the reign of absolutism. But they are incompatible with the high quality of genuinely bourgeois life and the verdict is spoken against these outdated commercial people in accordance with valid moral terms and up-to-date business principles. Freytag's anti-Semitism is unmistakable. The nobility consists of people who are unreliable, some of whom even have "dirt" on their hands—at best they are unsteady, weak and without true roots, so that only a competent bourgeois education could bring them back into shape.

Freytag's often cited tendency toward nationalism also becomes apparent here. The nobility is international; its lifestyle, seemingly at home everywhere, is the outdated remains of a historical epoch which, although it still sports some cosmopolitan customs, for example jousting rituals or court life, lacks those opportunities which can emerge from a life lived within national boundaries when capable individuals take over. For Freytag, then, the "national" always has a social element; it is the public life form of the industrious bourgeoisie. Nation and bourgeoisie become interchangeable concepts; the fact that this is not apparent at first glance only increases the measure of ideologic absolutization which Freytag imposes on liberal bourgeois society.

The protagonist Anton Wohlfahrt is the best example of this extolled lifestyle. He is a well-bred child of the bourgeoisie, comes from a solid family, grows up in a competent manner and completes his education with the graduation from high school. As apprentice he sits on the high swivel chair in the office, which is lowered as the business qualities of this outstanding young man develop, until he can finally exchange it for the upholstered deskchair of the business partner. From the very outset, this capable young man is assured of an unobstructed road because of his origin and the social connection between his family and the firm which he enters as apprentice.

The predicament of a man choosing from among two women has probably never been treated more "nondemonically" in world literature than in *Debit and Credit.* Anton is caught between a seductively beautiful aristocratic woman and the slightly oldish daughter of the proprietor of the firm. She is the one he marries. Toward the end of the novel, the story of this marriage is unfolded and one can read, not without amazement, how the road to the heart of this girl is mediated by the inscription "With God" on the first page of the "confidential ledger of O.T. Schroeter and Co." The radiant father once says. "When you left us, it was with anger that I saw my dearest hope destroyed.

Now we hold you, you dreamer, in the pages of the confidential ledger and in our arms."[13] Here, the romantic dream of love finally has its very bourgeois awakening. Probably there is no other passage in literature in which the founding of a bourgeois family as a social expression of an economic community of interest is expressed more naively and clearly. The marriage to Sabine Schroeter does not stand under the auspices of renunciation of the baroness Leonore, rather, it stands as the triumphant entry into true life.

Freytag's description of the economically dependent class corresponds to the self-satisfied attitude of the bourgeois. His picture of clerks and workers is patriarchal, much like the altitude which the businessman assumes towards his employees. They never play a decisive role in the life of those people who matter; rather, they lead a modest and marginal existence, which provides the occasion for slightly derisive and humorous depictions. Once it is said of the proprietor, who walks through the room of his actions, "He . . . returned to the second office where six pens were busily writing on the blue paper with such speed that the quills were bustling with excitement, because the wall clock had already started striking the hour."[14]

Freytag completely ignores the real needs of the proletariat, even though for someone engaged in objective observation this was hardly possible anymore in the mid-1850s. Here we have an example of modern ideology, of appropriate "false consciousness." Around the middle of the century, the economic base had already been transformed. Commercial trade was usually organized quite rationally; and the industries which supplied it or cooperated with it had grown into large-scale enterprises. As a consequence, a broad strata of white and blue collar workers were beginning to develop feelings of solidarity. Such facts, rather than proving *Debit and Credit* to be an anachronism, actually render it a highly contemporary book. After all, ideological transfiguration means that one regards the attained historical standpoint as essentially unchangeable precisely because it is considered to be valuable as it is. By presenting a picture of a generation the way in which it might have looked fifteen or twenty years prior to the actual date which he chose to give it, Freytag becomes the ideologue of the bourgeoisie of his time; he transfigures the comfortable center of a life whose very foundation has, in reality, already begun to slip away. By portraying the sober aggregates of such a life style—the scholar's desk or the office, the firm or the farm, the workshop or the editorial office, in short, the entire boring everyday world—including even price lists and marketing catalogues as legitimate material for the literary artist, the sun of poetic transfiguration shines over Freytag's world of imagination, i.e., the bourgeois world of the midcentury.

Debit and Credit is an educational novel. But, in contrast to Goethe or to romanticism, here an entire class is represented by an exemplary individual who is not very distinctive. The novel is the textbook of a teacher who knows to which group he belongs and who wants to educate all those into this group who are entitled to belong to it.

Notes

1. Friedrich Theodor Vischer, *Kritische Gänge*, vol. 6, ed. Robert Vischer (Munich, 1922), p. 558.
2. Gustav Freytag, "Dedication to Salomon Hirzel," *Pictures of the German Past I, Gesammelte Werke*, 2nd ed., vol. 17 (Leipzig, 1897).
3. Ibid., p. l.
4. Ibid.
5. Ibid.
6. Ibid.
7. Ibid.
8. In this context, we might remember that according to Emile Durkheim, "community" (*Gemeinschaft*), which corresponds to primitive society for him, knows only what he terms *mechanical* solidarity, while modern society exists—at least in principle—under the auspices of "organic" solidarity—a startling similarity! See Durkheim's *Division du Travail, passim.*
9. Freytag, ibid., p. 24.
10. Freytag, "Dedication to Crownprincess Victoria," *Die Ahnen I*, in *Gesammelte Werke*, vol. 8.
11. Quoted from Franz Mehring, *Gesammelte Schriften und Aufsaetze*, vol. 2: *Zur Literaturgeschichte, Eduard Fuchs* (Berlin, 1929), p. 67. Most recent edition: *Collected Works*, vol. 11, ed. Thomas Hoehle and Joseph Schleifstein (Berlin, 1961), p. 73.
12. *Soll und Haben I, Gesammelte Werke*, vol. 4 (1896), p. 68.
13. *Soll und Haben II, Gesammelte Werke*, vol. 5 (1896), p. 403.
14. *Soll und Haben I*, vol. 4, p. 42.

12

Friedrich Spielhagen: Bourgeois Idealism

If Gustav Freytag represents the first generation of the liberal bourgeoisie, then Spielhagen is the representative novelist of the second generation.

In contrast to the 1850s, liberal society around 1870 is marked by large-scale capitalism. The unleashing of forces of production and the development of new forms of organization was accompanied by economic crises, which had two principal origins. For one, they were precipitated by the economic downswing in those industries which supplied the railway construction; once the railroads were complete, the productive volume of these suppliers far exceeded the demand. The failure of businesses connected to the railways was an everyday occurrence. The stockmarket was the second source of crisis. The crash of 1873 in Vienna marked only the beginning, and was followed by crashes in other cities, including Berlin; all of them were results of a mania of speculation, especially in railway stocks.

In the 1870s, then, capitalism and crisis have become complementary concepts. But capitalism continues to perpetuate itself even in time of crisis. After the founding of the Reich, the haute bourgeoisie makes peace with Bismarck's state because he supported export industries by strengthening Germany and by implementing colonial policies that ensured access to cheap raw materials and new export markets. The customs restrictions which he imposed in 1878 to meet the demands of large farmers actually met the interests of heavy industry as well; only the finished goods industry was adversely affected by these policies. It was around this time, then, that a new economic type emerges: the patriciate and the large capitalist.

In our discussion of Freytag we pointed out that by the middle of the nineteenth century, the bourgeoisie had become the central social class; the position of all other groups in society was determined by their relation to this class. Gradually, feudal groups began to ally with the bourgeoisie. We have indicated the extent of their common economic interest in reference to Bismarck's protectionist policies. Politically, the classes are unified in the struggle against social democracy and gradually, these commonalities extend into a social peace treaty as well. The proletariat, on the other hand, became increasingly important for the bourgeoisie as an opponent. One immediate consequence of the great crises was a growing solidarity among the masses in opposition to the economic threats which they faced. The large stockmarket crashes increased the reserve labor army and decreased the general wage level, and wage increases could not keep pace with the rise in cost of living generated by the protectionist duties. German workers experienced a crash in the real wage level during this time and this made them receptive to socialism.

Increasingly, the bourgeoisie came to identify its life goal with the national ideal of the Bismarckian state. Between 1870 and 1880—the first generation of the bourgeoisie—that class had, by and large, concluded social peace with the aristocracy; thereafter, the reconciliation proceeded mainly by way of bourgeois imitation of the aristocratic lifestyle: the reserve officer came to embody the bourgeois ideal of happiness.

This predilection goes together with the love for the splendor and kitsch of the founding years, culminating in the Berlin "Victory Boulevard." This style is a bourgeois version of Versailles for a social group wanting to couch its economic and political superiority in grandeur. The ideal of the hard-working fellow relinquishes its hold on the propertied bourgeoisie, which comes into increasingly active contact with political praxis; instead it becomes an ideology for white collar workers, manual workers, and low-level civil servants. The connection between business and politics, which is always evident in the beginning periods of capitalist development—think of the Fuggers, the United States, or the England of Thomas Moore's time—is no longer a secret for German capitalism. "Behind the scenes" is a catchword that applies to the theatre of life as well.

This is the world in which Friedrich Spielhagen lived and worked. He reached the zenith of his fame in 1860; thereafter it dwindled gradually at first and then more rapidly. In the 1880s and 1890s, Spielhagen was attacked very bitterly by his critics, and today he is all but forgotten. Nevertheless, Spielhagen is important for us, and the strange story of his fame permits a better understanding of the social function of his *oeuvre*.

It simply cannot be a coincidence that a writer who is concerned with solidarity, duty, and with telling things as they are—rather than with fantasy or personality or "content," in short, a writer who formulates the demands of the bourgeois enlightenment—disappears so completely.

In an essay about Tieck, Friedrich Gundolf argues that the epigonic novels of Freytag and Spielhagen put an end to the notion that storytelling is poetry; instead they cultivated the notion of "reporting with or without a specific end."[1] Heinrich Hart's and Michael Georg Conrad's critique of Spielhagen must be seen in this connection. For Hart, Spielhagen is a man of reason who has only a literal imagination; Hart claims that Spielhagen has "no eye for the thousand fountains of real life from which new impulses and ideas spring up constantly."[2] And Michael Georg Conrad writes: "The likes of Dahn, Heyse, Freytag, Spielhagen and *tutti quanti* do not ignite heads, they do not revolutionize artistic realms, they do not even astound us with the courage of new world views."[3]

In order to understand the significance of this critique, one must take a closer look at the critics themselves. Hart's and Conrad's comments reveal the problems inherent in German naturalism. In Germany, the progressive and radical social tendencies of European naturalism were very quickly deflected into romanticism, and Hart's and Conrad's objections to Spielhagen are premised on their conception that trenchant discoveries and specific content are irrelevant, because rapture and genius alone make a true poet. But the Freytags and Spielhagens were not interested in Conrad's kind of revolution. They were not concerned with the shaking up of artistic worlds, but with the construction and consolidation of social relations. Gundolf, who sees Spielhagen's predecessors in Gutzkow, Dumas and Dickens—a writer who was, in his opinion, misunderstood—falls into the same category as Hart and Conrad. This affinity, which Gundolf sees as negative, actually does shed light on Spielhagen's position, because he, like these writers, is not concerned with esthetic enchantment but with a description of the real world. Hart, Conrad and Gundolf live one, two and three generations after Spielhagen, and they belong to a bourgeoisie for whom aesthetic enchantment was a way to veil the social problematic, which has become much sharper by this time.

Spielhagen is the founder of the liberal bourgeois aesthetic of the novel. He wants to consciously mirror society as it is in his works and thereby exert an unmediated influence on life. His aesthetic theory draws on the motifs of idealism. He takes seriously the notion that correct understanding can change the world. According to Spielhagen, not personal grandeur but the grandeur of the social facts must emerge in a text, and the writer must be aware of what he is saying. He serves as a communicator of understanding and knowledge; he should not only relate how things are, but at the same time, based on his insight, state how they should be. Thus the first basic aesthetic demand emerges; that the literary work must articulate the contemporary issues in the writer's own lifetime.

> I was always of the opinion—that is the beginning for the modern novel. The epic poet of our day has nothing to say except: I have these opinions regarding God and the human being, and this is how I arrived at these opinions.[4]

This constitutes a theoretical justification for the contemporary novel's right to exist—not as a nimble contemporary reportage or a publisher's venture, but as a moral bourgeois obligation of the writer.

From his demand for the depiction of contemporary situations follows the demand for objectivity in the description itself. The novel calls for closure, a systematically and logically structured construction, as well as causal consistency. Therefore, the ego of the writer must disappear entirely behind the matter he wishes to present. This is why Spielhagen wrote almost no novels or stories in the first person. In keeping with the tradition of bourgeois enlightenment, poetry is, for him—as it had been for Lessing—a modified form of theory and science. In Spielhagen, the conscious relegation of the poetic subject to the background finds its expression in dialogues or in multilayered conversations.

A third aesthetic demand follows: objective description and the shrinking of subjectivity in favor of a general worldview. For Freytag, and even more for Spielhagen, the writer traces what already exists, and the descriptions of the rising wealthy bourgeoisie of Freytag's epoch and the liberal-idealistic bourgeoisie of the period from the 1840s to the 1870s that Spielhagen describes are not poetic constructions; they are the representations of the world experience which the writers had of the poet.

Spielhagen was born on February 24, 1829, the son of a government architect in Magdeburg. A great part of his youth was spent in Stralsund. He changed his course of study several times; his first interest was medicine, then law and finally, philology. The unromantic tendencies of the young writer, who was interested in human as well as nonhuman nature, were already apparent in his selection of studies; as was true for

Freytag, studying philology permits Spielhagen an objective orientation within history. For some years, he lives with families of the landed aristocracy as a family tutor, then he tried his luck at journalism. He began writing in 1854, and moved to Berlin in 1860. He married, his wife died in 1900, and he died in 1911. This matter of fact account of his life, which lasted exactly as long as Goethe's, encompasses the closely circumscribed significance of the writer's biography for his work. Spielhagen's life story, like Freytag's, is no different from other forms of bourgeois existence; each day is a setting for work to be done. In the beginning of his life he appeared to be motivated by some trace of storm and stress, but the only important fact for his adult life was that he lived in Berlin, the center of the heyday of capitalism.

His works, just like his life, represent the final break with the attitude of resignation that permeated the bourgeoisie during the period of reaction. On the contrary, he emphatically rejected any attempt to escape social reality, to create a realm of pure fantasy or to flee into history. Poets and writers find satisfaction in the depiction of their own epoch because the world which they capture in their works opens itself up to them in real life; indeed, as members of the bourgeoisie they contribute to shaping this world actively and may even contribute to changing it. No longer does the environment frighten the poet into his interior self, as was true with Mörike; instead, the world in which the bourgeois has lived since the middle of the century is the source of his comfortable existence. The poet is permitted to wake up from the nightmarish dream of the jump into the dynamics of social development—his present life. In his *Theory and Technique of the Novel* (1883), Spielhagen expressed this secularized life feeling in the following words:

> I believe that there is general agreement with my conclusion that the most prominent feature, the essential characteristic of our contemporaries' physiognomy is the striving and the decision to take possession of one's heritage; to make one's home in a world that is not a preliminary stage to heaven or hell but solidly founded and lasting, a world that is the very source and the basic foundation from which our suffering and our happiness springs . . . it is the stubborn creed of Prometheus, it is his humble-proud expression: Have you not completed everything yourself, ardently glowing heart! which we see written—visibly and invisibly—on the front of each locomotive.[5]

Problematic Characters is the novel which made Spielhagen famous in one stroke in 1861. In this as well as in his following works, two of Spielhagen's preferences emerge. For one, he has a special ability to depict aristocratic figures. Sometimes they are likeable, more often he rejects them. Always, however, Spielhagen succeeds in making all members of that social stratum colorful and realistic so that they come alive for the reader, while the bourgeois often remains an abstract figure. Secondly, Spielhagen has a distinct penchant for describing landscapes, especially those of northern Germany, which are most familiar to him. The sea and the coast, the castle and the forest, all emerge exceptionally vividly. In this, his inclination toward the aristocracy and toward nature, the unromantic thirst for life proclaims itself again and again, a thirst which searches for a connection with the world and unconsciously grasps this world exactly where it appears to be the most vivacious and fulfilled. Even though the aristocracy is an object of criticism, Spielhagen's imagination is captured by it because it represents a vivid and ever-present form of life which—although it may be brutal in some respects—is similar to that represented for him by more neutral realms, for example, the landscape; he was mistaken about it because in it he always encounters a brutal but ever-present form of life, similar to that which he believed to encounter in a more neutral realm—the landscape.

At first glance, the novel appears to be dominated by the critique of the aristocracy. Again and again, Spielhagen lashes out against that stratum's conscious bearing and its class-arrogance. For example, a certain gentleman, von Cloten, has come to believe the nonsense that the Bible was probably written in the interests of the bourgeois classes. The following dialogue ensues, which seems to anticipate National Socialism:

> "Perhaps the man owes his life to a visit of the sons of heaven to the daughters of earth?"
> "What does that mean?"
> "Don't you know that was the way before Abraham to speak of the children of nobles who had married beneath their rank?"
> "No, never heard of it before! Sons of heaven? famous! Generally, Holy Writ too severe for me. Just imagine, baron—that idea—all men from a single pair! Nobles and not nobles!—Nonsense, impossible, ridiculous! Always thought Holy Writ must have been translated by men of low birth. Always annoyed when old tutor explained it otherwise."
> "Cloten," said Oldenburg, standing still and placing his hand on his companion's shoulder. "Cloten! You are a great man. That thought is worthy of the deepest thinker of all ages!"
> "Ah, pshaw!—are you in earnest, baron, or are you trying to chaff me again?"
> "My dear Cloten," said Oldenburg, passing his arm again under the arm of his companion and continuing on his way; "let me tell you

once for all, I am invariably and terribly in earnest in all I say, and the subject of which we were speaking is really of such immense importance that it won't bear joking. Hear then—but you must not make any improper use of what I am going to say—Cloten."
"Certainly not—*parole d'honneur!*"
"Hear then, that the same question which your genius has answered in an instant with unfailing tact, has occupied my mind for years. I also said to myself: The distinction between nobles and not nobles is not a mere distinction of name, of caste—it is a distinction of blood, of mind, of soul—*enfin,* of our whole nature. How can men so entirely different from each other, descend from the same original pair?[6]

Spielhagen amasses evidence in support of a bourgeois critique of the aristocratic life style. He indicts their brutal conduct, their foolish conversations, their ridiculous and coarse activities, their uncultivated manners. But he dispenses with long factual descriptions of conditions which would reveal the wretchedness of the aristocratic world. Instead, the conversations among different people suffice to reveal the writer's opinions and intentions. The conversation speaks for itself.

In order to further legitimate his criticism of the manner and attitude of the aristocracy, Spielhagen attempts to show the demise of this class in the era of the rising bourgeoisie. In what amounts to essentially a continuation of the bourgeois enlightenment, this critique has a rational cast both in terms of form and content. It is formal in that Spielhagen's presentation of the feudal order, of its representatives and sympathizers leads the reader to rejection and dismissal. The Protestant Church appears as the essential auxiliary of the Prussian aristocracy. The pastor goes so far as to praise primogeniture as good fortune, because it helps to preserve the status quo.[7] This pact between the Church and feudalism is even further strengthened because the sermon of the pastor appeals to those psychological predispositions of his listeners which are most likely to guarantee the immutability of the present order. In the novel, the pastoral glorification of primogeniture is separated only by seven pages from the condemnation undertaken by the authority of the pulpit, in other words, the exhortation to abdicate "the proud trust in reason." "the foolish reliance on your common sense,"[8] which follows closely the praise of the raison d'etat and the social status quo as the only criteria of "truth."

Here we are faced again with one of these intellectual situations of the nineteenth century in which material and ideological features are placed in close proximity, but are not yet comprehended in a social theory. If one were to compare Spielhagen to Voltaire, the following dialetical observation may be suggested: the French Enlightenment establishes a theoretical connection; e.g., by declaring religion to be a deceitful invention of priests, designed to satisfy egoistic needs. Spielhagen, on the other hand, as a spokesman of bourgeois enlightenment of German liberalism, is content to juxtapose particular situations, which appear to be characteristic for the life of a pastor. Nevertheless, precisely this juxtaposition contains a new social experience. By no longer assuming a strict relationship between the conscious material interests of people and the contents of their intellectual and spiritual lives, Spielhagen leaves room for a more truly differentiated and therefore more adequate method for the analysis of the complicated state of affairs: one that takes into consideration the unconscious mediations which either obstruct or promote such a relationship. Simultaneously, he refrains from postulating what amounts to a one-dimensional historical explanation. Granted, all liberal social theory is limited by its making all phenomena, in the last analysis, dependent on the bourgeois state as the highest standard, and Spielhagen is no exception.

The rational exposition and uncovering of feudal remnants is undertaken on its very representatives. Clearly, Spielhagen is heir to the thoughts and ideas of political romanticism when he depicts a count who elucidates his social theory as follows:

> "I consider the soldier's profession," he said, "not only the noblest, but also the most useful; the noblest, because here alone every faculty of man is roused and developed; the most useful, because it is the only security for all the other professions, which cannot exist without it. If the peasant wishes to raise his cabbages, if the mechanic wants to sit quietly in his work-shop, the artist in his atelier, and the scholar in his study—they must all thank the soldier, who for their sake stands guard at the town-gate, patrols the streets at night, disperses noisy revellers, and lights the enemy when he threatens the country. Compared with this profession, all others are low and vulgar."[9]

Here, one essential theme of political romanticism becomes very clear. It is commonly assumed that political romanticism sees its political ideal in the Middle Ages, but it is, really, the expression of the counterrevolution; its goal is the restoration of the absolutist state. This connection is somewhat obscured by the fact that the religious consecration of the Middle Ages helps to transfigure the contradictions within bourgeois society, and also because political romanticism finds appealing, for material-historical reasons, certain moments of the Middle Ages which recede into the background during the age of absolutism (for example, the greater power of particularist feudality in relation to the crown). But, most essentially, political romanticism unifies the real desires of courtly and aristocratic strata, who long for the return of a strong absolutist Europe, one whose states can guarantee their estate order and its privileges domestically and internationally with the power of the standing army. The enthusiasm for the Middle Ages is much more a part of that romantic writing which comes out of the bourgeois camp. Spielhagen's readers did not need any commentary in order to be able to judge such a social theory; indeed, Spielhagen's theory of the novel—which insists on persuading the reader with the facts themselves (in this case with the spoken word) and dispenses with supplementary interpretation and explanation—is most successful here.

He deals the greatest blow to the feudal order by denying its representatives any competence. In a comment about a Baroness von Grenwitz, the private tutor Oswald, who is the protagonist of the novel, explains:

> In small matters, she has good sense enough, but as soon as you approach the higher mysteries of our life here below, or as soon even as the question arises how a general conclusion can be obtained from the mass of details, she begins to talk nonsense, and produces such foolish aristocratic commonplace phrases that my head swims.[10]

The Pastor had denied the power of reason: here, he is told who might serve as his model; precisely that aristocracy which is still enthroned in its full political and social power. One might be able to forgive the aristocracy everything, but certainly not its inability to think. Its impotence to establish theoretical connections, to make observations meaningful through abstraction, is sufficient to pronounce judgment on this class. The essence of Spielhagen's bourgeois worldview is its rationalism, which—exactly as the Enlightenment stipulated it—knows no other sources of legitimate theoretical and practical behavior than rational insights based on unprejudiced observation.

In order to do justice to Spielhagen's first great novel, one must mention that he not only criticizes the aristocracy in order to legitimate the bourgeoisie, but that he also levels criticism against the bourgeoisie itself. This is contained already in the very title of the novel, *Problematic Characters,* which is taken from Goethe: "There are problematic characters. which are unable to deal with any situation in which they find themselves, and for whom no situation is ever right. Out of this emerges the tremendous conflict which consumes life, leaving no room for pleasure." Spielhagen wanted to capture and address the Young German generation, the youth which had a completely undefined negative attitude toward its own era. The Young Germans distanced themselves from romanticism at the same time that they were enamored with it; they tended toward collective political action even while they continued in the dreamy state of individualized feeling, they longed for definite duties to be fulfilled even while they were consumed by casual pleasures; they searched for a truly comprehensive theory and yet expended themselves in the small literary form of the feuilleton.

Spielhagen's novel had the conscious intention of tearing the bourgeois youth out of this meandering search, out of this restlessness and isolation, out of this nervous, unsatisfied haste, and to lead it to a consciousness of its theoretical and moral tasks. The novel was to help change attitudes, so that one would no longer see his "own life . . . [as being] without goal or purpose," and would no longer believe that "everything was without meaning."[11] For once and for all, interest in the transformation of the world was to replace the feeling of *Weltschmerz*.

Spielhagen's tendency to explain the defeat of the bourgeoisie in 1848 referred to the ignorance of the bourgeoisie itself, the unenlightened attitude of these people who do not have clear goals or objectives and "simply promenade along"—Romantics "in a modern waistcoat."[12] The establishment of such goals clearly predominates in this novel. An analysis of the text itself reveals his positive intentions. In the first place, we find the trend toward deromanticization. In a conversation, Oswald says:

> Love is the fragrance of that Blue Flower, which, as you said just now, fills the whole world, and you will find the Blue Flower, which you have sought in vain all your life long, in every being which you love with all your heart." A strange melancholy smile played around the baron's lips as Oswald spoke these words.

> You cannot solve the riddle" he said sadly, in a low voice; "for this very condition, that we must love with all our heart, if we wish to get rid of the torment which makes life a hell, is the impossible thing. Which of us can love with all his heart? We are all so driven, so weary, that we have no longer the strength nor the courage which true, real love requires. I mean that love which knows neither rest nor repose till it

has made its own every thought of our mind, every sentiment of our heart, and every drop of our blood.[13]

Here Spielhagen reveals an especially progressive methodological side. He does not want to "disprove" the mythology of the "blue flower," nor does he want to denigrate it; he simply relativizes it, revealing its conditional and limited existence by uncovering how inappropriate it is for the present. Even though this is a sad fact, he tells us, the romantic feeling no longer corresponds to reality. All eyes must begin turning toward the tasks of the times. Realist demystification is the primary bourgeois duty. The social order must be transformed—this much was shown by the critique of the aristocracy. Therefore it is essential, first of all, to see the world as it is.

The book *Problematic Characters* ends on the note that reason and science are indeed the greatest human power; they contain the only promise for the rectification of the bourgeois defeat. This theme appears in the first parts of the novel; Oswald advises the family tutor Bumperlein, who no longer feels a calling for the study of theology, to "happily turn his back on the paradise of naive thoughtlessness and harmless belief."[14] The fact that Oswald also advises Mr. Bumperlein to study medicine makes it conceivable that this advice to devote oneself to the eradication of individual suffering includes the desire to make all social-pathological symptoms disappear. After all, Oswald says that one should "not let oneself be locked in the same pens with whining and howling pretenders, the cowardly dogs clad in the sheepskins of humility."[15] In all of these passages, Spielhagen consciously invokes science as a weapon in the struggle against the existing state of affairs.

Spielhagen formulates his positive goals most explicitly in the sequel to *Problematic Characters,* entitled *Through the Night to the Light.* "The musty mist of fortification casemats and the suffocating air of the police state should disappear," and in its place, "a breath of free air" should come into "the fatherland."[16] How is this meant? Here, Spielhagen's justification of liberal bourgeois society is clearly revealed. He attributes to this society the motives of work and progress, of scientific development, and technical productivity; he sees it as engaged in the fulfillment of duty for the sake of all humankind:

> "We also, we—the children of this nineteenth century—are born to have no leave of absence. The enormous tasks given us in science, in politics, in every department of human activity, claim from childhood

up all our powers and consume them entirely. To arms! to arms! This is the unceasing cry which summons us also, whether our arms are the pen or the brush, the plough or the hammer, the compass or the lancet. And work—inexorable, imperious work—what does it care for the workman?—whether his temples are beating with fever, whether his brain is overwrought to insanity, or his limbs are trembling from exhaustion—work does not mind it. It rewards him with poverty, sickness, and suffering, and demands of the ill-treated, the oppressed, the labors of Hercules. Yes, my friends, we also are plebeians in the service of work as those Roman plebeians in the service of war, and we can complain with them and say, *'sine missione nascimur!* . . .*"*

Now the individual, however great he may he, counts for little; the whole strength of our day lies in the masses, which are pressing forward in close columns, slowly but irresistibly, in the path of progress. This is not yet clearly seen by many. Rulers, princes, and princes' servants, who have a dim apprehension of the matter, would like to bring back the olden times for the sake of their brutal selfishness and their frivolous vanity—the times when the individual was everything and the masses nothing; but it is all in vain. The army of progress, endowed with the death-defying instinct of the migratory lemur, marches on in long, unnumbered lines, shoulder to shoulder, each man stepping in the footsteps of the man before him, and when here and there a vacant space occurs the lines are closed up again in an instant.[17]

This passage contains elements that are typical of the bourgeois enlightenment: the optimism of progress, which is basically considered to be irreversible; the notion that science and politics are legitimate fields of human activity; the glorification of work as a mission that is burdensome in spite of the fact that it transfigures human fate. What the quoted passage lacks is any indication that there might be another, a more "profound" level of truth; it reveals no attempt to devalue the given reality, no effort to attribute "meaning" to the multifarious happenings with a religious framework. This is true even for the subject of death which is relativized by an awareness that each individual has contributed toward social progress and that descendents of these individuals will never have tasks other than those which the deceased have tackled before them. The concept of immanence is expressed clearly and precisely here, and the notion of transformation of social reality, formulated just as incisively, is tied to this. Reality can be explained only by means of reason and science and therefore it is seen only as the showplace of struggling humanity. With this conception, Spielhagen pays his ideological tribute to the rising bourgeois consciousness of Germany.

But the quoted passage contains yet another moment: while Freytag's glorification of liberal entrepreneurship is unbroken, Spielhagen, who lives in what we have called the second phase of bourgeois development in Germany, can no longer ignore the first signs of collective organization. Granted, he is an intellectual theorist and therefore the problem of collectivized activity appears to him primarily as a form of organization of scientific work; the conscious organization of capital is not yet visible to him, and he does not realize that in his juxtaposition of mass and individual he comes close to supporting the position of the proletariat. It was probably precisely those interpretations of his work which encouraged the negative criticism of Spielhagen and the all too quick demise of his fame in later years. Spielhagen satisfied his own demand that the literary artist must closely follow current events: he observed the economy and the entire material and spiritual life of his time and this is why he was able to capture events and phenomena much more differentiatedly than any other German writer of his century.

This very ability is probably the reason he came to live in social and political isolation in spite of the huge editions which his works initially had. After all, how important is a certain fascination with the aristocracy in relation to his consciously exercised critique? What are workers to make of his faltering attempts, in this as well as in later novels, to analyze their situation? And how, finally, is the bourgeoisie supposed to be able to keep a lasting peace with a man who persists, even after liberal goals have been realized, in seeing progress as an uplifting of the masses rather than as a triumph of individuals? One could almost call Spielhagen a radical materialist, because for him, the social division of labor is the reality of life, and the only chance for a meaningful life lies in the development of this division of labor for the satisfaction of all the various interests. Granted, all of this stays in the realm of freely suspended pathos, and Spielhagen's creed is restricted to the sphere of thought: he remains a bourgeois idealist. But he does not make the world the showplace of a super-temporal will, nor does he, like C.F. Meyer, make it the romping grounds of genius, who, with every justification, make people who do not count their victims.

Instead, Spielhagen's ideals, intentional and unintentional, correspond to the interests of all those groups who have a stake in desiring a transformation of the present state of affairs. It is true that in his enthusiasm for the aristocracy and for landscape, Spielhagen takes many breaths of that air which he later describes as musty; and it is also true that *Problematic Characters* in particular reveals itself, even in the title, to be a psychological enterprise and not a social analysis. The final paragraph of the novel, however, expresses the radical idea that the struggle against tyranny can only be carried out successfully in the "thunderstorm of revolution."[18]

The next novel, *The Hohensteins* (1863), takes place in 1848. Once again, the bourgeoisie and the aristocracy confront each other. *The Hohensteins* is a considerably more political and social novel, its themes are more realistic and its ending is more optimistic and more collectivist than *Problematic Characters*. And it more Clearly fulfills the function which Spielhagen attributed to the novel: to offer an informative stocktaking, to explain social reality by representing it objectively. The emphasis on political and social life rather than on the economic sphere is noticeable; the latter is, in comparison, neglected. While the later Spielhagen will not ignore the economy and will not shy away from reporting the material deprivations of the proletariat, in his early works he serves the public interests of the bourgeoisie, whose economic saturation and opportunities for social mobility are still in stark contrast to its weak political and social position, especially when seen in relation to the aristocracy.

The great emphasis on the political realm has a special significance in Spielhagen's novels. In Gottfried Keller's works, that realm becomes the consolation of the petit-bourgeoisie because, given the barely tenable economic situation of that class at the time, politics is the only sphere in which it can frolic; in Spielhagen's time, the political realm still provides a range of yet untouched opportunities to a rising bourgeois class.

The Hohensteins allows us a closer look at Spielhagen's concepts of social stratification. This work is especially differentiated and it is more appropriate to reality than *Problematic Characters*. Not only do bourgeoisie and aristocracy confront each other, status differences within these classes also become apparent. A conversation between a high-born President of Hohenstein and a Dr. Muenzer, a radical bourgeois politician, anticipates a sociological interpretation of language.

> Muenzer moved impatiently in his chair.
> "I am sorry to say I have not the remotest idea of what you are driving at," he said curtly.
> "I trust we shall soon understand each other," said the president, still in the same low, kindly tone. "It would be a marvel if we should have done so at once. For that is the curse of our day, that Babylonian

confusion has seized upon men, and no one any longer understands the language of others, although in the end all wish to gain
the same thing, though in different ways and by different means."
"Perhaps the difficulty is more serious than that," said Muenzer, who
began, almost unconsciously, to be interested in the conversation.
"Might not the difference in language be the necessary effect of a
corresponding difference in ideas?"[19]

To the aristocratic president, who can afford to be satisfied with the
world exactly as it is, who, indeed, must be anxious to transfigure existing reality, the world seems to be clouded only by small blemishes, by
"misunderstandings"; and mere rhetorical or logical artifacts seem to
be required to remove any discord which may arise. A false generosity,
which has always been a privilege of ruling individuals and groups, is
at the disposal of the President as well. Following all reality-mystifying
theories, which take care of the suffering and the unhappiness of history by regrading it as something that is "fundamentally," "basically"
secondary and which does not affect the essential "meaning" of history, this president also finds that, in spite of undeniable differences of
individual and social interests which might emerge, the primary fact
that finally remains is that "all . . . desire the same thing."

The President's elegant tone of voice, the artistically constructed
sentences of his expositions, reveal his contentment with the principles
of his time. His confident superiority, which expresses the world in
declaratory sentences and strives to actually mirror the existing social
order—which he holds to be organic and legitimate—in the language
itself, in the relationship of main to secondary clause, stands in contrast to the style of the revolutionary Muenzer, who smells problems
everywhere, who is unconciliatory and suspecting, and has a question-
ing style which always sees opposition and conflict as most essential.
One who goes on reading the quoted passage will find that Muenzer's
language continues to be defined by question- and exclamation-marks,
by appeals and entreaties, and by the particle "but."

It has already been conceded that Spielhagen may have been unconsciously infatuated with the aristocracy. In *The Hohensteins*, we find
next to unpleasant representatives of the aristocracy the congenial and
likeable Herr von Degenfeld. Spielhagen's attitude is certainly more
ambiguous than Gustav Freytag's. Freytag was unequivocal in grant-
ing the aristocracy a historic and contemporary right to life only to
the extent that this class constituted the preliminary stage of and the
preparation for the industrious bourgeoisie that followed. According

to him, the bourgeoisie can learn nothing from the aristocracy; according to Spielhagen, however, it can learn a great deal. Spielhagen's social nerves are rooted in the soil of feudalism, much like they had been for the Young Germany; he requires rational acts, constant and penetrating factual reports as well as incisive analyses to buttress his bourgeois position and to sharpen his critique of an antiquated social order. Perhaps the length of Spielhagen's novels can be attributed to his unconscious drive to emancipate himself from the affective fixation on his social "fathers." Perhaps this is the reason why Herr von Degenfeld, without apparent internal necessity, is made to articulate theories which coincide with the progressive political goals of the bourgeoisie of his time:

> Nothing is more absurd than the idea of most of our officers that a soldier ought to be a soldier and nothing else. If I am not much mistaken, we are rapidly approaching a period when the general who is not also a statesman, will be of little use in the world; and when statesmen who cannot strike a blow in case of necessity, will be little respected.[20]

In this passage, the type of the imperialist and, ultimately totalitarian general and statesman of late capitalism is anticipated.

Spielhagen's biting critique in *The Hohensteins* does not primarily hit the aristocracy; rather, it is intended to strike that group's bourgeois followers and imitators. His anger and his ridicule, which was focused on the clergy in *Problematic Characters,* is now directed primarily against the high bureaucracy and certain artistic circles. During the commotions of 1848, a major with the bourgeois name of Willibrod Dasch makes the following speech to the city council:

> Gentlemen! the decisive moment has come. I cannot doubt that any longer after what I have just seen and heard. A fanatical populace tyrannizes over the well-disposed; the militia threatens to desert us; we can rely no longer on any one except ourselves and the glorious army, the last support of the throne, the altar, and the hearth. The commandant of the city, Count Hinkel-Gackel, has this moment placed once more all of the regular troops at my disposal.

> Although we may be prepared to risk our lives in the good cause and to pledge our fortunes for its success, we are yet bound to secure the property of the city against a populace eager to rob and to plunder.[21]

In the end, the city's treasury falls into the hands of the alderman von Hohenstein, who embezzles it. Here, then, Spielhagen castigates the musty alliance between the bourgeois city government and the feudal state; he indicts the bourgeoisie for having one eye on the military while being simultaneously concerned with money, for its outmaneuvering of citizens' opinions and its vile disrespect for the broad masses of people. The city bureaucracy is condemned to an ahistorical death because it attempts to continue its parasitical existence with the help of a social stratum which has itself become obsolete.

Spielhagen's method for analyzing and deconstructing these individuals and strata is, once again, objective description and factual reporting. He does not make a direct value judgment about the mayor of that city, but the "hoarse whisper" in which he has the latter speak, his panting and sweating behavior, his language which is simultaneously bombastic and roguish—all suffice to accomplish Spielhagen's intended social criticism. A similar fate is in store for those artists who produce only when commissioned by the nobility and only in a courtly environment. A painter says:

> *Eh bien!* I am not so endowed as to be able to paint directly for immortality. For whom else can I paint then? For the gods of the earth, the rich, the great!—(who else wants to be painted? who else can pay me? . . . But I cannot imagine, by heaven, how Art can exist by the side of liberty—I mean your liberty. You want to abolish wealth, and Art is a luxury for the wealthy. The common people—in the best sense of the word, doctor— have no fondness for Art, no appreciation of Art. As long as Art has been known, it has found an asylum at the courts of princes. You need not suggest the republics of antiquity and of the Middle Ages! It matters very little in the end whether one rules or a few share the rule between them.[22]

Here, Spielhagen sits in judgment on the artist's lack of class consciousness, thereby making clear his own position as a fighter on the forefront of bourgeois liberty. He keeps himself apart from those artistic circles who are content to see their activity in isolation—as a value in itself—apart from those who reject their participation in the "universal solidarity of human interests"[23]

But the painter also expresses Spielhagen's longing, and here we can see, once again, the shadow of the Young Germany, which dictates a specific social mission to the writer; a mission that is difficult, weighty, and full of responsibility. Flaubert's rejection of artistic work as a bourgeois occupation was very emotional; Freytag happily welcomes the classification of artistic productivity into the bourgeois social order as a normalization process; Spielhagen has, for objective and rational reasons, a positive attitude toward his profession as a writer, which he exercises because of his talent and because of coincidence. Contrary to the frivolity of the "comedian" who flatters feudal circles, he has the inculcated seriousness of bourgeois morality.

Spielhagen's ability to differentiate within social strata is even more evident when he deals with social groups other than the aristocracy. For Freytag, matters were still quite simple: there is the bad or the stupid aristocrat on the one hand and the magnificent bourgeois citizen on the other; all the rest is rabble, the Jews, and the "assistants" of entrepreneurship who become the objects of folkloristic amusement. In Spielhagen, however, the very concept of people, of *Volk*, is broken up. In a discussion of Republican leaders during the revolution a spokesman says:

> "You look upon the people to-day as an inert machine, which you can manage as you choose, and to-morrow it is the essence of life, of energy and wisdom. It is neither the one nor the other, but simply a mass of more or less good men and more or less bad musicians, each one of whom has his own interests; and if you wish to make the whole company act in concert, you must first learn how to reconcile all these millions of individual ambitions. There is the mystery."[24]

With respect to language, this passage is similar to the one discussed above: the idea stays on a superstructural level because the difference of interests within the population is essentially attributed to differences in character. On the other hand, Spielhagen at times was quite able to recognize the economic differentiation in the population. An example is Muenzer's explanation of why the revolution foundered:

> Our revolution has miscarried, miserably miscarried. The heaving mountain has brought forth a mouse. Instead of a social—or at least a republican—uprising, we have only a small campaign for a romantic constitutions which will exist on paper only. The petit-bourgeoisie has betrayed the proletariat to the moneymongers who willingly offer themselves to the aristocratic fist which protects them from the petit-bourgoisie as well as the proletariat. The aristocracy will demand a high price for its protectorship, so high that finally—though years might pass before this happens—the bourgeoisie, made cocky and confident by the long period of social calm will refuse to pay and will proceed—in alliance with the proletariat and the petit-bourgeoisie— to topple the aristocracy, only to turn around at the very moment of victory and trample on the dumb dwarfs who fought its battle, so

that [the bourgeoisie] can rule—all powerful—from the money bags which serve him as a throne. This is the course of the movement, the *circulus vitiosus,* in which our [social] disease is likely to keep moving for generations.[25]

If one were to apply these statements to the relationship among aristocracy, bourgeoisie and proletariat during the period from the Bismarckian wars to the collapse after World War I, they would almost be prophetic. At the very least, they reveal an intuitively correct understanding of the class structure in the years 1848–49. No historical commentary is needed. We want to emphasize how close Spielhagen comes to formulating a concept of class society. This, of course, constitutes another reason for the eclipse of Spielhagen's fame after the final establishment of bourgeois society in Germany.

Next to the class question, the problem of leadership is the second important theme in *The Hohensteins.* Spielhagen's leader is represented by the figure of Dr. Muenzer. Once again, the writer's rational attitude toward the question of social transformation is revealed. For one thing, Muenzer falls passionately inn love with an aristocratic woman (how can we not think of Lasalle?). The unconscious infatuation with the aristocracy to which we have already alluded now becomes manifest and Muenzer himself articulates it consciously, admitting that his "love of humanity . . . did not [come] from the heart" but "from the intellect, from conviction" that his "compassion for people . . . was the compassion a doctor feels for his patients."[26]

Indeed, he goes so far as to separate justice and love of humanity: justice grows out of the recognition of the necessity of a new distribution of existing worldly fortunes, while love of humanity is almost entirely foreign to him. The leader has no illusions. In spite of all his resigned longings for romantic "beatific life, where there is no more virtue and vice, no more wisdom and ignorance, only pure beauty, wonderful, heartwrenching, bewitching, beauty that is not of this world,"[27] he himself knows that these wishes are irreconcilable "with worry, suffering, sickness—the terrible daughters of the earth";[28] but he only knows this "behind this forehead, between the narrow walls of his skull."[29] When Muenzer goes so far as to believe that he has to give up all individual feeling, pain as well as love,[30] when he demands that "the individual" must "disappear" into the "the collectivity,"[31] we can conclude that this confident and class-conscious bourgeois leader who believes in enlightened rationalism is, in fact, quite ambivalent toward the objectives which he has recognized and accepted as correct. And he expresses this ambivalence in the effusive pathos with which he describes his sacrifice of personal comfort and well-being. What he lacks is emotional identification with the work to which he feels called. Political leadership, in other words, remains a mere matter of reason; even the commitment to justice is only the product of rational deliberation.

This gives rise to a methodological sociologic observation. Evidently, it would be dogmatic to establish an unbroken unmediated relationship between the material interests of one who works with his head and his work products themselves. Individual psychological structures are more gradually transformed than economic structures or cultural institutions; in fact, they contain the most retarding moments in the historical process. Indeed, the only archaic moment which survives continues in the emotional life of individuals. It is no surprise then, that the archaic remnants of feudalism continue to be present in Spielhagen, in spite of the fact that he is an especially radical bourgeois.

Finally, we want to consider how positive ideals are presented in this novel: the impression of Spielhagen's vacillation between liberalist and collectivist objectives is reinforced; and the idealist point of departure of Spielhagen's social criticism is revealed even more clearly. In a rare outburst of fury, Spielhagen indicts the idolatry of keeping up appearances:

> In order to satisfy this moloch, the poor person was forced to lead a life which never at any moment allowed him to attain the feeling of human dignity; those from distinguished social circles were forced to indulge in pleasures which degraded them into animals; in order to please this moloch, the state had to be a domain of princes and their families; natural occupations had to split into unnatural castes which had to be closed off wherever possible, castes from which the privileged cruelly rejected the demands and aspirations of those who had been oppressed for centuries! . . . For the sake of this moloch . . . the blood of the best sons [of the fatherland] was uselessly spilled on inglorious battlefields; in even less glorious street battles, many good hearts were pierced by bullets.[32]

This outburst stands in contrast to the passage from *Problematic Characters* cited above. What is meant by the "Moloch of appearances"? Does not this notion imply a reversion to metaphysical themes? Is not a spiritual, very unmaterialistic apparition substituted here for the rationally criticized suffering of the masses? In any case, as with his sociology of language, Spielhagen is once again too abstract; his final reference point is some sort of nondeducible spiritual being. This contradiction between the liberalist secularization and the idealistic motivation of social critique is rooted in the peculiarity of bourgeois thought; it is as undeniable in Spielhagen as it is in Hegel. This is why the tasks of the revolution are not determined by the interests and instincts of the masses in revolt; the revolution is supposed to move only along a course prescribed by its intellectual and spiritual leaders. Spielhagen's pedagogical side is especially apparent in the discussion of socialism which he outrightly rejects:

> "This is why the socialist republicans are the most insidious enemies of freedom. . . . Not only do they not transcend the authority of the state which has drained us of all our vitality, but they actually strengthen it, thereby undermining the process of self-education of the populace. They are like the father, who gives his hungry child a rock instead of a piece of bread, and therefore they are guilty regardless of whether they are deceivers or the deceived, that is: whether they believe their theories or not.[33]

When the belief in the "solidarity of human virtue"[34] is mentioned further on in the speech, a causal and temporal relationship between morality and the material situation is meant. Despite all the materialist aspects of bourgeois thought, Spielhagen makes no connection between morality and spiritual structure on the one hand, and the concrete material situation as a determining factor on the other; indeed, he does not even consider the possibility that the two spheres interact. Spiritual forces are determining, whether they are good or bad. But at the same time, only certain of these phenomena are valuable, these spiritual values contain the very standard by which events in the material sphere of society are evaluated. Spielhagen does not criticize socialism for having an incorrect economic or political theory, but because it lacks the resources for an education of humanity. The "bread," then, is not actually bread, but the spirit.

Once again, Spielhagen demonstrates the fate of a person who is unable to consolidate his observations into a theory, in spite of his sincere intentions to analyze the social process. His positivist belief in the conclusiveness and persuasiveness of the presented facts and phenomena is really nothing more than a cover for his lack of a unified theory. Spielhagen, a member of the bourgeoisie with a penchant for feudalism, a man who does not close his eyes to the appearance of the proletariat and is therefore open to seeing social class differentiation, is unable to develop a scientifically founded "natural" history and theory of society. Describing and writing in themselves almost appear to be a way out from a position which is hopeless in its basic orientation. For him, the process of writing is an intellectual and spiritual method of justifying life in the social world, and the structure of that world is constituted intellectually and spiritually. Spielhagen is an idealist, and insofar as idealism is able to exercise ideological functions, it does so in his work. Bourgeois society is superior to feudalism because it is more right. It realizes its superiority through spiritual means, through insights and conviction, by its greater virtuousness and its willingness to sacrifice.

Therefore, the development of bourgeois society and the elimination of its still existing shortcomings, is dependent primarily, if not solely, on spiritual means. What matters in history are spiritual and intellectual qualities, therefore the material situation is no longer so important. As long as the material world corresponds to the wishes and intentions of the bourgeoisie—and this seems to be the case in those of Spielhagen's works which we have discussed—then this segment of reality is removed from criticism and at least retains the features of ideological transfiguration.

In his two following works, *In Reih und Glied* (1866) and *Hammer und Amboss* (1868), Spielhagen continues in the vein of idealist politics. Politics as well as general humanitarian considerations constitute the spiritual tone of these works; they preach a kind of free-thinking radicalism of opinion and go so far as to undertake an idealistic portrayal of a prison director. Socialism is discussed in both of these novels— Ferdinand Lasalle actually makes an appearance in the first one in the character of Guttmann—but solutions to urgent social and political problems are found only in the parliamentary process as the collective effort of all parts in the nation. The word "and" (instead of Goethe's "or") in the second title is a symbolic rendering of the function of each separate part of the national community, which serves the totality at the same time as it is strengthened by it. Spielhagen's use of metallic work instruments in his symbolic picture of social peace is only another expression for an organicist social theory.

What he criticized, almost derisively, as a romantic social theory of order in *Problematic Characters*, appears here—applied to bourgeois society—with all the signs of positive transfiguration. It never occurs to Spielhagen to consider the possibility that his observations of deplorable material and spiritual conditions might in fact be a sign that the entire social structure is unsound and this shows that we are indeed dealing with ideological transfiguration. He seems content to illuminate these conditions, and to advocate the institutionalization of formal legal equality and the opportunity for general spiritual freedom—which he does not define more explicitly. In both of these works, Spielhagen attempts to identify with the bourgeois life order and all of its appearances; therefore it is quite easy for him to bridge the gaps in this order in a generalized way, and to substitute the irrational sermon and the irrational song of praise for the rational critique which he exercised before.

But Spielhagen's liberal optimism did not hold out against subsequent developments; his view of the society after the crisis years, like so many people's, was more sober. He saw the crashes and their origins, the strange relationships between business people and the high bureaucracy, and the dangers to which propertyless groups were constantly subjected by the chaos of economic crises. The fight against the nobility that he carried out *a tout prix* in his first works—a fight that implicated even the realm of intimate feelings—recedes into the background, making way for a general critique of the disturbing trends of the new era. The novel *Sturmflut* is representative of this attitude. Today, this title—*Hurricane*—sounds very trite, but in its time, it had serious symbolic significance: from the raging sea, the wildness and the frenzy of the dance around the golden calf was audible. This novel was an analysis and a critique of the founding period.

Once again, we find the congenial aristocrat; in fact this type is portrayed even more distinctly, and one likely psychological reason for this is the fact that the social function of that entire stratum has by now been almost entirely eliminated. Spielhagen leaves it up to the aristocracy itself to recognize its new position and to draw the necessary conclusions; this is how a man of noble birth in a leadership position formulates it:

> In this century of decreasing class differences, we have come to be on the same level as those classes who were pushing behind us; or better who were confronting us. We are situated in the same dusty arena, in which the struggle for existence is fought.[35]

It is left up to General von Werben to distance himself from the exaggerated class pride of the bourgeois, especially the petit-bourgeois:

> "The man of the people remembers every small injustice precisely; even if it was inflicted a lifetime ago, he has forgiven nothing. The

aristocrat has not forgotten anything either, but he has learned to forgive; he has learned to appreciate his opponent's merits where he encountered these; he has learned not to close his eyes to the weaknesses of his own party; he has understood that the fight must be carried out on a different battleground; namely in the realm of law and justice; and he knows that victory will come to that party which learns how to solidly take root in this ground.[36]

It is characteristic of Spielhagen's psychology that now it is the aristocrat who speaks of the "solidarity of all human virtues." Can it be a coincidence that, at a time when the bourgeoisie is in crisis, the aristocratic general has to remind this class of its own ideals? It is his affection for the dying "fathers," which we sensed and expressed before, that breaks through here.

Granted, this should not cloud our awareness that in this work, too, Spielhagen portrays the liberal bourgoisie in a favorable light—at least that section which has not been morally polluted by the poison of the founding years. Above all, however, he continues with his destruction of the notion of genius, and with the critique of the conception of history that places heroic individuals at the center of human development, where Bismarck serves as his prime example. As in *The Hohensteins.* here it is also the uncle who imparts Spielhagen's basic views to the reader. Uncle Ernst makes it clear that the successes of the wars of 1864, 1866, and 1870 can certainly not be attributed to the Junkers—but not to Bismarck, either. In fact, they would never have occurred if they had "not dreamed of a United Germany—the hearts and minds of those men who were not rewarded for their services with noble titles or grants of land, and were not pardoned."[37]

Even though the nephew portrays his uncle—with the latter's approval—as a hater of Bismarck, this does not mean that the founding of the Reich hurt Spielhagen's bourgeois sensibilities; on the contrary, the bourgeoisie had, after all. made its peace with Bismarck precisely at the moment when its increasing power guaranteed economic and moral support for economic expansion. In Spielhagen's ideological sphere, of course, this fact reveals itself only in—comparatively speaking—a frenzy of normality. The new German Reich granted to its citizens the self-confidence that had hitherto been the privilege of foreign nations, and the emperor is only the symbol for the smashing of all remaining privileges and the certification of the equality of the citizens by the state:

> "It could be nothing less than a German Emperor, if we were to demonstrate to the English, the Americans, the Chinese and Japanese *as oculos* that henceforth they [could] no longer carry on trade and make

treaties with citizens of Hamburg, Bremen, Oldenburg, Mecklenburg, or even of Prussia, but [had to deal] with Germans, who sail under one and the same flag—a flag which has the will and the power to protect even the least and the poorest who shares the honor and the fortune of being a German."[38]

The person speaking these sentences became lieutenant during the war, but he actually feels pride when others use his "bourgeois name" and address him as "Mr. Smith."[39]

The bourgeois pride in unbroken economic development, however, came to an end after the era of depression began in 1870; thereafter, attempts to hold on to this pride no longer have the force of ideological transfiguration; instead, they take on the peculiarity of kitsch and of dishonesty—think, for example, of Rudolf Herzog. The more evident the relationship between capital and economic crisis becomes, the more this class, which sees itself as absolute, needs to ideologically justify the spirituality of its mode of life.

The fact that in this novel of the founding years, the proletariat is represented not by an industrial worker but by a small tenant farmer near the Baltic coast, is significant for a sociological interpretation of Spielhagen. It shows that Spielhagen avoids, probably unconsciously, the most burning social problems even though he is completely unable to ignore the situation of those groups which have to pay the cost of the general social development trends. The already mentioned tenant bitterly exclaims that the planned construction of the harbor does not serve the poor people, but only the property owners:

> "Many a tree will be cut down and turned into money, as well as many an acre of land that is not worth a penny, and many an acre of arable land on which a poor man ekes out a meager existence in the sweat of his brow, a person who will have to take his walking stick and emigrate to America, if there is still room for the likes of us."[40]

In his later works, Spielhagen continues to be essentially critical and accusatory and he does not pass over the deplorable state of affairs which he sees around hiim. But his positive proposals for change are always located in the ideal sphere. At the end of the novel *Was will das werden?* (1886), a colonel from the general staff explains that now, after the reactionary powers have failed, liberalism is under political and religious tutelage; he sees an enemy in every atheist and every social democrat, and fears that hypocrisy and cowardice of mind permeates even the "higher and highest strata of society" Once again, Spielhagen ends with an appeal for a return to decency, and awareness of prevailing social insincerity.

The novel *Sonntagskind* (1893) contains a very peculiar passage, in which the girlfriend says to the writer:

> "It is likely that your talent is more appropriate for a description of the higher social classes than of the lower groups, and that your psychological analysis of educated intellects and sensitive hearts will be more accurate than that of ignorant souls and crude minds. But I think this is why you should tackle that which is unfree, unpleasant, and ugly. You must examine this and study it especially carefully in order to be able to use it where necessary. I fear that otherwise the picture of the world that you design will lack the requisite richness and convincing truth. Your depiction of humanity cannot begin with the baron—like the newspaper feuillets—but it cannot end with the baron, or even much earlier, either—as does that of Zola and his various followers and parrots. You must include everything that has a human face. I have often teased you by calling you a crypto aristocrat; but I know very well that your soul is indignant toward any kind of pretension or presumption, toward all injustice, and that you have the deepest sympathy with the poor and with those who suffer."[41]

These sentences hold a key to Spielhagen's psychology; they explicitly mention the writer's love of aristocratic splendor; he is even called a "writer and crypto-aristocrat." Moreover, they clearly express the extent to which assistance for those who suffer is a matter of reason only, while emotions are turned to sublime spiritual matters. If one compares Spielhagen to Balzac and Zola, we see that he shares with Zola the tendency to analyze social problems, but he also has an affinity with Balzac, who was, like himself, taken with the splendor of the aristocracy. Indeed, even the moralistic demands of liberalism are seen, rightfully, as inadequate in their imprecise generality. One should certainly not read this passage as a conscious self-analysis undertaken by Spielhagen; nevertheless, the author's objectification is expressed, even if unintentionally.

We have already pointed out how frail and inconsistent Spielhagen's ideologies are. In a sociological analysis of literature, his place would be somewhere between Gustav Freytag and Conrad Ferdinand Meyer: between the transfiguration of the rising, middle, propertied bourgeoisie and the ideological illumination of the haute-bourgeois lifestyle. Spielhagen's ambiguous views mirror the fate of all middle groups in the developed bourgeois society: the process of concentration of modern capitalism decreases the opportunities for all middle strata; the more developed rationalization of the economy makes upward mobility more difficult; and the increasing social inferiority of the proletariat certainly does not make social decline more tempting. From the point of view of a sociological analysis, we can see that in Spielhagen, the affairs of the affected strata, their economic and social reality, appear in the twilight of an ideological construction which tends to fade and dim reality. He leaves a great deal of room for the illusion that people's views are to a large extent determined, not by real social situations, but by individual incidental events. Yet Spielhagen also shows a penchant for radical honesty which points a finger at the sore spots of the social order. It is for this reason that the history of his fame lies in the fact that he was silenced.

Notes

1.   Friedrich Gundolf, *Romantiker*, Neue Folge, (Berlin-Wilmersdorf, 1931), p. 126.
2.   Heinric Hart, "Friedrich Spielhagen und der deutsche Roman der Gegenwart," in *Kritische Waffengaenge*, no. 6, (Leipzig, 1884), pp. 50ff.
3.   Cited from Albert Sorgel, *Dichtung und Dichter. Der Zeit* (Leipzig 1928), p. 7.
4.   Friedrich Spielhagen, *Beitraege zur Theorie und Technik des Romans* (Leipzig, 1882), p. 174.
5.   Cited from Karl Lamprecht, *Deutsche Geschichte*, vol. 2 (Berlin, 1914), pp. 298ff.
6.   Friedrich Spielhagen, *Problematic Characters*, trans. Schele de Vere (New York. 1870). p. 171.
7.   Freidrich Spielhagen, *Problematische Naturen I. Saemtliche Romane*, vol. 1 (Leipzig, 1903), p. 65.
8.   Ibid., p. 58.
9.   Friedrich Spielhagen, *Through the Night to the Light*, trans. Schele de Vere. New York 1870. p. 171.
10. *Problematic Characters*, p. 145.
11. *Problematische Naturen*, p. 340.
12. Ibid., p. 422.
13. *Problematic Characters*, p. 210.
14. *Problematische Naturen*, p. 151.
15. Ibid.
16. *Through the Night to the Light*, p. 359.
17. Ibid., p. 337, 338.
18. *Problematische Naturen*, p. 564.
19. Friedrich Spielhagen, *The Hohensteins*, trans. Schele de Vere (New York, 1870), p. 232.
20. Ibid., p. 277.
21. Ibid., pp. 104–5.

22. Ibid., pp. 241–42.
23. *The Hohensteins,* p. 313.
24. *The Hohensteins.* p. 97.
25. *The Hohensteins,* p. 666. (This passage was omitted in the English translation.)
26. Ibid., p. 167.
27. Ibid., p. 164.
28. Ibid.
29. Ibid., p. 166.
30. Ibid., p. 169.
31. Ibid., p. 384.
32. Ibid., pp. 541ff. (This passage was omitted in the English translation.)
33. Ibid., pp. 499ff. (This passage was omitted in the English translation.)
34. Ibid., p. 501.
35. Friedrich Spielhagen, *Sturmflut I, Saemtliche Romane,* vol. 8, p. 47.
36. Ibid., p. 368.
37. Ibid., p. 114.
38. Ibid., pp. 72ff.
39. Ibid., p. 35.
40. Ibid.
41. Friedrich Spielhagen, *Sonntagskind, Saemtliche Romane,* vol. 3, p. 292.

13

Conrad Ferdinand Meyer: Apologia of the Upper Class

Meyer's prose fiction appears at first to have nothing to do with sociological categories in either form or content. The presence of sociological information will, however, be the subject of this investigation. The question will be whether the meanings and functions noted by the sociologist were intended or sanctioned by the author, and whether their effect among the readers can be traced.

The study of Meyer's concept of society is both challenging and simple: simple because all his stories are of an exclusively historical nature, challenging because the subjects of these stories are consistently taken from the more distant past, never from the present. If one considers merely the titles of his stories, one notes that they often contain the names of historical personages, such as Gustav Adolf, Pescara or Jürg Jenatsch. Otherwise they emphasize certain types of individuals—*The Saint, the Judge*—or refer to unusual situations—someone shoots from the pulpit, a monk marries. Everything is out of the ordinary, and the stories are consistently centered around an extraordinary individual.

All of Meyer's prose fiction can be considered novellas, even *Jürg Jenatsch*, which is often categorized as a novel. A novel covers the whole breadth of a network of relations, grasps the wealth of phenomena in human life and institutions, in short, "records" the world, as Zola put it.

Meyer's novelistic approach, however, as even the titles indicate, selects, focuses on what is special, creates a particular kind of order. The selection process alone would not give rise to sociological conclusions. The history of the novella's development in the Renaissance is closely tied to the selection of and the emphasis on certain situations. In the Renaissance context, however, subject matters that have already been given a literary form by tradition are retold. Further, German novels of the nineteenth century also may choose unusual events, as in Kleist's work. But Meyer's novels are always confined to specific times, particular persons and types. The individual is neither cradled in a basically harmonious, ordered world as in Goethe, nor is the individual driven out in search of fulfillment. Rather, Meyer's stylization of place, time and character expresses the constructs that an extraordinary man wishes to impose upon the world.

In order to make the sociological meaning of the selection process clearer, let us look more closely at the subject matter itself. The story *The Amulet* provides an especially appropriate and clear example. Here, the author makes selections in three areas—history, landscape and characters—until with great care the sole object of importance emerges.

First, the historic view is focused on the turbulent struggles of the sixteenth and seventeenth centuries in order to limit it to the especially adventurous Huguenot battles. Then, an episode is chosen that seems to be comprehensible from the vantage point of one particular great individual. When describing the confrontations of the opposing groups, which take the form of heated argument or bloody man-to-man combat, the author takes neither side. It means that the issues pertinent for great historical struggles are totally insignificant. They are important only insofar as they provide a colorful and fascinating backdrop for the great Admiral Coligny.

In relation to locale, there is a shrinking of area and distance. If characters in this story travel, one is tempted to think of the offhand tone in which the wealthy merchant speaks of his business trips. At the beginning of the third chapter, the narrator travels through Burgundy, then along the Seine to a small village outside of Paris. This journey, certainly requiring days and weeks, is dealt with in three lines,[1] and the one sentence that depicts this journey might have sufficed to include the arrival in Paris, if the narrator had not encountered an adventure in Melun, which prefigures the true hero of the story. The author captures the description of Paris, seen through the eyes of a Swiss man of rural origins, with a single line: "The first week passed with viewing the grand city." Paris gains external contours only at the point when the admiral's home and thereby the admiral himself enter the story.

This tendency to abbreviate is apparent also in the description of a journey that the fictitious narrator takes on Coligny's behalf, when he says, "Coligny dispatched me on a mission to Orleans where German cavalry were stationed. When I returned and entered my lodgings, Gilbert [of the admiral's party] came toward me with contorted features."[2] Here, the purpose of the shrinking of the landscape becomes clear. The journey— described in a half a sentence—begins with Coligny and ends with him. Time and place are not heroicized in the sense of a romantic mythology, but they are stylized into ornaments for the hero, for he alone is important. This fact is further emphasized by the selection of character. Coligny rules over everything. He is both ruler and leader, always great and always strong. He is also gifted with a superior inscrutability, which we shall analyze. The first-person narrator retreats completely into the background.

Such condensation and selection can be found everywhere in the story. Consider, for example, in the story *The Saint* the abruptly dramatic presentation of Henry's seemingly final break with Becket, which intentionally avoids any detail:

> Finally, Sir Henry came to a decision. He summoned the primate before a court of his barons, had him condemned as a traitor to the kingdom, and banished him forever from his territories. But on the same day that Sir Thomas was forced to flee across the ocean like a criminal, Lady Ellenor left her husband and Windsor Castle with a cry of woe that was heard far and wide.[3]

The composition of the novella *Jürg Jenatsch* reveals the same heroic stylization. It treats a mere episode from the Thirty Years' War in such a way that the grand milieu of a world war is evoked. All the powers, interests and passions of this turbulent epoch are concentrated in the Swiss landscape and in the figure of Jürg Jenatsch. Here, the German Empire, Italy, France, Spain, Switzerland all carry out their conflicts; great generals and politicians pursue lust for power, love, ambition; "fire and ice"—all can be felt in every sentence. Even the dynamics of the story are similar to *The Amulet*: it is constructed in individual isolated images of greatness or occasionally as background for starkly contrasting images.

The material provided here should suffice to illustrate that Meyer makes his selections in accordance with his hero-oriented conception of history. History becomes a stage for heroes, an opportunity for great individuals to carry out their portentious games. In *The Amulet*, a French officer plays the highest members of the court against each other without confiding in anyone. Pescara also plays a political game. And even such a harmless story as *The Shot from the Pulpit*, in which the old general has no opportunity for carrying out a daring deed but only a boyish prank, still sheds enough light on the dying protagonist so that he, who was a hero in the best days of his life, remains in age the hero of this story. The human being who "moves the world" is what matters.[4] At one point, Pescara lets the following statement slip out:

> "The finest thing in life is to move people and objects with invisible hands, those who have known this will not want to taste anything else."[5]

For the history of heroes, time is not recorded according to centuries or epochs, but according to genius. History becomes the great hall through which the great human being roams. One of Meyer's collections of poems is entitled "Anteroom." Other titles—"God," "Pious and Impudent," "Genius," "Men"—reveal what is paramount to the author: never the common, never the group, the hero alone is the endlessly variable theme of history. So for the people that Meyer celebrates, the task is never one of carrying out acts whose time has come; instead, it is the other way around: time is constituted by great deeds. Morone exhorts Pescara to action:

> "My dear Pescara, what a constellation of stars guides and supports you! The cause is ripe, and you, yourself, are mature! A decisive time, a desperate struggle, gods and titans, freedom rearing up against rule by force. Today the world still in motion and flux, tomorrow, perhaps, freezing to lava! And a deed that is prepared for you and for which you were born! Does not your forming hand twitch to carry out this deed?"[6]

But Pescara does not act, and thereby the world "hardens into lava."

One might be tempted to compare Meyer to Friedrich Hebbel. Not only do they share a love for historical themes, but their criteria for selecting these themes are similar. Hebbel's dramas tend to be situated at those turning points in world history where one epoch gives way to another. Transitions—from Germanic tribes to Christianity, from barbarism in Asia Minor to Greek culture, from feudal society to bourgeois liberalism—these are themes characteristic for Hebbel. Meyer, too, loves such turning points: Germanic tribes and the Carolingian Empire, Renaissance and Reformation, the Three Estates and Absolutism provide a background for several of his stories. Hebbel for his part wants to show that, in the last analysis, even the individual who strives to move against the flow of history is subservient to the overall historical process; world history runs over the individual blindly, and precisely these great situations of historical conflict show that even a great man is finally crushed by the wheel of events. For Meyer, on the other hand, the historical junctures exist for the sole purpose of giving great individuals their greatest opportunities to show what they truly are and what they are capable of doing.

Indeed, Meyer's stories express the conviction that it is "men" who give rise to the dialectics of history. Meyer thus stands Hebbel's Hegel on his head. Meyer transforms historical epochs into functions of the heroes, as can be seen by his use of dates. The first line of the *Amulet,* for example, contains a date but its only significance is that of an autobiographical reference. Generally, the chronological manner of speaking in Meyer's work takes the form "In those days it happened that . . ."[7] The exclamation of the short-tempered Armbruster in the same story (*The Saint*) is also very revealing: "Leave me alone with your meaningless numbers!"[8]

His casual attitude toward the multifariousness of people and situations makes the real course of history a matter of indifference for the writer. Therefore, he does not seek to capture it via research into primary sources, but takes it over in mediated form, such as that provided by Ferdinand Gregorovius or Jacob Burckhardt.[9] Their treatment of the past, which becomes meaningful as a backdrop to heroic deeds, is compatible with Meyer's own views. The social role of the study of history underwent several changes between the end of the eighteenth century and Meyer's time. During the Enlightenment, historical research is undertaken in the service of bourgeois progress; think of Arnold Heren, for example. The history of states is investigated in order to refute the inevitability of absolutism and to reveal its unsound structure of domination. During the Romantic period, one great era of bourgeois defeat, historical research aids the transfiguration of the past that is intended as consolation for the desolate state of affairs. Leopold von Ranke, for example, is not interested—at least in the beginning—in learning things from history that would be significant for the present; instead, he insists on looking at "how it really was then." And later historical materialism, which is oriented toward the proletariat, seeks to uncover laws of history which will permit an understanding and transformation of the present.

The writing of Renaissance history in the second half of the nineteenth century is closely connected to the extension of an upper class ideology which found in the history of "Great Men" and in the discovery of the "Renaissance Man" models for strong contemporary rulers. The Renaissance offered welcome objects of admiration for this view. In connection with the *Fuehrerideal*—the ideal of a strong leader—this epoch seems to be proof for a heroic concept of history.

From the standpoint of the revolutionary bourgeoisie or the proletariat, the fifteenth and early sixteenth centuries is the period during which secularization first met with success in European culture. The Renaissance then becomes the first stage of great bourgeois enlightenment in modern history—indeed, this was the view of the eighteenth century and of the Hegelian Left. Gregorovius and Burckhardt's works, therefore, can be called romantic insofar as their concept of history discovers a higher reality behind the "crude and transitory facts." This higher reality is the enduring, influential and exemplary role—for better or for worse—of great men. Of course, it must be noted that Renaissance historians, especially Burckhardt, did include other, even materialistic elements, but their impact, then and now, has been the fascination with the "Great Man." And this was also their main impact on Meyer.

One of the most peculiar consequences of Meyer's heroic concept of history is its application to the relationship between history and nature. This relationship has always been an important topic for the philosophy of history; it was discussed under the label of natural, mythical or archaic. To the triumphant bourgeois consciousness, with its stress on accumulation, nature appears as unquestionably physical, as material which exists, unchanging and inexhaustible, only in service to human society. The significance of the rise of the third estate lies precisely in the fact that it makes possible a direct and unembellished approach to nature; the exploitation of nature becomes a force of social development. The concept of nature that emerged in the French Enlightenment, which sees it as something good, something lawfully ordered, also contains its function as an economically useful resource. Rousseau depicts nature as both a real and a fictional historical factor; for him, the state of nature is a factual as well as a conceivable historical social order. Therefore, it would be inappropriate to search for a mythological thought construct in this, as if Rousseau believed that life in nature reveals ontological realities which are suppressed in a technically and organizationally structured society. On the contrary, the state of nature is that life-form, in which nature appears as a practical provider subservient to human economic purposes. Only in a physical-chemical sense did humanity "redeem" nature with the rise of the bourgeoisie.

In the Romantic period, which constitutes an era of depression for this class, the polar confrontation of man and nature disappears, and the relationship which dominated during the Enlightenment is turned into its opposite. Where before, nature was in the service of historical progress, in romanticism man abandons history to serve nature.

The mythical empire of the previous world, mythology and heavenly age on the one hand, and the mere vegetative quality of the world of children, are seen as the true home of humanity. Man's abdication to this "naturalness" appears as the key to becoming human. The rejection of the bourgeoisie by late feudal and absolutist society in the age of the Vienna Congress is transformed, by ideological magic, into the bourgeoisie's rejection of the present, in which such hostile powers make a claim to reality. One might even venture the supposition that in the Historical School in German philology, in the history writing of Ranke and his followers, history itself appears as something absolute and immutable. Such a categorical treatment permits historical reality to be treated as another "natural" element of nature. Even the organicism of the romantics shares with the Enlightenment the static concept of nature. But neither the Enlightenment's laws of history, nor the romantic organicism can conceal the fact that for both of these phases of bourgeois thought nature is seen as a given and appears as already ordained. For the eighteenth century, this has the ideological significance of guaranteeing the longevity of bourgeois society; for the romantics and their audience, nature is an emotional guarantee for having a link to the beautiful "reality" even in a contemptible world of appearances. Progress is possible only in the world of art, as expressed by Schlegel's concept of "progressive universal poetry."

For Meyer, nature and myth are not prior to history, but rather contained within it or following it. Meyer's attitude can be described as follows: gone are the great battles in which individuals or whole peoples appeared. Gone is the heroism, which is able to bestow the sanctification of a reality onto human life. Now, heroism—the secret of history—flees to nature, or rather, it takes the new morphological form of nature itself. History is not a continuation of nature, but nature is a continuation of history by other means; trees and rocks are the legitimate successors of Alarich, Saracens, the Hohenstaufens and Ceasare Borgia. It is nature that points to the grandiose, unique, victorious elements in every segment of life.

This becomes especially clear in *Jürg Jenatsch*. The disturbing conversation with Waser carries over into the gathering clouds and the darkening sky;[10] Jürg and Lukretia's journey is accompanied by a "southerly blue, clear and deep" sky.[11] Toward the end, when the hero's fate is sealed, the foehn wind is raging.[12] Immediately before the catastrophe, "pale yellow lightning tore through the low-hanging clouds."[13] Nature appears as a continuation of the hero's story.[14] From here, a sociological line leads straight to the circle around Stephan George, where the glorification of historical singularity found its last serious expression in Ernst Kantorowitz's book on Friedrich II.

There have been many attempts to make Meyer into a religious writer.[15] But neither his studies of Pascal nor his ties to Protestantism can hide the fact that his heroes are not guided by religion or morality. On the contrary, they are characterized by an amorality that crosses over into the demoniac. As we will see, it is misleading to even describe Meyer's heroes in this way, because in the last analysis we cannot really know what animates the souls of his heroes. Critical analysis reveals, however, that the realm of norms and conventions, of ethical constructions and practical moral demands diminishes in contrast to the dictates of a life of greatness. All of Meyer's heroes meet with temptation. That is, they all encounter situations where overpowering personal desires come into conflict with prevailing social norms. The hero resists temptation when he surrenders to his own demon; the triumph over conforming concepts of right and wrong is the criterion of genius. Giving in to convention becomes the sign of failure. Defeat in the battle with the forces of tradition is, at best, a consolation provided by the historian, because it confirms the hero's character. The quality of the individual—a more or less powerful expression of life itself—judges what is good and bad. The motto of *Hutten* expresses the sphere of amorality for all of Meyer's heroes: "I am not a completely thought-through book, I am a human being with contradictions."

In *The Amulet,* the French Admiral Coligny dictates the following letter to the Prince of Orange in a passage that permits a look into the world of Meyer's heroes:

> To bring about war with Spain at any price and without any delay is our salvation," thus wrote the admiral. "Alba is lost if he is attacked by you and by us simultaneously. . . . My plan is the following: a Huguenot volunteer army has invaded Flanders during these last days. If this army can hold out against Alba—and this will depend largely on your simultaneous attack on the Spanish general from Holland—then this success will move the king to overcome all obstacles and to proceed with determination. You know about the magic of initial success."[16]

Momentous undertakings are planned, daring combinations are at stake, the stakes are always great, and a great coup must be landed. The French officer, for example, is actively involved in high-level politics; he plays the highest members of the court off against each other without confiding in anyone; or he resorts to illegal means by arming irregular troops—in short, he acts as do all of Meyer's heroes who are faced with temptation. This completes the individualizing selection process: the lives of many depend on this hero and on his decisions; this is why they are worthy of the author's attention. Where history is produced by the acts of a few "big fellows"—by the machinations of a few figures—the author can confine himself to a small ensemble of characters. Only rarely does a person with a memorable face emerge from the confusion of the Paris streets, unless, of course, it is a hero.

Formally, this novella is a framed story, a tale within tale. The framing device itself points to the central theme of *The Amulet*: on the very first page, the narrator enters,[17] or rather, rides into the scene, providing a sharp contrast with the calculating and petty man of money who does not really lead a life at all. The 58-year-old narrator is not an old man, but one who has retained a strong bond with his livelier years. His memories are not pale ghosts of the past, but sharply articulated images.

Indeed, the category of the image plays a considerable role. In Lessing's aesthetics, presented mainly in *Laokoon,* literature has primarily to do with plots that fit the chronological form of language. Depiction belongs to the realm of the visual arts, and the image is banned from literature. It must be added that Lessing's spirited and exhortative *Hamburg Dramaturgy* reveals the extent to which he saw the variety of action in literature to be a sign that change was possible in a world badly needing it. Lessing would never have tolerated the following passage from *The Amulet:*

> I had time to observe and be moved by his face, which had been indelibly impressed upon me by a very good and expensive woodcut that has reached as far as Switzerland. At that time, the Admiral might have been fifty years of age, but his hair was snow-white and a feverish pink glow lay on his emaciated cheeks. On his powerful forehead and on his lean hands, the blue veins showed, and his expression was terribly serious. He looked like a judge in Israel.[18]

Jürg Jenatsch shares many traits with Coligny. Again, the hero finds himself in a situation of temptation. Jürg Jenatsch makes great history, but he does so objectively through treason. What is conventionally considered as evil is here completely vindicated as good, because it is grandiose, powerful and victorious. Jenatsch's decisiveness is superior to Cardinal Rohan's morality; the latter's truthfulness is less a virtue than a sign of weakness, deserving of defeat. It does, however, raise

Rohan into a sphere of heroic internationalism. When he is forced into a conflict of loyalties, his good name is more important to him than the fatherland:

> The duke's hand went to his heart. He knew already, but today he was being told for the first time: he had lost his fatherland. "Frenchman and a man of honour," he remarked softly, "then I chose the second, even if it means that I am without a country."[19]

Pescara's Temptation expresses in its title the typical predicament of all of Meyer's heroes. Even the virtuous Angela Borgia does not care much for the virtuous.[20] When the men who determine the course of history confront reality, all conventional moral precepts become irrelevant: "with violence, bribery, deceit . . . and wicked means . . . the empires are ruled."[21]

It would be difficult to catalog the virtues of Meyer's characters and certainly, patriotism would not be found among them. In a letter to his friend Julius Rodenberg, publisher of the conservative journal *Deutsche Rundschau,* Meyer himself claimed to have deleted all "ornament and chauvinism" from the second edition of *Hutten.*[22] It has been said that Meyer saw love of the fatherland as the key to the character of Jenatsch.[23] And it is true, the drive to power and domination in a personality that accepts every great gamble that comes along is the key to this character. The fate of Switzerland presents one such opportunity, but Lucretia represents a valid alternative. This is precisely what makes the story so singularly intriguing that the lover and the fatherland play equally important roles in initiating Jenatsch's actions. It is even difficult to decide whether Jenatsch's religious conversion and his betrayal of Rohan are done only for the sake of the country or also in order to win Lucretia's affections. Lucretia herself is a much more intimate opponent for Jenatsch than Cardinal Rohan. For him, the spark of the chosen personality is struck only at the last minute; Lucretia, on the other, is as much a creature of the demoniac powers as the beloved and hated Jürg. In Mörike's *Maler Nolten,* death seems linked to the defeats of the bourgeoisie of his generation, and transitoriness is seen as the essence of life. In Meyer's story, death becomes a highly intensified moment amid the fullness of life. Lucretia kills Jürg Jenatsch, and we may suppose that this act is also the beginning of her own physical destruction. But this implied double murder is the very expression of heroic life; only these two are worthy of each other; only they, who are bonded to each other by fate and by character, have the right to eliminate each other.

The solidarity of the international leading minority of leaders proves itself, in this case literally, to the death:

> With trancelike resolution, she now raised the inherited family weapon with both hands and brought it crashing down with all her strength upon the head she loved so much. Jürg's arms fell; with eyes full of love he looked at her standing tall before him; somber triumph flashed across his face; then he collapsed heavily.[24]

The same international atmosphere that we already noted in connection with Cardinal Rohan is evident in *The Saint*, as when the young Armbruster consoles the half-Arabian Becket with a quotation from the Koran,[25] when the rich rug merchant Ben Emir is introduced into court society in Ferrara,[26] or when the papal functionary Guicciardini glorifies the "great Germanic heretic Luther."[27] In light of this internationalism, where is the glorification of patriotism in Coligny or Leubelfing or Becket or Pescara or Wertmueller? In Gustav Freytag's works, the significance of nationalism is unmistakable. The rise of the German middle class is necessarily tied to the creation of a unified customs network, a policy of protective tariffs and the development of an administrative state, just as the upper middle class merchant and industrial interests require the expansion of international relations.

Certainly, Meyer's stories are not psychological; indeed, calling them antipsychological would be only a slight exaggeration. That is to say, the hero is not at all susceptible to psychological interpretation. He is a lord and master and therefore he is inscrutable. The inscrutability of the great ones is so great that it seems they are inexplicable to themselves as well.[28] No one can guess how Pescara will react "when a great wall rose within him against us, just at the point when we believed that we had won his soul"[29] To his political partners as well as his wife, he is "impenetrable and his thoughts and beliefs are concealed."[30] Thus a lesser being like Don Juan is therefore all the less able to know what Pescara will do.[31] The author himself doesn't really know what motivates his heroes:

> And he [Morone] embraced the general's [Pescara's] knee with such a fervent gesture that the latter, springing to his feet, withdrew from such adoration, but still appeared to be inwardly touched Perhaps he was spellbound by the honesty of feeling in such a dishonest soul, perhaps because his great intelligence involuntarily formed a viable whole from the hinted traces of his and Italy's possible greatness.[32]

311

Pescara's soul remains an "abyss and . . . a mystery" to all.[33] One would expect the love-hate relationship of Jürg Jenatsch and Lucretia to be a rewarding object of psychological analysis. But the author's interest lies elsewhere. These two are not exposed to critical investigation at all; rather, they are presented as rare and unique beings who must be accepted as they are.

In this context, one might mention the role of coincidence, especially in *The Saint* and *The Woman Judge*. At times it functions as a merely symbolic representation of invisible interior processes. But it also has a mythic side: fate eludes human influence and forbids probing into origins. In this second sense, the myth of the great human being remains an impenetrable riddle. They are riddles—another ideological element. Symbols and myths devalue the process of history. Events are not meaningful in themselves and cannot be taken as they are, as social reality with natural and material consequences. Instead, they all have a higher purpose, and are merely functions of the singular individual and his fate.

The inadequacy, indeed the rejection of a psychology of great individuals opens the possibility, if not an actual demand, for a psychological approach to the masses, the little people, the objects of history. They can be understood easily.[34] Consider the relations of Pescara to the Italians.[35] Waser, the good citizen of Zurich, is the object of psychological study in *Jürg Jenatsch*. With his categorizations and computations, he embodies narrow bourgeois caution and pedantry. To his mediocre mind it is even possible to envision Jenatsch leading "his troubled soul onto more peaceful paths by founding a home on his Davos estates."[36] This philistine is well-suited to psychological interpretation; in the literal sense, it serves him right. In recounting one of Waser's dreams. Meyer wants to expose the petty and insignificant world he symptomizes:

> After a short time, Waser was stretched out on the bed and tried to sleep, but sleep wouldn't come. He dozed for a moment; dream figures materialized before his eyes, Jenatsch and Lucretia, Professor Semmler and the old woman at the stove, the Moloja innkeeper and rough old Lucas, all of them seemed to mingle together in the strangest relationships. Suddenly, they were all seated at a school desk. Remarkably, Semmler was lifting the huge powderhorn to his mouth as though it were a Greek musical instrument. From it came the most amazing lamentations, which were greeted on all sides by peals of diabolical laughter.[37]

Meyer relates, not only the dreams of this stuffy mayor, but also one of the candidate in *The Shot from the Pulpit.* In it, the candidate possesses willful independence and powerfully dispatches extraordinary tasks, not as a hero, but as a scared rabbit. He awakes "not covered with his own blood, but bathed in cold sweat."[38] Hans Armbruster tells of a dream[39] that he has immediately before the catastrophe, a dream which promises a positive outcome. The horizon recedes grandly when the dreams of the great are at issue; as a matter of fact, none of their dreams are actually reported at all. They have, figuratively speaking, no time to sleep; dreaming itself becomes an aspect of their activity. Meyer speaks, for example, of Lucretia's "dreamlike" decision to kill Jürg Jenatsch.[40] To Morone's enticing speech, in which he offers the Italian crown to Pescara. Pescara replies: "Dream on, Morone!"[41] For the heroes, dreams do not have a psychological function. One may speak of a candidate such as Rosenstock or Wacholder in a psychological, that is to say, an almost mocking, way. Imagine Rosenstock transported into a novel by Adalbert Stifter or Mörike; there, a man refusing to become a "Venetian field chaplain" in order to avoid leaving his vineyard, would meet with nothing but compassion.[42] Meyer, on the other hand, describes ironically this "rooted man"[43] who has ties to home and fatherland as "being, in spite of youth, almost corpulent";[44] his reason is reduced to the nervous, cautious and petty common-sense wisdom of just one among many: "Stay in the country and feed yourself well."[45]

In the character of Krachhalder in *The Shot from the Pulpit,* these characters and their various ways of life are completely condemned.[46] This is not merely the mocking of a single farmer and his community; rather, of every moderate way of living that is capable of enjoying the advantages of material well-being and social respectability through a balanced harmony of interests. Here we find the literary predecessor of the modern petit-bourgeois, of Sinclair Lewis' Babbit or of Carl Sternheim's characters; they are used to demonstrate the mediocrity and insubstantiality, the inauthenticity and corruptibility of middle or lower bourgeois mass existence. The morally outraged Krachhalder sells his principles for a considerable expansion of the common forest.

When one recalls Gustav Freytag's glorification of bourgeois commerce, accumulation and respectable lifestyle, one senses that Meyer holds an opposite position. Not that Meyer is a critic of bourgeois society or that he is even aware of the phenomenon of crisis, which Spielhagen's consistent liberalism allows him to see. Such interest and deep concern for the actual life processes of society are completely foreign to Meyer. Instead, when viewed from his elevated post of command, all battles and skirmishes among the many who are not holders of power appear merely as illusions or as motions of puppets who are moved by the great ones. For the upper middle-class consciousness, the order of the world is indeed established and perpetuated by individuals, not by classes or by traditions.

In Meyer's novellas, the little people and the masses always occupy a servile position. There is only one point at which the author devotes more than a few words to the broad lower strata. It can be found in *Angela Borgia*. Ariosto pays a visit to the blinded Don Giulio, and his impressions are described as follows:

> From these remarks of the blind man, the poet deduced that young Este was beginning to make a place for himself in a different sector of life, amid a class of people that was different from that to which he had belonged until now, amid the unhappy and the suffering, the deprived and the disinherited; in a sphere of life subject to different conditions and laws than those of sensuous people who were entitled to enjoyment.[47]

This passage is perhaps exceptional because *Angela Borgia* is Meyer's last novella and, because of the impending melancholia of his old age, it does not follow the style of the rest of his prose. Still, it is interesting to note this exaggerated and historically distorted reference to a certain lower social stratum. Not only is this conglomeration of pitiable manifestations of misery an inappropriate description of the population of Italy toward the end of the fifteenth century, but Meyer's manner of referring to the "other class of people" is reminiscent of the descriptions of wild tribal peoples provided by European explorers. This kind of inclusion is motivated by folklore, not by compassion. And similar tendencies are evident in Armbruster's words, "it is one thing when kings and princes attack each other, and another when brawlers howl and stab in our Swabian tavern."[48] Only a declassed man such as the King's son Hans can laugh so hard that the earnest narrator says, "I have never in my life heard such a depraved laugh, neither in inns nor at the market place."[49] The author's concern is only for those "who are sensuous and entitled to enjoyment." "The jewelled world smiling to itself in the mirror" belongs only to them, as one can read a few pages earlier in the same novella.[50]

In a letter to Rodenberg,[51] Meyer talks about his main concern, the "connection of the small life with the life and struggle of humanity"

The word "small" can be taken quite literally here; little people are only present when they are foils for great events. We would never have heard of Hans Armbruster if his "little boat" had not taken a sudden turn "out of the channels of his own life and into the tide of a greater one."[52] The narrator of *The Amulet* would never have been noticed if his life had not touched the circle of the great Coligny. Petty private worries and joys mean nothing; the universally human is all too human to have a place in the life sphere of genius. And the framing story has a second function, aside from that which we elucidated earlier: to stress the distance between the great and the small. The little people in this world have no business except to tell about the great ones, and to reveal in the process that they are only objects of the great. They are not entitled to the best of life—beauty and a strong heart.[53] They have no access to enjoyment per se. After all, the great are the only ones who risk a tragic fall. They display "agonizing struggles and . . . pain-distorted features," while such a small-spirited man as the Zurich burgher Burckhardt expects to harvest only "a few stories and personages from the life of the saint."[54]

Meyer unabashedly submitted to his publisher the following sentence for an autobiography: "In German literature, Meyer is the representative of the historical novella and the chronicler of forces of world history."[55] But these forces are basically nothing other than the strong personalities.[56] In summary, one can say that, according to Meyer's conception, the shape of history depends on the deeds of single individuals. They meet the resistance of their adversaries, and the outcome of these conflicts is never predictable.

Essentially, nothing new ever occurs in Meyer's historical world. All that is important are the deeds of great individuals. What kind of deeds these are, whom they serve and whom they injure is completely irrelevant. World history is an indifferent prop, of which the masses are a part. All that we hear about them is the pettiness of their small miseries and calculations. One need not bother with their concerns; they would not contribute to our understanding of history. After all, history is the history of the struggles of individuals, not of groups protecting their interests. Economic questions, economic power struggles and social revolutions are left out, despite the wide range of material treated by Meyer's historical tales, and despite the fact that these stories from the Renaissance and from the Age of Absolutism would have offered many opportunities for the treatment of social struggles.[57]

If we ask ourselves what ideological needs are served by such a view of history and society, there is no doubt that this is, by and large, the worldview of the ruling class. This becomes readily apparent through a negative argument. The opposite of the worldview just presented would be the wishes of those not in power. For them, everything depends on important historical changes in the future. The "meaning" of their lives does not consist of chosen deeds, but is revealed in an uninterrupted labor process as their only means for survival. The misery of everyday life, of the physical, social and mental struggle for existence, makes up their world. But in Meyer's world we are dealing with the literature of the liberal upper middle class. Its members see the world as an opportunity for the development of personality; they raise themselves above petty and mundane worries of the little people and are constantly preoccupied with grand designs and grand ideals.

I do not use the terms "bourgeois upper middle class" as a mere economic category. True, the social strata most likely to identify with the lifestyle Meyer portrays consists mainly of southwest German industrialists, northern German merchants, bankers, and the corresponding intellectual circles. But the economic roots of the liberal and relatively unprejudiced mentality of these strata can be found, not only in German but also in English history. And this nineteenth-century upper-crust bourgeoisie has some traits in common with contemporary ruling groups; for instance, the tremendous economic influence and the contempt for average existence. They also share the wider perspectives of time and space which tend to make them independent of moral, philosophical and religious reifications. These common elements, however, arise from contrasting situations and have different meanings. Our monopolistic upper class is no longer part of a broad middle class, convinced of its mission in society, even though it did emerge from the same process of rapid concentration and centralization as did its liberal predecessor. The modern economic ruling class no longer tolerates and accommodates vigorous, independent small entrepreneurs, but is on the way to becoming the sole moving social force within the power groups now ruling all over the world.

With the ever-increasing gulf between this class and the rest of society, its functions and its ideology have become transformed. Meyer's positive view of education, which seems completely antiquated today, reflects a time when both individuals and society could expect real advancement from an increase in their scientific knowledge. His open admiration of the religious and national nonchalance of his Renaissance Men is anachronistic today, given the organizational responsibilities of the upper middle class within the larger socieety. The current view even tries to restrict the humanistic and revolutionary elements of the Renaissance by emphasizing instead its traditional aspects. Nevertheless, both—the German upper middle class of Meyer's time and that of today—present a sociological concept to which a literary work, like the present essay, can refer even without an economic analysis.

Of course, a serious objection could be raised here; namely, that the link we made between Meyer's concept of history and the ruling class of his time is improper because he was not a typical representative of the modern elite but rather a representative of a dying class: the Swiss patriciate. But Meyer does not draw his view of society from traditional sources, and his patrician background does not lead him to glorify the history of this class. Instead, he approaches social contradications from a disinterested perspective. General Wertmueller's speech is evidence of this: here, the arrogance of the aristocracy and the patriciate is rejected, the General is proud of the simple name Mueller, which does not receive its power from the past but from the extraordinary deeds of the one who bears it.[58]

The importance of Meyer's travels,[59] especially his stay in Paris, is a further example. In his biography, Robert Faesi writes of Meyer's opinion of Paris: "He had to condemn it ethically and praise it aesthetically."[60] This touches on an accurate point. Despite his pronouncedly Protestant superego, Meyer's innermost nature still sensed the grandness of bourgeois self-confidence in France, which he encountered in the Paris lifestyle of worldly elegance and its representations by Balzac or Stendhal. His visit to Rome in 1858 complemented what he found in Paris. "Come to Italy and sample life," he wrote later in *Engelberg*. The lively image of Paris is complemented by the grand style that he learns to appreciate in Italy. His friendship with Ricasoli, the Italian statesman, and his unqualified admiration of Bismarck fit well with this imagery of the cosmopolitan cities; both of these men are the synthesis of what his novellas preach: grandiose history, strong individual personality and extraordinary style.[61]

There is even more interesting and convincing evidence for Meyer's ideological function, largely ignored in literary history. An analysis of his correspondence, especially with Rodenberg, belies the image of the isolated, hermit-like poet and exposes it as a legend. Meyer was thoroughly acquainted with contemporary political and social issues. He had very particular views on them and his social impact can also be demonstrated. One could sum up Meyer's politics by saying that he would have belonged to the National Liberal party at the time when it

pursued its cartel policy with the conservatives. It stood for the promo-
tion of a large united national state; it consciously pursued economic
class politics, uniting industrial and merchant classes with big agrarian
interests and the military while it maintained a liberal cultural policy.[62]
It more or less stood for the politics of the upper-middle-class after the
founding of the German Empire in 1870–71.

Meyer's positive view of Bismarck, with whom he would go "through
thick and thin," is well known.[63] He said that his main interest in
Bismarck was psychological.[64] In a conflict between Bismarck and
Emperor Wilhelm the Second, he makes known his total sympathy for
the emperor,[65] but adds later that it may have been a grave error for
the emperor "to give up Bismarck."[66] In this context, his claim—that
he "occasionally" worried about the young ruler "because on the social
issue, for instance, Bismarck was clearly right"—is significant.[67]

This is clearly a class-specific confession, for which we can find other
evidence. After the elections in Saxony and Swabia in February 1887,
for example, Meyer expresses satisfaction at the "defeat of socialism in
the one case and of particularism in the other."[68] He writes to Haessel,
his publisher: "Italian democrats (and democrats in general) interest
me as little as they do you. In fact, in Davos I cut off short a Russian
(so-called nihilist) democrat who was boring me with his verbiage."[69] A
similar detachment from the general populace is evident in his July 1878
commentary about the Anti-Socialist Laws: "I can easily believe that
things are not running smoothly out there in the Reich. Here we have
had a popular veto of the Gotthard Subsidy (an unparalleled vulgar-
ity), and we have floods, hail, and I personally had to have a complete
change of servants."[70] This association of personal and general troubles
he had with the lower classes is characteristic not only of Meyer's highly
individualized idiosyncrasies, but of his class consciousness as well.

Aside from the exaggerated passage on the farmers from *Angela
Borgia* cited above, I know of only one other instance where Meyer
made some sort of positive reference to subservient groups. When he
was concerned about the printing of *Angela Borgia* at the time of the
great Leipzig printers' strike in 1891, he wrote to his friend Wille: "The
young managers are applying Draconian measures and many a poor
devil who had until now been able to shuffle along in a big publishing
house is now being mercilessly dismissed. [It is] neither clever nor
Christian."[71] Management is condemned, not out of consideration
for economic justice, but out of a clear sense of self-interest.[72] His
class consciousness in economic matters can generally be shown to

be absolutely antirevolutionary. In some places, he refers to himself as conservative.[73] But this does not mean merely a particularist Swiss political point of view and certainly not an opposition to German bourgeois liberalism. Rather, it is another formulation of a static, comfortable, upper-middle-class attitude; once he says disdainfully about lower-class people: "It is in the nature of things, that they are always the most vulgar characters."[74]

His love for Germany "in the last analysis" expressed the longing for upper-middle-class *Lebensraum*, "the longing and the need . . . to belong to a larger whole."[75] He wishes he could have lived in a German city where high society circles were as accessible in Germany as in Italy. If one reads the lists of recipients of complimentary copies of Meyer's works,[76] or if one studies his half aristocratic, half upper-middle-class acquaintances, it becomes apparent that the same circles who read his works were also those to whom he felt that he himself belonged.[77]

It was unmistakably Meyer's love of the upper-middle class lifestyle that led him first to France and Italy and then, after the founding of the Reich, to Germany. It is his affinity with the splendor of power that induced Meyer to change his chosen homelands, in 1881, Meyer wrote in the *Author's Album* of a German publishing house: "A Swiss writer should possess in equal degree the consciousness of his homeland's state sovereignty and the consciousness of its national affinity with Germany." In 1887, he referred to this affinity as an "immeasurable treasure" and considered its strengthening as the "exact barometer of a thorough education.[78]

Another indication of Meyer's class consciousness is his opinion of other writers. He wished to distance himself from the "brutal immediacy of contemporary topics." quite a transparent ideological process, since the atmosphere of his novellas lacks neither brutality nor personal opinions of contemporary topics—showing his cavalier way of treating the sufferings of the majority of mankind.[79] Therefore, he opposed those artists of his time who tried to expose the "brutality" of contemporary topics. He was an opponent of the naturalists because he was their ideological class enemy. Zola, Tolstoy and Ibsen are granted a certain degree of respect, but whatever their German imitator achieved was "pure horse manure."[80] For Spielhagen, who was, in a bourgeois sense, a very critical and radical thinker, he finds nothing but contemptuous words. Spielhagen, who allegedly exploited his writing skills in Berlin, faced great obstacles, while Meyer was, in his own words, devoting himself to "grand style" and "fine art."[81]

Finally, the reception of Meyer's writings corresponds to his own position. The fact that almost all of his stories are published, first in the periodical *Deutsche Rundshau* and later by Haessel is no coincidence. Both publishing houses, that of the brothers Praetel and the book publisher, counted the highest level of the bourgeoisie and leading political and military circles among their clientele. The *Deutsche Rundshau* especially has a thoroughly international readership among the upper crust. Rodenberg asserts correctly that "hardly another German periodical can offer an audience such as ours, one that is made up of the best of all nations. Our distribution network is universal: it includes America, Russia, the Scandinavian North, Holland and England—places where we caught on from the very beginning—and we gradually penetrated even into France."[82]

In Rodenberg's reports, one can follow especially well how an upper middle class audience forms around Meyer. When *The Saint* was published, Rodenberg reports the enthusiasm of the publishers who "represent the general public, are an echo for a wide group, and are themselves two highly intelligent, educated men."[83] And only a few weeks later he can report: "Politicians and business people, men and women—they all feel equally attracted by your work"[84] The following anecdote is also a notable illustration of this upper middle class audience: "Recently at a ball given by the Postmaster General Stephan, a young lady said to me, her face aglow, that she had read *The Saint* all day long, even while she was dressing, and that she could not get it out of her mind."[85] In 1883, Rodenberg, himself a well-situated intellectual, called Meyer's poems, which "march on victoriously" a "book for home and the entire family."[86] By the end of the year, he can again cite "the best audience and the leading press."[87] During the following year, highly respected individuals such as Julian Schmidt, Wilhelm Dilthey, Hermann Grimm,[88] and Wilhelm Preyer, "a fine and critical reader"[89] are among those who praise Meyer—a literary critic, a philosopher, an art historian and a natural scientist, respectively.

In 1885, "distinguished art circles"[90] join in, until the conclusion is reached that "your novellas and your poems already are among the indispensible possessions of all our educated people."[91] For this National-Liberal writer, however the word "educated" is only a collective term for the upper class. This includes the "enthisiastic admirer," Geheimrat Heinrich Geffken, a jurist, as well as the military author Max Jaehns—"one of our leading staff officers"—who keeps Meyer's poems on his desk because he is "strengthened and edified [by them] daily [like] the view or the air in the Alps."[92]

One might argue that attributing upper middle class ideology to Meyer is untenable because a heroic view of history is irreconcilable with the prevailing bourgeois liberal theory of history. Here, a study of Meyer can produce an important reappraisal: in Germany, liberalism was never properly the expression of ruling class consciousness. Instead, due to economic and political conditions, large landowners, merchants, and the military formed an alliance that was eminently susceptible to heroic irrationalism. At first glance, one might assume that Meyer's patrician background would create an imbalance between modern bourgeois ideology and the Swiss in him. But a closer analysis shows that, on the contrary, the bourgeois-patrician mixture was extraordinarily effective in ideologically reflecting and glorifying the alliance of the German upper classes.

Notes

1. Cf. *Das Amulet* in *Sämtliche Werke in vier Bänden*, Vol. 3, p. 19. English translations are from *The Complete Narrative Prose of Conrad Ferdinand Meyer*, 2 vols., trans. George F. Folkers, David B. Dickers, and Marion W. Sonnenfeld (Lewisburg: Bucknell University Press, 1976). English references will be provided when available.
2. *The Complete Narrative*, vol. 1, p. 61.
3. Ibid., vol. 1, p. 334.
4. *Die Versuchung des Percara* in *Sämtliche Werke*, vol. 4, p. 159.
5. Ibid., p. 184.
6. Ibid., p. 205 (English trans., vol. 2, p. 261).
7. *Der Heilige*, vol. 4, p. 75.
8. Ibid., p. 106.
9. Cf. the letter to Spitteler (1884?): "I have never looked for subjects, nor have I ever done so-called 'preliminary research.'" *Briefe C.F. Meyer*, Adolf Frey, ed. (Leipzig, 1908), vol. 1, p. 427.
10. *Jürg Jenatsch* in *Sämtliche Werke*, vol. 1, p. 15.
11. Ibid., p. 110.
12. Ibid., p. 229.
13. Ibid., p. 242.
14. The poem "Die Schlacht der Baume" ("The Battle of the Trees") expresses it in similar terms. Nature is the last conservatory of the heroic, after historic diversity has failed.
15. See, for example, Walter Köhler, *C.F. Meyer als religiöser Charakter* (Jena, 1911), as well as Otto Frommel, *Neuere deutsche Dichter in ihrer religiösen Stellung* (Berlin, 1902), pp. 143ff.
16. *Das Amulet*, pp. 39ff. (English: vol. 1, p. 53).
17. Ibid., p. 9.
18. Ibid., pp. 28ff.

19. *Jürg Jenatsch,* vol. 1, p. 206 (English: vol. 1, p. 46).

20. *Angela Borgia,* vol. 1, p. 316 (English: vol. 1, p. 200).

21. *Der Heilige,* vol. 4, p. 87. Cf. Meyer's thoughts on southern German politics, closing with the remark, "You see, that is very egotistical, but isn't that true of all politics?" written to Haessel, August 5, 1866, in *Briefe,* vol. 2, p. 6.

22. *Conrad Ferdinand Meyer und Julius Rodenberg: Ein Briefwechsel,* August Langmesser, ed. (Berlin, 1918), p. 200, August 24, 1884.

23. Robert Faesi, *Conrad Ferdinand Meyer* (Leipzig, 1925), p. 71.

24. *Jürg Jenatsch,* vol. 1, p. 256 (English: vol. 1, p. 231).

25. *Der Heilige,* vol. 4, p. 244.

26. *Angela Borgia,* p. 244.

27. *Die Versuchung des Pescara,* p. 160.

28. Cf. Morone's exclamation, "But you know not even yourself, Pescara!" Ibid., p. 211.

29. Ibid., p. 179. *Cf.* also p. 169, "If Pescara wil not . . . ," etc.

30. Ibid., p. 184.

31. Ibid., p. 187.

32. Ibid., p. 212 (English: vol. 2, p. 266).

33. Ibid., p. 236.

34. Franz Ferdinand Baumgarten's conclusion is much too simplistic: "Meyer rejected psychological analysis." in *Das Werk Conrad Ferdinand Meyer: Renaissance-Empfinden und Stilkunst* (Munich, 1917), p. 171.

35. *Die Versuchung des Pescara,* p. 170.

36. *Jürg Jenatsch,* p. 242.

37. Ibid., p. 29 (English; vol. 1, p. 90).

38. *Der Schuss von der Kanzel in Sämtliche Werke,* vol. 3, p. 105.

39. *Der Heilige,* pp. 61 ff.

40. *Jürg Jenatsch,* p. 256.

41. *Die Versuchung des Pescara,* p. 209.

42. *Sämtliche Werke,* vol. 3, p. 75.

43. Ibid.

44. Ibid., p. 74.

45. Ibid., p. 75.

46. Ibid., pp. 116ff.

47. *Angela Borgia,* pp. 311ff. (English, vol. 2, p. 343).

48. *Der Heilige,* p. 18.

49. Ibid., p. 44.

50. *Angela Borgia,* p. 263.

51. December 14, 1877, in *Briefwechsel,* p. 11.

52. *Der Heilige,* p. 27.

53. Ibid., p. 252.

54. Ibid., p. 138.

55. October 3, 1887, in *Briefe,* vol. 2. pp. 139ff.

56. In the words of Louise von Francois, Meyer "has turned his gaze to the pinnacles of life," and seeks "to portray the problems of tempestuous times and exceptional people." A. Schaer, "Betty Paoli and C.F. Meyer," in *Euphorion,* vol. 16 (1901), p. 499.

57. We are confident that our analysis has shown Baumgarten's view to be untenable. As he formulates it in the decisive passage of his book, "The

irony of life is the atmosphere which shapes Meyer's characters. Historical man is for Meyer the ironic tool of fate and no hero. Heroes shape the world according to their own laws. The course of history for Meyer's figures is a role in which fate twists and turns their lives, and this role often becomes their nemesis." Baumgarten, p. 84.

58. *Der Schuss von der Kanzel,* p. 91. One might suppose that the relative well-being of the Swiss industrial workers prevented Meyer from developing the guilty conscience which one would otherwise expect, given his psychological make-up; the rigidity of social thought can therefore proceed in an unbroken manner.

59. Even the eulogy in the *Beilage zur Allgemeinen Zeitung* (Munich, November 29, 1898) stresses the significance of the fact that Meyer "was a well-travelled man whose material independence made most incisive studies possible."

60. *Conrad Ferdinand Meyer,* p. 16.

61. Adolf Stern describes *Jürg Jenatsch* and its reception as follows: "As true as the historical setting appears, it was doubtless Meyer's personal experience of history through figures such as Cavour, Ricasoli and Bismarck, the greatest of all, which provided him an awareness and understanding of characters of political action who were guided by passionate yet impersonal feelings. The readers of *Jürg Jenatsch* were also unconsciously moved by this harmony between old and new atmospheres." *Studien zur Literatur der Gegenwart: Neue Folge* (Dresden and Leipzig, 1904), p. 51.

62. He had a decided distaste for the bourgeois-democratic opposition. This may also have clouded his relation with Graf Platen, of the neighboring estate. Cf. the letter to Haessel below, in *Briefe,* Vol. 2, *op.cit.,* p. 41, and the letter of January 29, 1889, *op.cit.,* p. 168: "I admit I am as unenthusiastic for Baron Roggenbach, who is supposed to have bought land here, as I am for Geffcken. Please in the name of Hell let Bismarck make you into a great imperial nation!" Further, after the election defeats of the Free-Thinkers in 1887 to Rodenberg, "I pity the erstwhile secessionists Forkenbeck, Bamberger, etc., but by God they deserved it." February 27, in *Briefwechsel, op.cit.,* p. 239. It is also interesting here that Meyer supported Wille's attempt to remove the passage in Heine's *Germany: A Winter's Tale* condemning the cowardice of the Prussian Junkers. Meyer called them "undignified verses." Cf. Karl Emil Franzos, "Konrad Ferdinand Meyer," in *Deutsche Dichtung,* Vol. 25 (1898-1899), p. 247, note.

63. To L.V. François, November 25, 1881, *ibid.,* p. 32; cf. also the letter to Calmberg, November 29, 1877, in *Briefe,* Vol. 2, *ibid.,* p. 232.

64. To Wille, March 1, 1886, in *Briefe,* Vol. 1, *ibid.,* p. 183.

65. To Rodenberg, March 28, 1891, in *Briefwechsel, op.cit.,* p. 297; cf. also the letter to Wille, January 16, 1891, in *Briefe,* Vol. 1, *ibid.,* pp. 210ff.

66. To Wille, December 7, 1891, in *Briefe,* Vol. 1, *ibid.,* p. 220.

67. To Wille, August 28, 1890. *ibid.,* p. 207.

68. To Rodenberg, February 27, 1887, in *Briefwechsel, op.cit.,* p. 239.

69. To Haessel, October 5, 1871, in *Briefe,* Vol. 2, *op.cit.,* p. 41.

70. To Haessel, June 15, 1878, in *Briefe,* Vol. 2, *ibid.,* p. 77; cf. also Meyer's lament over "the miserable state of our trade and railroads," to Meissner, April 14, 1877, in *Briefe,* Vol. 2, *op.cit.,* p. 270. Max Nussberger incomprehensibly identifies Meyer's German sympathies in the war of 1879 with "the century's

cherished democratic ideals." *Conrad Ferdinand Meyer: Leben und Werke* (Frauenfeld, 1919), p. 110.

71.   To Wille, October 17, 1891, in *Briefe,* vol. 1, p. 219.

72.   Köhler, cited above, succeeds in finding in Meyer "the deepest impulse of religious socialism . . . forward-moving love of mankind," pp. 230ff. He naively says of Meyer's stand on social issues, "The aristocratic and proper Zuricher that Meyer remained was repelled by the raw and calloused hands of workers. One might even infer a purely aesthetic antipathy on the part of this genteel poet of the aristocracy to anything related to 'workers.' For purely aesthetic reasons, Conrad Ferdinand Meyer would never have been able to write an *Arbeiterroman* or a social novella. That would mean alleys; he needed Renaissance palaces, the courts of sovereigns, warriors of course, but never the farmer." Köhler is doubtless correct in adding, "Socialism can therefore not count this author as one of its own." p. 230.

73.   E.g., to Rodenberg, December 9, 1881, in *Briefwechsel,* p. 101.

74.   To Haessel, September 5, 1866, in *Briefe,* vol. 2, p. 11.

75.   To Rodenberg, August 23, 1881, in *Briefwechsel,* p. 89.

76.   Cf. letter to Haessel, November 18, 1887, in *Briefe,* vol. 2, pp. 145ff. (a list of people who received a copy of *Pescara* with a card of dedication).

77.   Cf. the description of his contact with Frau D. of the "upper bourgeoisie" to his sister in Ghent in 1857, quoted by Adolf Frey, *C.F. Meyer, Sein Leben und seine Werke* (Stuttgart, 1900), p. 89. Cf. also in this volume the importance of the relationship with François. Wille and Ricasoli. Also the letters to Wille, August 8, 1877, in *Briefe,* vol. 1. ibid., pp. 157ff., and to Rodenberg, July 12, 1883, in *Briefwechsel,* p. 147. Cf. also the poetic phrase of W. Bolza: "The bitter misery of life never beat upon his door." "Keller und Meyer." in *Literarisches Echo,* vol. 2 (1899-1900). p. 1348. Similarly, Heinrich Kraeger, *Beilage zur Allgemeinen Zeitung,* 1900, no. 12, p. 5.

78.   Cf. Paul Wüst, *Gottfried Keller und C.F. Meyer in ihrem persönlichen und literarischen Verhältnis* (Leipzig, 1911), p. 6. Relevant as well is Pescara's sympathy with the Swiss, who, "lacking both leadership and the consciousness of a state, have given away what world position and foreign policy they had already won," p. 5. Cf. also the letter to Rodenberg, Easter, 1887, in *Briefwechsel,* p. 242: "I am treating my present Holy Father [i.e., Clemens VII of *Pescara*] purposely somewhat more gently than I otherwise would, because I will stand by both Kaiser and Reich through thick and thin." See also the letter of December 9, 1881, p. 107.

79.   Cf. Paul Wüst, ibid., p. 37: "Meyer alone has a weakness for such beatings and brutality. When he hears or reads such things, he cries out. 'Excellent!' "Keller described with these words a trait that would become of great consequence in C.F. Meyer's art: "'tragic desire' often, carried to the point of cruelty, an apt description employed by a later scholar."

80.   For the class-conscious opinion of naturalism, the following is also typical: February 12, 1890, Meyer writes to Rodenberg, "L. Tolstoy is probably the most prominent of the literary innovators (as far as he *is* one, since his is the religious impulse of rationalistic mysticism), but *The Power of Darkness* has greatness about it." *Briefwechsel,* p. 282. On the 15th Rodenberg answers, "You are right that we must not let the naturalists or realists take Tolstoy away from us," ibid., p. 283. But Meyer hadn't asserted it at all that clearly.

It is as if the two great upper middle class writers had unconsciously agreed on the enemy and his positions.

81. To Haessel, June 16, 1879, in *Briefe,* vol. 2, p. 86.

82. July 13, 1880, in *Briefwechsel,* p. 73. Cf. here also Rodenberg's report of his latest visit to Paris where he was pleased "to find the *Rundschau* so well respected in the leading circles of science and politics. Professors and high civil servants whom I met there spoke to me of the *Rundschau* in a way that showed me how carefully they read it, and how highly it is esteemed."

83. November 13, 1879, in *Briefwechsel,* p. 59.

84. December 6, 1879, ibid., p. 61.

85. February 6, 1880, ibid., p. 64.

86. February 5, ibid., pp. 138ff.

87. December 21, ibid., p. 184.

88. January 1, 1884, ibid., p. 186.

89. January 4, ibid., p. 187; cf. also March 13, ibid., p. 188.

90. November 26, ibid., p. 216.

91. Ibid.

92. January 3, 1887, ibid., pp. 234ff. A few references will show the close correspondence between the class-reflected reception by later critics, the reception by contemporary readers and Meyer's own intentions. Friedrich Dorn speaks of the "golden holiday mood" which "does not let the soft undertones of day-to-day suffering come through"; "the common man is missing from C.F. Meyer's writings," in "C.F. Meyer. Zu Seinem siebzigsten Geburtstag," in *Die Nation,* vol. 13 (1895–1896), pp. 19, 12. K.E. Franzos finds him "fine and elegant," *op.cit.,* p. 138; the "genteel artist" is no "democratic genre painter" and has "resisted the temptation to flatter the taste of the times." To Richard Specht as well, he is a "timeless artist" to those who come to him "from the confusion and the confusing noise of the much-too-living." In *Die Zeit,* Vienna, December 3, 1898, p. 152. His art "will not reach the common readership, but will remain confined to the circle of the truly educated," in W. Bolza, "C.F. Meyer," in *Das Literarische Echo.* vol. 1 (1898–1899), p. 419. He can "never become a writer for the growing spread of the generally educated." Adolph Stern, "C.F. Meyer," in *Westermann Monatshefte,* vol. 43 (1899), p. 702. Franz Ferdinand Baumgarten's interpretation is familiar, which speaks in sociologically unclear terms of the "opposition of a spiritual elite against realistic art and mechanistic life," p. 12. "Meyer was a misplaced bourgeois ... the seductions of his artist's blood troubled his bourgeois conscience," p. 54. Hans Corrodi says of Meyer's Novella, "it expresses, if not the outlook toward living of many people, then the 'ego' and 'world view' of a great and genteel poet," in *C.F. Meyer und sein Verhältnis zum Drama* (Leipzig, 1922), p. 118. Similar is Harry Mayne's formulation that "C.F. Meyer is not a writer for everyone," in *C.F. Meyer und sein Werk* (Frauenfeld and Leipzig, 1925), p. 337. Werner Kaegis' introduction to Ernst Walser's collection, *Geistesgeschichte der Renaissance* (Basel, 1932, p. xxx), asserts that "the novellas of C.F. Meyer were understood by few in their tragically affirmed tension between the aesthetic and the ethical life." Expanding upon Baumgarten's position, cited above, Thomas Mann attempted to interpret C.F. Meyer along the lines of his Tonio Kröger: "To be Christian, bourgeois, German . . . these are the central features of his artistry." *Betrachtungen eines Unpolitischen*

(Berlin, 1919), pp. 158ff. This selection from the literature will at this point be neither continued nor interpreted in detail. It should serve, however, to point out that Meyer's reception exactly corresponds to the "principle of selection" that we illustrated as his construction scheme for both form and content. We saw it again in his personal attitudes and reflected in his first readers. Selection is the glorification of the elite, but this elite is none other than the upper middle class. Its ideology can also serve as an example for imitation by other bourgeois social strata.

14

Gottfried Keller: Bourgeois Repression

Even more than was the case in previous chapters, our exposition of Gottfried Keller will be very basic and will focus on those aspects of his work that permit a sociological interpretation of this poet.

By way of introduction, I want to offer three questions: the title of the story *The Master of His Fortune,* a passage from the first chapter of "Epigram," and a passage from a diary.

> Come brave Lessing! It is true, every washerwoman knows your name, but they do not understand your true nature, which is nothing else than eternal youth, the ability to do all things, absolute good intention, without falseness and gilded in the fire. . . . Oh, I knew that one would only have to ask you a question in order to hear something clever."[1]

And in his diary entry for autumn, 1847, Keller reflects on his relationship to Freiligrath, Herwegh and several liberal Swiss politicians as follows:

> Secretly, I am very grateful to these men. I have developed from a vague revolutionary and partisan into a self-conscious and self-confident and thoughtful person, a person who knows how to honor the good of beautiful and marble-hard forms even in political matters.[2]

For each of these three citations, a misinterpretation is possible: a naive reader might misinterpret the title, Keller himself might misinterpret the two passages.

The dubious hero in the story *The Heroes of Selwyla* is not able to forge his happiness; all his attempts to do so turn into bad luck. Keller actually erases the very category of happiness, and this story is the best example. Successful renunciation of the satisfaction of libidinal drives and consciousness of duty fulfilled is supposed to take the place of a feeling of happiness: this is what is decisive for the character formation of a person as well as for his entire fate. Here we can see a great difference between C. F. Meyer and Keller. The former's moral standpoint strives for the optimal realization of all sorts of wishes and desires, regardless of whether they are directed toward self-preservation and intensification of life, toward the satisfaction of great longings, or the gain of material or cultural goods of outstanding value. Denial and moderation, everything that amounts to "economizing" in a narrow or in a broad sense, is rejected as negative and despicable. Meyer fondly legitimates anyone who manages to "forge his happiness"; he feels that it is the great individual who converts the world, nature and history into valuable objects; in fact their multifariousness attains significance only because a great person lives in it.

Keller represents the exact opposite of this attitude toward the world and life, an attitude which we have already characterized as upper bourgeois. He acknowledges that certain drives and needs of the ego clamor for realization, but if these cannot be made functional for the fulfillment of norm duties and obligations, Keller devalues them as fantastic: his characters either repress their drives and desires when they cannot realize them, becoming eccentric as a consequence, or they consciously reject them in an act of self-conscious denial—and this is the more valuable behavior. Again, the story titles reveal their respective attitudes: if we compare Meyer's *The Temptation of Pescara* and Keller's *The Banner of the Seven Upright,* Meyer's title connotes splendor, risk, adventure, the serving notice on moral conventions, and a fiery, strong individual; Keller's title, on the other hand, evokes number and measure, order and norm, morality and society. Meyer's hero becomes Keller's rogue: temptation is condemned, not transfigured.

According to Keller, Lessing's essential characteristic is nothing other than the formal virtues of youthfulness, ability, of honesty and modesty; in short, Lessing's significance is evaluated as an abstract ethical process. But does this really describe Lessing's essential character completely? Can we understand his innermost nature without reference to the issues in his works, the issues to which the virtues were directed? Can we understand him without remembering his struggle against all false authority in public, political and scientific life, his revolutionary esthetic theories and his enlightenment-oriented ideas? Doesn't the "literary figure" Lessing, who consciously, as a single individual, propagates new values, stand opposed to the generally binding conventional moral norms? Keller's misunderstanding lies precisely in his attempt to level all that is new and revolutionary about Lessing by deflecting it into a highly generalized catalogue of virtues. We must also note Keller's peculiar wording: "every washerwoman" knows Lessing's name. Without wanting to denigrate a washerwoman's general education, it certainly seems more appropriate to invoke a teacher or some other representative of general literary knowledge than to make this denigrating comment about a member of the lower classes. Consciously intended or not, such remarks have a social dimension.

Keller—so he tells us—feels gratitude toward revolutionary literary figures. What is more striking, however, is that he does not thank them for opening doors to knowledge, for insights into social life and into the means by which these intellectual discoveries might be helpful in creating more rational forms of society; he does not thank them for their revolutionary teaching, for their conviction that the polity must be radically changed. On the contrary, he is grateful to them for having taught him that one might attain harmonious and "complete" style in politics. Order and solicitousness in public life, a kind of political traffic regulation, is for him the fruit of his association with the precursors of bourgeois revolution.

These interpretations and misinterpretations of Keller share one thing: their common denominator is renunciation and self-denial. The individual in general should renounce happiness, and the "great" human being in particular should forego any emphasis on his personal uniqueness; the revolutionary, for his part, should give up the notion of smashing and radically transforming the social order. Such attitudes not only differentiate Keller from Meyer's patrician ideology, but it also distances him from the revolutionary movements of the lower classes. Much more clearly and less ambivalently than Spielhagen, Keller represents the petit-bourgeois "middle." In connection with Spielhagen we pointed out the peculiar historic dialectic of those middle class strata who find the road of upward mobility closed and fear social descent; and it is equally relevant for the Swiss petit-bourgeoisie which Keller represents.

These strata are neither capable of transfiguring the present situation, as are the upper classes, nor are they able, given their limited economic chances for the future, to reconcile themselves to the prospect of salvation in a secular or religious heaven, as are the lower classes. This is why ideologies of petit-bourgeois and middle-class groups are always torn. In general, however, one can say that they are more likely to support the upper than the lower classes. The specifically middle-class ideology centers around morality, as the above-quoted passages show.

The ethical rigor corresponds to a situation which—although it is not experienced as happiness—would only be worsened by transcendence and change. All that reality denies in the present and will deny in the future remains submerged in morality of orderly fulfillment of duty. These petit-bourgeois or middle-class groups cannot expect the fulfillment of their great desires in the political realm today or tomorrow, but this fact is veiled with an ideological attitude according to which people are not in this world to be happy but to fulfill their duties.

One might disagree with this interpretation and point out that the Enlightenment philosophy that accompanied the rise of the new bourgeois class in France and especially in Germany worked out normative moral teachings which demanded the fulfillment of duty as the primary guiding principle of practical activity—think of Kant. But a comparison between Kant and the men of the French Enlightenment should give us food for thought; Kant's moral philosophy which radically rejects any eudae-monistic justification for human action, has effect in a country in which the bourgeoisie's chances of social mobility are quite limited not only in political, but also in economic respects; a country, in other words, in which this class finds itself in a situation similar to that of the petit-bourgeoisie in Keller's Switzerland. The moral philosophy of the French, on the other hand, celebrates a harmony of morality and happiness as a concrete precondition for harmonious social relations as well as individual well-being; it calls for the acquisition of those virtues that are at the core of human nature. Here, the purpose of ethics is to bring about happiness. Following the stipulations of this philosophy promises success in the future. Keller's morality, on the other hand, is tied to self-denial and renunciation; the future holds neither possibility nor consolation. A difficult and hard present is legitimated ethically: Keller is the ideologue of the Swiss Protestant petit-bourgeoisie—a petit-bourgeois Kant dressed in the garb of a poet.

Keller's incomprehension of German conditions—although it is more or less play-acted—shows us how decisively Swiss conditions influenced hiim. This is what he has to say about Munich, the first large German city that he visits: "The females of the lower classes are incredibly crude. They swear and cuss just like the cowmen do at home, and every evening they sit in the pub and drink beer. Even the most noble ladies go to the coffeehouse and drink—not coffee—but, just for entertainment, a liter or two of beer."[3] Heidelberg does not fare much better; Keller writes to his mother and his sister: "In any case, this is a tattered and sloppy people, everyone lives off the students, half or three-fourths of the entire population are illegitimate children of students and run around in rags."[4]

And on March 10, 1849 he writes to Baumgartner from Heidelberg:

> I certainly do not want anything to happen here in the immediate future; I don't want to be in Heidelberg during a revolution, because I have never before seen a cruder or more distasteful proletariat anywhere else: one's life is in danger if one crosses the street alone at night; the most impertinent beggars just about eat one up alive even while they mumble about a Republic and about Hecker. And their so-called "leaders," the editors of the local rags are no better. I have never met more narrow-minded and brutal men than these second- and third-rate German republicans; they carefully nourish and tend all negative passions in the lower population: envy, vengefulness, bloodthirstiness, dishonesty.[5]

And Berlin is for him nothing but a "pigsty."[6]

These passages reveal Keller's aversion to all modern tendencies in Germany. His folkloristic approach hides a critique of social conditions. Overcrowding in the large cities, poverty and suffering connected to the industrialization process, a new bourgeois lifestyle that is just beginning to develop—all this stands in contradiction to the perception of public life that for Keller prevails in his home country. Like Montesquieu's Persian, he visits the regions of new capitalism, only to turn away in displeasure and disgust. Keller is not able to perceive the specific structures of new social realities; rather, he can perceive them only aesthetically. It is a consequence of the peculiar situation of the petit-bourgeoisie in Switzerland. His relationship to capitalism is that of a mere consumer, and he experiences all that is offered to him as an empty and unsatisfying pleasure.

Indeed, this is reminiscent of Gutzkow's sociologically interpreted nervousness, which grew out of the discrepancy between social wishful thinking and actual reality. The only difference is, of course, that the nervousness of the characters in Young German literature contain active and dynamic moments, while Keller's hypochondria is isolating and regressive. Both of these attitudes are appropriate to their respective situations: to the social opportunities of the rising liberal bourgeoisie in Germany on the one hand, and to the Swiss petit-bourgeoisie, whose viability is restricted, on the other.

Switzerland occupies a unique position in the middle of the nineteenth century. The goldrush of 1847 passes this country by and, while the bourgeoisie in France and Germany is largely differentiated as a class—1848 was the last occasion on which a bourgeoisie with "unified" interests appeared—in Switzerland it is united until the 1870s and 1880s; at the same time, the proletariat is numerically quite weak. In the last decades of the century Switzerland is finally drawn into the process of large-scale capitalism and, as the novel *Martin Salander* shows, Keller faces this new development quite helplessly.

In his hometown of Zurich, prevailing social relations were constrained and underdeveloped. Like the rest of the country, this city was relatively unindustrialized; neither raw materials nor an industrial reserve army existed and daily life transpired in very small parameters. The upper class lived by trade or became rich abroad; and occasionally, worked in cottage industries, such as watchmaking in the western part of Switzerland. Most of the petit-bourgeoisie made its living as artisans, small tradesmen, or silk spinners. Emigration also played a large role, since the Swiss could earn a livelihood everywhere in the world in the hotel business or the dairy industry. Life forms more suited to the late Middle Ages than to the nineteenth century were still possible, but barely. The Swiss petit-bourgeoisie leads something of an island existence. In Switzerland, some strata still made a living in small regional contexts, while everywhere else in Europe, industrialization led to the development of a mass proletariat.

The ideology of a democracy of feeling corresponded to this economic situation. Everyone felt a connection with everyone else; life passed within the organic ties of family, group and community. Economic differences played only a small role in the perceptions of the average Swiss. On the contrary, it follows from the precarious situation of the strata that the development of all class consciousness is impeded, and economic differences are psychologically repressed as allegedly nonessential.

Note the confident contempt with which Keller treats economic processes. "He travelled across the country in matters of business" is a typical comment about the economic affairs of one person. What do the people of Seldwyla actually do? We do not find out anything definite. The social structure of this small town is described vaguely and sketchily. The introduction mentions "business," "craftsmenship," "debts," "party-people," "regiment" and the "government," without giving any clear indication of even a single Seldwyler citizen's economic activity; in this connection one might also think of Keller's highly generalized economic designations in the novel *Three Just Kammacher.*

This disregard for economic differentiation has an important historical parallel in the ideology of the Jacobins, especially in Robespierre.
Even in these circles of petit-bourgeois politicians, the praise of virtue,
the morality of renouncing happiness comes first. The ideology of the
Jacobins also contains another moment, which is characteristic of
Keller's petit-bourgeois people as well as of all similar middle strata:
the exaggerated importance accorded to politics. The same thing that is
caricatured as *Bierbank* (tavern gossip) is consecrated and transfigured
in the wise conversations of the "just" about public affairs.

Victorious and defeated classes have always known that economic
interests use politics as an instrument of power expansion and in power
struggles. For this reason, bourgeois and proletarian struggles have
always been struggles between organizational forms, struggles that were
concerned primarily with economic goals, at least as long as it was not
a matter of private capitalists, of disagreements within a business or a
group of businesses. The notion that politics could be taken as an isolated
phenomenon, that it could be a separate sphere, alongside other spheres
such as art or economics or law, the notion that the realm of politics
could be entered as an arena of struggle in which public affairs might
be settled to the satisfaction of all—where, indeed, public affairs are
actually constituted—all these misleading conceptions are developed by
those strata whose actual situation in the economic struggle, while it may
not be desperate, does not offer great promise for upward mobility and
change. Stendhal's work also contains political themes, but, consciously or
unconsciously, he does without such artistic tricks because he attributes
an enlightened consciousness to the bourgeoisie of his time. For his hero,
Mr. Leuwen, political affairs are only an expression of large-scale economic disputes and governments are nothing but business adversaries.

Often, it is the middle strata of society that perpetuates the notion
of an equilibrium of forces in struggle with each other, of the notion of
a golden middle way in politics on which all can reach an agreement.
For them, the belief that the "middle" of society has a special mission
amounts to an ideological transfiguration of their social situation. All of
Keller's stories and novels accomplish this transfiguration of the middle.
They share the assumption that economic conditions are in good order
just the way they are. The marriage of a rich patrician daughter and a
petit-bourgeois man who is not very wealthy, as in the *Banner of the
Seven Upright,* is an exception. *Mrs. Regel Amrain* teaches that the
establishment of a family on a financially solid foundation is the core
of an orderly life; political interest should begin here and extends to

the community and the canton. *Pankraz, the Sulker* demonstrates that a fantastic roaming-in-the-world leads nowhere, and that the return to the upright life of the citizen holds the only possibility for a humanly valuable life. We can sense an air of resignation: this is how the world is. One must make a virtue of necessity; human substance is simply insufficient to grow and unfold in broad spheres, therefore, human existence is lived out in a constrained sphere of duties. This, Keller's patriarchal pathos, suggests typing him as a "petit-bourgeois Goethe"!

But Keller's development into an ideologic transfigurer of the Swiss petit-bourgeoisie did not proceed smoothly. Let us look at a few biographical facts: he was born on July 19, 1819, the son of a master wood turner. At the age of five, he lost his father, who was only thirty-three years old. Beginning in 1825, Keller attended the school for the poor: from 1831 to 1833, he attended the regional boys' school; in 1833 he was transferred to the industrial school and was expelled a year later for being the ringleader of a prank. Thereafter, he lived with relatives in Glattfeld and Zurich. He pursued painting, first himself and later through the instruction of poor teachers.

Without a steady job or any clear goals, he took up personal contacts with political refugees and he then wrote his first poems. With a travelling stipend provided by the state, he went to Heidelberg in October of 1848, studied literary history with Hermann Hettner, and attended Ludwig Feuerbach's lectures on philosophy and religion. He lived in Berlin from 1850 until December of 1855, when he moved back to Zurich. His plans to become the director of a Cologne art museum society or to be appointed as a professor in Zurich were shattered. Between 1861 and 1876, he held office as First City Secretary. In 1864, he lost his mother and his sister continued to manage his household affairs. On July 15, 1890 he died in Zurich; the city is his main heir.

Three moments of this biography are significant for our analysis: Keller's origin, his contact with radical currents, and the process of his final assimilation into the Swiss petit-bourgeoisie.

His parents already prefigure the petit-bourgeois life of the "ideal" satisfying existence of the "middle." Keller himself gives us a most precise description of this lifestyle in the first chapters of *Green Henry*. There, we encounter the bustling and alert father, who devotes himself to all kinds of enterprises within his occupation, and who, after taking care of his home affairs, spends most of his energy and possessions for the general affairs of professional associations, the community and the state; and we meet the energetic mother, a circumspect housewife, thrifty but not stingy, concerned about the welfare of others, but carefully guarding against luxury. Regardless of whether Keller gives us an idealized picture of his parents, he certainly succeeds in creating the ideal type of the petit-bourgeois family.

Keller found his way to this ideal via a detour: next to his strong instinctive rejection to the new capitalist world, we find him in relatively unmediated contact with radical bourgeois currents. Ludwig Feuerbach, for example, was not without influence. Keller related his first impression of the philosopher to his friend Baumgartner in January of 1849:

> How I will fare in [the lectures of] the latter [Feuerbach], I dare not say or even speculate about. Only one thing is certain: I will submerge all my previous religious convictions in a *tabula rasa* (actually this has already happened) until I reach the Feuerbachian niveau. The world is a republic, he says, and can tolerate neither an absolute nor a constitutional God. . . . I cannot resist this appeal, at least not for the time being. My God was only a kind of consul, who never enjoyed much prestige. I *had to* topple him. Only I cannot *swear* that *my* world will not vote itself another head of state one fine morning. Immortality is at stake. No matter how beautiful and full of emotion the thought is—if one turns it around the right way, the opposite is just as moving and deep. At least for myself, [I can say that] those hours which I devoted to the thought of death itself, were very solemn and contemplative. I can guarantee you that one will pull himself together and not become a worse person for it.[7]

Feuerbach deduced people's conceptions of God psychologically, from their egoistic needs; according to him, one confronts his own inner nature in God. Karl Marx interpreted this theory historically, he substituted horizontally and vertically ordered social groups for the "individual," and then inquired about the objective needs and interests that each particular group's specific conception of God revealed. But Keller is far from such a dynamic conception. While Marx does not pursue the question of correctness or incorrectness of theological conceptions but is interested in uncovering their ideological function, Keller—like Feuerbach himself—takes the content of these theological assertions seriously even when he declares them to be false. In the sphere of theology, Keller's atheism is more radical than Marx's abstinence, but the latter's abstinence contains a fundamental break from the social order which considers the isolated discussion of such questions meaningful, since for bourgeois thinking, the isolation of individual cultural spheres is maintained. The significance of politics in petit-bourgeois thinking is a most striking example.

Still, we must not overlook the fact that Keller's positive attitude toward Feuerbach contains the dialectical moment of discontent with the existing state of affairs. Granted, an unintended prophesy of his character development is provided by Keller himself when he says that he might "elect for himself another head of state one fine morning." We do not go astray if we evaluate his acceptance of the bourgeois-patriarchal lifestyle as a fulfillment of this prophesy. Even though Keller retains a secularized view of the world, this world is not without a religious consecration, which is conferred to it by the sanctified atmosphere of an existence bestowed by living in small circumscribed circles.

Keller's relationship to literature is similarly ambivalent. True, in his early years, he reads authors who are consciously bourgeois, like the young Tieck, Vulpius and Zschokke. But in 1856, he had only very smug comments about Gutzkow, and did not really examine Gutzkow's ideas with a single word.[8] It is almost as though he wished to avoid contact with all currents that might push him out of the atmosphere of a Swiss citizen's peace.

Similar tendencies are apparent in his search for an appropriate poetic form. After some early attempts at political poetry, he turns toward the theater. In a letter written to Hermann Hettner in March 1851, Keller formulates the function of the drama:

> The consecration of poetry will be accomplished by true poets, who are in a position to depict the will and the needs of the population, and it will not fail to come about when the virtuous content is created through *history*. Presently, everyone is concerned with the philistine and his misery, which is not a political subject matter, and with the wretchedness of present politics, to the extent that the police permits it. The latter is more worthwhile; but the real subject matter will only appear once the people are free, when worthy conditions and true statesmen and other carriers of culture exist. Then, the conflicts and differences of people will be of a worthy sort and they will provide appropriate content for true poetry.
>
> Meanwhile, it is quite a spectacle to see the population of such a smart metropolis as Berlin assembled in front of the stage, listening intently and hailing the actor who sings his innuendos in deliberately wistful moods.[9]

This passage almost reads like a sociology of dramatic arts; in his later years, Keller no longer wrote so comprehensively about the theater. One might suppose that during his stay in Germany he unintentionally came to identify somewhat with German social conditions, an identification which he otherwise resisted. Here, the drama appears to him as that artistic form in which the conflicts of history can be presented and brought to consciousness; he understands the role it played in the conscious struggle for emancipation of the bourgeoisie. He could have learned this from Lessing. But he never wrote a political comedy[10] and he almost always used the form of the narrative. Sociologically speaking, this form had the function of taking inventory of the world, a world with which one could afford to be, by and large, content. Personally, however, he had little reason to be so content.

In this connection, one might note his classification of things into small categories and his attention to order in even the smallest detail, which bordered on pedantry and peculiarity. A letter to Berthold Auerbach contains the following afterthought:

> I do not have a stamp at hand and I cannot walk to the post office. Therefore I expect you to mail your next letter without a stamp, so that we can preserve the world order at least on a small scale. You have, incidently, put too much postage on your last letter, as I remember, a letter to Switzerland cost only 4 Silbermorgen.[11]

The humorous note is unmistakable, but so is the seriousness with which Keller dedicates himself to the affairs of everyday life. Plenty of evidence can be cited to support this, for example a lengthy explanation to Emil Kuh as to why he should not address a letter to the "first head clerk" but simply to the "head clerk";[12] or when in a report about a great row he is having with his sister, he gives Theodor Storm detailed advice about the posting of letters;[13] or when, in line with his office duties, he instructs the state councilors not to leave the office rooms "without a prior notification or request."[14] These quotes reveal his concern with order and frugality, his scrupulous correctness in following prevailing public norms; in short, the virtues of a small man who takes his con- trained life sphere very seriously. *Einschweizerung*—becoming Swiss—is how Keller's adaptation into the bourgeoisie might be described.

This process becomes particularly clear in the history of the novel *Green Henry*. In a letter to his publisher Vieweg, Keller writes in 1850:

> The moral of my book is this: a person who is unable to keep his personal affairs and those of his family in balance is also unable to hold an influential and honorable position in bourgeois life. In many cases, society might be responsible for this, and then the content of the book would be that of a socialist tract. In the pres- ent case, however, responsibility lies with the hero—his character and his special fate—and this gives the novel more of an ethical significance.[15]

And in the year 1854, Keller explained to Hettner: "Green Henry comes to see, painfully, that it is not the earth, the vegetation, the atmosphere, but the human being himself who is the object of his potential talents. What matters is not the poet . . . but the pure feeling of humanness which, equipped with the personality or individual experience, enters or wants to enter concrete humanity (that of his fatherland) and wants to work in accordance with the laws of truth and simplicity."[16]

In the first-cited passage, the possibility for a tendentious political novel is left open in principle; even the word "socialism" is mentioned—and this is rare indeed in Keller's work. We can see that the original conception of *Green Henry* comes out of the same psychological context that gave rise to the dramatic plans; at the same time, however, Keller has already made a decision that this will not be a political book, but one that takes into account the role of individual factors in the forming of people's characters and fates. In the second passage, the social conditions of the individual's fate are not even mentioned; instead, the character of Henry serves to portray the general human condition in exemplary fashion.

Thereby, peace with the social order is extended from the posting of a letter to include the entire life situation. My description of Keller as the "petit-bourgeois Goethe" comes to mind again when, in the final version of *Green Henry*, the adaptation of the individual into the small sphere of activity is completed. What Goethe's Wilhelm Meister experienced in the patriarchal upper class happens to Green Henry in a more modest environment. The suicide of Green Henry in the first version of the novel may be reminiscent of Werther's suicide. Both literary artists have an initially critical attitude toward the social order, and the death of their heroes can in part be attributed to this; but both writers ultimately come to accept the social order as it was. At the very beginning of *Green Henry*, Keller once mentions the "open and trusting hope of the middle classes for a better, a more beautiful time in reality."[17] And in 1877 he makes the following comments about Wieland's statement regarding the *Wahlverwandtschaften*:

> [While you] elevate these [people] into the sky, you designate the others as crazy; what is right will lie somewhere in the middle! Let this be our wise statement of the year 1877.[18]

In both comments, the notion of the *middle* recurs, and in the letter it returns in a certain coquettish form. This is the key concept in

338

Keller's ideology: a feature of petit-bourgeois reality is ontologized, and it accords a glow to the entire reality. The notion of the middle is also, incidently, the foundation of all organicist social theories; it always serves as a justification—or at least confirmation—of an order that has superior and inferior parts. In short, it always supports power relationships per se. Think in this context of the concept of the *middle* in the poetry of the medieval courts. The *middle* is an approximation of the vegetative phenomenon. There is birth and death, there is the sequence of seasons, the coming and going of individuals and peoples, of war and of peace; there are the poor and the rich, the smart and the dull, men and women, but for Keller's position, the most essential aspect of all these phenomena is not their singular facticity, but something more in-between, something floating, a medium, the mere fact of being alive, the fact of existence, eternal recurrence and continuity.

We can make a general connection between the emotional aspect inherent in this general conception of "the middle" on the one hand, and the significance attributed to politics and the concomitant disregard of the economic sphere on the other: both share an acceptance of life as it is, with no expectation that the course of history will bring anything new or unexpected. If one looks, for example, at the table of contents of *Green Henry,* one is placed immediately in the environment of generalized and generalizable life situations, of a static attitude toward the world that is basically accepting the existing state of affairs. We find titles such as "The Praise of Origin." "Father and Mother," "Childhood," "Early Fault," "Dreams of home," "Change in the Course of Happiness," "Vocational Choice," "Spring Once Again." One moves through a landscape of human seasons, where rain and sunshine are sensibly distributed. The landscape can expect nothing from the movements of individuals or groups, rather it gives life to these people. The organic ordering of individual life is, seen from Keller's petit-bourgeois perspective, the return of the individual into the mother's womb or his acceptance of fatherly authority.

Keller himself once said that in *Green Henry* he was dealing with the problem of bringing up a "fatherless" boy. And in the novel he says, "I cannot help myself—even though I understand the silliness of it, I let my mind wander and I figure out what would have happened to me if my father had stayed alive, and if the world had been available in all of its life-vitality from my earliest youth on; each day this excellent person would have led me a bit further and he would have experienced his second youth with me."[19]

The individual fantasy which Keller draws here holds true on a larger social scale as well. In the conditions that are psychologically deduced from Keller's own fate, a social content appears: the existence of petit-bourgeois strata in Switzerland is not just tied to the "motherly" home ground, but also to the continued existence of the "fathers," the patriciate-patriarchal lifestyle. Keller owes his travelling stipend, which made it possible for him to acquaint himself with the world, to his "father," i.e., his home town; the just barely tenable situation of the Swiss petit-bourgeoisie is founded in Swiss bourgeois feudality which is not yet rationalized or captured in abstract industrial relations. Keller was convinced that the security of the "middle" of the family was an important value; its significance gradually becomes clear to "Green Henry," too. This security must also correspond to the ideological ideal of all petit-bourgeois strata in the specifically Swiss situation around the middle of the nineteenth century. In a letter to Lina Duncker, Keller writes:

> I, too, cannot admit that the arbitrary decisions of a publisher can interrupt the natural sequence of my products, so that the latter work might actually be published before that written earlier; because I am an author who is concerned, not just with his remuneration, but also with lawful, orderly development, in which the final opus should always be the best one and progress should be noticeable.[20]

The word "lawful" has to be interpreted through the word "orderly." The concept of law, after all, does contain a dialectical moment. It can signify a necessary succession, a dynamic that cannot be contained, in other words, a "lawful" change; lawful is by no means only an artistic unfolding but also a historical development, which leads to revolutions. The notion of necessity inherent here can be a consolation for that social stratum, which is interested in a transformation of the existing social order. But it is order per se, which seems to be the main attribute of the law that Keller is discussing. Lawfulness and legitimacy have always been the guiding principles of conservative ideology. The essential significance of Keller's casual statement is the notion that all things that transpire in the world are right; the statement is, in other words, a theodicy of the existing state of affairs.

Notes

1. Gottfried Keller, *Werke* (Zurich, 1965), vol. 5, pp. 386ff. All quotations are from this edition.
2. *Letters and Diaries 1830–1861*, ed. Emil Ermatinger (Stuttgart and Berlin, 1924), pp. 157ff.

3. *Collected Letters in four Volumes,* ed. Carl Helbling, vol. 1 (Bern, 1950), p. 19.
4. Ibid., p. 89.
5. Ibid., p. 280.
6. Ibid., p. 109.
7. Ibid., p. 274.
8. ibid., p. 433 (see also p. 438).
9. Ibid., p. 355.
10. Ibid., pp. 354ff.
11. *Gesammelte Briefe,* vol. 3/2, p. 190.
12. *Gesammelte Briefe,* vol. 3/1, p. 162.
13. Ibid., pp. 436ff.
14. *Gottfried Keller in seinen Briefen,* ed. Heinz Amelung (Berlin, n.d.), p. 145.
15. *Gesammelte Briefe,* vol. 3/2, p. 15.
16. *Gesammelte Briefe,* vol. 1. pp. 382ff.
17. *Werke,* vol. 2, p. 14.
18. *Gesammelte Briefe,* Vol. 3/1, p. 417.
19. *Werke,* vol. 2, p. 23.
20. *Gesammelte Briefe,* vol. 2, pp. 150ff.

Afterword

From Helmut Dubiel, Editor of the German Edition of This Volume

In the present volume, the author carries out the program for a sociological approach to literature as it is developed in his theoretical writings in Volume 1: namely, the treatment of prominent literary documents from the past as primary materials for a historically based study of social realities. Interpreting literature in this fashion becomes a means of analyzing society. This is not to say that the esthetic core of a work of art can somehow be glimpsed from the outside, through an analysis of extraliterary factors that impinge on the work. On the contrary, we see that objective social realities are always deeply embedded in the creative transformation of even the most subjective of experiences, such as fear, guilt and emotions of intimacy. It is here, in this esthetic dimension, that social realities can be grasped.

The predominant theme of the present collection is bourgeois mentality and its historical development. For example, the works of Lope de Vega, Calderon, Cervantes and Shakespeare are analyzed within the historical framework of the decline of feudalism and the rise of the absolutist regimes. Those of Molière and Goethe are set against the background of an evolving and consolidating bourgeois society in Western Europe. Foreshadowings of a late bourgeois contemporary totalitarianism are detected in the plays of Ibsen and in the novels of Hamsun.

While Part I of this volume broadly follows the parabolic rise, consolidation, and decline of bourgeois mentality, as documented in major works of Western literature, Part II is marked by an intensive analysis of a particularly rich segment of German literature, and accordingly should be read as supplementary to the earlier part, complementing it with precision and detail. Assuming narrative literature as his focus, the author traces the development of bourgeois mentality peculiar to Germany in the nineteenth century. The antimodernism of the romantics, the theoretically empoverished social critique of the "Young Germany," Mörike's neurotically disturbed embourgeoisement, Freytag's bourgeois materialism, Conrad Ferdinand Meyer's glorification of upperclass bourgeois "heroic" style, and so on, are all shown to be symptomatic of a single syndrome—that of the miscarriage of a bourgeois revolution in Germany. In these "Studies on the German Novel of the Nineteenth Century" the question is posed, on the basis of literary materials, why an enlightened bourgeois mentality never managed to become consolidated in Germany.

The essays on the sociology of literature collected in this volume are the product of three decades of work. The author composed "Studies on the German Novel in the Nineteenth Century" (Part II) during the early years of his association with the Institute for Social Research in Frankfurt. Forty years later they were published for the first time under the title, *Erzählkunst und Gesellschaft.* Part I is based for the most part on a study written during 1955-56 at the Center for Advanced Studies in Stanford. It was first published in 1957 as *Literature and the Image of Man,* and subsequently in German translation in 1966. An earlier version of the chapters on C. F. Meyer, Ibsen, and Hamsun was published in issues of the journal "Zeitschrift für Sozialforschung" during 1936 and 1937.

A further detail concerning the Hamsun essay is worth mentioning: It is a literary-political document in its own right. When the author wrote this essay in 1934 for eventual publication in 1937, no one would have imagined that Knut Hamsun's latent sympathies for national socialism, which are detected and brought to the surface in this essay, would achieve the blatancy they did by 1940.